The Soul of New Orleans

a legacy of rhythm and blues

also available from Swallow Publications...

I HEAR YOU KNOCKIN'

The Sound of New Orleans Rhythm and Blues

by **Jeff Hannusch** (a.k.a. 'Almost Slim')

"I Hear You Knockin", the Sound of New Orleans Rhythm and Blues by Jeff Hannusch. This well written and lavishly illustrated volume presents colorful and informative portraits of more than two dozen important New Orleans Rhythm and Blues figures. In most cases, the subjects tell their own stories, sharing their successes and joys, as well as their failures and sorrows. Included are singers, producers, instrumentalists, DJs and record label entrepreneurs. Some have scaled to the top of their profession and earned international reputations. Others have tasted success on a smaller scale and just play fun fun and a little extra money on the weekends. Together they tell the fascinating story of the rise of New Orleans Rhythm and Blues. A must for fans of rhythm and blues and New Orleans music!

Jeff received an **American Book Award** in 1986 for this book and the book is now in its fourth printing.

Available in **soft cover only**, **388 pages**, (5.5" x 8.5"), list for **$16.00**.
ISBN 0-9614245-0-8

Swallow Publications, Inc.

Post Office Drawer 10 • Ville Platte, Louisiana 70586
ph 337-363-2177 • fx 337-363-2094 • e-mail - info@flattownmusic.com

The Soul of New Orleans

a legacy of rhythm and blues

by Jeff Hannusch

Swallow Publications, Inc.

The Soul of New Orleans, a legacy of rhythm and blues

Jeff Hannusch

Copyright © 2001 by Jeff Hannusch
Published by Swallow Publications, Inc.

ISBN 0-9614245-8-3

Swallow Publications, Inc.
Post Office Drawer 10
238 East Main Street
Ville Platte, Louisiana 70586
(337) 363-2177
(337) 363-2094 fax

Find us on the world wide web at:
http://www.swallowpublications.com

E-mail inquiries to:
info@flattownmusic.com

Library Of Congress Cataloging-in-Publication Data

Hannusch, Jeff.
 The soul of New Orleans : a legacy of rhythm and blues / by Jeff Hannusch
  p. cm.
 Includes bibliographical references (p.) and index.
 ISBN 0-9614245-8-3 (pbk.)
  1. Rhythm and blues music--Louisiana--New Orleans--History and criticism.
  2. Musicians--Louisiana--New Orleans. I. Title.

 ML3521 .H36 2001
 781.643'09763'35--dc21

                2001049917

Printed and bound in the United States of America.

Acknowledgements

This book could never have been completed without the assistance of the following cherished friends, supporters, killjoys and relatives not necessarily listed in terms of importance: Dr. Janis Johnson, Philip and Sandra McCarthy, John and Helen Hannusch, Cosimo Matassa, Arthur Okazaki, Bunny Mathews, Billy Delle, Joseph Irrera, Jan Ramsey, John Broven, Phil Rupp, Louis Nugent, Jerry Brock, Barry Smith, Lynn Abbot, Lance Slom, Glen Smith, David Booth, Gary Rouzan, Tex Stevens, Cilla Huggins, Freddie Salagi, Dave Howard, Mike Hurtt, Kevin Aucoin, Isaac Bolden, King Ellis, Scott Barretta, Paula Burch, Rico, Terry Gilroy, Heather West, Hammond Scott, Nauman Scott, Wolf Stevenson, Tommy Couch, the New Orleans Jazz & Heritage Festival, David Jones, Joe Banashak, Scott Jordon, Tulane University's Hogan Jazz Archive, Patricia Gorman, Marshall Sehorn, King Ellis, the University of New Orleans Library and Natorium, Shelly Schubach, Rick Coleman, Antoinette K-Doe, Ernie K-Doe, Scott Billington, Warren Hildebrand, Peter Guralnick, Chris Strackwitz, Chris Soileau, Mike Ledbetter, Cleon Floyd, Mary Katherine Aldin, Tee-Beaux, Jin and Floyd Soileau, Louis Maistrios, Kathleen Joffrion, St. Jude, Woody Sistrunk, Connie Atkinson, Boomer, Pat Cline, Leo Gosserand and of course all of the great musicians and entrepreneurs for telling me their fascinating stories.

Cover designed by Arthur Okazaki.
Back cover photograph courtesy of Paula Birch

Dedication

To all of New Orleans' great rhythm and blues
musicians: past, present, and future.

Contents

Introduction

"I'm not sure, but I'm almost positive, all music came
from New Orleans."
-Ernie K-Doe, 1980

Upon the publication of *I Hear You Knockin': The Sound of New Orleans Rhythm and Blues* in 1985, I honestly didn't imagine I would ever write a companion volume. At the time, I thought I was ready for other journalistic and professional challenges, some which I achieved, some which I didn't. However, the research that went into the book, the people I encountered compiling it, the positive reviews, the encouragement from many supportive readers served to deepen my fascination, and curiosity into the New Orleans R&B tradition. In retrospect, it gave me an even greater appreciation for the genre, love, and respect for the fascinating and talented people who were responsible for creating it.

Luckily, the portrait format of *I Hear You Knockin'* leant itself well to a sequel/epilogue and I've spent many years interviewing subjects and compiling research which is collected here. I'd also like to point out that not only have many of the subjects I've written about in *The Soul of New Orleans* been neglected and overlooked, but so too has the great New Orleans rhythm and blues music and culture they created. If in even some small way I have focused attention on them, convinced even one reader to go hear live New Orleans rhythm and blues, purchase a CD recorded by one of the artists profiled here, purchase one of their scratchy 45s in a thrift store, or learn to play this music, then this book has served it's purpose.

Many of these profiles have partially appeared in magazines, journals, fanzines, newspapers and liner notes. However, rather than conveniently recycle them, I went back to the original notes and interviews in order to add pertinent information and correct inaccuracies in order to tell a more complete story. Indeed, rereading the original stories and essays induced me to relisten to more music, compare facts, ask more questions, and reread and correct the errors that often seemed to leap off the old clippings.

Keep in mind this is not a definitive or chronological history of New Orleans rhythm and blues, nor was it intended to be. Rather it is series of profiles of artists, club owners, promoters, sidemen, observers and record label owners. The individuals profiled here were chosen because of their importance in the development of the music, their creativity, were personal heroes, or whose contributions have been previously ignored by journalists and researchers. While they may not be directly linked, these individuals share a common trait—they created and were part of proud, innovative and influential musical tradition.

The title of the book has a deeper meaning than once might initially assume. While it's true that several artists were exponents of soul music, this is a collection of essays that define the music that gave New Orleans it's soul and helped define it's unique culture for decades. I have tried my best to let the subjects tell their story and keep my insights to a minimum, but that's obviously not always possible. I sincerely hope that readers enjoy this book as much as I did writing and researching it. I'm very proud of the result.

Part I

The Founders

For better or worse, New Orleans is a city shaped by tradition. This deep sense of tradition permeates the city's language, architecture, food, social structure, dress, politics, literature and most definitely it's music.

Settled by the French in 1718, because of its location near the outlet of the Mississippi River, New Orleans became home for people of diverse origins, including those from Spain, Italy, the United Kingdom, Haiti, Canada, and quite obviously Africa.

It is absolutely impossible to overlook the importance of Africa as a shaper of New Orleans music. While other American outposts feared black slave uprisings in the early 19th Century, slaves in New Orleans were allowed and encouraged to assemble so they could sing tribal chants, play their instruments and dance. These gatherings, held Sunday afternoons in Congo Square, preserved African music traditions that might otherwise have otherwise been lost forever. Inevitably, these African rhythms filtered into the city's indigenous music—particularly after former slaves began to play European instruments and formed their own bands. This unlikely combination produced New Orleans' syncopated polyrhythmic "Second Line" beat—a cadence where the drummer and bass instrument hit on the beat and the after beat. This sound was first heard in Dixieland jazz and of course eventually rhythm and blues.

The first signs of national recognition for New Orleans R&B came in 1947 with Roy Brown's "Good Rockin' Tonight." However, it wasn't until three years later when the arrival of the New Orleans R&B sound was signaled by Fats Domino's' recording of "The Fat Man." Produced by Dave Bartholomew, "The Fat Man" had a fairly simple formula. Bartholomew backed Domino's up front vocals and bright piano with solid bass and drums, horns that played whole notes in unison, and a guitar that doubled the bass line. The record sold over one million copies and it's success drew out-of-town record companies like a magnet, who were eager to exploit the abundant talent found in the city.

The breakthrough year for New Orleans R&B occurred in 1955 when the style began the metamorphosis into rock and roll and attract an even broader audience. That was the year Domino's records began appearing in the national pop charts. He was followed by Little Richard, Huey Smith & the Clowns, Clarence Henry, Paul Gayten, Frankie Ford, Lloyd Price and Lee Allen, before the end of the decade.

The artists profiled in this section are artists from the first generation of New Orleans rhythm and blues. Some who became national stars via hit records, some who didn't get the breaks they needed to sustain a career and unfortunately remained neighborhood celebrities. Nevertheless, together they created an instantly identifiable sound that would please listeners and eventually create history.

CHAPTER ONE
~ Jack Dupree: The Champion ~

Because the late pianist Jack Dupree lived away from his home town for the last 50 years of his life—most of it abroad—his importance as a shaper of the New Orleans blues and rhythm and blues tradition has been largely overlooked.

Nevertheless, Dupree was one of the most prolific and entertaining New Orleans artists of all time. He created music which evoked the flamboyant milieu of black New Orleans during the early part of the 20th Century—the world of gamblers, good timers, drug addicts, pimps, prostitutes, poverty, oppression and colorful musicians. One of his most powerful songs in the genre, "The Junker Blues", was the inspiration for Fats Domino's "The Fat Man", a record which put New Orleans rhythm and blues on the commercial fast track in 1949.

Sheer longevity also has a lot to do with Dupree's importance. He probably summed it up best in a 1990 interview when he stated: "I'm the last living barrelhouse piano player that came from New Orleans. The only one left is me."

William Thomas Dupree was probably born July 23, 1909. Press kits, articles, as well as album and CD liner notes have listed July 4, 1910 and July 4, 1909 as his date of birth. However it is probably safe to assume Dupree claimed July 4 to coincide with Louis Armstrong's alleged birthday or the American independence day. Dupree was the youngest of six children and raised in New Orleans' Irish Channel on St. Andrew Street. His father—from the Belgian Congo—and his mother—of Creole and Cherokee decent—ran a neighborhood grocery and raised their family in an apartment located above the business. Dupree often claimed his parents were killed in a fire set by the Klu Klux Klan, a tale most journalists swallowed whole. Dupree's parents did perish in a fire, but the blaze was caused by an exploding container of kerosene stored in the grocery. The eight-year-old orphan was sent to the Colored Waif Home, the same institution which earlier was home for Louis Armstrong. It was here that an elderly Italian priest taught Dupree how to play the piano.

"That place was way back in the graveyards," said Dupree, referring to the building which was located behind Holt Cemetery on Rosedale Drive. "The priests sent us out to get them King Edward cigars. One day when I was about 10, they gave me and a friend a quarter to go buy five. We had to go through the cemetery to get to the store. I saw the grave diggers in there and the hearse in the corner behind the weeds. We were hiding behind the tombstones watching. They dug up a casket and dumped a body out and put the casket back in the hearse. A tall white man saw us and sneaked up behind us. He said, 'What are you kids doing here?' In those days they had false teeth that went in and out of your mouth and he popped his out while he was standing over us. He gave us 50 cents and told us that if we ever told anybody what we saw he'd come and get us. A couple nights later we were in bed and the nuns came around. They used to wear those big white hats on their head. Well I was laying in bed and I saw one of those white hats and hands reaching for my friend and I screamed. Then about 100 of us started screaming. I thought it was the man from the cemetery coming to get us."

Once Dupree learned the rudiments of the piano he would often sneak into the city where the gin mills, beer joints, speakeasies and whore houses that hired piano players to entertain. He saw and learned from Tuts Washington, Sullivan Rock, and Yellow Burch, who would all occasionally turn the piano over to the youngster when they wanted a drink.

"The first guy I saw was Don Bowers who was a writer for *The Chicago Defender*," said Dupree. "He was a barrelhouse guy. After him there was Drive Em Down [Willie Hall]. He played at Noonie's Place on Calliope and Franklin [now Simon Bolivar]. He was the best I ever heard. He worked for an Italian guy. He had cars parked around there for three blocks when he played. I picked up a lot from Drive Em Down by sitting in the corner and watching his hands."

Dupree would become a protege of Drive Em Down who died around 1930. Like many New Orleans barrelhouse players, Drive Em Down had a hard time being heard above the din of a rowdy clubs. To overcome this, he would tuck his left thumb under his fingers and smash the piano with his fist. This caused the bass to jump off the keyboard and rise above the din. With his right hand he played the song's melody. Dupree adopted this technique as did Archibald, Cousin Joe, and Professor Longhair. Later, Dupree would pay tribute to his mentor by recording the menacing "Drive Em Down Stomp." At the age of 14, Dupree had left the orphanage and got a job working in diary. During his spare time, he continued to be drawn to the rowdy joints along the Mississippi and Central City's Battlefield where the piano players hung out and played.

"In my day there were a lot of young piano players," said Dupree. "Bill Bugle, Clarence Love, Walter Davis—but we weren't always all working. If one of us got a job we all went and then split the money. I'd start playing and then I'd turn the piano over to the next guy. Then I'd go get some chicken. You see by having a lot of good piano players, people would stay in the joint until until 12 o'clock the next day drinking and carrying on. We'd put a glass on the table and sometimes split $80 between us. During cane cutting time, we'd all go to Plaquemine, Louisiana, and play on the plantations. We could live for a month on the money we made up there."

When the Depression and Prohibition arrived, there was far less demand for music and less money around for those who played it. Dupree decided to take up boxing and he trained at Kid Green's gym on South Rampart Street. Assuming the professional name "Champion Jack," he boxed in New Orleans and around Louisiana in medicine shows for a decade.

"I got so good none of the pros could hit me," said Dupree. "You see I was a left-hander and they couldn't handle that. My first fights were here with Kid Blue, Class Black and Tony Moret—I whipped them all. Later I fought in New York and Chicago."

Dupree's travels also took him to Indianapolis in 1934 where he befriended pianist Leroy Carr. Carr's playing would have a profound influence on Dupree. He would adapt Carr's intricate right hand runs and he cherry picked his repertoire. While in Indianapolis, Dupree often played with Carr at the Cotton Club along with guitarist Scrapper Blackwell. The duo remained friends until April 1935 when Carr succumbed to cirrhosis of the liver. Dupree continued to work in Indiana and had taken over as headliner at the Cotton Club where he built up a strong reputation. Part of his show included risque duets with Orphelia Hoy which were a throw back to the days of vaudeville and medicine shows. This brief portion Dupree's career was also very influential, as humor would became an important element of Dupree's recordings and live performances.

During the late 1930s Dupree often made forays to Chicago where he met Big Bill Broonzy and Tampa Red, blues artists who had made records for the Okeh label. Dupree would make his first recordings for Okeh in June 1940.

"I was working at the Cotton Club when Lester Melrose came down [from Chicago] and found me," said Dupree, referring to the owner of Okeh Records. "Melrose had beat all of the bluesmen out of money but I didn't know it at the time. He gave me $200 and I had never seen that much money in my life. He baited me and a few weeks later I went to Chicago to record. That's when I did 'Cabbage Greens.' Back then I didn't know anything about royalties or copyrights. Melrose just smiled and said, 'Sign here.' I didn't know I was signing everything over to him. Big Bill Broonzy, LeRoy Carr, Big Boy Crudup—all of us did it."

On Dupree's initial session he was accompanied by Indianapolis guitarist Bill Gaiter and bassist Wilson Swain. His first release, "Warehouse Man Blues," was a social commentary and didn't solely concern a warehouse man. At the time the federal government was trying to combat the Vitamin C deficiency among poor blacks by giving welfare recipients canned grapefruit juice. In the song, Dupree complains his grandmother went to the welfare office to get food but was offered only grapefruit juice. The other side, "Chain Gang Blues," is a strong example of Dupree's New Orleans barrelhouse piano style and included some sarcastic lyrics. However, of the seven songs he recorded at his first session, the gem was the double-entendre, "Cabbage Greens," which featured sharp boogie-woogie piano, slap bass and lyrics which celebrated his hometown. It was a good seller in the race market.

Dupree's third Okeh session from January of 1941 yielded "Junker Blues" which became one of Dupree most famous and influential numbers. A hammering New Orleans barrelhouse boogie-woogie, Dupree warns of the perils of "junk"—marijuana, cocaine and heroin. While "Junker Blues" and his other magnificent Okeh recordings helped elevate his career, in later years Dupree was bitter about them because Melrose claimed composer credit on all of his Okeh releases. As a result, Dupree never saw much more than the $200 he received when he signed with Melrose. Nevertheless Dupree's Okeh recordings rank among his best. Suddenly though, his career came to a temporary halt once the United States entered World War II and he was was drafted by the Navy.

"By me being an A-1 cook, I was one of the first to get shipped out," said Dupree. "A lot of old piano players had to be good cooks. When the pressure was on, a lot of women had to go to work while the men stayed home. Some mornings you could look in the yard and see the man hanging out baby diapers while the women was going off to work."

While Dupree claims he was in a Japanese prison camp for two years, he recorded at least one session while on leave for Folkways. When the War ended, Dupree was discharged in New York. He decided to stay there likely lured by the many opportunities to work and record. He would record for several companies, the first being the Joe Davis label. On the Joe Davis sessions, Dupree performs solo, slamming the piano with his left hand and shouting the blues the way he did in the rowdy New Orleans joints. Since he wasn't provided accompaniment, Dupree's technical ability was prominently displayed as his right hand floats along the treble end of the piano hitting all the perfect notes.

The highlight of these recordings was topical two-sider "FDR Blues" and "God Bless Our New President"— recorded six days after Franklin

Roosevelt's death—and the masterful New Orleans stomper, "She Makes Good Jelly." "You've Been Drunk" and "Gin Mill Sal" are also New Orleans alley music at it's best.

After leaving Joe Davis in 1946, Dupree spent the next seven years recording for several independent labels in New York including Abbey, Derby, Harlem, Red Robin, Gotham and Apex. One of the most prolific portions of his career, beside recording as Champion Jack Dupree, he also used the alias' Lightnin' Junior, Meathead Johnson, Tom Collins, Brother Blues, and Duke Bayou in order to avoid breaking contracts.

"If you had a contract you were supposed to record for only one company," said Dupree. "But we would record for another company and use another name. Me, Sonny Terry, Brownie McGhee, Peetie Wheatstraw—we all did that. I went under the name Willie Jones once. We had to do that to make money."

According to Bobby Robinson, who recorded Dupree for his Red Robin label in the early 1950s, Dupree was living in a one room kitchenette Harlem apartment at the corner of 126th Street and Lennox Avenue, with a piano and seven dogs. In August 1953, Dupree, who was billed as "the Tongue-Tied singer" made a rare trip back to New Orleans and appeared at the Dew Drop. Earlier in the year he'd signed an exclusive contract with the Cincinnati-based King label, one of the country's premier R&B labels. Using studios in New York and Cincinnati, Dupree's output for King rates with his best. The New York sessions produced numerous classics including "That's My Pa," "Stumblin' Block," and "Failing Health," which featured Mickey Baker's sparkling guitar and mellow saxophone from Willis Jackson. However, Dupree's first and only R&B chart entry, the relaxed "Walkin' the Blues," was recorded in Cincinnati. On it Dupree plays and sings unspectacularly, but he tells a humorous tale about a hard working man that appealed to record buyers.

After more than a dozen King releases, in 1955, Dupree signed with RCA which assigned his work to the subsidiary labels Groove and Vik. Dupree cut four sessions in New York for RCA, but only three singles were released. The highlights of this period were "Just Like A Woman" and "Dirty Woman," songs which still had strong links to New Orleans. During this period, Dupree supplemented his income, by hustling session work with other artists and acting as a talent scout for labels like Ember and Old Town. He would record behind numerous New York artists including Larry Dale, Cousin LeRoy, Bob Gaddy, and Mr. Bear.

In 1958, Dupree was signed by Atlantic's Jerry Wexler who suggested he cut an album's worth of traditional blues favorites. Backed by a gin fueled four-piece Harlem band—Pete Brown on saxophone, Larry Dale on guitar, Willie Jones on drums, and Wendell Marshall on bass—Dupree recorded the rowdy *Blues From the Gutter*. One of the very first albums by a blues artist, it included his unique readings of "Stack-O-Lee" and "Frankie & Johnnie"—songs which he often heard in New Orleans—as well as songs about narcotics—"Can't Kick the Habit"—and a remake of the "Junker Blues." The album ranks as one of the highlights of his career.

Dupree had heard Sonny Terry, Brownie McGhee, and the late Big Bill Broonzy rave about Europe after they performed there, and how it was an untapped market for blues artists. They also said it was largely free from racial prejudice. Annoyed by the conditions blacks were forced to accept in America, Dupree was anxious to see what Europe was like.

"I was recording in New York and working for gangsters at the time [1959]," said Dupree. "They booked me some dates and they sent me to Europe. I cashed in the return ticket and didn't go back. I lived in London for a long time."

Obviously Dupree enjoyed his new surroundings, marrying a 20-year-old English woman and eventually settling in Zurich, Switzerland. Dupree continued to record prolifically, cutting six mostly solo albums for the Danish Storyville label. A 1966 date for England's Decca label paired him with John Mayall and Eric Clapton. Throughout the 1960s, he performed regularly throughout Europe and built up a sizable following playing festivals, concerts and clubs.

Since 1970, he recorded almost two dozen albums for several labels on both sides of the Atlantic. Unfortunately, many of these latter recordings were rushed and unimaginative, leading to criticism and the occasional unfair negative reappraisal of his career .

In April of 1990, the still energetic 80-year-old—who was then residing in Hanover, Germany—returned to New Orleans for the first time in 36 years to play at the New Orleans Jazz & Heritage Festival and make new recordings for the Bullseye label. During his visit to the Crescent City he was reunited with a step-sister and a son.

"I didn't even know they were alive," said Dupree. "My son was in the service and I thought he got killed in Vietnam. I wrote to Washington to find out about him but they wrote back saying he was missing in action. I gave up finding him but low and behold he was here all the time. I lost her [his step sister's] address. Her mama took me from the orphan home when they already had six kids. It was a great feeling being taken into a family because I never had that family-type feeling growing up. She would lend me money so I could go to the show."

After a splendid set at the Festival, Dupree cut the aptly titled *Back Home In New Orleans* in just one evening at Ultrasonic Studio. Using a small band that included Alvin "Red" Tyler and Walter Payton, Dupree sounded especially content to be back home and playing with New Orleans musicians. He returned to New Orleans the following year to play the Jazz Fest and to record again for Bullseye. However, Dupree's health had deteriorated between trips to America and he was forced to sit in a wheelchair in order to play. In December 1991, he was hospitalized in Hamburg, Germany, with cancer of the spinal chord. It was the Champion's second bout with the disease as he had been diagnosed with cancer of the prostate and had a tumor removed from his back in 1989.

The elder statesman of New Orleans blues died at his apartment on January 21, 1992. Over 500 people attended his funeral in Hanover and his casket was draped with an American flag. On it rested the head-dress of a American Indian chief. In the tradition of his home town, a Dixieland band played at the service. Dupree was buried at sea.

CHAPTER TWO
~ Clarence Samuels: Chicken Hearted Woman ~

New Orleans has been home to many great blues shouters including Roy Brown, Smiley Lewis, Tommy Ridgley, Mr. Google Eyes, and Joe Turner. That list should also include the great Clarence Samuels. Although Samuels rarely recorded in New Orleans, he was instrumental in the development of the city's early rhythm and blues style and has enjoyed a prolific career. Samuels had been away from the Crescent City for over four decades, but returned in 1997 to recover from a serious illness and to be near his family.

Samuels was born in New Orleans October 30, 1923, and raised in Baton Rouge. His father Eddie Collins, a. k. a. Eddie Samuels, played trumpet and led the Roseland Six, a popular society band.

"My father got me interested in singing and he started letting me perform with his group when I was young," said Samuels. "His band broadcast every day on WJBO. They strictly played white clubs. One was Club 66 that was secretly part-owned by [future Louisiana] Governor Jimmie Davis. I had to learn a lot of standards. My father was strict about singing in the right key and pronouncing all the lyrics clearly."

In 1943, Samuels married and moved to New Orleans. Although the United States was in the midst of WW II, he found plenty of work entertaining in several clubs, eventually landing a regular job at the Palace Theater off of Canal Street. In 1947, Samuels met another former Baton Rouge native, Ernest Riles, who owned the Down Beat club located at 712 South Rampart Street. The Down Beat served as a front for Riles' more profitable businesses—prostitution and selling bootleg whiskey.

"Riles had bands on weekends but the place never did much business," said Samuels. "He asked me if I wanted to take over the club and perform there. I didn't have anything to lose so I gave it a try."

Once Samuels began working at the Down Beat, he was approached by a singer who had just got to town from Beaumont, Texas—Roy Brown.

"Roy was down-and-out then," recalled Samuels. "I had to lend him my clothes even though they didn't fit him. He was a pretty good singer so we came up with the idea of the Blues Twins. We put a band together [which included guitarist Edgar Blanchard, saxophonists Leroy Rankin and Red Tyler, as well as drummer Bob Ogden]. Pretty soon the place was packed every night. We never sang together—Roy did a set, then I'd do a set."

Brown of course became famous via "Good Rockin' Tonight," a song some have suggested is the very first rhythm and blues record. Although Samuel's recollection of the incubation of "Good Rockin' Tonight" varies markedly with Brown's, it can't be completely discounted because Samuels wrote the B-side of the hit, "Lollipop Mama."

"Roy was doing 'Good Rockin' Tonight' at the Down Beat," recalled Samuels. "I didn't really think it was that good of a song because it didn't get as much reaction from the audience as when I did 'Lollipop Mama.' But Wynonie Harris came around the club to listen to it. [Harris covered the song for King Records] I couldn't understand why the man [Dave Braun of Deluxe Records] was interested in recording him [Brown] and not me."

"Good Rockin' Tonight" took off quickly and so did Brown. He dissolved the Blues Twins and took the band from the Down Beat with him, initially to Gert Town's Starlight Inn and then on a Midwest tour.

"Roy was selfish," contended Samuels. "All of a sudden he got popular and forgot the people that helped him get started."

Samuels though would not have to wait long to see his name on a record label.

"Sammy Goldberg came by the Down Beat," said Samuels. "I'd never met anyone like him before—he was a black Jew. He was a talent scout working for the Chess Brothers in Chicago. He wanted me to come to Chicago and make records. The Chess' were just getting into the record business and didn't have any artists. They owned a club then on Cottage Groove in Chicago, the Macambo."

Trying to capitalize on what Braun overlooked in New Orleans, Goldberg sent Samuels a train ticket to Chicago. Samuels became a popular attraction at the Macambo and became the first artist to record for Aristocrat, the label which preceded Chess. With the Macambo's house band, Dave Young's Orchestra, in support, Samuels' initial outing included his version of "Lollipop Mama." His second release, "Baseball Blues," was inspired by the legendary Jackie Robinson.

"I went to Wrigley Field and Jackie made a play that won the game for the Dodgers," said Samuels. "I wrote 'Baseball Blues' after that and the Chess Brothers would have recorded Robinson doing it. When Robinson was in Chicago he stayed with Monte Irvin [a Negro League baseball star] and I knew where Irvin lived. I brought the song to Jackie but he told me that his wife took care of his business and that I should show the song to her. When I told Jackie's wife the title of the song she got mad and said, 'My husband isn't going to sing no blues.' So I wound up cutting it myself."

During his Chicago sojourn, Samuels attended several recordings sessions produced by the Chess Brothers, including some by Muddy Waters, the transplanted Mississippi blues guitarist who became one of the label's top selling artists. According to Samuels, Muddy's timing was so bad that at one session, he tapped Muddy on the shoulder so he would know when it was the right time to start singing. Samuels was in Chicago nearly a year when Goldberg—who had since moved to Los Angeles and hired as a talent scout for Jack Lauderdale's Down Beat and Swing Time labels—called with an offer. He lured Samuels west with the promise of a recording contract and a two-week stint at the prestigious 5-4 Ballroom.

"Those were black market recordings," admitted Samuels, referring to his two Swing Time 78s. "At the time the Musicians Union had a ban on recording. Nobody was supposed to be making records, but Jack said he knew a place where we could record and we got paid under the table. The day I was in the studio Charles Brown, and Ray Charles also recorded."

Goldberg began booking Samuels, Turner, and Wynonie Harris on a Battle of the Blues package that toured the country. During a stop in Houston, Turner and Samuels went to visit Peacock Records' Don Robey to see if he was interested in recording them. Robey was out of town, so they went to see Saul Kahn at Freedom Records, Peacock's local competition. Kahn was more than willing to record both artists.

Samuels had three releases on Freedom including "Stack Em, Stack Em" which Imperial leased, "Lowtop Inn"—a popular New Orleans record— and "She Walk, She Walk, She Walk" a song Professor Longhair appropriated and recorded for Atlantic as "She Walks Right In." Eventually, Samuels settled in Houston and used it as a home base for several years. Robey's partner, Evelyn Johnson, ran the Buffalo Booking Agency and booked dates for him throughout the region. In 1950, Samuels traveled to Cincinnati to record for Deluxe but "Stompin' At the Jubilee" failed to sell. In 1952, he was in New Orleans and recorded "How Many More Years" with Edgar Blanchard's Gondoliers issued on a rare 10 inch album. He wouldn't record again until 1954 when he signed with Lamp, a subsidiary of the Aladdin, where he recorded the brilliant "Crazy With the Heat" and "Lightnin' Struck Me."

"I had moved to New York then because I was working at some Upstate clubs," said Samuels. "When I signed with Aladdin I went to Jesse Stone's office. [Stone was Aladdin's East Coast A&R man] He asked me if I had any material. I said, 'No but I can have four songs ready tomorrow.' He didn't believe me, but the next day I had them. Jesse was amazed and told me that I should concentrate on being a songwriter. I never did, but now I wish I'd have gone in that direction."

In 1956, Samuels was back in Texas looking for another record deal.

"I sent a demo of 'Chicken Hearted Woman' to Excello's Ernie Young in Nashville. He said he liked it and he'd record me next time I was in Nashville. Johnny Copeland was my guitar player—he was still in high school then—I told him how I wanted that chicken sound on the guitar and he played it just right. One weekend we were booked into the New Era Club in Nashville and we cut the session."

"Chicken Hearted Woman" was Samuel's biggest seller and was often played on the John R's show on Nashville's WLAC. It has since appeared on numerous blues anthologies. Although Samuels never had a record reach the national charts, he was popular enough to constantly tour throughout the country during the 1950s. One of his regular stops was Macon, Georgia, where he met Richard Penniman.

"Little Richard came to watch me sing when he was a teenager," recalled Samuels. "He stopped me after a show and said he was going to be a singer just like me. He wanted to know how I kept such a good band? I told him, 'You have to pay your musicians decently.' The next time I came to Macon, Richard was singing with a band and he invited me to see him. I went by the place, but after listening, I knew he was going to have to find his own style if he was going to make it. Richard was trying to sound like Billy Wright [Atlanta's premier female impersonator/vocalist] who I didn't think could sing anyway. I didn't understand what he was trying to do. The next thing I know, Richard's got 'Tutti Frutti' out and he's a big star. Right after that, we were both staying at the same motel near Houston. He invited me to his room and he said, 'Clarence you taught me a lot about this business. But let me show you something.' He had a table with stacks of bills on it and a big pistol. One by one, the guys in the band came in the room and looked at the money and the gun. Richard gave each one of them a stack of bills and they left. Finally Richard told me, 'Clarence that's how I keep a good band.'"

In 1958, Samuels was back in New York and was signed by Apt, a division of ABC Paramount.

"That's when I did 'We're Going To the Hop,'" said Samuels. "That should have been my biggest record. Everybody at the company said it was going to be a hit but it was released the same time as Lloyd Price's 'Personality' [on ABC]. His record stopped every record cold. I couldn't even get my record manufactured because all the presses were pressing 'Personality.'"

Samuels returned to Houston and worked clubs in the immediate area. He wouldn't record again until 1966.

"I started my own label Sharon," said Samuels. "I did 'Charlie Loan Me 50¢.' It did a little bit around Texas but I got out of the business not long after. I moved to Orlando, Florida, and the woman I was staying with didn't want me traveling. I stopped performing and booked bands."

Samuels later started the Duplex label in 1973 with Jimmy Liggins, an old friend from Los Angeles, who had also moved to Florida.

"Our first record was 'Come Into My Bedroom,'" said Samuels. "That was Deloris Ealy and Harmonica Fats. Then we did Bobby Williams' 'Funky Super Fly.' It sounded just like a James Brown record and I sang background on it. Henry Stone [at Tone Distributors in Miami] was interested in leasing it. He said he could make it a hit because he had connections. We didn't do it because we thought we could make it a hit on our own. Unfortunately it didn't turn out that way. Our other single was by A. C. Jones who was a guitarist from Florida. His singing reminded me of Johnny Ace. I produced one or two other singles on him for another company but I can't recall the name of the label"

Eventually Samuels returned to Los Angeles and started a profitable T-shirt/promotion company that had the Jackson Five as a client.

"I went 10 years without remembering my singing career," said Samuels. "I never really thought about it until I got sick. At that point, I realized I might die without anybody knowing what I had accomplished as an entertainer."

Luckily, Samuels regained his health after several blood clots were removed from his legs. Revitalized, he has started writing new material and in 2000 he recorded *The House of the Blues* CD which included several imaginative new songs and some of his original recordings. A rare Clarence Samuels performance, at the Tommy Ridgley tribute in August of 1999, proved that even as a septuagenarian, he still has strength, energy and possesses a unique stage presence rarely seen. At the end of his short cameo he had most of the audience on their feet

"I can still sing, I can still write, and I can still perform" concluded Samuels. "I haven't used up all my talent."

CHAPTER THREE
~ Paul Gayten: True ~

A major, although often overlooked, figure in the early development of New Orleans rhythm and blues is the late Paul Gayten. Gayten's accomplishments were numerous. His initial 1947 recording, "True," was the city's first R&B hit, and his early recordings would influence Fats Domino, Professor Longhair, and Dave Bartholomew among others. Gayten led one of New Orleans' most popular bands and served as a talent scout, songwriter, promoter and producer—overseeing hits by Annie Laurie, Larry Darnell, Clarence Henry, and Bobby Charles.

An extremely skilled pianist, Gayten could play anything from blues to bebop and Bach. The nephew of renown barrelhouse piano player, Eurreal "Little Brother" Montgomery, blues was his initial influence and he learned to play many of his uncle's signature tunes including, "The 44 Blues" and "Special Rider Blues." Later he would learn to read music, play Tin Pan Alley standards, show tunes, and learn most of Duke Ellington, Count Basie, and Jimmy Lunceford's repertoires. Mac Rebennack recalled Gayten rarely played a song the same way twice, often alternating the tempo to keep the audience entertained and his band alert.

Gayten was born at Charity Hospital in New Orleans, January 29, 1920, and raised in the Tangipahoa Parish town of Kentwood. His family owned a white baby grand piano which the entire Gayten family played. In a 1950 biography published by his booking agency, Gayten recalled that his uncle (Montgomery) would often push the piano onto the back porch and entertain their neighbors. According to Gayten, he was quite young when he learned to play. "I learned to walk by holding onto the keys of the piano," he claimed. "With each step I took, I learned another note."

At the age of 14, Gayten moved to Jackson, Mississippi, where he lived with his Godfather. A year later, he joined Doc Parmley's 16-piece band before eventually hooking up with the Royal American Show band, and later the Silas Green Show band. The Royal American and Silas Green shows constantly toured the Southern states, performing in theaters, warehouses, baseball parks, city squares and farmer's fields. This continual traveling exposed Gayten to several different styles of music and he came in contact with many musicians. In 1938, he returned to Jackson and formed a six-piece band, the Southland Troubadours, the first black musical group to broadcast over Jackson's WSLI. In 1940, Gayten was drafted and stationed at Biloxi, Mississippi. His music skills helped him avoid most of basic training, as he organized a small combo that entertained the troops at service clubs and USOs.

"Paul was playing at the officer's club at Keesler Air Force base," recalled trumpeter Frank Mitchell. "He got to know a white sergeant from playing there. One night the sergeant brought a girl to the club and they sat down and listened to Paul. At the end of the night, the sergeant asked Paul if he could drive the girl home. Paul agreed. On their way there, he talked the girl into having sex with him. Paul took the girl to her rooming house, but somebody saw them and called the police. The Sheriff caught them in bed and they pulled Paul out of there. They drove him to the county jail in Gulfport, which was 12 miles away. Paul said they whipped his ass in the police car all the way there. He stayed in jail for a couple of days before they let him go. When they did, the police told him he had 20 minutes to get his things and get out of town. The next bus out of town was headed to New Orleans and Paul was on it. When he got here, Paul started playing at the Robin Hood on Jackson Avenue with just a trio. Gradually he added more musicians until he had seven or eight in the group. They became the hottest attraction in town."

By 1946, the Paul Gayten "Trio" consisted of himself on piano, Edgar Blanchard on guitar, Robert "Sweet Pea" Green on drums, and George Pryor on bass.

"Paul got out of the service before Dave Bartholomew," recalled Billy Diamond, who occasionally filled in on bass with Gayten. "When Dave saw what Paul was doing at the Robin Hood it really opened his eyes. Dave didn't necessarily copy Paul, but he was a big influence on him. Paul was a sharp cat. He wore expensive clothes, diamonds and drove flashy cars. He was a very good musician and expected the best out of the people that played with him."

Gayten's revue also included two vocalists, Earl Williams and Annie Laurie. Gayten had earlier met Laurie in Miami when she fronted Snookum Russell's band. Laurie was in New Orleans with Dallas Bartley's Small Town Boys when he lured her away. Around this time, Gayten had befriended Al Young, the proprietor of the Bop Shop on South Rampart Street. The Bop Shop stocked releases on several independent labels including De Luxe, a Linden, New Jersey, label owned by David and Julian Braun. The Brauns had only been in the record business since 1944, but built a successful label by recording black music that the major labels ignored. Always on the trail of emerging talent and trends, they told

Young they were coming to New Orleans, and inquired if he could recommend talent they might be interested in recording. Young obliged, referring Gayten.

Gayten's initial De Luxe session took place in January of 1947 at the J&M Studio and was split with Earl Williams. Williams' record stalled, but Gayten's rendering of the standard, "True," backed by the risque, "Your Hands Ain't Clean," spent eight weeks at the top of *Billboard's* Sepia record chart. "True" didn't sound like a New Orleans record, as stylistically it was closer to the relaxed style of West Coast music popularized by Nat "King" Cole and Johnny Moore. The success of "True" sustained the Brauns interest in New Orleans, who besides Gayten, also recorded Roy Brown, Cousin Joe, Smiley Lewis, and Dave Bartholomew.

In May 1947, *The Louisiana Weekly* noted Gayten was, "New Orleans' newest jukebox sensation, packin' 'em in at the Robin Hood." During that month, Gayten backed Laurie on a cover of Ella and Buddy Johnson's "Since I Fell for You." It proved to be a bigger hit than "True." The following month's *Louisiana Weekly* reported, "Annie Laurie has become one of New Orleans' popular disc artists. Hear her waxing of 'Since I Fell For You'—terrific!"

Between October and December of 1947, Gayten and Laurie cut seven sessions at J&M so that De Luxe could stockpile material for an impending recording ban planned by the Musicians Mutal Protective Union. During these sessions, Gayten cut "Hey Little Girl"—later recorded by Professor Longhair as "Hey Now Baby," and Fats Domino, who called it "Hey Little School Girl." A 12-bar blues with a rumba beat, this was clearly one of the first distinct examples of New Orleans R&B on wax.

Gayten and Laurie spent the early months of 1948 on the road, headlining at the Apollo in Harlem, the Howard in Washington, the Savoy in New York and the Regal in Chicago. Neither artist recorded during the lull in the strike in the fall of 1948, although Gayten arranged Chubby Newsome's hit, "Hip Shakin' Mama." Apparently the duo had a falling out (perhaps over Gayten working with Newsome) as Laurie began performing with Dave Bartholomew's band around New Orleans, while Gayten toured with Bea Booker.

By February of 1949, they'd mended their fences and they were back in the studio. Gayten cut the lovely "Creole Gal Blues," and Laurie accounted for the tough "Annie's Blues." These recordings featured Lee Allen on saxophone, the newest member of Gayten's "Trio." Gayten would also produce more recordings by Newsome and Eddie Gorman. Later in the year, De Luxe was absorbed by King Records, so the Brauns formed a new label, Regal. The Brauns continued to rely on Gayten's expertise and he relocated to New Jersey to be closer to their operation. Gayten had success with his interpretation of Leadbelly's "Good Night Irene" and with Laurie's "I'll Never Be Free." He also produced Larry Darnell's "I'll Get Along Somehow" and "For You My Love." the latter which reached number one in *Billboard's* R&B chart in 1950. However, the following year, Regal was on the verge of bankruptcy so Gayten returned to New Orleans and began a six year run as bandleader at the Brass Rail on Canal Street. Many consider Gayten's Brass Rail group one of the finest New Orleans rhythm and blues groups of all time. Besides Gayten, at one time or another, the group boasted Lee Allen, Jack Willis, Chuck Badie and Frank Fields as members.

In 1952, Gayten signed with Danny Kesler's Okeh label, the R&B arm of Columbia Records. However, Gayten's stint at Okeh was largely uneventful, primarily because Columbia had difficulty promoting and selling black records. Outside of his superb rendition of Clarence Davenport's "Cow Cow Blues," which was popular in New Orleans, and a raucous version of "They All Asked For You (Down At The Zoo)," his Okeh releases didn't sell particularly well.

In 1954, Gayten recorded "Get It"/"I'm Tired," for Checker, a subsidiary of the Chicago-based Chess label. The following year he was hired by Mel Mallory, who ran the local Capitol office and had formed the Mel-A-Dee label. Gayten and his band backed up Little Leo (Lloyd Price's brother) and Roy "Boogie Boy" Perkins on the initial Mel-A-Dee sessions. Perkins' splendid swamp pop ballad, "You're On My Mind," made it to number one on several New Orleans radio stations and did extremely well in South Louisiana. The Perkins session marked the first time a black band played behind a white artist on a New Orleans recording session.

Gayten cut more titles for Checker in 1955 but none were issued. However, at the time, Chess owner Leonard Chess was keenly aware of the success Imperial, Specialty and Aladdin were having with their New Orleans recordings and he wanted a piece of the action. The label earlier had regional success with the Hawkettes and Sugar Boy Crawford, but Chess wanted a stronger presence in the city. To accomplish this, he hired Gayten as his New Orleans A&R man. The deal would pay dividends the following year when Clarence Henry brought him "Ain't Got No Home."

"Paul's wife Odellia was my high school teacher at L.B. Landry," said Henry. "When I was 15, I used to work at a gas station. To get home, I had to get off the street car and transfer to a city bus in front of the Brass Rail where Paul played. The club's clientele was real classy and so was his band—the place was always packed. Paul had this high class way about him. I used to think it was really cool the way he left teeth marks in the filter of his cigarette when he smoked. After I wrote 'Ain't Got No Home,' I took it to Paul. He was looking for something to go up against Imperial and Fats Domino. Paul thought I might be the one to do it. He convinced Leonard Chess to fly down and listen to me play at the Brass Rail. He liked me and I got signed. Before we went in the studio, we rehearsed at Paul's house on Paris Avenue. He was great to work with. I liked the way he got that chinky-chinky-chink New Orleans back-beat going in the studio. He had lots of good ideas for material and he was a guy that really respected other musicians."

"Ain't Got No Home" became a hit, but Henry couldn't immediately repeat his initial success. Gayten would later produce some memorable records on Chess by Bobby Charles, Eddie Bo, Charles Williams, as well as Myles and Dupont. However, he might well have exploited more talent in New Orleans with a freer hand. Gayten was required to get Chess' approval before he could sign an artist. This meant sending an audition tape to Chicago, getting Chess to listen to it, and then wait for an answer. In comparison, Gayten's competition, Dave Bartholomew, had no such restrictions. Bartholomew was given carte blanche by Imperial's owner Lew Chudd to sign any artist and hustle them into the studio if the situation warranted it. As a result, on more than one occasion, Bartholomew was able to procure an artist Gayten was initially interested in.

Gayten also continued to make records on himself and his solid band. He would reach the charts with two instrumentals, "Nervous Boogie" and "Windy." His last Argo (another Chess subsidiary) release, "Windy." was a respectable number 78 in the *Billboard* Hot 100 and became a huge hit in the West Indies. In a subtle example of 1950s payola, "Windy" credited John Richbourgh as co-writer. Although he had no input in composing the song, Richbourgh, a. k. a. John R, probably the country's most powerful R&B disc jockey—at Nashville's 50,000 watt WLAC—was obviously inclined to play the record knowing he would benefit when Chess dispersed the composer royalties for "Windy." Gayten also recorded a snappy jingle for Richbourgh ("Hey John R, whatcha gonna do? Hey John R, play us some rhythm and blues.") which aired on his show for over a decade.

As Chess A&R man, Gayten also promoted records in the South. On Mondays (his day off from the Brass Rail where he now owned a 15 percent stake) he often flew to Dallas, Houston or Atlanta, promoting new releases at distributors, one stops and radio stations. Gayten was also on the look out for regional hits on small regional labels that Chess might be interested in leasing. Gayten would prove to be such a valuable promotion man that Chess moved him to Los Angeles in 1958 to expand and run the label's West Coast operation.

"Paul did a few gigs in Santa Monica when he got out here but he pretty much concentrated on the record business and got away from playing," said Billy Diamond. "He and Earl Palmer [who worked for Aladdin] were the first black record executives on the West Coast."

Late In 1959, Gayten had one last minor hit, "The Hunch," a cover of a Ray Peterson Quintet instrumental which reached number 68 in the Hot 100. Released on Anna, a Detroit label co-owned by Barry Gordy's sister, Chess distributed the label so he didn't mind Gayten moonlighting. His Anna follow up, "Beatnik Beat," did nothing and nor did the Gayten produced Larry Darnell's reworking of "I'll Get Along Somehow" on Argo. More importantly, Gayten increased Chess's presence on the West Coast as he continued to promote the label's new releases. Gayten recorded one last session for Chess in 1967, but it was never issued.

"Paul did real well out there," said Henry. "He owned a couple of houses and at one time lived across the street from Nat "King" Cole. He'd come back to New Orleans once in awhile on business but he didn't play music."

Gayten remained an executive with Chess until the company was sold to GRT in 1969. He then formed his own record company. Pzazz, whose motto was, "Put some pzazz in your jazz."

"Paul had Pzazz," said Diamond. "He had a big record with Lorez Alexandria. He also recorded Louis Jordan and Rick James. He did that for a few years but the record business had started to change and he got out all together. After that, Paul and his wife started a direct marketing company."

Gayten died of natural causes in Los Angeles on March 26, 1991.

CHAPTER FOUR
~ Tommy Ridgley: The New Orleans King of the Stroll ~

For a half-century, the late Tommy Ridgley was one of New Orleans' greatest rhythm and blues artists. A regal, confident, and engaging performer, he never had a national hit, like several of his contemporaries, but he made an impressive string of recordings that date back to November 1949. His music entertained three generations of New Orleanians and reached listeners in all corners of the world.

Born Thomas Herman Ridgley Jr., October 30, 1925, he was the third of 17 children and grew up two miles from New Orleans in the Shrewsbury section of Jefferson Parish. As a child Ridgley sang spirituals on the corner of Andover Street and Harlem Avenue (now Causeway Boulevard) with neighborhood pals. During his three year Navy enlistment, which took him to Okinawa, Ridgley taught himself to play blues on the PX pianos. After his discharge in 1946, Ridgley returned to Shrewsbury and studied music under the GI Bill at Grunewald's School of Music. Evenings though would often find him on La Salle Street hanging out and listening to music at the Dew Drop Inn.

"The Dew Drop had a Monday night talent show that was big," recalled Ridgley in 1985. "I'd been there a couple of times to see what the competition was like but it took me a couple of weeks to build up enough confidence to enter it. I knew I could sing but I didn't know what would happen when I got on stage. Finally, I built up the nerve and entered. The emcee, Sporty Johnson, called me to the bandstand and Edgar Blanchard and the Gondoliers were the house band. I asked them to play 'Piney Brown Blues.' I stood behind the microphone and didn't move anything but my lips. I got a tremendous ovation though and won first prize. I went home that night and looked at that $5 bill over and over."

With stage fright behind him, Ridgley began singing the Bama Band and Al Anderson's group at Gerttown's Starlight Inn. One evening in November 1949, bandleader Dave Bartholomew, who had recently been hired by the Hollywood-based Imperial label as an A&R man, dropped by the club in search of talent. Sensing Ridgley had potential, a week later Bartholomew returned to the Starlight with Imperial's other local rep, Al Young, who also heard the singer's promise. Ridgley was subsequently hired to sing with Bartholomew's band and was offered a recording contract. On November 29, 1949, Ridgely and Jewel King, Bartholomew's other vocalist, became the first New Orleans artists to record for Imperial Records. Ridgley's initial outing "Shrewsbury Blues" was a braggadocios slow blues with some memorable lyrics about his rough and tumble neighborhood.

"It was a good seller around New Orleans," confirmed Ridgley. "I'd been doing 'Shrewsbury Blues' on stage for a couple years before going in the studio. I wrote it around Roy Brown's 'Along About Midnight.' We needed a fast tune for a flip side so I came up with 'Early Dawn Boogie.'"

A productive songwriter, Ridgley also wrote both sides of his second Imperial release, "I Live My Life" (later covered by Fats Domino as "I Lived My Life") and "Lavinia."

"I have to admit that 'Lavinia' is the only song I ever stole," said Ridgley. "A guy named Blazer Boy [George Stevenson] was playing the piano in the Tiajuana. He was singing this song 'Loberta' and I couldn't get it out of my head. The next time I went in the studio I told Dave 'Let's try this.' I changed the words a little but I did it just like Blazer Boy."

Ridgley also wrote other Imperial sides including "Good Times" and "A Day Is Coming."

"'Good Times' came from the old 'Junker's Blues,'" said Ridgley. "Everybody was doing a version of it and I thought mine came out pretty good. 'A Day Is Going To Come,' is a tune I wrote and recorded twice. Once for Imperial and later for Herald as 'I Wish I'd Never.' That was real big around here."

Another popular local record was his cover of Melvin Smith's "Looped."

"Lew Chudd instructed us to do that song," said Ridgley. "He heard 'Looped' in California and thought it was going to be a big hit. Lew air mailed a copy of the record to New Orleans and had us wait at the studio for it. When it got here, Cosimo's secretary typed out the words for me to learn. The guys in the band listened to it and ran it down a couple of times. In half-an-hour it was done."

Other great sides on Imperial included "Junie Mae" and "Monkey Man."

"Those were tunes we got together on the bandstand," explained Ridgley. "'Junie Mae' was a regular 12-bar blues. You had to do something like that every night for the audience. 'Monkey Man' was a B-flat shuffle. When you hit the bandstand, you'd tell the band to play it because it was good opener."

Ridgley's recordings for Imperial especially benefited from the quality musicians Bartholomew used on his sessions.

"No question Dave had the best band around," emphasized Ridgley.

"Earl Palmer drums, Salvador Doucet piano, Frank Fields bass, Ernest McLean guitar, Lee Allen [who referred to Ridgley as 'Pregnant Eyes'], Herb Hardesty, and Red Tyler on saxophones. Those guys could play any-thing—jazz, blues, rhythm and blues. They were the real reason all those companies started coming to New Orleans to record."

Under Bartholmew's direction, Ridgley also recorded with King, Waldorf and Decca. His first Decca single, "Tra La La" was a popular local record and was covered by Tommy Brown, who had a minor nation-al hit with it on Dot in 1951. Two years later, Ridgley struck out on his own.

"Dave went to California and left me the band," said Ridgley. "We were playing at the Pelican Club and a guy came in and offered me $150 a week to sing at his club in Nashville. That was good money and I want-ed to go. The owner of the Pelican let me out of my contract so I put a band together and went to Nashville. I had Milton Batiste on trumpet, 'Guitar Red,' Edwin Mollier on drums, Sam Noel and Eddie Smith on sax-ophone. A guy named 'Woo Woo' played piano—he was high on wine all the time. We played in Nashville for six weeks and then came home. [In 1953, Ridgley was a regular attraction at Ruby's Inn in Kenner fronting Ben Johnson's Orchestra.] After that I got with a guy named Big Curtis who booked us and we stayed on the road from 1954 to 1956."

After leaving Bartholomew, Ridgley's Imperial contract wasn't renewed. Atlantic was interested however and he signed with them in 1953. In August he cut "I'm Gonna Cross That River"/"Ooh Lawdy My Baby," with Ray Charles backing on piano as well as Edgar Blanchard and the Gondoliers. He also cut the wild sax-driven instrumental "Jam Up" which narrowly missed the R&B charts. By 1956, Ridgley was working regularly at the 1202 Club on South Carrollton Avenue before moving across town to Natal's Club on Chef Menteur Highway.

"That was when Justin Adams joined the band," said Ridgley, refer-ring to the late guitarist. "It was the beginning of the Untouchables band. In 1957, I signed with Al Silvers' Herald label and we had a big record with 'When I Meet My Girl.' Al promised me a new Cadillac but I told him I preferred the money. Things were going pretty good, I was playing at Tulane, LSU, USM, Mississippi State, and Ole Miss—strictly white colleges."

By the end of the 1950s, Tommy Ridgley and the Untouchables had taken residence at the Dew Drop where they became the house band— playing the talent shows, backing out of town acts, and playing the early morning jam sessions. Ridgley and the Untouchables also backed Sam Cooke, Clyde McPhatter, Ivory Joe Hunter, and Little Willie John when they performed at Municipal Auditorium or at the Lincoln Beach amusement park. Ridgley would begin the 1960s by signing with Joe Ruffino's up-and-coming Ric label. His tenure at the label would be one of the most fruitful and musically enjoyable portions of his career.

"When Ruffino heard I was available, he sent for me," said Ridgley. "Me and him were alright."

On the label of Ridgley's Ric debut, "Is It True"/"Let's Talk It Over," Ruffino billed Ridgley as *The New King of the Stroll*.

"Ruffino wanted to make that a stroll record. Chuck Willis [who was billed as *The King of the Stroll*] had just died and Ruffino thought that he and I had a similar style. That was a big record around New Orleans. I remember Ruffino thought he was pretty shrewd for signing me at that point. Right after that record came out he said, 'Tommy we have to get some more songs together and get back in the studio.'"

Ridgley had numerous local hits on Ric including "My Ordinary Girl," "Please Hurry Home," "The Girl From Kooka Monga" and "Double Eyed Whammy"—which was covered by guitarist Freddy King as instrumental retitled "San-Ho-Zay" for King Records.

"'Double Eyed Whammy' was inspired by Evil-Eyed Fleagle, a character in the Li'l Abner cartoon strip who cast his whammy on people at the drop of a hat," laughed Ridgley. "'The Girl From Kooka Monga' was my interpretation of Jessie Hill's 'Ooh Poo Pah Doo.' It was a song that went over well on the gigs."

Ridgley's most popular record on Ric was the Eddie Bo composition "In the Same Old Way" from the summer of 1961.

"Larry McKinley was responsible for making that a hit," specified Ridgley. "He was the hottest jock in New Orleans [at WYLD] then. If he played your record there was a pretty good chance it was going to take off. After Larry got on 'In the Same Old Way' it was picked up by every other station on New Orleans. There was a lot interest in that record from major labels, but after Ruffino got burned by Roulette on Joe Jones' 'You Talk Too Much,' he started distrusting people from the North. When my record was out, Barbara George had just recorded 'I Know.' In New Orleans 'In the Same Old Way' was selling better. 'I Know' got picked up by another label [Sue distributed it] and they had a big national hit with it, but my record just stayed local."

Ridgley and Ruffino kept plugging away though, following with "My Ordinary Girl"/"She's Got What It Takes." Both sides were taken at a medium New Orleans two-beat tempo and did well regionally. His Ric session from December 1962 though had an unexpected lack of creativity. It consisted of three ballads, including a cover of Bull Moose Jackson's lugubrious "I Love You Yes I Do" and "Honest I Do," a note-for-note cover of "In the Same Old Way." Sadly, these would be Ridgley's last Ric recordings. Ruffino's death in 1962 briefly left Ridgley without a label, but that was a small hurdle considering what was around the corner.

"A turning point in my career came with the Beatles," said Ridgley. "There was a change in music and people at that time got away from R&B. All the college work disappeared. Mostly I started playing for middle-aged audiences. It was tough but I hung in there."

After lone releases on Blue Jay and Cinderella, in 1964 Ridgley cut "All My Love Belongs To You"/"I Want Some Money Baby" for Johen, a short-lived subsidiary of Watch Records that was distributed by London. Produced by Wardell Quezergue, the brassy arrangements were very much influenced by Bobby Bland's then popular style.

"When we got out of the studio we just knew we had a hit," laughed Ridgley. "Joe Assunto [Watch's co-owner] was positive we just cut a number one. But Dave Bartholomew said, 'Man that record ain't going nowhere because London doesn't promote their records.' Well Dave was right. Nothing happened and there wasn't a thing we could do because the ball was in London's court."

By the late 1960s, not only was Ridgley's brand of music pretty much off the charts, but many of the clubs that previously featured rhythm and blues were closed or began booking rock or soul bands. However, while many New Orleans R&B artists that had hits were reduced to clerking in department stores, driving cabs, waiting tables, or repairing cars, Ridgley continued to hustle gigs and get the occasional recording date. Singles on International City, Dew Drop and White Cliffs were neighborhood records, but they kept him working.

"I've always been the kind of guy who jumped at the chance to record," said Ridgley. "I never concerned myself with contracts or money. I just wanted to see my name on a record."

By the 1970s, the initial revival of New Orleans R&B, partly fueled by John Broven's book *Walkin' To New Orleans* and the emergence of the New Orleans Jazz & Heritage Festival, benefited Ridgley. Outside of Clarence Henry and Fats Domino's groups, most of the New Orleans R&B bands of the 1950s and early 1960s had dissolved once their style of music fell out of favor. However, Ridgley and his band remained untouchable over the years. Once past hit-makers like Irma Thomas, Bobby Mitchell, Ernie K-Doe, Aaron Neville, Benny Spellman, and Robert Parker began working again, they needed a crack New Orleans band to back them. Quite often, Ridgley and the Untouchables got the call.

During the decade he waxed creative new singles on Hep Me, Sansu,

Basin Street, River City, Ronn and Sound of New Orleans that sold around town. In 1977, Ridgley was also the subject of one of the first New Orleans R&B album reissues, *Through the Years*, which collected most of his Ric material. In the 1980s, Ridgley kept busy working around New Orleans and occasionally accepting European festival dates. Reissues of earlier work appeared on Rounder and Pathe Marconi, while new singles appeared on Sound of New Orleans, Maison de Soul, Tudor and Du Bat. Although there were several collections of Ridgley's vintage material available, he didn't cut his first contemporary album until 1990 when *How Long* appeared on Sound of New Orleans. Two years later, he recorded *She Turns Me On* for the Modern Blues label. However, his best effort during the decade was clearly *Since the Blues Began*, backing Snooks Eaglin and George Porter, released on Black Top in 1995.

"We cut a lot of songs that had been in my head for a long time and material I cut before but felt was improved on," said Ridgley. "It reminded me of the sound we used to get back in the old days."

Unfortunately, Ridgley fell ill shortly after *Since the Blues Began* was released and he was unable to fill dates that might have helped promote the CD. Although he regained enough strength to continue playing, Ridgley cut back his schedule and turned several dates over to his brother Sammy who fronted the Untouchables. In the spring of 1998, Ridgley had a kidney transplant that temporarily took care of his health problems. After the operation, Ridgley reflected on his career.

"I've never had a big hit but I've cut some pretty good records that could have gone national with a a little luck. I've been able to play music all these years when a lot of guys that had hits lost it all and are doing nothing. I've said it before and it's still true—around New Orleans I'm still a star."

In January 1999, Tommy Ridgley received *Offbeat* magazine's annual Lifetime Achievement Award. Three month's later, he made his 28th consecutive appearance at the New Orleans Jazz & Heritage Festival. Unexpectedly, Ridgley died of lung cancer on August 11, 1999.

CHAPTER FIVE
~ Jewel King: 3x7=21 ~

Just barely a one-hit wonder, Jewel King accounted for one of New Orleans' earliest rhythm and blues hits with the raucous "3 X 7= 21," a record which became the Imperial label's initial calling card into the field of R&B. Details concerning King's career are sketchy but we do know this:

Jewel King was born June 21, 1910 and came to New Orleans from Texas after WW II. By 1948, she was making a name for herself as a vocalist at Club Desire, Club Rocket and the Dew Drop. She also appeared on vaudeville shows —"Midnight Rambles" —that were held at neighborhood movie theaters. In the summer of 1949, King was an occasional attraction at the Paddock Club on Bourbon Street.

The late saxophonist Alvin "Red" Tyler, a member of Dave Bartholomew's Orchestra, and who played on several of King's recordings recalled, "You have to remember that in those days the band was the big attraction. The vocalists just came up to sing as part of the show. It wasn't uncommon for a band to have three or four vocalists at one time. Jewel sang with us quite often, She was tall, attractive, and she had a lot of stage presence. Jewel wasn't as good a singer as Annie Laurie [Paul Gayten's vocalist] but she worked real hard and was a good draw."

Bandleader Dave Bartholomew, who hired King and gave her the chance to record added.

"We'd been working around the Robin Hood with Jewel and she was sounding good. When I did my first session for Imperial [November 1949] I told Jewel to come down to Cosimo's Studio. [Actually J&M] We did a split session. Tommy Ridgley recorded 'Shrewsbury Blues'—Jewel cut '3 X 7 = 21.' Red Tyler played a beautiful solo on '3 X 7 = 21' which I think was what really sold the record. The tune took off around New Orleans with a bang and started to look like it was going to make some noise across the country."

King however threw a wrench into the works.

"Her record looked like it could have been even bigger than 'The Fat Man,'" continued Bartholomew, referring to Fats Domino's debut. "Lew Chudd arranged a series of dates all the way out to the West Coast with Fats, Jewel and my band. Just before we were supposed to leave, Jewel said she wasn't going. Her old man, Jack Scott, who played guitar and did arrangements for Paul Gayten, told her that I was making too much money and she wasn't going to get paid for her records. Jewel didn't want to leave New Orleans. I told her I thought it was a big mistake on her part but what could I do? We had to leave without her. [Ridgley replaced her and sang "3 X 7= 21" on the tour.] I think time proved me right—her career stalled."

"3 X 7= 21" stopped selling once it approached 100,000, narrowly missing the charts. Bartholomew was able to coax her back into the studio for one more session, but, "I'll Get It" and "Broke My Mother's Rules," didn't catch the public's attention the way "3 X 7=21" did. Her last recording session took place in Houston in 1952 when she recorded "Lost Lover" and "Round About Love Time," the latter an attempt to emulate the success of her Imperial debut.

"Jewel started working with Jack Scott's new band," concluded Bartholomew. "The last I heard, they moved to San Antonio and she was working at the Keyhole Club. That was back in the 1950s. That's the last I heard of her."

King died in San Antonio November 25, 1997.

CHAPTER SIX
~ Fats Domino: The Fat Man ~

Fats Domino... Even the name bounces rhythmically off your tongue.

So far, no other New Orleans artist has created a sound that has consistently been more recognizable, more influential, and more profitable, than Antoine "Fats" Domino. During the 1950s and 1960s, Domino had a phenomenal run of chart success, selling upwards of 70 million records while chalking up 23 Recording Industry of America Association certified gold records in the process.

However, unlike the more flamboyant rock and roll idols that would emerge during the era, Domino made his way into the charts, and the hearts of America, quite leisurely. He wasn't threatening or outrageous, a harbinger of a radically new sound, and his personal life was absolutely wholesome. Domino established himself by simply continuing to play and develop the inimitable type of music he had always performed—New Orleans rhythm and blues. Through his warm relaxed creole vocals and catchy piano, Domino transformed the New Orleans sound into a very commercial entity. Initially his records sold in the black community, but when rock and roll became popular in the mid-1950s, his style was embraced wholeheartedly by white record buyers as well.

Antoine Domino Jr. was born in New Orleans on February 26, 1928. The youngest of nine children, Domino's parents, Antoine Sr. and Donatile, had moved to the city several years earlier from Vacherie, Louisiana, a town located upriver on the west bank of the Mississippi River. Like many black families, the Dominos came to New Orleans hoping to find employment that bustling port offered. It has incorrectly been written that Domino's first language was French. Domino spoke English, albeit a unique dialect, heavily influenced by creole patois and the unique speech patterns of the New Orleans Ninth Ward neighborhood where he grew up.

When Domino came into the world, his family lived in a simple shotgun house at 1939 Jourdan Avenue near the Industrial Canal. Later they moved to a larger, more comfortable house, at 2407 Jourdan. During his childhood, Domino's neighborhood was still primarily rural and many homes still had outdoor privies. The Ninth Ward then primarily consisted of first generation European/American families (mostly Italians) and black families, lured to New Orleans with hopes of finding better paying jobs. Most Ninth Ward families maintained large gardens and livestock to help make ends meet.

"When I was real young, I remember catching crawfish in the ditches near my house," recalled Domino. "People kept cows and chickens in their yards too."

In addition to it's countrified ways, the Ninth Ward was alive with music that emanated from honky tonks, jukeboxes and brass bands that accompanied parades and funerals.

Domino also heard the rhythmic way that fruit and vegetable vendors would advertise their products when they pushed their carts through his neighborhood.

"'I got o-o-o-k-r-e-e-e,' they'd shout," said Domino. "Wa-a-a-terme-e-e-l-o-on, Red to the rind. Let me show you."

Dominos father supported his family on a modest $26 a week salary he earned working at the Fair Grounds race track stable. Although Antoine Sr. played violin and Donatile the accordion, their son's musical inspiration came from his brother-in-law, Harrison Verret.

A veteran Dixieland musician, Verret played guitar and banjo with the Kid Ory and Oscar "Papa" Celestin bands. Although 21 years older than Domino, Verret took a special interest in his nephew, encouraging him to play the piano Domino's family inherited from a relative. To assist Domino, Verret printed the name of all the notes on the piano keys, showed him chords and how to run the scales.

"He was the one that taught me the foundations," said Domino, referring to Verret. "Once he showed me the chords, I could play with just about any band."

A grammar school friend of Domino, the late Irving "Lee" Dorsey, recalled that Domino rarely played games with his pals after the school bell, instead preferring to head home and practice the piano.

"When I was nine years old, I used to deliver ice for an old man," said Domino. "When people asked him where I was he'd say, 'Just find out who has a piano on his route. That's where you'll find him.'"

Domino was tutored by a Ms. Celestin for two years. Initially, timing and singing on key were problems for him, but as he practiced, Domino rapidly improved. At the age of 10, he was already performing in public and occasionally accompanied Verret's to jobs in the French Quarter. After Verret was confident in Domino's ability, he began booking small jobs for him around the neighborhood. Domino didn't complete high school, so in his mid-teens he began working as a laborer to help support his family. Besides hauling ice, Domino was employed at a bakery, cut grass, waxed cars, collected scrap metal, hauled lumber, stacked bed springs, and worked with his father at the Fair Grounds.

"I only worked at the Fair Grounds two weeks," said Domino. "They wanted me to get in the back of a truck with two horses and ride all the way to St. Louis. That was the end of that. I didn't even go back and get my little $12 for the week."

Through the various trails of Domino's labor, music remained his passion. By the time he was in his mid-teens, Domino was performing three nights a week, occasionally venturing beyond the boundaries of the Ninth Ward.

In 1947, Domino was hired to play with Billy Diamond's Band, a regular attraction at the tiny Hide Away Inn, located at 2800 Desire Street. Diamond was a colorful energetic hustler who played the string bass and led one of New Orleans' hardest working bands.

Diamond was the first one to refer to Domino as "Fats," an apt moniker for a 5'6", 220 pound 19-year-old.

"I used to be kind of small," explained Domino. "But I started picking up weight and Billy started calling me 'Fats.' Then everybody started calling me 'Fats' Domino."

After Diamond hired Domino, Verret took his brother-in-law to the Musician's Protection Union Local 496 and bought him his first union card. That same year, Domino married his childhood sweetheart, Rose Mary Hall, a YMCA receptionist, and they moved into a small house not far from his parents. Together they would raise a family of four boys and four girls, all with names that begin with the letter A.

By the late 1940s, a new style of music was being created in black America. Initially it's development was shaped by economics more than any other factor. As Dave Bartholomew explained, "It got too costly to keep up a big band. Bandleaders had to scale down so they could keep working and making money—that had a lot to do with the evolution of the sound we called rhythm and blues."

Almost exclusively recorded by independent labels, rhythm and blues discs were hustled to regional distributors, jukebox operators, record shops, and the few small stations that programmed their records. As the music became more accessible, Domino began to listen to the latest rhythm and blues artists.

"I listened to Roy Milton, Camille Howard, Charles Brown, Amos Milburn, Joe Turner, and especially Louis Jordan," he pointed out. "Back then it seemed like Louis Jordan put a new record out ever two weeks."

Domino also listened to boogie-woogie pianists Albert Ammons, Pete Johnson, and Meade Lux Lewis. His local influences included Champion Jack Dupree, Paul Gayten, Archibald, Professor Longhair, and Isadore

"Tuts" Washington.

It was Diamond who first encouraged Domino to start singing a few numbers during their sets. According to Diamond, Domino immediately displayed the talent which would set him apart from other entertainers and he would become the chief draw at the Hide Away Inn.

The first printed references to Domino appeared in Dr. Daddy-O's Louisiana Weekly column on July 9, 1949:

"Say Papa have you been to the Hideaway lately??... Fats Domino is out there making them holler!!!...Yeah that Fats Domino outfit is much mad..."

Several months later, when he was "making them holler" at the Hide Away, Lew Chudd, and Dave Bartholomew visited the club to see what the fuss was about.

Bartholomew's name will forever be linked with Domino. Together both men would leave a bold and permanent mark on popular music. A blunt man who refers to himself as "a slave driver" when describing his work ethic on the bandstand and in the studio, Bartholomew produced and arranged most of Domino's records, but nearly every other significant New Orleans rhythm and blues record during the 1950s.

Lew Chudd was a intelligent and innovative businessman who set up Imperial Records in California in 1946. Initially, Chudd sold records to migrant Mexican field hands who worked in the California orchards and fields. Later he tried to expand the market, releasing big band and urban blues records, but with little success. However, once Chudd began releasing rhythm and blues discs, he began making his mark in the industry.

Like all of the successful independent record entrepreneurs of the era, Chudd spent a lot of time on the road, visiting radio stations, distributors, and record stores to promote current releases. He also looked for new trends and talent to record. While in Houston during the fall of 1949, Chudd heard Bartholomew and his band at the Bronze Peacock club and thought they were original and had what he was looking for. Committed to taping the growing market for rhythm and blues market, Chudd signed Bartholomew as a talent scout, producer and artist.

"Lew had never been to New Orleans before," said Bartholomew. "When he came here he asked me what was going on around town. I told him about this guy who was supposed to play pretty good boogie-woogie piano down at the Hide Away.

"It was Friday night and I wasn't working, so Lew and I went down there. [Al Young, a South Rampart Street record shop owner and also a talent scout for Chudd, also made the trip.] That was the first time we heard Fats Domino. He was singing 'The Junkers Blues,' and Lew really liked it. At the intermission, I introduced Fats to Lew Chudd and that's how things got started."

As Domino recalled:

"That was 1949. Lew Chudd came down here looking for talent and I had a big name in New Orleans playing at the Hide Away. I was playing there one night with Little Sonny [vocalist Johnny Jones]. Lew and Dave came in and asked me if I wanted to make a record."

On sound advice from Verret, Domino signed a contract with Imperial that called for royalties rather than a purchase of his services outright. This wasn't the general practice at the time, but the deal turned out to be very advantageous for Domino.

Just prior to the session, Domino went to Bartholomew's house to rehearse material. Bartholomew was interested in Domino redoing "The Junker's Blues" but he wanted to eliminate the references to narcotics. At the time there was a popular radio detective series called "The Fat Man" and Bartholomew thought that would make a good title for a song to be recorded by an artist referred to as "Fats." Together, Domino and Bartholomew reworked the lyrics to fit the title. They also wrote bluesy numbers about Detroit and the Hide Away.

On December 10, 1949, an anxious Fats Domino arrived for his recording debut at the J & M Studio on North Rampart Street in New Orleans' French Quarter. Bartholomew's band was used, rather than Diamond's, which contributed to the 21-year-old's trepidation. Engineer, Cosimo Matassa, positioned three microphones in the studio to achieve the desired balance. Domino and the supporting musicians— Ernest McLean on guitar, Frank Fields on bass, Herb Hardesty and Clarence Hall on tenor sax, Alvin "Red" Tyler on baritone sax, Joe Harris on alto sax, and Bartholomew on trumpet—were all recorded on one track. The recordings were transferred to a Duo-Presto acetate disc cutter which produced the master recording.

The late saxophonist Red Tyler recalled the session:

"We talked our way through those tunes but it was a long and drawn out session. We just made suggestions to each other about what we should play. Nothing was written down on paper. Most of Fats' sessions were like that."

Initially, producer Bartholomew wasn't satisfied with the session.

"Fats' piano was too loud and it didn't fit right. But there was nothing we could do because we were working with with just one track. It was a mistake but we sent the record out anyway."

Originally, the pensive "Detroit City Blues" was the side Imperial promoted but that changed once listeners heard "The Fat Man" with it's frantic boogie-woogie intro and Domino's rich creole vocals.

The record immediately broke in New Orleans. In a *Billboard* ad, Imperial claimed they sold 100,000 "The Fat Man" singles in just ten days. *The Louisiana Weekly* commented that "Fats Domino, recorder of that big jukebox sensation, 'The Fat Man Blues' is becoming nationally famous. The chubby faced little fellow set them on their ears at Lloyd's Place 1/24 with Dave Bartholomew backing."

"The Fat Man" entered the *Billboard* R&B chart on March 24, 1950, rising to number six during it's three week stay. The single proved to be Imperial's first national hit, selling 800,000 copies during 1950. Eventually it would top one million and earn a gold record. Many have called "The Fat Man" the first rock and roll record.

"At the time it came out, mostly black people bought that kind of record," said Domino. "But Lew Chudd told me that everybody was buying my record."

Not only did "The Fat Man" introduce a new artist, but Domino's New Orleans style of rhythm and blues would quickly become a dramatic influence on other artists throughout the country.

Los Angeles bandleader Johnny Otis recalled the first time he heard "The Fat Man".

"I was in a restaurant with my band when a guy came and changed the records on the jukebox. He left some free plays and somebody played "The Fat Man." We all ran to the jukebox to see whose record it was. It seemed like collectively everyone said, 'I wish we would have cut that.'"

With "The Fat Man" hot, Chudd arranged a California/Southwest tour for Domino and Bartholomew that initially was to include another Imperial artist from New Orleans, Jewel King. King, whose "3 X 7 = 21" was beginning to build steam declined when her husband, bandleader Jack Scott, convinced her to remain home and work with his band instead. Domino was also reluctant to leave the Crescent City because he thought he might flop. However, once the tour began, things went extremely well.

"By the time we got home everybody pretty much knew Fats was going to be a big star," said Red Tyler, who played saxophone on the tour.

Back in New Orleans, Domino picked up where he left off, knocking them dead at the Hide Away and other local clubs. Nationally though, his rise to the top was more arduous. Bartholomew hustled Domino back to J & M in late January hoping to cut a follow up hit, but neither "Boogie Woogie Baby" or "Little Bee", caught the public's ear. The highlight of the session would turn out to be the rhythmic reworking of "Hey! La Bas Boogie," a demonstration of how rhythm and blues could be adapted to tradition two-beat Dixieland. The band's performance is so strong that only audiophiles are aware that the drums and Domino's piano were nearly inaudible.

"It was something we put together right quick," said Domino. "'Hey! La Bas' was an old Dixieland tune I used to hear all the time. It was my brother-in-law's idea to cut it."

Domino's third single paired the remaining tracks from his initial session, "Hide Away Blues" and "She's My Baby," but they didn't generate sales outside of New Orleans either.

Domino and Bartholomew didn't return to the studio until September 1950, when they cut "Every Night About This Time," a number five R&B record. The hook on "Every Night About This Time" was it's 6/8 triplet style of piano, which would become a trademark on many Domino recordings. Although Domino had played triplets on his initial session ("Detroit City Blues" and "Hideaway Blues") it was "Every Night About This Time" that made the style popular for the first time with record buyers.

"That triplet piano came from a guy out in California—Little Willie Littlefield," said Bartholomew, referring to the Modern Records recording artist who had a hit in 1949 with "It's Midnight." "That got to be Fats' style. Once he started, he couldn't leave it because that's what people wanted to hear. After that we toned down Fats piano to sell records."

No slouch behind the 88s, Domino would latter get to show off his dexterity on instrumentals like "Swanee River Hop," "The Fat Man's Hop" and "Fats' Frenzy," but most of his more adventurous performances stayed on the shelf for several years and weren't issued until Imperial needed album and EP tracks in the mid and late 1950s.

With "Every Night About This Time" climbing the charts, Bartholomew and Domino embarked on a Midwest tour with Professor Longhair. This time the tour ended disastrously when the band got stranded in a Kansas snow storm and Longhair won most of Domino's earnings gambling between shows.

Shortly after the band returned to New Orleans, Bartholomew and Chudd had a sudden and acrimonious falling out. Bartholomew found out that Al Young received a $1,500 bonus from Chudd but Bartholomew got nothing. Stung by Chudd's slight, Bartholomew resigned from Imperial

Without Bartholomew and his band, Domino began recording with his regular ensemble. Distinguishing between the two groups is quite easy. Bartholomew's group played with more swing and polish. Domino's quintet was much more brash and occasionally less disciplined. However what Domino's band might have lacked in technique, they certainly made up it in enthusiasm. Domino's group then consisted of, Billy Diamond on bass, Buddy Hagans on tenor saxophone, Emmett Fortner a.k.a. Wendell

Ducong on alto saxophone, Walter "Papoose" Nelson on guitar, and
Clarence "Teenoo" Coleman on drums.

Domino was particularly fond of the late Coleman's aggressive drumming:

"Teenoo was left-handed and could really keep a beat. I used to have
him set his drums up right next to the piano because the drummer is where
I get my drive from."

With Bartholomew absent, in January 1951 Domino cut "Tired of
Crying"/"What's The Matter Baby," both bluesy, but with some jagged
edges. The following month Domino was back at J & M reworking Tampa
Red's "Don't Lie To Me" and "Rockin' Chair," an original tune that was
a one week visitor to the charts in December.

At the time, Chudd placed Al Young in charge of Imperial's New
Orleans sessions including Domino's. However, Young had difficulty dis-
cerning between a mediocre performance and outstanding one. Without
Bartholomew at the helm, Domino's recordings began to often sound
chaotic, as they suffered by not having formulaic arrangements and more
skillfully crafted material.

In January 1952, Chudd, who was becoming concerned with lagging
sales, was in New Orleans on a promotion stop when he attended a recording session with Domino and Young. One of the songs Domino recorded
was the bluesy "Goin' Home" that shot up the charts later in the spring. It
became Domino's first number one R&B record. Despite a poor audio
mix, an out-of-tune saxophone solo, and some of bizarre guitar chording
by Nelson, the lyrics to "Goin' Home" hit a familiar chord with listeners
who had moved from rural areas to the fast moving cities.

"That was our big song back then," said Domino. "We closed all our
shows with it and the audience would always fall out. We had to play
'Goin' Home' several times every night."

Just as "Goin' Home" was being shipped to distributors, Domino and
his band were in Nashville playing at Grady's. Still looking for another
hit, and a suitable replacement for Bartholomew, Chudd arranged for Tad
Jarrett, a Nashville deejay/songwriter/artist to produce a session on
Domino. Jarrett did an excellent job on "Poor Poor Me"/"Trust In Me,"
but both sides missed the charts.

Chudd though was immensely pleased with "Goin' Home" although
it might have remained at number one much longer than it did (one week),
had it not been supplanted by another New Orleans record, Lloyd Price's
"Lawdy Miss Clawdy."

"I'm the one that played piano on 'Lawdy Miss Clawdy,'" said
Domino. "I was driving past the studio when they were recording it. Dave

[Bartholomew] asked me to come in and play. I came up with the intro on 'Lawdy Miss Clawdy.' It was number one for two months while 'Goin' Home' was number two."

Bartholomew produced "Lawdy Miss Clawdy" for one of Imperial's competitors Specialty Records. He also used the same band that backed Domino on his initial Imperial sides. According to Joe Banashak, who ran A-1 Distributors and wholesaled both Imperial and Specialty in New Orleans, he played a dub of Price's record over the telephone for Chudd after the March session. Both realized the song would have been perfect for Domino. Chudd, who surely fumed knowing Bartholomew was successfully directing talent and material to labels other than Imperial, continued having second thoughts about taking Bartholomew"'s work for granted. Banashak arranged for Chudd to meet with Bartholomew at his office and eventually they settled their differences. Together they cemented a relationship that guaranteed Imperial and Domino's success for the next decade.

However, just before Domino returned to the studio with Bartholomew, he was involved in a car wreck on his way to an appearance in Rayne, Louisiana. Domino walked away from the accident, but his manager, Melvin Cade, a New Orleans club owner, was killed. Cade had signed Domino to a management contract when he began making records. Cade's death voided the contract .

In September 1952, Domino and Bartholomew were reunited at J & M, but curiously cut a dull session, outside of the note-for-note cover of Professor Longhair's "Mardi Gras In New Orleans." However it was held back until early the following year when it became the B-side of "Goin' To the River." A sizable hit, "Goin' To The River" reached number two on the R&B charts, but might well have done better as Domino explained:

"I had recorded 'Goin' To the River' but it hadn't come out yet. We were doing a show in Dallas when Chuck Willis [also on the bill] heard me play it. He kept saying, 'Fats play that song again.' After the show he asked me if he could cut it. I told him to contact Lew Chudd to see if it was okay. Lew didn't care how many people cut it because he had the publishing on it.

"Two weeks later I heard somebody play Chuck's record and mine still hadn't come out yet. I called Lew about it and he said, "Well I guess we better put your's out too."

With "Goin' To The River" still in the charts, Imperial released the infectious "Please Don't Leave Me," which featured Nelson's slashing rhythm guitar interweaved with Domino's sparkling boogie-woogie piano. Recorded in Hollywood at Radio Recorders Studio during a West

Coast tour, the song had only two verses. Domino explained it's origin.

"When I first made it ["Please Don't Leave Me"] my wife said, 'Fats, what's the matter? You ain't singing too much. You must have run out of words.'

"I said, 'Well I don't know any [more].'

"So she said, 'Why don't you do a record where you go 'woo-woo-woo' in it. So I did, and it was called 'Please Don't Leave Me.' When we went to the studio I said, 'I only want to cut this song one time.' That's what we did.

"After the record came out, I was in a Chinese restaurant in Philadelphia with Dave and a guy sits down next to us. He didn't know who we were and he started complaining to the waiter. 'All day long, all I hear is, 'woo-woo-woo.'"

Dave points to me and said, 'That's the man that made that record.'

He looked at us and said, 'Woo-woo-woo.'"

Domino's wife also inspired another hit from 1953, "Rose Mary," a song that was recorded at two different sessions. It also made the R&B charts.

"That's the only song I ever wrote about a real person," said Domino. "I wrote a lot of songs with people names in them, but they weren't real people."

Suddenly on a hot streak, Domino had sold over four million records by the end of 1953 for Imperial. Anxious to resign his best selling artist, Chudd inked Domino to an unprecedented nine year contract.

To this point, Domino's records were mostly purchased by black listeners, programmed on juke boxes in black establishments, and sold in black record shops. However several white deejays, including Hunter Hancock in Los Angeles, Poppa Stoppa in New Orleans, and Alan Freed in Cleveland, had begun programming rhythm and blues records for a curious and attentive white teenager audience. These new listeners began purchasing Domino's records, as well as those by other black artists, which expanded the market for R&B records.

In terms of record sales, 1954 was slow for Domino. "You Done Me Wrong" charted, but for only a lone week. However, tunes like "You Can Pack Your Suitcase," "Where Did You Stay," "Little School Girl"— styled on Paul Gayten's "Hey Little Girl"— and the remake of Tommy Ridgley's "I Lived My Life" were worthy performances. Domino and his band maintained a busy schedule throughout the year including a string of one-nighters that began in March and didn't conclude until the end of July. A few weeks later they appeared at Brooklyn's Ebbet's Field with Muddy Waters, Buddy Johnson, Little Walter, the Clovers, and the

Orioles, as part of Alan Freed's Moondog Jubilee of Stars Under the Stars concert. In September, Domino was sidelined after his tonsils were removed, but the following month he was back on the road. On one memorable date, Domino appeared at Los Angeles' Wrigley Field before 25,000 people and was introduced by fellow New Orleanian Louis Armstrong.

With 10 R&B chart records behind him, by the mid-point of the decade, Domino was a well established star in black America. However the amalgamation of black and white musical culture would soon manifest itself as rock and roll and eventually explode in popularity across the country. Domino would be part of the fireworks.

The year 1955 would be a key one for Domino and the development of popular music. In January, he appeared at Alan Freed's Rock and Roll Ball at Harlem's St. Nicholas Arena. Later in the month, he recorded the frantic "Don't You Know" with it's socking back beat at the J & M Studio. The record got him back in the charts as it climbed to number seven on the national R&B best seller list.

Domino's next release, "Ain't It A Shame," was recorded while on tour in March at Master Recorders Studio in Hollywood, California. Like all of Domino's West Coast sessions, it featured his regular New Orleans band. On "Ain't It A Shame," guitarist Nelson doubles Domino's left hand and Herb Hardesty plays an economic sax solo that is married to the song's melody. The record turned into Domino's best selling single to date, topping the R&B charts for 11 weeks.

"Ain't It A Shame" also captured *Billboard's* prestigious Triple Crown, an award bestowed on singles that topped their R&B dealer, juke-box, and disc jockey charts. Previously, only Johnny Ace's "Pledging My Love," had earned the award. "Ain't It A Shame" was also the first Domino single to enter the *Billboard* pop chart, checking in at number 86 for one week. "Ain't It A Shame" was the first of many Domino tunes that would be covered by a white artist. Dot Records rushed Pat Boone into the studio to cut a toned down version of "Ain't It A Shame" which reached number 21 in the pop chart.

"That hurt," admitted Domino. "It took me two months to write 'Ain't It A Shame' and his [Boone's] record comes out around the same time as mine and sells more records."

The B-side of Domino's "Ain't It A Shame" was the alluring "La-La," a tune Domino pointed out was and example of his primary theory about songwriting:

"I wanted to make a record people could sing along with. I thought everybody could remember 'la-la.' When I write a song, I like to keep it simple. People can't remember all the words to a song, but they can remember a phrase."

Bartholomew concurs that "La-La" was indeed mesmerizing:

"After the song came out, we were on the West Coast and someone came up to us and said, 'Do you fellows realize that 'La-La' is the song the Stanford football team warms up to?' It must have been pretty catchy."

Suddenly Domino had a very hot hand. The pulsating "All By Myself," also recorded at the March Hollywood session followed and reached number three in the R&B charts. His next release, the hammering stop-time, "Poor Me," also checked in at number three. Both records were too authentic for the taste of pop record buyers, but they solidified Domino as one of the most popular black entertainers in the country.

The hillbilly streaked "Bo Weevil"—with Ernest McLean's brilliant guitar solo— kicked off 1956 and provided Domino his second crossover record. The song rose to number 35 in the pop charts but likely have done better had it not been covered by Teresa Brewer, whose version reached number 17.

In a bid to attract white listeners and expand their catalog, Imperial released the first of several Domino albums *Rock and Rollin' with Fats Domino* which made it to number 18 in *Billboard's* album charts. It included current hits like "Bo Weevil" and "Ain't It A Shame," along with earlier successes like "The Fat Man" and "Goin' Home."

The brilliant "I'm In Love Again" became Domino's third number one R&B hit single and his first top 10 pop release. The interplay between Domino's vocals, and Herb Hardesty and Lee Allen's tandem tenor saxes. was a major reason the record was so popular.

Present on more than 100 Domino recordings, the late Lee Allen recalled that he made $42.50 for a standard four-song Domino session during the mid-1950s:

"Sometimes we'd work all day and half the night, but we never looked at the clock and we didn't worry about money. We just kept trying until we got it right. Back then we were trying to find a sound and we worked together to get it."

Domino's other key saxophonist was Herb Hardesty.

"I played on 90 percent of all solos on Fats records," pointed out Hardesty. "I play on 'I'm Walkin,' 'My Blue Heaven,' 'Ain't It a Shame,' 'Let the Four Winds Blow,' 'All By Myself,' and several others. At the time I was spending long hours in the studio with Fats as well as recording with Smiley Lewis, Lloyd Price, Shirley and Lee, Joe Turner, Jewel King, and Archibald. When Fats approached me about going on the road with him, I sacrificed my studio work to do it. During that time, we often played to segregated audiences. Nonetheless, Fats was popular with all races of people, and gave the audiences their money's worth."

The B-side of "I'm In Love Again," the standard "My Blue Heaven," made it to number 21 in the pop charts and became Domino's first British hit. It became one of many of his two-sided Imperial hit singles.

"Dave and Fats worked extra hard on those standards," said Matassa, referring to "Blue Heaven." "A lot of producers and artists would come in the studio and cover the exact arrangement of a song and be happy. Those two weren't finished until it had 'Fats Domino' stamped all over it."

Musically, Domino hadn't changed his style as he continued to record pulsating straight ahead New Orleans rhythm and blues. However he gradually became recognized as a rock and roll artist rather than a rhythm and blues artist, a situation that initially puzzled him.

"Everybody started calling my music rock and roll, but it wasn't anything but the same rhythm and blues I'd been playing here [New Orleans]," said Domino. "I think Alan Freed was the first one to call it rock and roll."

As early as 1954, *Billboard* reported: "Teenagers are instigating the current trend towards r. & b. and are largely responsible for keeping the sales mounting. The teen-age tide has swept down the old barriers which kept this music restricted to a segment of the population... Some California juke box ops say that the machines located where youngsters congregate will show popular records taking a secondary position to r. & b. recordings."

However not all rhythm and blues artists had the ability to attract teenage listeners. One of many examples was Domino's label mate, Smiley Lewis. The New Orleans blues shouter's recordings were more than equal to Domino's in quality (they often used the same musicians on sessions) but Lewis often sang about going to jail and staying drunk all weekend. Domino's themes were far more wholesome. He sang about waiting for his sweetheart in the rain and mending a broken heart, lyrics that wouldn't upset white deejays or the parents of white teenagers. Lewis remained a hard-luck R&B artist and died in poverty. Domino became a multimillionaire and an American icon.

Chudd was very careful in the way he presented Domino to the public. Album jackets, trade advertisements, and photos released to the media, without exception portrayed an immaculately dressed Domino flashing an inviting smile back at record buyers. Domino's processed flat top hair cut, which a writer once aptly described "Looks like it got caught in a pants-pressing machine and then got trimmed by a lawn mower," actually accentuated his innocent appeal.

Aimed at teenage record buyers, "When My Dream Boat Comes Home" climbed into the top 20 of the pop chart in the summer of 1956. Its B-side "So Long," featured well timed pauses and lonely alto sax break by Wendell Duconge. It reached number 44 in the pop charts and was played by Domino and his band at the conclusion of their shows for several years.

If Domino wasn't already a major rock and roll attraction by the fall of 1956, he certainly was with the release of "Blueberry Hill," an R&B chart topper and a number four pop single. Another standard, Domino and Harrison Verret enjoyed Louis Armstrong's 1949 version and they lobbied to record the song while the band was in Los Angeles in June. However, Bartholomew wasn't enthusiastic about recording the song in the least.

"I didn't think 'Blueberry Hill' was hitting on shit," admitted Bartholomew. "It took all day to record and it still didn't sound right. Lew Chudd put it out because he didn't have anything else on Fats. I said, 'No don't put that thing out. It's no damn good.' So Lew calls me back two weeks later and says, 'Dave, from now on cut nothing but no-good records. We just sold three million.'"

When Domino recorded "Blueberry Hill," he had a problem remembering the lyrics and was unable to finish a complete take. Master Recorders' engineer Bunny Robyn instructed Domino and the band to play the parts of the song that they knew and he'd take care of the rest. After the session, Robyn spliced together two different takes of "Blueberry Hill" to create the final master tape, quite an uncommon practice at the time.

The flip of "Blueberry Hill," "Honey Chile"—from the same session— was originally tapped by Imperial as the hit side and Domino performed the song in the movie *Shake, Rattle and Rock*. However the public chose otherwise and it became Domino's biggest hit ever.

With several records in the charts, Domino spent the last half of 1956 on the road touring major theaters and auditoriums from coast to coast, including a November appearance on *The Ed Sullivan Show* where he performed "Blueberry Hill." Domino didn't record during the last half of 1956 but he still had one more hit before the year ended with a cover of Smiley Lewis' "Blue Monday," a song Imperial had on the shelf for 18 months. It was his second straight number one R&B single. Not as bluesy as Lewis' declamatory treatment, Domino's approach was smoother and he sings the lyrics almost matter of factly. Especially fond of "Blue Monday," Domino has referred to it as one of his favorite records.

"I like 'Blue Monday' because it tells a good story," stressed Domino. "Anybody that works can appreciate the words in the song."

The flip of "Blue Monday," "What's the Reason I'm Not Pleasing

You" was an oddity because for the first time Domino cut a record that sold pop but was ignored by R&B buyers.

Domino's third consecutive number one R&B single was the strutting "I'm Walkin,'" a rare song Bartholomew "had a good feeling about" before he went in the studio in January of 1957. Again the guitar figure follows Domino's left hand.

"'Papoose' [Walter Nelson Jr.] was responsible for that arrangement," said Bartholomew. "I wanted something simpler but he said, 'No, lets put in a sixth note.' We did and that's what made 'I'm Walkin'" so catchy."

Domino's original was covered, this time by teenage television star Ricky Nelson who redid "I'm Walkin'" with a rockabilly arrangement for Verve. Chudd was so impressed by the cover, he signed Nelson when he found out Verve didn't have Nelson under contract. It would be a shrewd move as Nelson would eventually supplant Domino as Imperial's top selling artist.

"Valley of Tears," another Los Angeles recording, complete with a weepy overdubbed female chorus showed Bartholomew and Domino were capable of adapting their style to attain success in the pop charts. Far more satisfying to R&B buyers though was the bold "Wait and See," recorded at the "Valley of Tears" session.

An obscure gem from 1957 was "The Rooster Song" released on the *This Is Fats* album and on the EP *Here Comes Fats Domino*.

"Back in those days we had a lot of guys out in the streets selling fruit, vegetables and meat," recalled Domino. "One day I heard one singing this song about a rooster. I took the idea to the studio, kicked it around and came up with, 'The Rooster Song.'"

The rock and roll boom of the 1950s was not lost on Hollywood as several studios cashed in with low-budget hastily made films. Using similar formulas—stringing together several clips of rock and rollers lip-synching their hits and interspersing B-movie players acting out sketchy story lines—these movies were extremely popular with teenagers. Chudd's arranged for Domino to appear in *Shake, Rattle and Rock, Jamboree, The Big Beat* and *The Girl Can't Help It*. The latter, arguably the best, as it was filmed in color, starred Jayne Mansfield, and featured Domino and his band doing "Blue Monday."

"It was all right but it was hard work," said Domino. "I was only singing one song but it took five or six hours [to film]. I knew I was no movie star and I wasn't an actor—I was just singing my song. It was a job I had to do because it brought my music to more people and helped sell records."

The title track to *The Big Beat*, with it's economic piano solo, and it's flip, the exquisite "I Want You To Know," both made the pop charts before the end of 1957. In just over two years, Domino had 18 releases in *Billboard's* Hot 100, far more than any other R&B artist.

The Domino hit parade continued throughout 1957. At the time, he and his band were making $2,500 a show and the trades projected Domino would become the first rhythm and blues artist to earn one million dollars. Recording success continued with, "When I See You," "I Still Love You" and "Yes My Darling," a record Domino wasn't particularly fond of.

"They speed that record up," said Domino. "I don't remember cutting it that fast. When we recorded it we did it a lot slower, but after it came out, we had to play it like the record. Lew Chudd told me that they did it to make me sound younger."

According to Cosimo Matassa, "Yes My Darling" wasn't the only Domino recording that was altered.

"They sped the tapes up to get a brighter sound and maybe to make them a little faster for the kids. It also made it impossible for another company to cover a song note-for-note. Imperial had a real good engineer, Bunny Robyn, that did their transfers. He always got a real bright sound."

Chudd had Robyn repeat this process when transferring pre-1955 master tapes to albums in the late 1950s. This would present a problem decades later when preparing Domino's recordings for CD reissue. Of the existing Domino analog master tapes, most had been speed up by Robyn and no longer were a true documentation of Domino's original recordings. Engineers putting together digital Domino compilations in the 1990s had to find the true playing time from the labels on the original 78 and 45 records. Then with the aid of computers, they adjusted the speed of tape machine to play back the tapes at the original speed.

The piano in Matassa's studio also contributed to Domino's sound.

"I learned a trick from a piano tuner that made my piano sound brighter on records," said Matassa. "I cheated on the treble end of the keys. I had it tuned just a bit higher than normal so the instrument would stand out more."

Off Matassa's piano in February of 1958 flew "Sick and Tired," a song that was a local hit the previous year for Chris Kenner. Domino's relaxed version broke nationally and made it to the number 22 position in the Hot 100.

On the personal front, the 30-year-old recording star and his family moved into a spectacular newly constructed $60,000 mansion—complete with a roof built with imported Italian tiles, central air conditioning, a spectacular grand piano, a bar with hundreds of silver dollars laminated on it's top, and a garage containing two new Cadillacs. A pink and yellow contemporary castle in a village of traditional New Orleans shotgun hous-es, Domino built his house on the corner of Caffin Avenue and Marais Street not far from where he grew up. Pressure had been put on Domino to move to the more affluent Ponchartrain Park subdivision in Eastern New Orleans, but he preferred remaining close to his friends and his roots.

After a 21 month absence from the pop chart's top 10, Domino regained those heights again in November of 1958 with "Whole Lotta Lovin'," a song that again incorporated the traditional New Orleans parade beat— a sound characterized by the extra syncopated "second line" beat on the bass drum.

"I didn't invent that sound," said Bartholomew, who often instructed drummers to duplicate the beat on Domino's recordings, "I just took it off the street. I remember when I was playing in one of my first bands, there was an older musician who used to say, 'I don't know why they don't make the bass drum stand out more when they arrange music. That's the biggest instrument in the band, but they forget to play it.' What he said always stuck in my mind."

Other songs rooted in New Orleans second line tradition were the parade standards "Little Liza Jane"—with another brilliantly guitar solo from Nelson—"Dark Town Strutters Ball," and "When the Saints Go Marching In," which replaced "So Long" as Domino's set closer. The B-side of "The Saint's," "Telling Lies," was recorded at Master Recorders and arranged by Earl Palmer, Bartholomew's ex-drummer who had recently moved to Los Angeles. Both sides reached number 50 in the Hot 100.

The intense "I'm Ready," which benefited by an overdubbed clapping track, proved Domino could rock with the likes of Little Richard, Elvis Presley or Jerry Lee Lewis if he wanted to. "I'm Ready" climbed to num-ber 16 on the pop charts and number seven on the R&B side, continuing a growing string of gold records. It's flip, the standard "Margie" made it to number 51 in the pop charts.

"When I made a record I put two good sides on it," insisted Domino. "I never wanted to put just one good side on."

The hit parade continued with another two-sided top 20 single, "I Want To Walk You Home"/"I'm Gonna Be A Wheel Someday". The latter was written by Baton Rouge's Roy Hayes and originally recorded two years earlier by Bobby Mitchell. Bartholomew's regular guitarist, Ernest McLean (again substituted for Nelson) played a rapid guitar figure which made Domino's version verge on rockabilly.

Domino would close out 1959 with his seventh Top 10 pop hit, "Be My Guest," inspired by a popular television game show, and the bluesy

"I've Been Around." With the 1950s coming to a close, Domino could look forward to a new decade secure in the knowledge that the only Elvis Presley had sold more records in the past ten years than he had.

Imperial released five Fats Domino singles in 1960 and each side reached the pop charts. The biggest seller was the unforgettable "Walking to New Orleans," a number six record recorded in April. It was the first of several Domino releases to include overdubbed strings.

"Walkin' To New Orleans" was written by Abbeville, Louisiana, swamp pop singer/songwriter Bobby Charles (nee Guidry). Originally influenced by Domino, Charles had several regional hits on Chess Records in the mid-1950s and later was signed by Bartholomew to Imperial in 1959. His songwriting was obviously well suited to Domino's style.

"I got to know Fats from being around the studio," recalled Charles. "I wrote 'Before I Grow Too Old' and he recorded it [February 1960]. It didn't do much [number 84 pop] but Fats told me if I came up with anything else let him know. One night Fats came to Lafayette and I went backstage to see him. He was glad to see me and asked me to visit him in New Orleans. I told him I was broke and couldn't afford it. Fats just laughed and said, 'Why don't you walk to New Orleans?' That was my hook. I went home and wrote it ['Walkin' To New Orleans'] and next time I came to New Orleans I gave it to him. I think it was one of his biggest hits. I had to give up two-thirds of the rights to those songs to Dave and Fats. That was the only way they would record them. I'm not bitter about it, that's just the way things were done then."

"Bobby's a great songwriter," declared Domino. "He offered me 'See You Later Alligator' before Bill Haley put it out but I turned it down and missed out."

Another swamp pop artist/writer who was a source of good innovative material was Gulfport, Mississippi's, Jimmy Donley. Donley who had regional singles on Decca, Chess and Teardrop, showed up at Domino's home in the fall of 1960 hoping to audition some of his songs. After an awkward exchange, Domino invited Donley into his living room. He listened to Donley sing and play his guitar and was impressed. Domino was especially taken with the bluesy, "What A Price," and began playing a pattern on the piano to match Donley's lyrics. Domino was eager to record it, and encouraged Donley to continue submitting material.

Domino's emotional treatment of "What A Price" was reminiscent of earlier blues hits like "Goin' To the River" and " Every Night About This Time." The single went to number 22. Donley, a great talent who tragically took his own life in 1963, also wrote several of Domino's latter hits, including "Rockin' Bicycle," "Bad Luck and Trouble" and "Hold Hands."

As events transpired, Charles and Donley came along at an opportune time as Chudd was beginning to press Domino and Bartholomew for more material to release. In addition to singles, Imperial continued to issue a steady string of Domino albums with attractive titles like *A Lot of Dominos*, *The Fabulous 'Mr. D* and *Let's Play Fats Domino*. The 12 track albums usually included a couple of current hit singles, flip sides, EP tracks and the occasional unreleased performance. However, by the early 1960s Domino and Bartholomew were running out of material to keep up with Imperial's album, EP and 45 rpm release schedule. In addition to material submitted by Charles, Donley and occasional other writers (the talented Earl King began submitting material to Domino), an increasing amount of Tin Pan Alley material was being recorded at Domino's sessions.

Tracks like "The Sheik of Arab," "Easter Parade," "Am I Blue" and "Isle of Capri" seemed marginal choices, and Domino often sounded stiff preforming them. On the other hand, "Margie," "Prisoner's Song," "I'll Always Be In Love With You" and "Put Your Arms Around Me" fit Domino's style and were actually enhanced by his treatment.

Now that Bartholomew felt comfortable working with the New Orleans Philharmonic Orchestra, he often hired them on Domino's sessions. Their presence was especially effective on, "Don't Come Knockin'" and "Three Nights A Week," both solid sellers.

By 1960, Matassa had patched two Ampex tape recorders together to make available three tracks in his studio. This allowed Bartholomew to experiment with overdubs. When an arrangement called for strings, a beefier horn line, or vocal accompaniment, Matassa left a track open so that later Bartholomew could overdub whatever musical embellishments were called for.

Multi-tracking also allowed Bartholomew to record foundation tracks at Cosimo's for Domino while he was on the road. Pianists James Booker, Edward Frank and Allen Toussaint—who could each duplicate Domino's technique—were often hired for these sessions and their playing was saved on a separate track. When Domino would return to New Orleans, he'd meet with Bartholomew and listen to the prerecorded material. Usually the existing piano track was erased after Domino's piano was recorded, but on several occasions, the initial piano track was kept and only Domino's voice was overdubbed. Even Matassa, who was behind the board for each of Domino's Imperial sessions, can't recall who played piano on each recording. However, he does remember that Domino's sessions had a habit of taking longer than most artist's he worked with.

"Fats wasn't exactly a joy to record," pointed out Matassa. "He was a nice guy, and let me tell you he was creative, but sometimes Fats lost sight of the fact we were trying to make a record. Sometimes he'd stop in the middle of a perfectly good take and ask, 'How do I sound?'"

Matassa recalled that after every session, Domino would insist on taking home test pressings of the material that were recorded so he could learn to play the songs exactly the way they were recorded.

"I always play my songs just like I recorded them," insisted Domino. "I never change anything because that's the way people want to hear them. Sometimes I'd play a song and tell the audience that it was my new record but people would say, 'Fats you've been playing that song for two months.'"

When Domino was back in New Orleans, he would often drive downtown in a late model Cadillac to A-1 Distributors on Baronne Street in order to check the progress of his latest release.

One single he followed was "Fell In Love On Monday" which featured a lavish production and checked in at number 32 in the pop charts. Once again Bartholomew added a bank of background singers to the orchestra to complete the pop effect. A more familiar Domino was heard on the upbeat "Shu Rah" (number 32 pop), the lamentive "It Keep's Raining," (number 23 pop) and the brilliant New Orleans second line parade beat classic "My Girl Josephine" (number 14 pop).

"I wrote that song ["My Girl Josephine"] in about 30 minutes," said Domino. "Everybody whose name is Josephine thinks I wrote that song for them. But I didn't have anybody in mind when I wrote it. After it came out, I heard somebody across the railway tracks telling folks, 'That's me in that Josephine song.' But it wasn't. Josephine just rhymed with the lines I was writing in the tune."

Domino returned to traditional blues on the Louis Jordan cover, "Ain't That Just Like A Woman," and the previously mentioned "What A Price." Both tracks made the top 40 early in 1961. However his next major hit was the cover of Roy Brown's "Let the Four Winds Blow," which included an especially attractive Lee Allen sax break. It reached number 15 on the pop charts during the summer.

The B-side of "Let the Four Winds Blow" was an innovative and influential ballad "Good Hearted Man." While it missed the national charts, the song was an especially popular, and often covered song in South Louisiana, an area where Domino has always been extremely popular.

Although Domino continued to appear regularly in the charts after "Let The Four Winds Blow," his releases were no longer reaching the lofty heights they once had, and their stays were becoming briefer. It wasn't that the quality of Domino's releases had declined, instead the public's musical tastes were starting to change and there was more competition. Vintage rock and roll and rhythm and blues was becoming passe as it was being replaced on the charts, and in the record shops, by surf music, pop, country as well as Memphis and Motown soul.

Imperial continued issuing Domino 45s and albums at a measured pace—about five singles and two albums annually, occasionally dipping into the vaults for material to keep up with their release schedule. Domino maintained the tempo, continuing to record some great New Orleans music. The alluring "What A Party," complete with an overdubbed house party track, made it to number 22 on the pop charts and "Rockin' Bicycle," a Jimmy Donley song, rolled in at number 83.

"A rocking bicycle is a bicycle built for two," explained Domino. "After we did that song, I bought my eldest daughter one because I wanted to know what one looked like. We'd go riding in the neighborhood and people would stop and say, 'Look at that rocking bicycle.'"

Released in November of 1961, "Jambalaya"/"I Hear You Knockin'," was one of Domino's best singles ever. His treatment of the Hank Williams classic was incomparable. The surging rhythm and rolling piano set the pace while Domino handled lyrics perfectly suited to his style and heritage.

"I always liked country and western music," remarked Domino. "Hank Williams songs especially seemed to fit my style. I did several of his numbers."

"I Hear You Knockin'," a cover of Smiley Lewis' 1955 hit, was equally spectacular. Held back from release by Imperial for three years, the song was another natural for Domino. Nevertheless the public's reaction to "Jambalaya" —which topped out at Number 30—and "I Hear You Knockin'"—it stalled at number 67—had to puzzle Domino, Bartholomew and Chudd. Two years earlier, both sides probably would have reached the top 10.

Domino continued to constantly tour and would make his first of what would be several trips to Europe to perform. Domino and his band's first overseas excursion was in 1962 when they appeared at two jazz festivals in France. Later they would stop in Hamburg, Germany, where he met the Searchers, Jerry and the Pace Makers, and the Beatles, groups visiting from England. Domino found Europeans extremely receptive to his music and it became a lucrative touring route for three decades. However, Domino quickly learned he needed to take a little bit of New Orleans along on his trips to keep himself and his band happy.

"I can't get the food I want over there," pointed out Domino. "Creole food is my favorite and I love to cook it—red beans, gumbo, jambalaya. My older sister taught me to cook. Now I bring my own pots, canned foods, dry foods and spices on the road. I always try to get a room in a hotel with a kitchenette so I can cook."

Early in 1962, Imperial released another track from their vaults, "You Win Again," a Hank Williams composition, that served as Domino's last top 40 single for Imperial when it reached number 22. In April, Domino cut five songs at Cosimo's including "Dance With Mr. Domino," a rocking twist record, that hit the wall at number 98. Whether Bartholomew or Chudd realized it at the time, it was Domino's last recording session for Imperial. His nine year contract with the label had concluded and although he was loyal to Chudd, he was interested in listening to offers from other labels. Imperial had been stockpiling a considerable amount of unreleased material that allowed them to continue releasing Domino singles and albums at a steady rate, but with diminishing commercial success. Only the silky standard "Did You Ever See A Dream Walking" reached the charts .

The year 1963 signaled the end of an era for the New Orleans record industry and a time of transition for Domino. Chudd didn't make a serious effort to resign Domino once he became interested in ventures beyond the record business. Feeling the majors squeezing him out of the market place, and without his big guns, (Ricky Nelson left the label in 1962) Chudd decided to sell his labels to Liberty Records. After weighing his options, Domino, who had 78 chart records for Imperial, also made a move.

"I didn't really have a reason to leave Imperial," said Domino. "But something else came up."

Something else was a five year, $50,000 per year guarantee from ABC-Paramount Records for his services. At the time, ABC was aggressively making in-roads into the rhythm and blues market and had signed Lloyd Price, Ray Charles and B.B. King, all who experienced substantial chart success. Obviously, ABC was sure Domino would follow suit.

Domino though would make a rough and awkward transition to his new label. Because there was a feud between New Orleans' Musicians Union and Cosimo's studio, and because ABC felt they could sell Domino in the country market, his sessions took place in Nashville. Initially, ABC kept Domino quite busy as their emphasis was on albums rather than singles. Producers Bill Justis, Sid Feller and Felton Jarvis oversaw Domino's sessions, and although they used Domino's New Orleans band in the studio, their pop approach—overdubbed strings and bubbly backup vocals—

marred several good performances.

The initial ABC album, *Here Comes Fats Domino,* did contain some fine New Orleans sounding material, the best being "Just A Lonely Man," "There Goes My Heart Again," "When I'm Walking (Let Me Walk)" and "Red Sails In the Sunset." The latter two which were released on singles and reached the middle of the pop charts.

Liberty, who was obviously eager to profit from Domino's Imperial catalog, released an album late in 1963 with a similar title, *Here He Comes Again!* They went as far as designing a similar cover as the ABC album and overdubbed all 12 tracks with a chirpy vocal group in order to try and sound like Domino's Nashville recordings. Liberty continued to recycle Domino catalog, reissuing all of his Imperial albums and compiling several LPs that contained Imperial sides that were issued on, Sunset, their budget label. They also extended the "Gold Standard Series" which reissued his biggest hits on singles, issues that were especially popular with collectors and jukebox operators.

Meanwhile, ABC kept Domino busy in Nashville. They issued *Fats On Fire*, an album with a great cover but unfortunately mediocre music, further marred by Bill Justis' sugary pop arrangements. None of the singles pulled from the album reached the charts. The third ABC album from 1964, *Getaway With Fats Domino*, was marginally better as the overdubbed choruses and strings were eliminated. The album contained only one chart record,"Heartbreak Hill," which slipped into the pop charts at number 99. Two other ABC singles, Lazy Lady" and "Sally Was A Good Old Girl" also checked in near the bottom of the pop chart in 1964. These tracks, and whatever remained in the ABC vaults, was collected and later issued in Holland as *The Best of Fats Domino*. However, after 1964, ABC decided to cut their losses and released Domino.

The following year, Domino was signed by Mercury, but the label insisted him recording oldies and uninspired country material. To their credit, Mercury did release a rousing live album recorded at the Flamingo Hotel in Las Vegas. Using his great New Orleans band, Domino ran through most of his hits including "Please Don't Leave," "So Long" and "Let The Four Winds Blow." Unlike most of his post-Imperial output to this point, Fats Domino was truly on fire. The album certainly ranks as one of his best. Unfortunately it was released at a time when the British rock sound was dominating the airwaves and the charts, therefore it's sales were disappointing. Mercury planned to issue the Southland U.S.A. album, but unexpectedly withdrew it just before it's scheduled release. Apparently this prompted Domino's departure from the label.

In spite of waning record sales, the demand for Domino appearances remained extremely high. By the mid-1960s, Domino and his band were spending as much as 10 months a year working lucrative casino dates in Las Vegas, Reno, and Lake Tahoe. Domino was a welcome visitor, as he was one of the top draws on the Vegas strip, and an avid gambler. Domino particularly enjoyed his tenure in Nevada because it allowed him to pursue two of his favorite indulgences: adding to his lavish wardrobe and extensive collection of jewelry.

Domino's cache of jewelry is especially spectacular and extensive. At times he wears so much on stage that he appears to have just emerged from a buying spree at Tiffanys. Over the years he has accumulated hundreds of cuff links, tie-claps, pins,watches and bracelets. Perhaps his most ostentatious piece is a watch with a jeweled six-sided star face. The band is studded with 352 diamonds, some which spell out the word "Fats."

In addition to headlining, Domino rubbed shoulders with gamblers, gangsters, movie stars, and many of the other entertainers who frequented the casinos.

"One of my best memories of Vegas was meeting the great Elvis Presley," recalled Domino. "Elvis came into my dressing room the second time he played there. He said, 'Fats I'm a little nervous. The last time out here I fired a blank.' Man, that night he went out and tore that place down."

In March 1967, British fans had their first chance to see their New Orleans idol in concert when Brian Epstein booked him into London's Seville Theater. Later that year, Domino was reunited with Dave Bartholomew at Cosimo's new Jazz City Studio and cut enough tracks for an album. Two singles, "Work My Way Up Steady" and "Wait 'Til It Happens To You," were issued on Bartholomew's Broadmoor label. Domino and Bartholomew didn't reprise the Imperial sound, rather they managed to capture a relaxed, more contemporary New Orleans groove. When back home, Domino usually played at Al Hirt's Bourbon Street club, where he rarely played to an empty seat, even during three week long engagements.

The following year, Edward West at Warner Brothers/Reprise signed Domino to a five year contract and dispatched him to New York to record with an all star band that included James Booker on piano, King Curtis on sax, and Earl Palmer on drums. The resulting album, *Fats Is Back*, produced by Richard Perry, was an entertaining set, but it could have benefited by eliminating a couple of mediocre songs and replacing them with songs better suited to Domino's New Orleans style. The highlight of the LP was his cover of "Lady Madonna," a Lennon-McCartney composition that was right up Domino's alley. Released on a single, "Lady Madonna" spent two weeks in the charts at number 100. It was his last entry in the pop charts.

Unfortunately after *Fats Is Back*, Warner Brothers had no idea what to do with Domino. He wasn't keen on the way label wanted to record him, so in exchange for letting him out of his contract, Domino gave Warner Brothers the Broadmoor tracks he recorded in 1967. Issued on an album simply called *Fats*, with zero promotion, it didn't sell and was quickly deleted.

Domino seemed to lose his zest for recording in the 1970s, perhaps aptly feeling he could finally rest on his laurels. He stayed busy touring though and cranking out his hits 50 weeks a year. Tragically, a fatal car wreck in North Louisiana decimated Domino's band early in the decade. Bassist James Davis was killed, and soon after several members of the band defected. However, by 1975, Bartholomew was back working with Domino along with Lee Allen and Herb Hardesty.

"I felt like I was following my catalog playing with Fats," said Bartholomew. "We'd been a team for a long time. We've been very successful and have had a lot of fun together over the years."

In 1978, Domino cut a self-produced album at SeaSaint Studio, *Sleeping On the Job*, that was released in Europe on the Sonet label. It contained a few enjoyable moments, but Fats playing a synthesizer didn't really endear old or new fans. Two years later, Domino released the album on his own label, F. D., adding two tracks and retitling it, *Fats Domino 1980*.

During the 1980s, Domino was primarily accessible to the public through live performances which continued to be stupendous. He did enter the studio in 1980 to cut "Whiskey Heaven" for the soundtrack to Clint Eastwood's film *Any Which Way You Can*, which entered the country charts. Four years later, Domino teamed up with Doug Kershaw to cover Rockin' Sidney's novelty hit "My Toot Toot" that got lots of radio play.

In July of 1986, Domino, along with his 11-piece orchestra, embarked on an ambitious two month, 60 concert tour. Just prior to leaving, he taped a one-hour HBO special in New Orleans, *Fats Domino and Friends*, with Jerry Lee Lewis and Ray Charles.

"We strictly had fun," said Domino. "I've known Ray since 1953 when he played around New Orleans at the Dew Drop. I go pretty far back with Jerry Lee too. We used to play shows for Dick Clark in the 1950s."

At the time, the 58-year-old Domino reflected.

"I don't like to work as hard as I used to. I hate to admit it, but now some days I don't even touch the piano. I've got an album recorded that's ready to go. It's got some new material that's on it and I reworked some of my old tunes. There's a song on it called, 'I've Got New Orleans On My Mind', that really has the feeling of my old hits. But I don't just want to sign a contract with the first company that comes along because I'm trying to be a lot more careful about my business. In the past, a lot of my old masters got sold or ended up with record companies I've never heard of. They change the cover, sell thousands of my records, and I never see a penny from them. I've lost millions of dollars that way and I don't want it to happen again."

Outside of the closed door HBO filming, Domino didn't perform in New Orleans on the tour. Domino insisted that he shouldn't play in his hometown more than once or twice a year, because he feels overexposure would cause him to lose some of his New Orleans fans. Later in the year, Domino, along with Jerry Lee Lewis and James Brown, were of the original inductees into the Rock and Roll Hall of Fame.

By the 1990s, Domino had reached his mid-60s and continued taking life progressively easier. Attrition had affected his group, especially with the death of Lee Allen, drummer Smokey Johnson's illness, and the defection of Bartholomew. Domino cherry picked no more than a handful of jobs a year, as he no longer felt the need to crisscross the globe to play his music.

"I've been all over the world," said Domino, who was given a commemorative day and the key to the city of New Orleans on October 24, 1991. "There ain't too many places I haven't been to or places I haven't seen. It's not that I don't like other cities, but I'd just as soon stay home in New Orleans when I can. Besides I don't like to fly too much. It makes me nervous."

In 1992, EMI, who now controlled his Imperial catalog, released a 100 track box set, *They Call Me the Fat Man*. The following year they issued *Christmas Is A Special Day* — later retitled *Christmas Gumbo*—a collection of seasonal offerings. To date it's been Domino's last album, although collections of his material continue to be reissued both here and abroad.

To date, Domino hasn't left New Orleans since 1995. He turned down a 1998 invitation from President Clinton to accept a National Medal of Arts award at the White House, begging off by claiming that it wasn't the right time for him to travel. In his place he sent his oldest daughter to accept one of Americas highest honors.

The year 1999 saw a slightly rejuvenated Domino. In January he played at the fifth anniversary celebration for the New Orleans' House of Blues club where $100 tickets sold out well in advance. He also performed breath taking shows at the New Orleans Jazz and Heritage

Festival, where he was reunited with Dave Bartholomew. In the fall he played at the opening of Harrah's downtown casino. However, recording again doesn't seem to be high on Domino's agenda.

"I would like to record again," said Domino. "But the situation has to be right."

Hopefully the "right situation" will occur at least one more time.

CHAPTER SEVEN
~ Ray Charles: Genius + New Orleans = Soul ~

Unbeknownst to many, Ray Charles, "The Genius," has a strong tie to New Orleans, and in fact was briefly a resident of the Crescent City. This period has often been downplayed by music historians, biographers, and even the man himself. However, New Orleans, and it's rhythm and blues tradition, had a measurable impact on Charles during his formative years.

Most people are familiar with Charles' background. Born Ray Charles Robinson, in Albany, Georgia, he grew up in Greenville, Florida. At the age of six he began to lose his sight from glaucoma and his mother enrolled him at the St. Augustine School for the Blind where he learned to read and write music in braille, play piano, saxophone and trumpet. His early influences included Chopin, Artie Shaw, and Art Tatum. At the age of 15 his mother died and he quit school in order to move to Jacksonville, and later Tampa, to become a professional musician.

Charles played in bands that covered Count Basie, Cecil Gant, and Louis Jordan material, as well as sitting in with the Florida Playboys, a popular country band. In 1947, he moved to Seattle and played spot jazz gigs and later formed a group, the Maxim Trio, which styled itself after the Nat "King" Cole Trio. During this period he changed his professional name to Ray Charles, as not to be confused with the champion boxer "Sugar" Ray Robinson. He also began a two decade long heroin addiction. Charles was signed by Swing Time Records and he cut nearly 50 titles for the label and had a couple of decent R&B hits in the late 1940s, and early 1950s. However there wasn't yet an identifiable Ray Charles style as most of his material was in the Nat Cole/Charles Brown vein.

In 1950, Charles went on the road with label-mate Lowell Fulson who had several hits at the time including "Everyday I Have the Blues" and "Blue Shadows." In addition to abbreviated cameos at the beginning of the show, Charles wrote charts and played with Fulson's band. In 1952, Atlantic took an interest in Charles and purchased his Swing Time contract. Their investment didn't pay immediate dividends however as Charles' initial Atlantic releases didn't sell very well.

In December 1952, Charles was booked into the Pelican Club on South Rampart Street and according to the Louisiana Weekly broke all previous attendance records. Confident that he had a large enough following to use the city as a base, Charles moved to New Orleans fɪ Dallas five months later.

"There were good musical sounds in New Orleans then," related Charles in his 1978 autobiography *Brother Ray*. "I sat in with as many cats as I could. The blues was brewing down there and the stew was pretty nasty. I was experimenting with my voice and doing fewer imitations."

Charles moved into a room at Hotel Foster at 2926 La Salle Street and immediately took up with Betsy Rudell who was a stout, good looking cook that lived across the street in the Magnolia Projects. Like most New Orleans musicians, Charles' daily routine included stopping at the nearby Dew Drop to eat red beans and rice, hang out, and hustle available gigs. The Shaw Agency in New York was handling his occasional national bookings, but around the New Orleans he was booked through the Dew Drop's owner Frank Painia, or his associate Hosea Hill, the proprietor of Thibodaux's Sugar Bowl club. For the first time Charles was paired with bands—usually six pieces which included two saxophones and two trumpets— that were familiar with his repertoire. Charles was impressed by the quality of musicians in the city, to the point where long after he'd left New Orleans, he still returned periodically when he needed to recruit new band members.

Everyone in New Orleans that knew Charles from this period was amazed by his independence and self-reliance.

"If you didn't know he was blind you would never have suspected it," said saxophonist/bassist Bill Sinigal, who had first met Charles on the road in Florida in the 1940s. "Everyday he'd walk from Foster's to the Dew Drop [one block], cross Sixth Street and walk right in the front door and sit down. We'd all be standing on the street watching and wondering how he did it. Ray was very intelligent and very sensitive. He only had to hear your voice once. From then on it was, 'How you doing Bill.'"

The secret to Charles mobility was his ability to hear the echo that his heels on his shoes made when he walked. If he heard them reverberate, he knew there was a wall nearby. If he didn't, he was walking next to an open space or a doorway. According to Sinigal and others, Charles was also an ace gambler.

"Best black jack player I ever saw. [Charles played with cards pin pricked in braille.] He hardly ever lost. He won a whole lot of Bobby Marchan's money and plenty of other peoples too."

Trumpeter Frank Mitchell, who recorded and gigged with Charles, recalled he was normally quiet and reserved.

"He sort of kept to himself. He wouldn't have much to say to you if you weren't a musician. He traveled a lot so he lived out of a suit case. He black suit, tie and white shirt] and maybe one change he was up in his room he listened to spirituals on the

New Orleans recording session took place at the J & M 18, 1953. Atlantic's Ahmet Ertegun and Jerry Wexler came down from New York for the session which was split with Tommy Ridgley. Unlike most visiting record companies, Ertegun and Wexler didn't use Cosimo's "A Team" of Red Tyler, Earl Palmer, Lee Allen and Ernest McLean. Instead, Edgar Blanchard and the Gondoliers (Blanchard on guitar, Auguste "Dimes" Dupont and Warren Hebrand on saxophone, Frank Fields on bass, and Alonzo Stewart on drums) were booked for the session. The Gondoliers had backed Atlantic's Joe Turner on the number one hit "Honey Hush," recorded at J & M four months earlier, so Wexler and Ertegun were comfortable using them.

Ridgley recorded first with Charles joining the Gondoliers on piano, but both sides were uninspiring. On "Oh Lawdy My Baby," Ridgley simply recycled the same arrangement as B.B. King's current hit "Woke Up this Morning." Although Charles latin-tinged playing boasted the arrangement, overall it was a mediocre effort. The same can also be said about "I'm Gonna Cross That River" which borrowed it's charts directly from Fats Domino's "Goin' To The River." Uncharacteristically, Charles plays Domino-like triplets, and apparently at one point was scolded by Wexler and Ertegun for deviating from the formula.

With Ridgley finished, it was Charles' turn and for the first time he went to church in the studio. Charles chose to record Guitar Slim's "Feelin' Sad," which was a regional hit the previous year. Charles had been floored by Slim's passionate voice (Charles had sat in with Slim) although he likely winced at his primitive musicianship. When Charles listened to Slim he felt a revelation. Here was a blues artist baring his soul the same way an emotion charged Baptist preacher would (Slim had at one time been a jack-leg preacher in Mississippi) in front of his Sunday congregation. If an undisciplined musician could successfully combine gospel and the blues, why couldn't a skilled and schooled one like Ray Charles?

Charles' version of "Feelin' Sad" was fervent and technically better than Slim's, right down to the gospel changes and coda ending. However it wasn't nearly as spellbinding as the original. Charles initial move towards gospel-blues, or what would become known as soul, was tentative—especially considering the other track he cut, "I Wonder Who," was a standard blues— but he'd taken the first step in a new musical direction. "Feelin' Sad" sold in the Deep South where Charles toured, but not elsewhere.

During August, Painia booked Charles into the San Jacinto Ballroom in the Treme section of New Orleans. He also played a weekend at the Dew Drop with a band billed as "Joe Tillman's Orchestra," a group which included Tillman on saxophone, Oscar Moore on drums, Wallace Davenport on trumpet, and Lloyd Lambert on string bass. However most weekends, he worked clubs and dance halls in Mississippi, Louisiana, and Alabama, with groups Painia or Hill assembled.

"I played one gig with Ray but he didn't hire me because I couldn't read fast enough," said Bill Sinigal. "He used to like to hire tenor players to mess with 'Fathead.' [David Newman, Charles on and off saxophonist from Texas] Fathead would set up next to the piano and all night long they'd argue about who was going to kick whose ass. It was kind of funny, but those two would get so loaded you didn't know if they were kidding or if one of them would pull a gun out."

In October, Charles would be invited to play on Guitar Slim's initial session for Specialty Records.

"Frank Painia had hooked Slim up with me and Ray," said Frank Mitchell, who played on the date. "Slim ran the songs down, Ray came up with the horn charts and arrangements. I wrote them down for the other musicians."

Engineer Cosimo Matassa watched the session unfold:

"Johnny Vincent [Specialty's field rep] was there but he was more or less a cheerleader. Ray became the producer by default. He was real confident in his abilities and he showed each musician what they should play. He kept the reins on Slim as best as he could, which believe me wasn't easy. Slim had a tendency to jump meter and sing off mike, but Ray was real patient and eventually got what he wanted."

It took two days to finally get an acceptable version of Slim's "The Things I Used To Do," (Charles can clearly be heard yelling "Yeah!" in relief at the song's conclusion) on tape, but the hard work paid off when the record shot to number one in the R&B charts, an accomplishment which didn't go unnoticed by Ertegun or Wexler.

"When Atlantic found out Ray was on Slim's session they got pretty hot," recalled Sinigal. "But Ray was a hustler and he needed the money to buy dope. He would score it in the projects or on Sixth Street. There was a guy named Cheatham that sold him weed and heroin for $10 a cap. I remember seeing Ray with ice cream in both hands walking up and down La Salle Street. He was over-dosed and the ice cream was keeping his temperature down. Cheatham was keeping him moving so he wouldn't die. The dope didn't hurt his music though, in fact it made him even more focused on it. Actually, a lot of your better than average musicians then were strung out on drugs at the time."

Late in October, Charles, who was billed as "King of the Jukeboxes" in *The Louisiana Weekly,* returned for a weekend at the Dew Drop and he played some dates at the Labor Union Hall. Charles second and last Atlantic session in New Orleans occurred in December. According to Mitchell, who played on the date, Painia hand picked the musicians for the session. Once again Wexler and Ertegun flew in to oversee the proceedings.

"That was a bootleg session," laughed Warren Bell Sr., who played alto saxophone on the date. "I don't know if they [Atlantic] didn't have time to file the proper paper work or if they didn't want the Union to know Ray was recording. We couldn't do the session at Cosimo's [actually J & M], we had to use the WDSU [radio] studio in the French Quarter. [Besides Bell, O'Neil Gerald also played alto on the date. The other musicians included Lloyd Lambert on bass, Oscar Moore on drums, Frank Mitchell and Davenport on trumpet, Charles Burbank on baritone saxophone, and Joe Tillman on tenor sax.] The first time I ever laid eyes on Ray Charles was that night when we started to rehearse. That wasn't like a regular R&B session where the musicians played something off the top of their heads—we had written arrangements. If you listen to those horn charts, you can tell Ray had a different approach and he was very much influenced by jazz. His singing was also real churchy which was something you didn't hear other blues singers do at the time."

Charles first recording at WDSU was "Don't You Know" which featured a punchy horn line and a playful, but pleading vocal that would soon become his trademark. "Don't You Know" would become Charles first chart record at Atlantic and began a landslide of hit records. The rest of the session included some magnificent blues including the minor-keyed "Nobody Cares," (which Guitar Slim appropriated five years later as "Along About Midnight" after he'd moved to Atlantic's subsidiary Atco) "Ray's Blues," and "Mr. Charles Blues".

However, as artistically great the session seemed, Wexler and Ertegun thought differently at the time.

"They loved 'Don't You Know' but they didn't like the other tunes," said Mitchell. "They wanted to throw them in the garbage. They wanted low-down gut bucket blues. What they got was blues, but they thought the songs were too progressive. If you listen to the horns on there it sounds like there's 17, not five."

Indeed, "Nobody Cares" was kept on the shelf for two years and then released as a B-side. The other tracks didn't see the light of day until Charles had left Atlantic when the label assembled the *The Genius Sings the Blues* album in 1962. Mitchell added that the Musician's Union eventually found out about the surreptitious date and fined each musician $50 for participating on it, more money than they were paid by Atlantic.

During the Yuletide season, Shaw booked Charles on several one nighters, including a New Year's Eve show in Houston. It was there that he met Della Bee Howard, a woman he fell in love with and would marry. Charles briefly returned to New Orleans, collected his belongings from Foster's, stopped at the Dew Drop to bid adieu to his new Orleans friends, and headed back to Texas. By the end of 1954, Charles had recorded "I Got A Woman," a song which was the veritable blueprint for soul music. Soon after his career exploded and he would become one of the biggest names in popular music.

While New Orleans was undeniable an influence on Charles, when listening to his early Atlantic repertoire one can't definitely say that he was influenced directly by the New Orleans rhythm and blues sound of the 1950s.

"I don't think Ray was influenced that much by the music they had around here," said Mitchell. "He was too good a musician and he was looking for his own sound to make a name for himself. He had a lot of friends here though and he liked hanging out in New Orleans."

"I don't hear New Orleans when I hear Ray Charles even on the things he recorded here," added Bell. "If anything, Ray influenced the musicians here. After he started having all those hits, all the bands around here covered his tunes."

Charles may well have had the last words on the subject when he told writer Robert Palmer, "When I went to New Orleans, I was already pretty much into what I was doing. New Orleans had very little influence on me."

Concerning Guitar Slim, Charles said, "I gave to him, he gave to me."

It might best be said then that New Orleans was a source of inspiration and a good place for Ray Charles to discover his hidden potential.

CHAPTER EIGHT
~ Chuck Carbo: I Didn't Want To Do It ~

New Orleans' most underrated vocalist might well be Chuck Carbo. Bandleader and producer Dave Bartholomew, who obviously knows a thing-or-two about singers, considers Carbo perhaps the best vocalist in the city.

"Chuck has a beautiful voice," concurs Cosimo Matassa. "Outside of Johnny Adams, I don't think there was another vocalist in New Orleans as good as Chuck. Johnny could reach those high notes, but nobody sang with more emotion than Chuck Carbo."

Carbo has embraced three styles during his career. He's sang in a gospel quartet, was the centerpiece of a 1950s doo-wop group, and has been a successful solo R&B and soul singer.

Born Hayward Carbo, January 11, 1926, at Houma, Louisiana, Carbo moved with his family to the Zion City section of New Orleans in the early 1930s. His father was a minister, and each Sunday he and his brother Leonard ("Chick") sang in their father's choir. The Carbo brothers had several musical influences as they grew up, including the King Cole Trio and the Golden Gate Quartet.

After both serving in the Coast Guard during World War II, the Carbos were invited to join the Zion City Harmonizers gospel quartet. In 1952, the group—which also included Howard Wicks, Oliver Howard, Joe Maxon and Matthew West—changed it's name to the Delta Southernaires. As one of the city's most popular quartets, the group began broadcasting Sunday mornings on WWEZ, in addition to appearing on several local gospel bills. The following year, on the recommendation of promoter Phyllis Boone, the group auditioned "Bye and Bye" and "John the Revelator" for Cosimo Matassa. Matassa saw potential in the group, but not as a gospel group.

"Cosimo asked us if we could do rhythm and blues," said Carbo. "He was looking for a group like the Dominos or the Orioles, but we really didn't know any blues numbers—we were gospel singers. Cosimo thought we had good voices and convinced us we had potential with R&B. He told Dave Bartholomew at Imperial about us."

Carbo had to do some soul searching before deciding to make a secular record. But with the assistance of guitarist, Adolph Smith, the group began working on R&B material. Smith wrote two memorable tunes, "I

Didn't Want To Do It" and "You're the One," that the group recorded on their initial Imperial session.

"When we got to the studio Edward Frank and the rest of the musicians didn't know what to make of us," said Carbo. "They'd never played behind gospel singers before. Even Dave wasn't really sure what to do with us."

The group insisted on using another name on the record because they intended to continue performing gospel as the Delta Southernaires. Carbo's wife Gloria came up with the Spiders, but once the record started getting local air play, deejay Ken Elliot—"Jack the Cat"—revealed that the Spiders and the Delta Southernaires were in fact one and the same. According to Carbo, the New Orleans gospel community was outraged and the group was no longer welcome at spiritual programs.

Luckily, "The Spiders" wound up with a two-sided hit. The strutting "I Didn't Want To Do It" made it to number three in the R&B charts in February of 1953, and the silky, "You're The One," followed it to number eight.

"'I Didn't Want to Do It' probably would have gone to number one but they wouldn't play it in Los Angeles, Detroit or Chicago because the stations there thought it was suggestive. Of course they played it in New Orleans because we were from here. We did get a lot of airplay on 'You're the One.' In fact, a lot of people that bought our record because of 'You're the One,' discovered 'I Didn't Want to Do It' by flipping it over."

The Spiders toured extensively off their debut, appearing at the Apollo in Harlem, the Howard in Washington and the 5-4 Ballroom in Los Angeles. However, the group couldn't get a decent paying job in their own hometown.

"Nobody in New Orleans would pay us what we got paid on the road," said Carbo. "They thought because we were from New Orleans, we'd work for whatever we were offered. Fats Domino is the only New Orleans artist that got paid decently in this city."

When the dust settled, the Spiders signed a management contract with Boone and Matassa. At the same time, Carbo was unexpectedly summoned to Hollywood by Imperial prexy, Lew Chudd.

"Lew Chudd told Dave he wanted to meet me," said Carbo. "I went out to California with Dave and met him. He wined and dined me, and said I had a great voice. Lew wanted me to sign a separate contract and record without the Spiders. I told him I couldn't do that because the group had been together a long time and it wouldn't be right. But when I came back to New Orleans, the rest of the group was mad at me."

The Spiders unfortunately wound up in a tangled web of jealousy.

"I got more involved with the Spiders than I should have," admitted Matassa. "I bought them uniforms and a station wagon. I spent a lot of time and money on them that in retrospect I should have put in the studio. They were a great group, but once they got popular, they started bickering about women, money, who was the boss, and who took the station wagon home at night."

Although turmoil within the group didn't affect their recordings, they didn't get back in the charts for two years. The Spiders' early style blended gospel and the close harmony popularized by the Five Keys and the Ink Spots. Supported by a crack New Orleans band directed by Bartholomew, the group had a snappy syncopated sound. Adolph Smith continued to supply superior material for the Spiders, including "For A Thrill," "Tears Began To Flow," and "Why Do I Love You," but their records didn't break outside of New Orleans. However, it was a Bartholomew tune, "I'm Slippin' In," that made more noise for the group, breaking in New Orleans and on the East Coast. Nevertheless, the Spiders continued to splinter. Maxon and Carbo quit to stay at home. Chick took the reins of the group and sang lead on the group's next regional success, "Bell's In My Heart."

Chuck Carbo and the original Spiders reunited in August 1955 to record one last national hit, "Witchcraft," which made it to number seven in the R&B charts late in 1955. However, Carbo, who sang lead on the song, didn't benefit from its success because Chick, and rest of the new Spiders, wouldn't allow him to sing with the group when they performed. Chick continued to lead the Spiders for two years while Chuck cut two good singles under his own name for Imperial.

Imperial released Carbo in 1957, but he continued to work at clubs like the Dew Drop and the Tiajuana. In 1960, pianist Edward Frank produced a Carbo for Carleton Picou's ERAH (Every Record A Hit) label but the session was never released. In 1961, Carbo began working with Mac Rebennack, who was then an A&R man for Johnny Vincent at Ace Records.

"I met Chuck somewhere in the mid-1950s," recalled Rebennack. "I was always a big fan of Chuck because he had such a mellow hip voice. I had the pleasure of writing some songs for him and we did a few records at Cosimo's. He was a real special cat to work with. If I was short a tune, Chuck was one of the few artists I knew that could write a tune on the spot and he always sang his ass off. He's just one of those rare type singers. He would take a piece of material he'd never heard before and he would cut the damn thing. He was one of the easiest singers to work with."

Carbo's first single for Vincent was "Lover of Loves"/"I Wake Up Crying," issued on Teem.

"That was a new label Johnny started for some reason," said Carbo. "Mac didn't have anything to do with the session, Earl King produced it. I wasn't happy with it because it sounded cheap and rushed. Lee Dorsey had 'Lover of Loves' out at the time and we covered it. It got some airplay in New Orleans but it didn't sell."

The initial Carbo/Rebennack collaboration appeared on Rex.

"Rex was Cosimo's label but Johnny Vincent distributed it," said Carbo. "We did 'Promises' which was number one around New Orleans. It got up to number eight in Philadelphia and it did real well in New Jersey. Cosimo and Johnny sent me on a promotional tour of the Northeast when the record started to hit. It was the biggest record Cosimo had on Rex. Johnny tried to tell me it didn't sell, but I knew better than that."

"Promises" was a dreamy Rebennack ballad absolutely perfect for Carbo's smooth voice. The flip, "Be My Girl," also penned by Rebennack, was a jaunty New Orleans shuffle reminiscent of his work with the Spiders. Carbo's second Rex release, "Picture of You"/"Lucy Brown," featured a pop arrangements with abrasive intrusions of brass and vocal group accompaniment. It didn't sell. In 1962, Matassa folded Rex and Carbo wound up on Ace. His first Ace release, "Tears, Tears and More Tears," was a moving pop ballad that made an impression on New Orleans listeners, especially teenagers eager to dance the Jamaica.

"Those Ace things were recorded with Mac's regular record-hop band although Red Tyler usually played saxophone," said Carbo. "Mac was playing piano then because he got shot in the hand and couldn't play the guitar."

Carbo bowed out on Ace with "Cutting Out"/"Out On A Limb" just before the label folded. Soon after, Rebennack left New Orleans and Carbo took a job in a lumber yard.

"I had a family growing up and I had to put food on the table," said Carbo. "It was great being known as a performer but I had to look at reality. I had to get a regular job."

In 1969, Carbo resurfaced with the funky, "Can I Be Your Squeeze"/"Take Care of Your Homework Friend" on Eddie Bo's Fire Ball label which was leased to Canyon. A few local gigs materialized, but Carbo wasn't ready to abandon his day job. His next trip to the studio was in 1971, when he recorded "I'm Gonna Marry Your Daughter"/"Black People's Music" on Senator Jones Superdome label.

"I did that with Dave Bartholomew," said Carbo. "Edward Frank was on piano, Dave sang background and so did the late Leonard Lee. But that record just didn't sound right to me."

Carbo was comfortable in a nine-to-five lifestyle when in 1982, he was invited to sing at a WWOZ benefit held at Municipal Auditorium.

"I hadn't sung in years, but when I picked up the microphone that night it seemed like magic," said Carbo. "I thought to myself, 'Hey, I can do this again.'"

With the encouragement of other musicians and fans, Carbo gradually started performing again. He began sitting in with James Booker and Red Tyler at the Maple Leaf Bar, and appeared at the New Orleans Jazz & Heritage Festival. In 1988, Carbo caught a break and recorded his first solo album, *Life's Ups and Downs*. Produced by Edward Frank, and featuring guitarist, Alvin Robinson, the LP was issued on Mike Dine's British label, 504 (504 is the New Orleans area code).

"When we finished, I asked Mike if he could put out a single to help get some work," said Carbo. "One of the songs I wanted to put out was, "Second Line On Monday" which I wanted to be out by Carnival."

Released just in time for Mardi Gras of 1989, Carnival listeners later flipped the single over and began playing Carbo's treatment of the Doc and Innez Cheatham's blues shuffle, "Meet Me With Your Black Drawers On." Word got around and quickly the single and album were hot items. 504 moved several thousand 45s and several hundred LPs in New Orleans, virtually with no airplay beyond WWOZ.

"It was a big jukebox record," said Carbo. "'Meet Me With Your Black Drawers On' wasn't a nasty song—I thought it was cute and it's got a catchy beat. When I walked down the street, the kids would yell, 'There goes the black drawers man.'"

"Meet Me With Your Black Drawers On" led to two CDs on the Rounder label, *Drawers Trouble and The Barber's Blues*. Tastefully blending blues,standards, gospel, and past successes, both CDs benefited by the presence of Carbo's old buddies, Edward Frank and Mac Rebennack.

"I didn't want to get pigeon holed as a rhythm and blues singer," said Carbo, referring to his work on Rounder. "I know I'm more than that. If [those CDs] sound like old New Orleans R&B it's a surprise to me. I think we went into left field and really got some up-to-date sounds, even though I still felt the emotion just like I did back in the gospel days. I pride myself on my phrasing and my diction—I know how to sing and I practice. I've cultivated my voice over the years and I've improved. When I perform, I'm Chuck Carbo. I don't try to sound like anybody else."

In 1999, Carbo and the Spiders were inducted into the United In Group Harmony Association's Hall of Fame at the ninth annual awards ceremony at the Symphony Space Performing Arts Center in New York.

"It was a great honor being there," reflected Carbo. "Just to be mentioned along with groups like the Drifters, the Orioles, the Ravens, the Ink Spots, and the Moonglows is a compliment. But being inducted into a Hall of Fame with them is a dream of a lifetime."

CHAPTER NINE
~ Eddie Bo: Check Mr. Popeye ~

If sheer quantities of singles were a measure of achievement, Eddie Bo would certainly be one of New Orleans' most successful recording artists. A prolific and colorful rhythm and blues performer, Bo is often referred to as "The Maharaja," because of his penchant for wearing colorful turbans on and off stage. During the 1950s and 1960s, his music was the perfect embodiment of the classic New Orleans R&B sound that was popular across the country. Although Bo couldn't score a national hit at a time when many of his Crescent City contemporaries were in *Billboard's* Hot 100 and R&B charts, it was a matter of simply not being in the right place at the right time—not a matter of talent.

Edwin J. Bocage was born in New Orleans on September 30, 1930, and he grew in Algiers and the Ninth Ward. Bo's mother played blues piano and was his initial musical inspiration. After a hitch in the army, in 1950, Bocage enrolled at Grunewald's School of Music where he studied piano, arranging and music theory.

"I was a turncoat," laughed Bo. "I started out playing jazz and that's what I really wanted to play. But I switched to rhythm and blues because that's where the money was at the time."

Bo got his R&B chops together as "Spider" Bocage, initially at Caffin Theater playing with the Lastie Brothers band, and later as the leader of the house band at the Tiajuana Club on South Saratoga Street. By the mid-1950s, the Spider Bocage Orchestra was often hired by booking agent Percy Stovall who sent the group as far as Mexico and the Carolinas backing Earl King, Big Joe Turner, Guitar Slim, and Smiley Lewis. In 1955, Bo was spotted at the Tiajuana by Johnny Vincent who was just getting the Ace label off the ground. As "Little" Bo, he cut "I'm Glad"/"Baby" and played on Al Collins' "I Got The Blues For You." Neither record did much and Vincent temporarily lost interest in both artists. The following year, Bo signed with the New York-based Apollo label. His Apollo debut reworked Collin's "I Got the Blues For You," but he called the song, "I'm Wise." It did well in New Orleans and was a Southern territorial hit. Little Richard heard the song and later recorded it as "Slippin' And Sliddin'." It was one of his biggest records.

Vincent attempted to take advantage of Bo's sudden popularity and issued a leftover track from his Ace session, "I'm So Tired." Vincent didn't have another track for the B-side so he used Huey Smith's "We Like Mambo," but Bo's name appeared on both sides of the single. To Smith's dismay, "We Like Mambo" began selling in New Orleans.

"I got a lot of calls for work off that record," admitted Bo. "I felt bad for Huey but what could I do? People asked for 'We Like Mambo' so I started doing it on my shows."

Bo was signed by New York's Shaw Booking Agency and he put a band together that included bassist James Prevost, saxophonists David Lastie and Robert Parker, guitarist Irving Banister, as well as drummer Walter Lastie. The group toured the country and backed the likes of Joe Turner, Ruth Brown, Charles Brown, and Amos Milburn. When in New York, Bo and the group cut more sides for Apollo including "Hey, Bo" which made noise around New Orleans.

After five singles on Apollo, in 1957 Bo moved over to the Chicago-based Chess label where he cut two Paul Gayten-produced singles. The initial release, "Dearest Darling" was covered by Etta James and was a major hit in 1960. It's flip, "Oh-Oh," powered by Edgar Blanchard brilliant guitar, was as close as any New Orleans R&B artist ever got to rockabilly. Bo then briefly returned to Ace with "I Love To Rock and Roll"/"I'll Keep Trying," a great single that did well in the South. Around this time, Bo suffered a gunshot wound during an argument with his first wife. Shortly after, his hair was burned off while he was getting his hair straightened and processed. To conceal the damage, Bo began wearing turbans that matched his stage clothes. He continued wearing them even after his hair regrew as he felt they added to his stage presence.

In 1959, Bo signed with Joe Ruffino's Ric label. While at Ric, Bo recorded several memorable songs including his label debut, "Hey There Baby"/"I Need Someone." Propelled by Walter Lastie's superb drumming and Robert Parker's driving saxophone, both sides showcased Bo's soulful vocals. During his Ric tenure, he also served as producer, talent scout, songwriter and audition coordinator. Ric and Ron artists he wrote for and produced included, Martha Carter, Tommy Ridgley, Robert Parker, Johnny Adams, and Irma Thomas. A skilled carpenter, Bo even built a small studio behind Ruffino's office where several sessions took place. On his own Ric recordings, Bo usually wrote his own material, although many of his compositions were credited to his second wife, Dolores Johnson.

"I always felt Eddie was one of the most talented songwriters to come out of New Orleans," said the late Tommy Ridgley. "He was always coming into the studio with with great ideas for songs and arrangements. Joe Ruffino realized he had something in Eddie Bo and he gave him free rein in the studio."

An exemplary example of Bo's songwriting ability can be found on his second Ric single, "You Got Your Mojo Working." A clever answer to the Ann Cole/Muddy Water's hit "Got My Mojo Working," the song also played on Bo's mystical maharaja image. His third Ric single, "Tell It Like It Is"/"Every Dog Got His Day," spent several weeks bubbling under *Billboard's* Hot 100. "Tell It Like It Is" was especially a natural for the New Orleans market as it perfectly captured the city's parade beat. The flip side was also popular, but unfortunately Ric's limited promotion budget and their scattered distribution network prevented the single from breaking nationally. In March of 1961, Bo cut "It Must Be Love"/"Dinky Doo," another strong New Orleans seller that Capitol leased. For the first time, Bo experimented with the New Orleans Symphony which proved to be interesting and tasteful.

Eddie Bo's best selling Ric single "Check Mr. Popeye"/"Now Let's Popeye," featured the AFO Combo. An extremely popular local single that captured a syncopated laid back New Orleans beat, it nurtured the local Popeye dance fad and opened the door for a rash of Popeye related records. Belatedly, Ric leased the single to the Philadelphia-based Swan label, but by the time the Swan pressings hit the market, the Popeye was yesterday's news.

"Ruffino was the kind of guy that was satisfied with just selling 25,000 copies of a record," said Bo. "He never really looked any further than selling records around here. We had plenty of other records that Ruffino could have leased nationally, but it meant giving a piece of the record up to a larger company. Ruffino didn't go for that. He felt like they were stealing something from him."

Bo's ninth and last single for Ric was "Baby, I'm Wise," a remake of his Apollo hit, and the aptly titled "Roaman-itis." Bo's tenure at Ric would end abruptly after he and Ruffino got in a pistol waving dispute over royalties.

"Normally Bo was pretty easy going," said Ridgley. "But he could get hotheaded if he thought he was being taken advantage of. He got interested in the Muslim religion and he got down on white people for a while. He told me he'd never record for a white man again."

Bo temporarily made good on his promise to Ridgley. In 1962, he cut two good singles for the AFO subsidiary At Last, and then waxed four more on Rip Roberts' Rip label. One of the Rip singles, the pleading "Your With Me," started selling around New Orleans and was quickly leased by Chess at the recommendation of Paul Gayten. Chess also picked up "Fare Thee Well," which originally appeared on Arrow. Bo also recorded a single on Irvin Smith's Cinderella label and four more for Blue Jay. He then stopped briefly at NOLA, leaving "Heap See (But A Few Know)."

In 1966, Bo signed with Joe Banashak who ran the Instant, ALON, and Seven-B labels. Again he served as an artist, producer, talent scout and straw boss around the studio. He cut several great records on Seven-B under his own name and using the alias, Roy Ward. Highlights from this period were the ballad "Let Our Love Begin," the funky "Fence of Love," and the splendid duet with Inez Cheatham, "Lover and a Friend," which Capitol leased. Bo would also produce local hits on Skip Easterling, Oliver Morgan, Eddie Lang, Chris Kenner, and Art Neville. He was also responsible for the overdubs and remixing on Roger and the Gypsies time-less instrumental, "Pass the Hatchet."

Banashak and Bo eventually split after a disagreement so Bo began working for Al Scramuzza's Scram and Power labels. While at Scram, Bo produced neighborhood hits by Mary Jane Hooper, Little Sonny Jones, Walter Washington, and Benny Spellman. In 1969, he finally got that well deserved national hit when the funk laden "Hook and Sling," was leased to Scepter and reached number 13 in *Billboard's* R&B charts and number 73 in the Hot 100. Scepter distributed one other Scram/Bo single, "If It's Good To You (It's Good For You)," but it remained a New Orleans record. Scram folded shortly after, but Bo's furious pace of recording didn't abate. He started his own label Bo-Sound and began experimenting with modern funk and jazz. He recorded several singles on the label including "Check Your Bucket", which made a local splash in 1972 and was leased by Atlantic. However, by the mid-1970s, music became a sideline as gigs slowed down and Bo began working as a carpenter.

In 1977, he recorded *The Other Side of Eddie Bo*, a self-produced jazz album released on Bo-Sound. Two years later he opened the El Grande club on North Broad Street, a club he partially funded from a winning long shot ticket at the Fair Grounds. Bo performed at the club most week-ends, but it folded after being open just a couple of months. In 1980, *Watch For the Coming of Eddie Bo*, another jazz album appeared on Eboville. Bo spent most of the 1980s in Florida searching for spiritual peace and working as a carpenter. However, by 1990 he was back in New Orleans and rededicated himself to his music. Bo began playing at sever-al French Quarter clubs and as you'd expect, began recording again. His 1998 self-produced Bo-Sound CD, *Nine Yards of Funk*, explores jazz and funk but retains a flavoring of New Orleans R&B.

CHAPTER TEN
~ Li'l Millet: Rich Woman ~

Being that the late Li'l Millet had only one single—albeit the classic "Rich Woman" from 1955—he was one of New Orleans' more obscure rhythm and blues artists. However, although he was curiously under-recorded, Li'l Millet remained a popular live local attraction for nearly 25 years.

Born McKinley James Millet in New Orleans on October 25, 1935, his childhood was spent on Jourdan Avenue, the same Ninth Ward street Fats Domino grew up on. The son of a carpenter, Millet and his four brothers eventually moved to General Taylor Street in the Uptown section of the city.

"My mother encouraged everyone in the family to study music," recalled Millet in 1989. "In fact my first band was with my brothers. We took lessons from Professor Wilcox and he played bass with us. I played piano and all my older brothers played a horn or a drum."

As a student at Xavier Prep, Millet spent time listening to his mother's Ink Spots, Paul Gayten, and Roy Brown 78s. Possessing a quick ear, Millet could reproduce a song after just a couple of listens.

"The first band I played in worth mentioning was the Hawkettes," said Millet. "That was the trombone player's band—Carl Joseph. They had eight or nine pieces when I joined and they stayed pretty busy. [This was before the group recorded "Mardi Gras Mambo"] I played with them for quite awhile and then me and another guy quit because the band got too big. That's when I started my own group."

Millet formed a five-piece ensemble that included himself on piano and vocals, Tyler Van Scott on trumpet, Bill Smith on drums, Ernest Meyer on guitar, and John "L" on tenor sax. By 1954, Millet's group was a regular attraction at the Blue Gardenia club on the corner of Frenchman Street and Esplanade Avenue. They also started playing in many of the nearby small towns.

"We got the name Li'l Millet and the Creoles from a guy named Bismark Parker," said Millet. "He owned the Gables Inn in McComb. He booked us and had some placards made up for the job that said 'Li'l Millet and the Creoles.' We didn't know what to make of the name at first, but everybody liked it and it stuck."

The following year Millet and the Creoles were playing at the Sugar

Bowl in Thibodaux when Specialty Records producer Bumps Blackwell was in the house. He thought the group had a unique sound and approached Millet between sets.

"Bumps said he liked the way we played Bo Diddley's 'Diddley, Diddley, Daddy.'" said Millet. "We changed it around and gave it a different horn line and a new beat. He said he could get a woman [Dorothy La Bostrie] to write new lyrics for the song and he wanted us to come down to the J & M Studio and record it."

Just a few days after meeting Blackwell, Millet and the Creoles were in the studio and completed a standard four song session. To fill out the Creoles, Blackwell added Lee Allen on tenor, Earl Palmer on drums and Frank Fields on bass. Two sides were issued from the session, "Rich Woman," the remake of "Diddley Diddley Daddy," and "Hopeless Love."

The hypnotic "Rich Woman" was everybody's pick. Played at a mambo tempo, Millet's nasal vocals are answered by a spectacular second line horn pattern. Today "Rich Woman" is considered a New Orleans R&B classic, having been covered and reissued several times over the years. However, as Millet explained the record didn't do much when it was released.

"It got a few plays around here and in Tennessee [on WLAC] but that was about it. People asked me to play it at our dances but I don't think Specialty gave it much of a push because they had Little Richard and he was their money maker."

Ironically, a song Millet auditioned for Specialty, "All Around The World," was recorded by Little Richard

"We did that tune for Bumps but it never came out," said Millet. "We had a job in Houma and Richard came with us. That's when he first heard 'All Around the World.' When Richard got back to New Orleans he went in the studio and cut it. I didn't like his version because he didn't do it the way I meant it to be played. On top of that, Bumps tried to steal the song but somebody in Hollywood convinced him to keep my name on it. He still got credit as a co-writer even though he didn't have anything to do with the writing it."

Although Blackwell gave Millet his first break, Millet felt that the Blackwell and Specialty didn't give him or other lesser known New Orleans Specialty artists a fair opportunity.

"Bumps was always in a rush," said Millet. "He'd call at 2 a.m. and say, 'Get your band down to the studio and lets cut.' You can't make a good record that way. And Bumps was always trying to mess with your tempo. You'd have a good groove going and he'd try to make you drag it."

Millet recorded on several occasions for Blackwell, but great songs like the rousing, "Rock Around the Clock," and the fantastic ballad "Someday Mother," languished on the shelf for 30 years until the British Ace label issued them. Millet pointed out that once Little Richard abandoned rock and roll, and Blackwell started producing Sam Cooke's pop recordings, he turned his back on New Orleans.

Although his recording career never got on track, Li'l Millet and the Creoles were never short of work.

"We were always busy," said Millet. "We played the Town & Country in Donaldsonville, the Bama Club in Prairieville, the College Inn in Thibodaux, the Southern Club in Opelousas. I never worked a day job."

Booking agent Percy Stovall also used the Creoles to work behind headliners like Nappy Brown, Earl King, Smiley Lewis, and Jimmy Reed. The group also opened shows at Dave Brown's Blue Eagle. Unfortunately, in 1958, just when the Creoles were building a head of steam, Millet's draft notice arrived which took him out of circulation at a period when he and the Creoles could certainly have done more recording. When he was discharged in 1960, Millet wasn't keen about playing music again, but Ernest Meyer convinced him otherwise. On Millet's second go-around, he made an important change to the band. Instead of piano, Millet began playing electric bass, an instrument which gave the band a very different sound. According to Millet the reason for switching was simple.

"There were too many ragged pianos out there that had dead keys and they were always out of tune. You'd have to cross chord just so you could tune up to a B-flat with the horns. The bass was much easier to deal with."

Eventually Millet and the Creoles returned to playing several of their old haunts which kept them busy during the 1960s. Work began to slow up though in the early 1970s, when many night spots closed, or no longer featured R&B music. Later in the decade, their bookings primarily consisted of dances at New Orleans social aid and pleasure clubs.

Millet disbanded the Creoles in 1980, when disco eliminated what little work the band had left. With music behind him, Millet drove a school bus and took care of a couple of apartment buildings he had purchased in the 1970s. Although a hit record proved to be elusive, Millet looked at his career with understandable pride.

"I had plenty of good times and made plenty of money," he said. "I always thought music was good to me."

During the the 1990s, Millet occasionally performed on benefit shows, but before a serious comeback could be undertaken, he died of cancer on June 29, 1997.

CHAPTER ELEVEN
~ Clarence Henry: The Frogman ~

Because of the continued major media use of "Ain't Got No Home," some listeners consider Clarence "Frogman" Henry a one-hit wonder. This certainly isn't an accurate observation however, as Henry's body of spectacular recordings has elevated him to legendary status. Nevertheless, Henry points out that while being considered a rhythm and blues pioneer is great, having a timeless hit—one that has generated millions of dollars—makes life a lot easier.

"'Ain't Got No Home' was in *Forrest Gump* and Paramount Pictures was very generous with me," said Henry. "It's been in several other movies too. My man Rush Limbaugh plays it all the time. You can't buy publicity like that. I get fan mail (often simply addressed 'Frogman, New Orleans, USA') every day of the year."

The easy going Frogman lives in a comfortable Algiers bungalow surrounded by frogs. Not only is his yard and garden filled with ceramic and plastic frogs, but the inside of his home is crammed with every conceivable frog-like knickknack.

"I've probably got thousands of frogs," points out Henry. "Statues, dolls, salt and pepper shakers, rugs, plates—you name it. I get them from fans and friends all the time. They've just sort of accumulated over the years."

Clarence Henry, Jr. was born in New Orleans on March 19, 1937, the son of a railroad porter and his wife Ernestine. As a youth, he followed his sister Lizzie to classical piano lessons and took her place when she decided music wasn't for her. At the age of 11, he and his family moved across the Mississippi River to the New Orleans suburb of Algiers. Henry attended L. B. Landry High School where he picked up a second instrument, the trombone. Landry's band director was William Houston, the owner of a North Claiborne Avenue music school, who doubled as president of the Musicians Mutual Protection Union Local 496. To encourage his students to pursue music, Houston would get stars like Shirley and Lee, and Fats Domino to perform at school assemblies.

As a teenager, Henry also took musical field trips.

"I used to sneak in the Pepper Pot (in nearby Gretna) to see Professor Longhair," said Henry. "It was just him and a drummer, but it sounded like a whole band in there. When I played talent shows at school, I played his numbers, and dressed just like him with tails and a long Indian wig."

However, Henry's major influence was Fats Domino.

"Fats was my inspiration," admitted Henry. "When I sat down at the piano, I tried to play everything he did. As far as I'm concerned, Fats is the real king of rock and roll."

In 1952, he met fellow Landry student Bobby Mitchell, who led a vocal group called the Toppers.

"My first professional job was playing with the Toppers," said Henry. "We all went to school together. Lloyd Bellaire was their regular piano player, but he couldn't make all the gigs and I'd fill in for him occasionally. We played a lot of hops and high school dances, but not many clubs—we were too young."

The Toppers auditioned for Imperial's Dave Bartholomew, who thought the teenagers had potential. Henry played trombone on the group's first session but eventually got fired because he missed a gig in order to attend his own shotgun wedding. After graduating from Landry, Henry turned down a music scholarship from Southern University and started his own R&B group. Concentrating solely on piano, Henry worked Westbank clubs like the Fat Man and the Chicken Shack. At the Chicken Shack, Henry was spotted by Pascal "Pops" Perez, who ran a Gretna gambling joint, the Joy Lounge. Perez hired Henry in 1956 and paired him with saxophonist Eddie Smith and his band. The combination proved to be a success as they kept the Joy packed six nights a week.

"On Sunday we normally played until 2 a.m.," said Henry. "But one night there was a full house and we played until eight in the morning. I wanted to go home but Pops kept telling us to keep working. The sun had come up and we had run out of songs to play. Finally I just hit an old blues riff on the piano and started to sing, 'Ain't got no home, no place to roam.' Then I added the part about, 'I can sing like a frog and I can sing like a girl.' The audience really went for it."

After Henry went home and got some sleep, he went to work on "the frog song." He auditioned the composition for bandleader Paul Gayten, who in the mid-1950s was the local A&R man for the Chicago-based Chess label. Gayten heard the potential in Henry and he alerted his boss, Leonard Chess, who flew from Chicago to hear Henry play. Chess agreed that the Algier's teenager had potential and in September 1956, Henry signed a Chess contract. Gayten and Chess picked up on the Fats Domino influence in Henry's style and enhanced it once they got to the studio. On Henry's recording debut, Gayten assembled a band that included two regulars on Domino sessions, saxophonist Lee Allen and guitarist Walter "Papoose" Nelson. Gayten played the Domino like piano accompaniment while Henry concentrated on getting the multi-voiced lyrics correct. The frog song (retitled "Ain't Got No Home") and the frantic "Troubles, Troubles," were issued on Argo—a Chess subsidiary label. Initially, there was no reaction to Henry's record, even in New Orleans. However, that soon changed.

"Chess pushed the wrong side," said Henry. "Finally, Poppa Stoppa [Clarence Haymen] at WWEZ flipped the record over and played 'Ain't Got No Home.' Right away people called the station asking for the frog song. Poppa Stoppa was the first one to start calling me 'Frogman.' People were calling him and asking for the frog song by the 'Frogman.' Back then everybody called Fats Domino 'The Fatman.' Poppa Stoppa told me, 'Clarence you got this song about a frog. We'll have to start calling you the 'Frogman.' The name stuck."

Chess quickly changed it's marketing strategy and "Ain't Got No Home" raced to number three in *Billboard's* R&B chart and number 30 in the Hot 100. Henry quickly went from playing New Orleans clubs to auditorium shows around the country. Before the end of 1956, Henry was wowing them at New York's Apollo and the Howard in Washington. The following year, he toured Jamaica with Bull Moose Jackson and the Teenchords.

Quite often, after an artist has a hit with a novelty song, they have difficulty reaching the public again. Unfortunately this happened to Henry. Chess released the other songs from Henry's initial session, "Lonely Tramp," and "I'm A Country Boy," but they didn't sell outside of New Orleans. In June 1957, Henry returned to Cosimos's and answered "Ain't Got No Home" with "I Found A Home." This time though the multi-voice gimmick wasn't bought by the public. His next Argo single, "It Won't Be Long," driven by Papoose's inspired guitar, fizzled. Touring abruptly ended, but Henry found work on lucrative Bourbon Street. However, his career didn't start hopping again nationally until 1960, when Leonard Chess unexpectedly came by the Court of the Two Sisters where Henry was working at the time.

"Leonard said we were going in the studio the next day," said Henry, who hadn't recorded in two years. "I didn't have any material but we got "But I Do" together. That record put me back on top and I started touring again."

A Bobby Charles swamp pop ballad that Henry nearly recorded at his first session, "But I Do" peaked at number four in the pop charts. Arranged by Allen Toussaint, Nat Perrilat's saxophone provided the distinct introduction that helped make the song so attractive. Suddenly, Henry was inundated with work. In order to cut a follow up, Chess had to catch him between dates in Chicago. In March 1961, Toussaint flew to the Windy City to produce Henry's cover of the the Mills Brother's ballad, "You Always Hurt the One You Love," which made it to number 12 in the pop charts. Another chart record from this session was "I Love You Yes I Do," a Bull Moose Jackson standard.

Other lesser hits followed including "Lonely Street" and another Bobby Charles song, "On Bended Knees." Chess/Argo issued an album, *You Always Hurt The One You Love*, that included his early 1960s hits, B-sides and some unreleased material. Henry then joined Dick Clark's Caravan of Stars tour with Chubby Checker, Duane Eddy, and Paul Anka which crisscrossed the country. In July 1961, Henry traveled to Memphis where Bill Justis produced his next batch of recordings. The session yielded great tunes like "Standing In the Need Of Love" and "A Little Too Much," but they missed the charts. Chess continued to record Henry once a year, but like many R&B artists whose roots were in the 1950s, his record sales began to tumble.

Nevertheless, in 1964, Henry opened 18 dates for the Beatles on their North American tour, including a New Orleans show at City Park Stadium. Those were good paydays for Henry, but the hysteria the Beatles created ensured that the audience totally ignored him. On top of that, the style the Beatles brought with them swept Henry's New Orleans style out of the charts. That year, he returned to Bourbon Street, where the people still remembered his hits. Henry and Chess parted again and he subsequently signed with Texas-producer Huey Meaux. Henry recorded five great singles for Meaux that were leased to Parrot Records including the classic "Cajun Honey."

"My manager, the late Bob Astor, was responsible for me getting with Huey," said Henry. "In some ways I thought that was some of the best stuff I ever cut. You see Huey is a country boy and he wanted to get me into a hillbilly bag. I always liked country music, but I would never have tried to play it if he hadn't pushed me. Those were all country musicians on those records so the sound was authentic. There was a guy out of Biloxi, Jimmy Donley, that wrote great country songs. He used to write and record for Huey so there were a lot of his songs around. He wrote 'Think It Over,' which was one of my favorite tunes."

Meaux didn't confine Henry to just country material though, giving him free rein to rock on the remakes of "Ain't Got No Home" and "Sea Cruise." After Meaux's leasing deal with Parrot ended, Henry cut a couple of singles for the the Nashville-based Dial label, but they were largely overlooked outside of New Orleans. In 1969, Henry recorded the album *Clarence Henry Is Alive And Well, Living In New Orleans And Still Doing*

His Thing... for Roulette. Henry sold and autographed thousands of them at his gigs, but the album was totally ignored elsewhere. In 1973, he reconnected with Meaux and had a couple of singles released on the Pla-Boy label, but they too only reached the local market. Nevertheless, Henry still had a good thing on Bourbon Street, as his name drew tourists in droves. Not only did he earn a comfortable living, but his band featured many of the top New Orleans R&B players.

"I played on Bourbon Street for 19 years," said Henry. "The 544, Court of the Two Sisters, La Strada, The Backstage—I played nearly every club on the Strip. Six hours a night, six nights a week and I had the best band in town."

But by 1981, Henry finally had enough of the French Quarter.

"I was burned out," admitted Henry. "I enjoyed the work, but I was becoming a physical wreck and I needed a change."

Henry began to take it easier, but in 1982, he decided to undertake a lengthy tour of England. The dates paired him with comedians Cannon & Ball, who also hosted a popular television program. Taken with Henry's out-going personality and music, the duo convinced him to return to England to tape a year's worth of shows. During his stay in England, Henry recorded *The Legendary Frogman Henry* for the Silvertone label, which did well overseas. To date these have been his last commercial recordings.

In the mid-1980s, Henry began working for Blaine Kern, a Mardi Gras float builder who also staged elaborate Carnival balls and provided entertainment for them. Henry worked several lucrative jobs for Kern in between festival and occasional "oldies" gigs in New Orleans and around the country. At this time, Henry's catalog of songs began to pay him dividends. His old records were being programmed on syndicated oldies shows and his material was included in several films and television programs.

"With most of my recordings, everybody made money but me," said Henry. "I'm pleased with the new company [MCA/Universal, which now controls the Chess catalog] and they've been fair with me. Still, I see my old records come out in Europe that I've never been paid for."

Henry's lucrative catalog allows him to enjoy life and spend more time around the house with his frogs. He no longer plays piano on shows and only works frequently around Mardi Gras and during the New Orleans Jazz and Heritage Festival. In the last few years, he has also picked up occasionally work at the casinos along the Mississippi Gulf Coast. While Henry admits he's slowed up, he contends he's never going to stop playing music.

"As long as my health allows me, I'm going to keep performing because it's what I truly enjoy," he concludes. "People want to see the Frogman, but you know the Frogman wants to see the people too."

CHAPTER TWELVE
~ Al Johnson: Carnival Time ~

Since 1960, Al Johnson's "Carnival Time" has been considered a Mardi Gras anthem around New Orleans. For two weeks every year, "Carnival Time," with it's get up and shake something second line rhythm, blares from Crescent City jukeboxes, radios, sound systems and televisions, 24 hours a day.

Nevertheless, despite possessing a great blues voice and a solid rhythm and blues piano technique, Johnson has curiously remained under-recorded and under-appreciated. His entire recorded legacy is limited to four singles. Frustratingly, because of shoddy business practices, as well as unsound professional and legal advice, Johnson only began to benefiting from the royalties generated from "Carnival Time" in the new millennium.

"Sometimes I wish I'd have never cut 'Carnival Time,'" lamented Johnson. "I made the record so people would be happy, but it seems like it's brought me nothing but a lot of problems. The situation soured me towards the music business and I've never really felt comfortable pursuing music as a career."

Johnson was born in 1940 and grew up in a family that encouraged him to play music. His father, a railroad porter, bought his son a trumpet and a piano which he mastered quickly. Spiritual music was his original interest, but he later began to play Dixieland, ala Louis Armstrong, and later rhythm and blues.

"I started playing music in public during grammar school," recalled Johnson. "When I got into high school, I started going around to all of theaters that sponsored talent shows. First prize was $5 which was plenty of money back in the 1950s. I won lots of $5 bills playing Sugar Boy Crawford's 'I Cried.'"

Besides Crawford, Johnson also cited Smiley Lewis, Fats Domino, and Professor Longhair as his early influences. Not only did he hear their records on radio and jukeboxes, he also saw them perform around town. In 1956, while Johnson was still in high school, he cut a single for Aladdin Records, "Old Time Talkin'"/ "If I've Done Wrong."

"I don't remember much about the session," admitted Johnson. "I've never even heard or seen the record. [It does on very rare occasions appear on auction lists but might not have been released to distributors.] My mother had to sign for me to record because I was under 18 at the time. We cut it at Cosimo's Studio down on Governor Nichols Street. Dave "Fatman" Matthews played piano and arranged the session. All I did was sing."

After the Aladdin single, Johnson joined the Twilighters, a group that featured himself on piano and vocals, his brother Curtis on tenor sax, Steve Kelly on drums, and "Junior" on guitar.

"We played the Cadillac Club on Poland Avenue and Jessie's in Marrero," said Johnson. "We played most of the popular R&B songs of the day, but I like to think we did them in our own style."

Pianist Reggie Hall eventually joined the Twilighters and Johnson was forced out of the group. Johnson then formed his own four-piece band which caught the ear of Edgar Blanchard who was recruiting talent for the newly formed Ric and Ron labels.

"I graduated high school on June 4, 1958," said Johnson. "Two days later I was in the studio. Edgar brought me to Joe Ruffino who owned Ric Records. Ruffino liked my audition so we cut 'Lena' and 'You Done Me Wrong.'"

Both sides were superb examples of late 1950s New Orleans R&B, especially the raucous "Lena" which was in the Smiley Lewis bag.

"I never signed a contract with Ruffino," detailed Johnson. "I was just interested in getting a record out and thought I'd be taken care of later. 'Lena' did pretty well around New Orleans and I heard it was played in a few other cities. After the record died down I went to Ruffino and asked for some money. He told me that I still owed him $11 for the session, but it was okay—he'd let me slide."

Miffed, Johnson returned to playing New Orleans dates, determined to write a song that was unique enough to catch the public's attention. The song was "Carnival Time."

"I had a friend named Frank Miller," said Johnson. "He told me he was going to help me write a song. He gave me the lines about the Green Room and the Plaza. [The lyrics were actually lifted from Archibald's 1952 Imperial recording of "Soon As I Go Home."] Those clubs were near the corner of North Claiborne and Basin Street— there's a fire station there now. The song says let them [the clubs] burn down, but those places weren't really on fire, I just meant the people there were having a good time. My in-laws helped me with the rest of the song. I was always told that to be great, you had to be different. Well 'Carnival Time' was so different that the musicians had a hard time playing it. I still don't think we got it 100 percent right."

Apparently several takes of the song were recorded, some with

Johnson playing piano, some with Mac Rebennack. The issued take of "Carnival Time" had Rebennack on piano with James Rivers taking the driving tenor sax break. Recorded in December 1959, it was released just before Mardi Gras two months later.

"When 'Carnival Time' came out Jessie Hill had just recorded 'Ooh Poo Pah Doo,'" said Johnson. "You couldn't go anywhere without hearing 'Ooh Poo Pah Doo.' That was the Carnival record of 1960. It buried 'Carnival Time.' I was really disappointed."

Johnson had little time to dwell on his dismay as he was drafted soon after the single was released.

"I was stationed at Fort Bliss, Texas," he said. "They had me firing missiles, but I got a hold of a trumpet and started working on my chops again. Eventually I got into the army band. They liked me because I could play loud and long. I started getting letters the year after I enlisted saying that 'Carnival Time' was tearing it up back in New Orleans. I thought to myself, 'How about that.'"

Johnson's military hitch ended in 1964, a disastrous year for New Orleans music.

"There was almost nothing left of the music business when I got back," said Johnson. "The Beatles [music] put almost all of the New Orleans bands out of work and most of the record companies had left town. I couldn't get any money from 'Carnival Time' because Ruffino died while I was in the army. There was no future in music at that time."

Johnson attended welding and refrigeration school, but found he didn't want to pursue either profession. Johnson wound up getting a cab license and began shuttling tourists to-and-from from the airport in a White Fleet cab and picking up fares in the French Quarter. He'd get an occasion booking around Mardi Gras, but little else as no one was interested in recording him.

In 1976, Mardi Gras Records reissued "Carnival Time" on the *Mardi Gras In New Orleans* album which drew attention to Johnson from inside and outside of New Orleans. Three years later, he launched a brief come back, playing at Tipitina's, Jimmy's and the Jazz Fest. He also began trying to get royalties and secure the rights to "Carnival Time." Johnson hired a series of lawyers to represent him, but since he never signed a writers contract with Ric's Ron Publishing Company, he wasn't in a good position. In 1984, his former Ric label mate, Joe Jones, assumed control of Ron Publishing while Rounder Records purchased the reissue rights to his Ric recordings.

"I got some checks but they weren't for what I felt was fair," he said. "If I cashed them I was agreeing with terms I didn't feel were right so I sent them all back."

The situation got even more bizarre when Jones sued Johnson claiming Johnson sold him his writers stake in "Carnival Time" in the early 1960s so he wasn't due any royalties. After more lawsuits and over a decade in court, in the fall of 1999, Johnson got the rights to "Carnival Time" back and he's finally receiving proper writing and performance royalties. Nonetheless, the ordeal scared him away from the music business. Although he listens to music and plays the piano everyday, he rarely performs in public, even during Mardi Gras when he could take advantage of the popularity of "Carnival Time." As a result, a great New Orleans rhythm and blues talent has sadly going to waste.

Part II

The Supporters

❖

Naturally, one first thinks of the artists who got their names on the record labels and in the charts when listening to or discussing New Orleans rhythm and blues. However the contributions of the supporting musicians—sidemen for lack of a better term—can not be ignored, as their hard work and creativity helped develop and nurture the genre.

During the early 1950s, even though there was a large pool of New Orleans talent, there was only a small clique of studio musicians, most which had connections to Dave Bartholomew's band. However, by the end of the decade, as more labels descended on Cosimo's Studio looking for the successful New Orleans sound, the circle of musicians used at recording sessions gradually expanded. The circle continued to stretch after the monopoly the out-of-town labels had on recording in New Orleans ended in the 1960s. Dozens of homegrown labels sprung up, many with a desire to sound different from the competition. While many labels continued to use studio regulars, innovative producers like Allen Toussaint, Mac Rebennack, Harold Battiste, Wardell Quezergue, George Davis and Eddie Bo were willing to use newcomers to spark their recordings.

Until the bottom fell out of the local record industry in the late 1960s, many musicians maintained a comfortable living playing club dates and augmenting their income with studio work. Few though survived the 1970s without adjusting—i.e. taking a day job or leaving town. Some even abandoned the profession entirely. However, several of the more creative musicians who started their career as sidemen—Huey Smith, Allen Toussaint, James Booker, Mac Rebennack, Robert Parker to name a few—were able to springboard from the role of supporter and forge a successful solo career.

What follows are the stories of a select group supporting musicians who helped create the New Orleans R&B sound.

CHAPTER THIRTEEN
~ Billy Diamond: Providing The Bass ~

Producer and bandleader Dave Bartholomew, as well as Imperial Record's owner Lew Chudd, are justifiably given the lion's share of credit for making Fats Domino a recording star and international icon. However, if it weren't for Billy Diamond, it's conceivable that Domino might have wound up playing Dixieland on Bourbon Street, or perhaps abandoning music all together. Diamond hired Domino to play in his band in 1947 and gave him the "Fats" moniker. He was also the first person to encourage him to start singing.

Diamond, a short chubby man with a perpetual grin, now resides in Los Angeles. He is well aware of his place in music history, but matter of fact about it.

William Diamond was born in New Orleans on October 5, 1916 and grew up at 2215 Louisiana Avenue. Like many teenagers, Diamond became interested in music at an early age via watching brass bands march through his neighborhood.

"Louis Armstrong actually gave me a trumpet in 1930 but I never learned to play it," said Diamond. "I used to make guitars out of screen wire and basses out of old inner tubes tied to washtubs. That's how I learned to play bass. Later I got a Kay bass when I was 15 and learned from Tom Copelin and Marvin Kimble—they were Dixieland bass players."

In the early 1930s, Diamond moved with his family to Andry Street in the Ninth Ward.

"I lived right next door to the Rumboogie," said Diamond, referring to the legendary Ninth Ward bar. "I helped build the place. My aunt owned the joint. There was no live music there because it was too small. It was a place you'd go to get a beer or some wine. They had a jukebox though and it was a real popular neighborhood bar."

During WW II, Diamond was stationed at Camp Poche in nearby Harahan, Louisiana, where he drove trucks and later dispatched them. After the war he thought he'd take on music as a profession.

"It was real competitive back then and there were a lot of good bands and great musicians," said Diamond. "I'm talking about Joe Robichaux, Snookum Russell, Herbert Leary and William Houston—those were the guys that played all the society jobs and played on the river boats. A lot of the Creole clubs and organizations only wanted to hire creole bands—not black bands. That didn't really change until Dave Bartholomew busted the walls down with his band.

"My first band was Billy Diamond and the Mellow Riff Trio. Besides myself, I had Johnny Fernandez on piano and Rupert Roberts on guitar. We didn't get a lot of good gigs, but we worked around the Ninth Ward at Club Desire, the Cougar Club, Bogger's Patio and Rose Dixon's place on North Derbigny. We played a lot of high school dances too. I was pretty good about selling the band."

Diamond and the Mellow Riff Trio became part of the "Dawn Patrol," a radio program that was sponsored by Jax Beer and advertised in *The Louisiana Weekly* and on WWEZ radio.

"Every Monday night we played a different club with Dr. Daddy-O or Ernie the Whip emceeing the show," said Diamond. "We'd back Patsy Valdalia or Annie Laurie and it would be a promotion for Jax beer. They paid us $40. Every place we played was packed because of all the publicity."

In 1947, Diamond formed another band, the Solid Senders, that consisted of Diamond, Frank Parker on drums, Harrison Verret on guitar and an untested piano player, Antoine Domino.

"I knew Fats' brother Joe from hanging out at a grocery store on North Rocheblave," said Diamond. "Fats had a band at the time with Buddy Hagans playing at the Ballerina Club. Buddy was a sax player—I went on the road with him once backing Roy Brown. Fats had a lot of talent even back then. He reminded me of Fats Waller and Fats Pichon. Those guys were big names and Antoine—that's what everybody called him then—had just got married and was gaining weight. So I started calling him 'Fats.' It stuck."

Initially Domino didn't sing with the Solid Senders, as Parker sang most numbers. Later Little Sonny Jones was hired as the band's vocalist.

"Paul Gayten was real popular at the time and Fats really liked his records 'True' and 'Hey Now Baby,'" said Diamond. "I convinced him to start singing on the gigs and those were the first numbers he tried. Later on he started singing 'Junco Partner'—the James Wayne tune."

One of the first breaks the band got was playing the Sunday matinee replacing Gayten at the swank Robin Hood Club on Jackson Avenue. However, it was at the Hide Away Inn on Desire Street, nestled deep in the Ninth Ward, where the band picked up a large and loyal following.

"That club was owned by Ed Wein," said Diamond. "His brother Tony had the Green Room downtown. It wasn't much of a place but the Desire Projects had just opened about a block away so it was packed all the time. Fats loved to perform there because people came just to hear him play 'Swanee River Boogie.' We made $12 a man at the Hide Away. We made $12 at the Robin Hood too, but they [the Hide Away] paid our union pension dues. Dave [Bartholomew] heard about us at the Hide Away and he brought Lew Chudd down there one night. Obviously they liked what they heard because they signed Fats and made a lot of records with him."

Bartholomew preferred to record Domino without the Solid Senders and used his own orchestra. That meant that Frank Fields played bass on "The Fatman"—and most of Domino's New Orleans recordings—rather than Diamond. The Solid Senders however continued to play with Domino around the city and eventually on the road.

"Frank was probably a better bass player than I was," said Diamond. "But I was a good entertainer and I worked hard. Fats went on the road with Dave a couple of times, but they didn't do so well. He felt more comfortable playing with my band."

Diamond explained that besides playing the string bass, his job was to keep the crowd entertained. He accomplished this by riding, walking, slapping, and generally clowning with his instrument.

Diamond did play on Domino's number one R&B hit, "Going Home Tomorrow," recorded in 1952, during a period when Bartholomew temporarily left Imperial and Diamond's band was employed. He also played on most of the sessions Domino cut on the road including "Blueberry Hill" and "Blue Monday."

Once Domino's records started climbing the charts, Diamond began spending more time on the road. As the band grew, and dates were more scattered across the country, Diamond also assumed the role of road manager, a job that included driving, and making sure the band's vehicles were working properly, reserving accommodations on the road, making sure the band's uniforms were laundered, as well as hiring and firing musicians. Unfortunately tragedy struck in 1952.

"We were going to a job in Rayne, Louisiana," said Diamond. "I took the band and the instruments in the station wagon up Highway 61 and 190 to Opelousas and then drove down to Lafayette. That was all straight highway. Fats rode in his Cadillac with Melvin Cade. Melvin was our first booking agent and he owned the Rhythm Club on Jackson Avenue. They took Highway 90 which was 15 miles shorter, but it was all winding road. They got into a wreck and Melvin was killed. Fats was shook up but he was okay."

By the mid-1950s, the New York-based Shaw Agency was handling Domino's bookings. Shaw convinced Diamond to put the bass down and concentrate solely on being Domino's full time road manager. Diamond spent five years in this capacity and only played bass occasionally. When in New Orleans, Diamond got to know several New Orleans up-and-coming R&B artists and became their advisor in many cases, imparting wisdom and advice.

In 1962, not long after accompanying Domino on his first trip overseas, Diamond opted for a career change.

"Fats stopped working for a long time," said Diamond. "When we played on the West Coast we played the 5-4 Ballroom in Los Angeles which was owned by Charles Sullivan. Charles was the guy behind Motown moving out West and had been after me to work for him. I had just gotten married and my wife didn't want to raise kids in New Orleans because it was segregated. So we moved to L. A. I already knew a lot of New Orleans cats already here like Plas Johnson, Earl Palmer, Ernest McLean and Paul Gayten. I hired the bands and managed the 5-4. I met all the West Coast R&B people—Johnny Otis, Big Mama Thornton, Guitar Shorty, Philip Walker and T-Bone Walker. I did that until 1969 when Charles got killed and the club closed."

With numerous connections in the music industry, Diamond decided to venture into the record promotion business. Today he still hires himself out to record companies looking to promote their latest releases on the West Coast. There aren't many people in the music industry you can name that Diamond doesn't know or whom he hasn't had dealings with. Most of his waking hours are taken up with calling dee jays, program directors and record labels.

Over the years Diamond has remained close friends with Domino and they often get together during his frequent visits back to New Orleans.

"I saw Fats in New Orleans at the House of Blues earlier this year [1999] and at the Jazz Festival," said Diamond. "Fats complained that his band doesn't like to rehearse, but you can't keep a band and get them to rehearse if you only work once every six months. It would be great to see Fats get out there and playing again. It would make me feel a little bit important because I was there when he started out."

CHAPTER FOURTEEN
~ Edgar Blanchard & The Gondoliers: Let's Get It ~

One of New Orleans' most talented but underrated rhythm and blues musicians was the late guitarist Edgar Blanchard. Blanchard played on and arranged hundreds of recordings with Roy Brown, Little Richard, Eddie Bo, Johnny Adams, Ray Charles, and Big Joe Turner among others. As a musician, Blanchard was incomparable.

"Edgar was one of the top guitarists in the country," declared the late Alonzo Stewart, who played drums behind Blanchard for over a decade. "A guy like George Benson couldn't even hold the light for Edgar to stand under. He could do it all."

As an arranger Blanchard was a rhythm and blues pioneer.

"I knew Edgar from playing at the Dew Drop in the early 1950s," said Harold Battiste. "He was the first guy from New Orleans I'd consider an arranger. He wrote charts for every instrument in the band and that was something no other bandleader was doing then."

Blanchard was born August 17, 1924, at Grosse Tete, Louisiana, a village located 20 miles west of Baton Rouge. As a child, he moved with his parents and three brothers to New Orleans. Blanchard was already a talented guitarist as a youth. Trumpeter, Frank Mitchell recalled playing a job in New Sarpy, Louisiana, in the 1930s with Blanchard when he couldn't have been much more than 10.

During WW II, Blanchard was in the US Army and saw action in Europe. He returned to New Orleans in 1945 and studied music theory and arranging at Grunewald's School of Music under the GI Bill. Upon graduation Blanchard formed a band with Albert "June" Gardner on drums, Otis Ducker on saxophone, Ed Blackwell on piano, and Stewart Davis on bass. Blanchard called the group the Gondoliers, a name inspired by a trip to Venice, Italy, during the War where he saw gondoliers serenade their passengers in their boats as they rowed through the city's canals.

In the late 1940s, the Gondoliers were making the rounds of clubs like the San Jacinto, the Robin Hood, the Gypsy Tea Room, the Dew Drop and the Downbeat.

"Outside of Ernest McLean, Edgar could outplay ever other guitar player in New Orleans," said Mitchell, who often crossed paths with Blanchard. "By being a guitar player he was a natural arranger. His band was playing stuff other bands in town couldn't handle."

The Gondoliers were playing regularly at Percy Stovall's Pelican Club on South Rampart Street. To supplement his income, Stovall began booking artists like Roy Brown and Chubby Newsome around the area and he needed a dependable band to back them. In December of 1948, Blanchard and the Gondoliers were signed to an exclusive contract by Stovall, who had decided to sell the Pelican and concentrate solely on the booking business. The following year, Stovall got the Gondoliers an extended engagement at Houston's Bronze Peacock, a club owned by Don Robey, who also ran Peacock Records, and was always on the lookout for new talent. He recorded Blanchard and the Gondoliers and used them on a session with harmonica player Papa Lightfoot.

Blanchard sings on "Creole Gal Blues" and "She'll Be Mine After Awhile," displaying a confident and smooth style. His playing on these sides is more country flavored than the more urban style he would later become known for. The single didn't sell though and Robey requested no more material.

In early 1950, the Gondoliers were back working at the Dew Drop, but Blanchard broke the group up and took a job with Roy Brown's band, the Mighty Mighty Men. After several months with Brown, most of the band quit and Blanchard assumed the role of bandleader, earning $125 a week. Besides touring with Brown, his playing and arranging can be heard on several of the blues shouters masterpieces including "Hard Luck Blues" which topped *Billboard's* R&B chart in 1950.

"Edgar was playing the baritone chart on the bass strings of his guitar," recalled Mitchell, who joined Brown's group when Blanchard was bandleader. "Our tenor player quit and we had a hard time finding a new one. Edgar just stepped in and played the treble clef and the baritone chart simultaneously on his guitar."

Blanchard was a Mighty Mighty Man until the fall of 1951, when he had a disagreement with Brown while on the road and quit. Wanting to begin working as studio musician, Blanchard returned to New Orleans hoping to pick up session work at the J & M Studio. However, at the time guitarist Ernest McLean was getting most of the studio work in New Orleans and nobody called Blanchard. Frustrated, he quit playing music entirely.

"Edgar came in the Famous Door where I was playing around 1952," said Stewart. "I told him I was going to start my own band and asked him if he'd be interested in joining. Edgar had laid the guitar down and was planning moving up North and get a job in an automobile factory but I talked him into staying. I told him, 'You take care of the music, I'll take care of the business.' We kept the name Gondoliers because people already recognized it."

The new version of the Gondoliers included Warren Hebrard on tenor, Edward Santino on piano (another former Mighty Mighty Man), Mitchell on trumpet, Stewart on drums, and Blanchard on guitar. Saxophonist Lee Allen was going to be in the group, but he took a job with Paul Gayten's band at the last minute, and August "Dimes" Dupont replaced him.

"We did nothing but rehearse for a month," said Stewart. "I put some money up to get the band off the ground. I bought uniforms, a P. A. system and music stands. We really sounded great after that month. Our first job was at the Hide Away Inn where Fats got started. That first night, we had every musician in the city come out to see us play and the place was packed. We were a hit from the beginning."

The Gondoliers' first regular job was substituting for Sharkey Bonano at the Famous Door. The group did well but eventually was terminated.

"We sat down and read music," said Mitchell. "The guy that owned the place, Mr. Hip, wasn't used to that. He was accustomed to Dixieland guys standing up and just playing off the top of their head. One night after the gig he said, 'Your band is good but I'm gonna have to give you your notice. I like you guys, so I'm gonna make sure you keep working. I get calls all the time from people looking for music.'

"The next day he got a call from one of the Perez brothers. They owned the Perez Lounge on Airline Highway. It was a big dinner club that catered strictly to rich white people. He had Pete Fountain's Basin Street Six working in there. That band was half whiskey heads and half pot heads. One night the pot heads and the whiskey heads got in a fight and the band got fired. The Perez that ran the joint decided to hire a black band."

The Gondoliers worked the Perez Lounge for several months and also began working at the Dew Drop. They also accompanied headliners that Frank Painia booked on the road.

"We backed Johnny Ace at the Stable Club in Bilioxi," said Mitchell. "We tore the house up and the club owner wanted us back. The next night, the Stable's owner called our job and Perez answered the phone. We were taking our break in his office, because we couldn't sit in the club. Until then, Perez thought we were just a local band. He came in and said, 'You must be some high class niggers playing all over the place.' Edgar was cocky and said, 'Yeah we sure are. We travel all over the country.' The next thing we knew, we had to take our breaks in a tiny storage room behind Perez's office where they kept the brooms and mops.

"One day we came to work and Perez had written some songs in a Negro dialect that he wanted us to perform. Edgar took the sheets of paper the songs were written on and tore them up right in his face. After that we took our breaks in the room where they kept the onions and potatoes."

The owner of the Stable eventually lured the Gondoliers to Biloxi, where they played six nights a week during a two year stint. When they came back to New Orleans they played at the Dew Drop or toured with Joe Turner and Ray Charles.

In 1953, the Gondoliers worked on Joe Turner's "Honey Hush" and Blanchard provided the distinctive choppy two string intro. Blanchard also played on several other Atlantic sessions including Professor Longhair's "Tipitina," Tommy Ridgley's "I'm Gonna Cross That River," and Ray Charles' "Feeling Sad," where he was especially brilliant.

Blanchard also began doing sessions for Specialty Records producer Bumps Blackwell, who was beginning to record regularly in New Orleans. Blanchard's playing would enhance several Specialty recordings including Little Richard's "Slippin' and Slidin,'" "Ready Teddy," and "Miss Ann." On Richard's sessions, he primarily doubled the bass line on his instrument and didn't solo. His playing was far more extroverted on the two singles he cut under his own name for Specialty, "Mr. Bumps," a hot rock and roll instrumental, and "Stepping High" which included some country picking, ala Chet Atkins.

When Blanchard wasn't in the studio, he and the Gondoliers kept extremely busy. At one point they worked 96 consecutive weeks at San Antonio's Keyhole Club, followed by 28 weeks at Pensacola's Piccadilly. In New Orleans, they worked the Dream Room, the Famous Door and of course the Dew Drop.

"The Gondoliers were a complete floor show," stressed Stewart. "Besides dance music we did a vocal group thing just like the Ink Spots. We also had a comedy routine that went over well. We'd clown on numbers like 'How Come My Dog Don't Bark' and 'Tom Dooley.'"

After Blackwell stopped recording in New Orleans, Blanchard became a favorite of Paul Gayten, who was producing sessions for Chess. While working with Gayten, Blanchard did some of his most innovative playing. On Gayten's instrumental "Driving Home," he played a variation of the guitar pattern that propelled Bill Doggett's "Honky Tonk." He also put a guitar intro on Eddie Bo's "Oh-Oh" that sounded like a rockabilly lick Scotty Moore might have played on one of Elvis' Sun recordings. Blanchard also backed Charles Williams, Clarence Henry, and Bobby Charles during this period. The Gondoliers also got to record for Chess under the guise of "Myles and Dupont" doing a vamp on Huey Smith's style on "Loud Mouth Annie." Blanchard also recorded a vocal, "Lawdy Mama"—complete with a one note 24 bar solo—which wasn't issued until researchers found the track in the Chess vaults in the 1980s.

In 1958, Blanchard cut two instrumentals for Ace, "Lets Get It" and "Lonesome Guitar," which were loaned to Joe Ruffino and issued on his newly formed Ric label. Blanchard subsequently was hired by Ruffino as his A&R man. His arranging and playing became the backbone of the early Ric, and later Ron sound, as he worked with Eddie Bo, Al Johnson, Tommy Ridgley, and Irma Thomas. Blanchard's second Ric single, "Bopsody Blues"/"Blues Cha-Cha," was mastered but withdrawn at the last minute in favor of a Johnny Adams side he arranged, "I Won't Cry." Blanchard and the Gondoliers recorded Ric's only album, *Let's Have A Blast,* which captured the vaudevillian element of the group's stage show, but unfortunately didn't include very much of the group's creative musical skills.

By 1960, bassist Frank Fields, saxophonist Warren Bell, and Guitar Slim's former pianist, Lawrence Cotton, had become members of the Gondoliers. At the time the group was a fixture at Natal's on Chef Menteur Highway.

"We spent more than five years at Natal's working six nights a week," said Stewart. "But the place got sold in 1964 and they made it into a bowling alley. After that, we worked at a white club in Mobile. We were supposed to play there three months, but after a couple of weeks, George Wallace came to Mobile and held a rally. The owner got worried about violence and he paid us off and told us to go home. We played a couple of weeks at the Safari, but after that there was no more work and we broke up. I stayed in music, but Edgar took the Civil Service exam and got a day job."

By the mid-1960s, Blanchard's taste for Old Cominsky whiskey began to catch up with him.

"Edgar was in and out of the hospital," recalled Mitchell. "The doctor cut a piece off his liver and told him to put the bottle down. He did pretty good for awhile, but then he started playing in the French Quarter and he started drinking again. The doctor had to cut another piece off his liver and told him that was it—they couldn't cut no more."

By 1970, Blanchard was playing banjo and guitar with Dixieland groups in the French Quarter and performing Ink Spots tunes weekends at Genero's on Airline Highway with trumpeter Henry "Hawk" Hawkins. Several of his contemporaries said Blanchard was in poor health because of his weakness for liquor, but he was still healthy enough to hold a day job and pick up work occasionally playing music. However, on the morning of September 16, 1972, Blanchard, who was then working as a security guard at the Milne Boys Home, succumbed to a heart attack. His premature death obscured his sizable contribution to the music of New Orleans.

CHAPTER FIFTEEN
~ Frank Mitchell: Lefty ~

Among the dwindling group of rhythm and blues musicians that were active in the 1940s and 1950s, one of the most entertaining and interesting individuals is the sharp-witted trumpeter Frank Mitchell. Referred to as "Half-A-Hand," and "Lefty," by his contemporaries, Mitchell's tone and playing style is unique as he is a rare left-handed instrumentalist with a handicap.

"I consider myself the greatest left-handed trumpet player in the world," said Mitchell. "In fact I don't even know any other left-handed players besides myself."

Mitchell did take lessons, but for the most part he is a self-taught musician. As a result, he has a unique approach to the instrument that combines his own findings—some which most trumpeters consider backwards—and more conventional techniques he was taught.

Frank Sherdon Mitchell Jr. was born August 15, 1917, between Pearlington and Logtown, Mississippi. When he was quite young, he lost two fingers off his right hand in an accident, but Mitchell considers himself a natural southpaw.

"I was raised by my grandmother," recalled Mitchell. "We lived in a lumber camp. The only way you could get there was by boat. On holidays like Labor Day and the Fourth of July, Dixieland bands would come to the camp and perform. They would play on the boat when they arrived to advertise the dance. I was fascinated by the coronet player. I couldn't get that sound out of my mind and I'd always be looking at the coronet player."

At the age of eight, Mitchell and his grandmother moved to Slidell, Louisiana. Although it was a small country town, Slidell attracted several Dixieland groups from nearby New Orleans.

"Kid Rena, Kid Sheik, Bob Anthony—I saw a lot of guys like that," said Mitchell. "Sam Morgan though was the most popular, he had the town sewed up."

A friend of the family had a coronet and offered to sell it to Mitchell.

"I'd huff and puff but couldn't get a sound out of it," admitted Mitchell. "He offered to sell it for five dollars, but at the time there was no way my grandmother or I could come up with that much money."

The Mitchell's eventually moved to New Orleans and rented a cold water flat in the French Quarter. The move intensified Mitchell's interest in music.

"I had a job working as house man at the Monteleone Hotel," said Mitchell. "I had an uncle that had a common-law wife that took a liking to me. She took me down to Werlein's on Canal Street and bought me a used trumpet for $35. My payments were $1.50 a week. I started taking lessons from Professor Valmar Victar that were 25 cents each."

Mitchell soon found that Victar was more interested in the quarter than teaching him how to adapt to playing a right-handed instrument left-handed.

"I really had to work at it," said Mitchell. "It was frustrating but I was persistent and I kept practicing."

Eventual another teacher, Eddie Collins, took on Mitchell and showed him the chromatic scale. His older sister who played in the St. Mary's school band showed him some fingering technique.

"I started sitting in with some older musicians but I never thought I sounded too good," said Mitchell. "I was going to sell my horn, but some guys I played with said they'd buy me a another one if I ever did. One night a musician stopped by my house and whistled for me to come out. Back then musicians had a secret whistle they used when they wanted to call to each other. He wanted me to come with him to the Japanese Tea Room [later renamed the Caldonia Inn] and play with some other guys. I went, but I was scared and not playing very well."

A member of the audience noted Mitchell's anxiety and suggested that during the band's break that he follow him outside. The man produced a homemade cigarette and passed it to Mitchell.

"It was marijuana," laughed Mitchell. "I'd heard about it but I'd never tried it. I smoked some, got real relaxed, and went back inside to play. The next day people in the neighborhood came up to me and said, 'Man you sure sound good. How long have you been playing?' That never happened to me before."

In 1942, Mitchell received his draft papers but never served overseas. After he was discharged, Red Tyler convinced Mitchell to take advantage of the G.I. Bill and study at Grunewald's School of Music to sharpen his skills. Besides Tyler, Mitchell's classmates included Edgar Blanchard, Ernest McLean, and Earl Palmer.

New Orleans was booming in the late 1940s as the era of rhythm and blues was about to explode. Mitchell was there when it ignited.

"I started playing with the Mid-Riff Trio," recalled Mitchell. "We played at Elbert Ellis' Horseshoe Bar. We weren't really a trio. There was myself and Leroy "Batman" Rankin on saxophone, Lester Alexis on drums, Alex Burrel on piano, and the bandleader, George Miller on bass. We used to have guys like Lester Young and Jo Jones sit in with us. After that we moved to the El Morocco on the corner of Bourbon and Iberville Street."

In 1948, most of the Mid-Riff headed to California but Mitchell stayed in New Orleans and joined the Four Hair Combo which worked regularly at the Caldonia Inn.

"That group consisted of me on trumpet, Warren Hebrand on tenor sax, Clarence 'Big Slick' Fritz on drums and Johnny Fernandez on piano," recalled Mitchell. "The Caldonia had the best female impersonator show in the city. It was so popular that the white sissies started coming there until the police ran them off. We'd back their show and then play two sets of dance music. Professor Longhair played there during intermission. He played with Charlie Lamb on drums, and Papoose [Walter Nelson Jr.] on guitar. The Caldonia was just a hole in the wall in Treme but we kept the place packed. The owner, Mike Tessatore, renovated the place but it didn't go over with the patrons. People stopped going there so I got a job leading the house band at the Dew Drop. The Dew Drop was the place to go then. Just about anybody who was anybody in show business could be found at the Dew Drop. [Owner] Frank Painia made it a home for entertainers. Earl King, Guitar Slim, Joe Turner, Jimmy Nelson, and Wynonie Harris all lived at the Dew Drop at one point. Those were happy times. I was playing there every night to a packed house presenting some of the greatest floor shows in the city."

In 1951, Mitchell was hired by New Orleans-based Roy Brown to play with his band, the Mighty Mighty Men. With several records in the charts, Brown and his group spent a great deal of time on the road.

"Roy could be a real hard guy to take sometimes," said Mitchell. "He was okay when it was just the guys in the band around, but when his wife was around, he was a different person. He wouldn't ride in the same car as us because he was a star. He wouldn't let us curse and he would fine us for the stupidest little things.

"We did a tour of all the little towns up in Mississippi. We went in the fall because that was the only time the share croppers had money. Greenwood was our base and we stayed at a rooming house. We played in places like Clarksdale, Greenville, Leland and Indianola. One night we were going to play in Greenwood when the guy that owned the place got in a fight with a state trooper. Well right after that a bunch of state troopers came back and cleared the place out. The man had to give everybody their money back and he had a packed house. They made us march back to the rooming house and get all out stuff. The state troopers told us to get out of town and they followed us to the county line to make sure we did. Not long after that I had a disagreement with Roy after a gig and I came back to New Orleans."

Mitchell then joined Edgar Blanchard's new Gondoliers that often played at the Dew Drop for Painia, who in addition to running his club, was also booking artists in surrounding towns. One of them was Big Joe Turner.

"Joe would perform at the Dew Drop from Thursday to Sunday," said Mitchell. "During the week Frank would book him around the area in towns like Slidell, Gulfport and Biloxi. We sounded real good behind Joe. He called his record company [Atlantic] and told them, 'Look, I got a good band and some new material. Let me go in the studio and cut.' I lived around the corner from the J & M Studio, but I never got in it until I went in with Joe in [May] 1953. At that session we did 'Honey Hush' and 'Crawdad Hole.' After the session me and Edgar came back to the Dew Drop. Frank said to us, 'Y'all ought to be ashamed of yourselves. That was some of the worst shit I've ever heard.' We just looked at each other because we thought we did pretty good. But a month later the record was number one in the country and Frank was walking around with his chest stuck out because it was his band on Joe's record."

Five months later, Mitchell participated on Guitar Slim's initial Specialty session. Painia, who was booking the capricious guitarist at the time, handpicked the musicians for the session. He augmented Slim's regular band with Mitchell and Ray Charles—the latter who acted as straw boss arranger.

"I remember that session like it was yesterday," recalled Mitchell. "I went down to the Dew Drop to get Slim and he was glad I was on the session. I got there in the morning and Slim had already smoked three sticks of weed and had drank a half-pint of gin. We got about two blocks from the Dew Drop when Slim made the driver stop so he could by a pint of gin. That was gone by the time we got to the studio. When we got there, the man from Specialty [Johnny Vincent] said, 'What do ya'll want to drink?' Before anybody could say a word, Slim yells, 'Gin.' Then he [Vincent] sent a guy out for two more bottles.

"That first day we didn't even get one good take. Slim's timing was very bad, plus he was drunk. It got to where he couldn't play the guitar. The man from Specialty knew what he wanted from Slim, but he couldn't get it that day. He had two men hold Slim up to the microphone but that didn't work. We finally had to give up about 5:30 in the afternoon.

"Frank was really mad and told Slim, 'I'm ashamed of you.' He had somebody stand outside of Slim's room until the next day so he couldn't get drunk again.The next morning Slim was given a stiff shot to steady himself. After an all day grind, we managed to cut 'The Things I Used To Do,' 'Well, I Done Got Over It,' 'A Letter to My Girlfriend' and 'The Story of My Life.' They were all good, but 'The Things I Used To Do' really took off and put Slim on the upgrade."

Before 1953 concluded, Mitchell was present on Ray Charles last New Orleans session.

"Whoever first called Ray Charles 'The Genius' hit the nail on the head," said Mitchell. "I've never seen or heard a better musician than Ray Charles. When Ray lived in New Orleans he stayed at Foster's Hotel which was down the street from the Dew Drop. Like every musician in town, at some point in the day Ray would come by the Dew Drop to eat, see what was happening, or hang out. A lot of us would stand outside the Dew Drop and wait for him. Because he was blind we were amazed how he knew exactly where he was going when he walked down the street.

"The session I did with Ray was a bootleg session. We didn't cut it at J & M, we cut it at a radio station [WDSU] in the French Quarter. I don't think Atlantic wanted the Union to know Ray was recording. Wallace Davenport was the other trumpet player, Lloyd Lambert was on bass, Joe Tillman on tenor, Warren Bell played baritone, and Oscar Moore was on drums. We cut a standard four song session, but the man from Atlantic, Armet Ertegun, got mad and wanted to throw three songs in the garbage. They were just blues but he thought they were too progressive. The only song he liked was 'Don't You Know Baby' [which briefly charted]."

Mitchell eventually left the Gondoliers after his wife complained the group traveled too much, a move he eventually regretted. Mitchell then rejoined the Dew Drop house band and played with them until 1956, when a New Orleans Police Department officer threatened that if he didn't leave the city, he'd be arrested on a narcotics charge. At the time, a possession of marijuana conviction meant a one way ticket to the State Penitentiary at Angola. Mitchell moved for Houston.

"Houston was a guitar town back then," pointed out Mitchell. "I had a hard time getting a job. [guitarists] Joe Hughes and Cal Green had a group called Blues For Two that had the town wrapped up. The only job I could get was playing one night a week with Piano Slim. Later I got a job working with a band at the Four Palms. It was a club where elderly white people went. We played a lot of standards there."

In the early 1960s, Mitchell was approached by a then up-and-coming blues guitarist, Albert Collins, who needed a bandleader and arranger. Mitchell took on the assignment.

"Albert was a good guy and a great guitar player, but he did a lot of things that worked on your nerves," said Mitchell. "Like you'd have a job playing somewhere 500 miles away and Albert would put just $2 of gas in the car when we'd leave Houston.

"All he wanted to do was make records. He signed a deal with a couple of gangsters who said they'd get him a record deal. They did, but they got a lot Albert's money too. Those records 'Sno Cone,' 'Frosty' and 'Backstroke'—I arranged those. We were supposed to get $40 a man for doing those sessions but we never got 40 cents. Albert had a regular gig at Walter's Lounge playing every weekend. He had that gig for three or four years. Then his records started selling a little bit and his head got big. He'd take a one night gig for more money than Walter paid and then not tell Walter he wasn't going to show up. Well he messed that gig up and lost it.

"Then he got a job in our neighborhood playing Friday to Sunday night at Betty's Playhouse. About two weeks after we started working there, Buddy Ace [a Houston singer who recorded for Duke] talked Albert into doing a promotional tour of Florida and Alabama with him. The first date was in Pritchard, Alabama, where nobody ever heard of Albert Collins or Buddy Ace. Their records weren't even on the jukeboxes. We played for the door but nobody showed up and we made no money. That happened in every town we played in. Finally in Panama City, Florida, they had to call Don Robey [Duke's owner] to get him to wire $400 so they could pay the hotel bill and get back to Houston. In the meantime, Medgar Evers had got killed and we heard that the service stations in the South weren't going to sell gas to blacks because they were worried about rioting. Well we had to drive through Alabama, Mississippi and Louisiana to get back to Houston. At about 3:00 a.m. we're halfway through Louisiana when we start running low on gas. We pulled into a station and Albert talked to the guy that worked there. Well you never heard more 'Yes sirs' and 'No sirs' in your life. But we got the gas and made it back to Houston. We went through all of that and didn't make a nickel. We could have worked three nights in Houston for good money and walked to the gig. Finally I couldn't put up with Albert anymore and I quit."

Mitchell worked with several other Houston R&B bands until he moved back to New Orleans in the late 1970s. Once back, he scuffled playing various low paying Dixieland gigs until he took matters into his own hands. Along with a banjo player he found in the Musicians Union directory, Mitchell began playing for tips Jackson Square.

"Most weeks we'd make around $1,000 each," said Mitchell. "On weekends, I'd fly to Houston and visit my family. I did that for 10 years. I put my application in at Preservation Hall several times but they never hired me."

When interviewed in October of 1998, he hadn't picked up the trumpet in several months because all his front teeth had recently been removed and he was waiting to be fit for a plate. However, Mitchell was anxious to play music again.

CHAPTER SIXTEEN
~ Alvin Tyler: Simply Red ~

A mainstay in New Orleans' greatest studio band, the late saxophonist Alvin "Red" Tyler enjoyed a career spanning over a half century, making his mark in the genres of rock and roll, rhythm and blues, pop and contemporary jazz.

Tyler recorded with virtually every significant New Orleans R&B artist of the 1950s. He also acted as a producer, composer, and arranger for several labels, as well as acting as a brilliant front man when called upon. He recorded a rock and roll instrumental album in the late 1950s and two contemporary jazz albums in the 1980s.

Tyler was born December 5, 1925, and grew up in New Orleans' Fourth Ward on Bienville Street. He was introduced to music via brass brands that led funerals to nearby St. Louis Cemetery. After WW II, he took advantage of the GI Bill and attended Grunewald's School of Music. He played briefly with Clarence Samuels and Roy Brown, but in 1949, he was invited to join Dave Bartholomew's Orchestra, then the most popular band in New Orleans.

"Dave's band was doing a lot of big band tunes," recalled Tyler in 1998. "We used to do stock arrangements on stuff by Dizzy Gillespie, Count Basie, Woody Herman, and Jimmy Lunceford—a lot of things that were built around a soloist. The rhythm and blues thing didn't really start until later when we started backing up vocalists. I really think if rhythm and blues wouldn't have taken off like it did, Dave would have had one of the best swing bands in the country.

"Right after Dave hired me he started working for Imperial Records as a producer and talent scout. That's how I got my start in the studio. I started recording with Fats Domino, Jewel King, Tommy Ridgley, Shirley and Lee, and Smiley Lewis. On those early sessions we didn't always know what we were going to play until we got to the studio. Even though most of the musicians could read music, nothing was written down except sometimes the vocals. Somebody would have an idea for a riff and we'd work on a rhythm to complement it. A lot of times we got in a situation where we had to pull something out of the hat. Musically you had to be a quick thinker. We didn't always finish sessions right away, but we were good musicians, and most of the time we made the records pretty good. We had a lot of success recording that way."

"A basic R&B tune is a repetitive 12-bar song that's built off of one riff. A jazz song normally has a number of riffs that don't repeat themselves. There are a number of R&B tunes that borrow their riff from the catchy part of a jazz song. A good jazz musician has no trouble playing R&B. I enjoyed playing both—it kept me thinking."

After Bartholomew productions began climbing the charts, other out-of-town labels began coming to town looking for the New Orleans magic. Tyler played on Specialty sessions with Lloyd Price, Guitar Slim, and Little Richard. Atlantic hired him to play behind Tommy Ridgley, Joe Turner, and Professor Longhair. Chess used him to back Bobby Charles, Paul Gayten, and Clarence Henry.

"Often Lee Allen or myself were called on to play the solo," said Tyler. "I also played the baritone which I didn't like carrying around, but it gave me a two-edged style and brought me more work."

Tyler earned a reputation as a clever and reliable musician. Never a showman, Tyler was inventive but not undisciplined, traits that studio owner Cosimo Matassa noted and appreciated.

"Red was a calm hard working guy who contributed a lot in the studio, often without anybody noticing. A lot of sessions were credited to what I'd call, 'Default producers.' Guys who wouldn't be anywhere near the studio during the recording. They'd just turn the session over to somebody in the band. A lot of times they chose Red. Later, when I was out on the West Coast with Jimmy Clanton on some shows, Red came with us and saved us from disaster several times. We got paired with some really bad bands but Red showed them how the songs were played and he led the way."

Matassa recommended Tyler to Ace Records' Johnny Vincent who was often at his Jackson, Mississippi, office when sessions were being cut in New Orleans. Tyler quickly piled up credits at Ace, arranging Clanton's "Just A Dream," Frankie Ford's "Time After Time," Calvin Spear's "Doin' The Rock and Roll," and Joe & Ann's "Where You May Be" among others. An avid photographer, Tyler also shot the cover photos for Frankie Ford's *Sea Cruise* and Huey "Piano" Smith's *Havin' A Good Time* albums.

"Working for Johnny Vincent wasn't like working for other record companies," said Tyler. "He kind of ran the label out of the trunk of his car. I never signed a contract with Ace. All the agreements I made with Johnny were verbal. There were a lot of promises, but very little money. One day Johnny came in the studio and said, 'Red, how about doing an instrumental album?' I'd never thought about recording one but I guess Johnny saw Bill Doggett do well with instrumentals like 'Honky Tonk' and 'Tanya.' He thought I could do likewise."

Vincent also took note that Tyler's partner Lee Allen had jumped into the charts with, "Walkin' With Mr. Lee," on Ember and felt his producer might be able to sell some records for Ace. Tyler cut two solo sessions for Ace which resulted in a couple of singles and an excellent album *Rockin' and Rollin'*. "Junk Village" and "Peanut Vendor" are the tunes New Orleanians remember best.

"I'll tell you who played on that album," said Tyler. "June Gardner was on drums, Frank Fields on bass, Justin Adams on guitar and Allen Toussaint on piano. James Booker might have been added on organ [he's certainly present on "Junk Village"], Rufus Gore played the other saxophone and helped with arrangements. At the time Rufus, who we called 'Nose,' had just come down here from King Records in Cincinnati.

"I had worked the same kind of session on Allen Toussaint's *Wild Sound of New Orleans* album which was also instrumentals [It contained "Java" which Tyler co-wrote and was later a hit for Al Hirt] and also Lee Allen's, "Walkin' With Mr. Lee." I wrote "Promenade" for Lee but I never got paid for it. Allen Toussaint produced that record and after it came out, he wanted to know when I was going to write another hit.

"I had worked out a few simple instrumental arrangements before we went in the studio [on my album]. We did 'Peanut Vendor' but that wasn't my song. I heard a version of it by Stan Kenton and thought I'd cover it. Johnny didn't do his homework and put my name on the record as the writer and Ace as the publisher. I named some of the songs like 'Dippy', 'Stinky', and 'Walk On', but Johnny came up with the other titles. There wasn't a concentrated effort to sound like we were from New Orleans on those recordings—that's just the way we play here. I don't know how any of those records sold since Johnny didn't do any bookkeeping. I never worked behind those records because I didn't have time to. I was busy in the studio then."

"Even when we made all those R&B and rock and roll hits at Cosimo's, I still considered myself a jazz musician. During the day we might go in and cut a session on Fats or Smiley, but at night I'd be playing jazz somewhere in a club. I supported my family that way for years."

In 1961, Tyler left Ace but he continued doing sessions for other labels. That same year he played on Lee Dorsey's Fury hit "Ya Ya," and produced Little Junior Parker's "Foxy Devil" and "Yonder Wall" for Duke. He and Harold Battiste also formed AFO Records, the first black-owned record label in New Orleans.

In 1963, Tyler and most of the other musicians associated with AFO moved to Los Angeles where he did sessions for Sam Cooke's SAR label and recorded with Cooke at RCA. Tyler eventually returned to New Orleans the following year and joined pianist Ed Frank's Quartet. Still wishing to be part of a successful record label, in 1966 Tyler became a co-owner in Par-Lo Records which launched Aaron Neville's "Tell It Like It Is." Unfortunately, Par-Lo folded after just a handful of releases.

In the early 1970s, Tyler became a salesman for a New Orleans liquor distributor, a job that allowed him to augment his income from music and provide he and his family with pension and health insurance benefits. It also allowed him to cherry-pick gigs and concentrate on playing the music he enjoyed most—jazz. During this decade Tyler performed weekends with the Gentleman of Jazz at the V.I.P. Club, part of Mason's Las Vegas Strip on South Clairborne Avenue.

During the 1980s, Tyler picked up session work with Rounder Records backing Gatemouth Brown, Johnny Adams, and James Booker. This led to two excellent solo contemporary jazz albums, *Graciously* and *Heritage*.

In the 1990s, Tyler—who'd retired from selling liquor—divided his time leading a jazz group that often played at Snug Harbor and touring with Dr. John. In 1997, the City of New Orleans declared July 9 "Alvin 'Red' Tyler Day," and presented him the key to the city. Two years later, Tyler injured his back playing on a gig and spent several months recuperating at home. He was looking forward to performing again when he died unexpectedly from a heart attack at home on April, 3, 1998.

CHAPTER SEVENTEEN
~ Bill Sinigal: I Had To Be A Hustler ~

Bill Sinigal, the composer of "Second Line"—arguably the most popular song associated with Mardi Gras—is oddly one of New Orleans' least recognized musicians. Nevertheless, Sinigal has made an enormous contribution to the Crescent City's rhythm and blues tradition—albeit one largely behind the scenes.

"Bill Sinigal was a role model for a lot of musicians and bandleaders," pointed out guitarist/bandleader Deacon John. "He always had a good band, was reliable, and ran a band like a business. His group was always on time and sharp. Bill showed me the way to run a band. How to take out money out of the musicians' checks for taxes, pension and union dues. Bill worked with a lot of New Orleans artists and for several national booking agencies. If the Shaw or Buffalo Agency needed a band to back somebody for three weeks, Bill would go from here to Alaska at the drop of a hat. Not too many people have heard about Bill Sinigal because he didn't record much. But he didn't have time to because he was on the road all the time."

William Sinigal was born in New Orleans, May 13, 1928, and grew up in Uptown section of the city. After residing in the Magnolia Projects for 40 years, today he and his wife reside in the peaceful Gentilly section of the city.

"I was crazy about music even as a kid," revealed Sinigal. "My first instrument was a C-melody saxophone that I bought at a pawn shop. They sold it to me cheap because I thought it was a tenor saxophone. A C-melody saxophone has limitations. If the band plays in a key besides C, you have to play in a concert key. Later I bought a tenor which allowed me to be more of a complete musician."

"I loved all kinds of music—standards, blues, Dixieland. You might even catch me listening to hillbilly music. Basically I was self-taught on the saxophone. I got to the point though where I could play a few riffs and got hired by a few bands around town."

Hoping to improve himself as a musician, in the late 1940s Sinigal enrolled at Grunewald's School of Music.

"I wanted to learn to read music and play the bass," said Sinigal. "My teacher was a German gentleman, Professor Otto Fink. He was probably the biggest influence on me as a musician. He'd sit down with you for a

30 minute lesson that would often stretch to two hours. Your wrists and fingers would ache when you finished the lesson."

Now a double barrel threat, by the early 1950s Sinigal had already backed Fats Domino, Roy Brown, Joe Turner, Tommy Ridgley, Sugar Boy Crawford, and Snooks Eaglin.

"Back then if you wanted a gig, you brought your instrument, a black suit and a black tie to the Dew Drop," said Sinigal. "If somebody needed a musician they came to the Dew Drop to find one. Frank Painia hired musicians to play at the Dew Drop and he also booked bands on the road."

One of Sinigal's first regular jobs was accompanying the grand imperial wizard of the electric guitar, Eddie Jones—a.k.a. Guitar Slim.

"Slim was a preacher in Greenwood, Mississippi," laughed Sinigal. "A fellow he knew killed a white man and sold his guitar to Slim to get some money so he could get out of town. Word got around what Slim did and he had to leave town too. With the money he had left, Slim bought a bus ticket as far as he could ride—New Orleans. When Slim got here he worked at a sausage factory in Arabi and lived at the Gold Leaf Hotel over top of the Club Tiajuana."

"Slim worked at that guitar because he wanted to sound like Gatemouth Brown real bad. He couldn't but Slim found his own style. The Bolden family that owned the Tiajuana were crazy about Slim and let him play there. I started playing bass in his band with Huey Smith on piano and Oscar Moore on drums. Sometimes Charles Burbank or Joe Tillman played tenor saxophone. Occasionally I played sax and Willie Nettles would play bass. Slim was a comical country guy but he drove the audiences crazy. We played a lot of dates around New Orleans and in the country. Slim could spend a whole day matching his shoe strings with the suit he was going to wear that night. At least once a week he'd fire the whole band. Slim would come in the dressing room and say, 'Gentle-mules, y'all should have done better tonight. As long as you fellas shit between the heels of your shoes, you ain't playing with Guitar Slim no more.' The next day we'd be in the Dew Drop and Slim would walk in just like nothing happened. He'd say, 'Come on fellas we got a gig tonight.' We'd say, 'Slim you fired us last night.' He'd answer, 'Well y'all is hired back,' and we'd go make the gig. Slim had written 'The Things I Used To Do' a couple of years before he recorded it [1953]. He used to call me to his room and say, 'Sinigal come here and listen at this—nothin' can stop this from being a hit.' Well Slim was right. Later he got with Hosea Hill and his band. They played with Slim after the song got hot and went all over the country."

In the late 1950s, Sinigal worked with the house band at the Dew

Drop and spent time on the road with numerous groups in need of a reliable saxophonist or a bass player— for an evening, a weekend, or a couple of months. With the popularity of New Orleans R&B at it's apex, Sinigal realized it was time to take advantage of the trend. In 1960 he formed his own group, the Skyliners.

"It was a very young group of musicians," detailed Sinigal. "Besides myself on bass, there was Himas Ankle on baritone, Marcel Richardson on piano, Milton Batiste on trumpet, James Rivers on saxophone, Edwin Maire on guitar, and Madison Marshall on drums. We were as good as any band in New Orleans. When I started the band, I bought a Ford station wagon from a junk yard for $500. I fixed it up and wound up putting 600,000 miles on it. During the day I worked for a pharmaceutical wholesaler. In the evening I'd drive to country towns and arrange gigs. On the weekends we'd go out and make the dates. I don't know how I had the energy to do it. But I had six kids to feed at the time—I had to be a hustler."

"Just about every New Orleans artists with a record we played with. I remember sneaking Irma Thomas away from her husband Andrew for some dates in Florida. He followed us all over the state in a Greyhound bus trying to catch us. Sometimes we booked Irma as Etta James and got away with it. Back then before television and videos, you could fool people because they didn't know what the artists looked like. When Irma got home though, she had a pocket full of money so Andrew wasn't too mad."

Thomas recalled that Sinigal would begin lengthy tours with only one or two gigs booked when they left New Orleans. Amazingly he'd find engagements along the way by calling to the next town and setting one up at an armory, club, fraternity or road house.

While Sinigal lived out of a suitcase for the better part of two decades, in 1962 he was in New Orleans long enough to complete a most historic recording.

"I got to know Henry Hines, a producer who had a connections with Cosimo Matassa," recalled Sinigal. "We went in the studio and cut a lot material. Each musician got $15 for every song we did, so I wanted to record as many songs as we could. One of the songs we cut I called 'B-flat Blues.' It was a song the band did on gigs that got a good reaction. The introduction was the same one Dave Bartholomew played on 'Good Jax Boogie.' But that riff came along way before Dave was born. Dave played it when he wanted the musicians to get back on the bandstand after the break. The rhythm came from a song called 'Joe Avery Blues' that used to be popular. The break was just a thing marching bands played around here for years to get people to shake their booty."

"When I was at Grunewald's, one of our assignments was to take four bars out of several songs and create our own composition. That's really how I put the song together. Cosimo didn't want to call it 'B-flat Blues,' so I thought 'Second Line' would be a good title. It was the first record to come out on the [Matassa's] White Cliffs label. We didn't do it as a Mardi Gras song, but as it turned out it made a lot of noise around Carnival."

Sinigal received one royalty check from White Cliffs before the label folded. In 1964, he did some sessions for producer/bandleader Al White but would never record under his own name again. However, even without a record, he and the Skyliners stayed extremely busy as they were under contract with the Shaw Booking Agency for most of the 1960s.

"Whoever had a hot record that Shaw booked we backed," said Sinigal. "Their New York office would send us an itinerary and the artist's the music charts. We'd learn the material and then meet who we were going on tour with. Bobby Marchan, Dee Clark, the Impressions, Curtis Mayfield, Joe Simon—like I said, I put six engines in that Ford. I played music until the late 1960s when we did some dates in Florida that didn't turn out well. It was sort of the last straw. I was tired of the hassles of running a band—buying strings for the guitar player, replacing the drummer's snare. I'd had an interest in photography, so I decided to start taking pictures for a living. I felt dealing with a camera was easier than dealing with musicians."

Sinigal maintained a busy schedule taking photographs at parties, weddings, social events, and concerts. Although he no longer played music, he still kept in touch with many musicians and paid attention to what was going on in the record business. In 1974, Sinigal was instrumental in getting "Second Line" re-recorded.

"I knew Senator Jones and he was looking for material to cut," said Sinigal. "I said why don't you redo 'Second Line.' He did with the group Stop Inc. That's the version people are familiar with hearing. I didn't like what they did to the song because they messed the bass line up. Senator asked me how much money I wanted so he could recut the song? I said, 'Just give me $100.' Senator said, 'All I got is $65.' So I said, 'Okay I'll take that.' Outside of that, and the one check I got from White Cliffs, that's the only money I ever got for 'Second Line.'"

CHAPTER EIGHTEEN
~ Chuck Badie: Count Me In ~

Anyone with an interest in New Orleans music has undoubtedly heard Chuck Badie, but probably never realized it. Badie's string bass provided the bottom on several significant New Orleans hits including; Ernie K-Doe's "Mother-In-Law," Barbara George's "I Know" and Chris Kenner's "I Like It Like That."

The spry and energetic Badie enjoys dispensing advice to younger musicians, talking about New Orleans music, but above all, playing his bass, which he still does a couple nights a week at the Palm Court club on Decatur Street.

Peter "Chuck" Badie Jr. was born in New Orleans on May 17, 1925, the son of Myrtle and Peter Badie Sr. He was raised in the Carrollton section of the city and attended McDonogh 24. Badie's father played alto saxophone with Percy and Willie Humphrey's Dixieland band, but he was never inclined to pick up his father's instrument. After Badie finished school, he began working as a carpenter. When WW II began, he was drafted into the Navy and served overseas. After returning home, like many future great New Orleans musicians, he enrolled at Grunewald's School of Music on Baronne Street under the GI Bill.

"Back in 1940 and 1941 I used to go to dances at the Rhythm Club on the corner of Jackson and Derbigny," recalled Badie. "A lot of big bands played there like Lucky Millander, Tiny Bradshaw, Erskine Hawkins and Billy Eckstien. They would park their big buses with their names on the side in front of the club. I remember the musicians pouring talcum powder inside their shirts before they got on the bandstand because they were probably wearing the only white shirt they had left and couldn't get it to the cleaners."

"I really enjoyed listening to the way the bass fit into the band. At the time, I started listening to Jimmy Blanton and Junior Raglan, they played on Duke Ellington's records. They made the double bass into a solo instrument when before it was just a rhythm instrument. When I enrolled at Grunwald's, I wanted to play the bass. I was lucky and had a great teacher, Otto Fink, who was a trained classical musician."

Badie graduated Grunewald's in 1949 and joined a band called the Buccaneers which included, Earl Anderson on trumpet, Eddie Smith and

Joe Tillman on tenor, Oliver "Snow" Berry on drums, and a piano player
Badie recalls named "August." The Buccaneers played several local clubs
including the Dew Drop. Many singers and musicians dropped by the La
Salle Street club, including hit-maker Roy Brown who was looking to put
together a new band in 1951.

"I heard Roy was having auditions at Foster's Hotel," said Badie. "I
went down to check it out and got hired. That's when I went on the road
for the first time. I played nearly a year with Roy and did some recording
with him in Cincinnati. Roy wasn't a bad guy to work for, but there were
cliques in the band. He hung out with certain guys and ignored everyone
else. I didn't fit in with his pals so I finally quit his band in Little Rock
and took a bus back to New Orleans. The first night back in town, I went
to a club in the Ninth Ward where Paul Gayten was playing. He hired me
on the spot. Paul had a regular gig at the Brass Rail on Canal Street. I started playing the electric bass then. The first night I played it in the Brass
Rail, the owner ran in and told Paul, 'I don't want two guitars in my
place.' Paul said, 'That's not a guitar man, it's new instrument called the
electric bass.'"

Badie worked primarily with Gayten's group but he took spot jobs
with other bands when his schedule allowed it. One night, Dave
Bartholomew needed a bass player at the last minute for an engagement at
the Municipal Auditorium, opening for Lionel Hampton. After the show,
Badie was approached by Hampton who needed a replacement for his
bassist who had just quit.

"Lionel asked me if I could travel," laughed Badie. "I told him, 'Can
a fish swim?' The next night we played in Houston and then we headed
west. After that we spent a lot on time playing in Europe. I was pulling
down a bill and a quarter every night. I was in Europe so much that I felt
I could speak like the people over there after awhile. I loved working with
Lionel, but my father got sick in October of 1956 and wanted to be with
him. I quit then and came home."

Once back in New Orleans, Badie continued to do spot gigs and play
regularly with Ellis Marsallis' Modern Jazz Quartet. Around 1960, Badie,
who had done some studio work for Ace and Specialty, was playing at the
Dew Drop when Allen Toussaint approached him about playing on some
of the sessions he was producing for Minit and Instant Records.

"Toussaint admired my playing and I said, 'Sure.' Back then there
were only a few clubs around to play at. You only got a chance to play
two maybe three nights a week at most. Recording sessions then paid
$41.50. If you did one or two a week, it was like having a day job. I
remember Nat Perrillat [a tenor sax player on several Toussaint produced

sessions] calling me and say, 'Man, I wish Saint would call, I need the bread.' [Guitarist] Roy Montrell called Toussaint 'Two Cents.' After we made all those hits, I told him [Toussaint], 'Man you ain't Two Cents anymore, you're a nickel now!'"

In 1961, Badie became one of the original members of the AFO Executives, New Orleans' first exclusively black owned and operated record label.

"It was a wonderful organization and I was proud to be a part of it," said Badie. "We did something that at the time had to be done. Until then, it was companies from out of town that came here and made most of the records. We got paid for playing on the sessions, but those companies made the real money. When Harold called and said what kind of label he wanted to start, I said, 'Count me in.'"

"With Harold Battiste and Red Tyler, we had two guys that had been A&R guys for other labels so they had some expertise. Melvin Lastie and Roy Montrell had played on a lot of sessions, so we had a lot of experience too. John Boudreaux, Ellis Marsailis, Tami Lynn and myself weren't amateurs either. We were lucky and had a big hit with Barbara George right away, but we had some unfortunate business dealings. Eventually we realized AFO wasn't going to be successful in New Orleans. It just wasn't happening here."

Badie and the other Executives still believed in AFO, but they felt the only place they could succeed was on the West Coast. In 1963, Badie and his family piled into Battiste's station wagon and headed for what he thought were greener pastures. Once in Los Angeles, Badie picked up session work with Sam Cooke, and few spot gigs, but he eventually came to the conclusion that Los Angeles wasn't the promised land.

"With Sam I cut 'A Change Is Going To Come' and 'Tennessee Waltz,'" said Badie. "It was my idea to speed up 'Tennessee Waltz' and play it in 4/4 rather than 3/4 time. It was a pretty good little hit. I made a few gigs with Sam including a week in New York. King Curtis's 10-piece band was on that gig. I heard him tell his band, 'Listen to that New Orleans cat play that second note on the bass. That's the only place where they play like that.'"

"But L.A. was too tough. There wasn't much work and what work there was did didn't pay enough money to raise a family decently. After a year I came back to New Orleans. I was going to make a living as a carpenter but I wound up playing with Snooks Eaglin and Smokey Johnson at Rip's Playhouse on Orleans Avenue. A week after I came home, Red came back too. Right after that we heard Sam had got killed."

Badie later joined Tyler and June Gardner (Cooke's regular drummer also back from Los Angeles) to play with Ed Frank's jazz group which played weekends at the Forest Inn and the Haven.

"I didn't get any calls for sessions after I got back from L.A.," said Badie. "There wasn't much recording going on then because there weren't many labels left here."

In 1967, Edward Frank's band got hired to work at the newly opened Mason's V.I.P. Club on South Clairborne Avenue.

"We opened Mason's," said Badie. "We played there six-nights a week. Nobody believed a black club could hire a band six-nights but we kept that place busy. I left Mason's in 1969 and went to Vernon's Steak House on Louisiana Avenue where I had my own band. They booked a lot of jazz artists that we backed including John Coltrain. I went back to Mason's in 1971 and played with Red's group until 1974. After that I quit and put the bass down. There wasn't enough money in playing music anymore. I got a job waiting tables at the Royal Sonesta. I did that for 15 years and retired from there in 1988."

Around that time, bandleader Emory Thompson called Badie and asked him if he was still playing music.

"I told him 'I am now,'" said Badie. "I went over to Walter Payton's house and borrowed a set of strings for my bass. The job with Emory was on the Creole Queen and my old buddies David Lastie and Justin Adams came by to see me. It was just like old times. After the gig my fingers were killing me, but everybody said I sounded just like I did 20 years ago. The next thing I knew, Teddy Riley called and said he had seven gigs he wanted me to play with his band. I said, 'Teddy, maybe I'll take two. I just getting started again.' Then Danny Barker started calling me because he had a lot of work. Man the phone still hasn't stopped ringing."

Badie has since recorded with Doc Cheatham, Sammy Remington and Butch Thompson. Looking back on a his career, Badie, one of the greatest and most influential bassist New Orleans has ever produced, feels that's the key to being a great bassist comes from within and from above.

"I believe it's gift from God but you have to take advantage of that gift and put it to use," said Badie. "There are guys that woodshed all day, but if they can't play in meter, they ain't gonna cut it. I'm just lucky that I was blessed with the talent to play the bass as well as I do."

CHAPTER NINETEEN
~ Lloyd Lambert: Playing the Good Notes ~

The late Lloyd Lambert was perhaps the prototypical bass player. A man of few words, he let his instrument do the talking. While he made a name for himself in the field of Dixieland music, he was also an important pioneer in rhythm and blues. During the 1950s he led perhaps the nation's best R&B band, that which backed Guitar Slim. Adaptable and innovative, Lambert was also one of the first musicians to switch from the ungainly acoustic upright bass to the compact and louder electric bass.

Lambert was born in Thibodaux, Louisiana, June 4, 1928. His father, Adam, taught music and all of his brothers and sisters played music professionally.

"I played my first job on piano in Morgan City when I was nine years old." recalled Lambert in 1987. "It was with Teddy Johnson's jazz band. My father played guitar with Teddy. Teddy told my dad, 'Prof your son sounds pretty good, bring him out when we get these little jobs.' So every Saturday we'd play up and down Bayou Lafourche, from Donaldsonville all the way to Grand Isle. Teddy had a good band. He used to book a lot of musicians out of New Orleans like Kid Howard and Kid Clayton. Thibodaux was a good town for entertainment because there were a couple of musical families. There was my family and the Gabriel family. Joe Gabriel led a band something like Claiborne Williams' jazz band out of Donaldsonville. Those were the two most popular bands on Bayou Lafourche."

Lambert stayed with Johnson's band until he was 14. At that point his father began to teach him how to play the trumpet and soon after he landed a spot playing with Hosea Hill's Serenaders.

"Hosea wasn't a musician," pointed out Lambert. "He was a good timer but he loved music. Hosea was the most important Negro in Thibodaux. If you got thrown in jail, or you needed to borrow some money, Hosea was the guy to see.

Hill owned the Sugar Bowl, Thibodaux's hub for black entertainment on Lagarde Street. When Lambert joined the Serenaders, the band was playing swing music three nights a week at the club. In the late 1940s, the Serenaders began venturing beyond Thibodaux and traveled throughout the Deep South. It was during this period that Lambert sensed black music was moving in a new direction.

"Rhythm and blues and be-bop came in after swing," said Lambert. "Our band was pretty advanced so we made the switch pretty easy. I'm not bragging, but compared to people like Lionel Hampton and Louis Jordan, our band was better."

In the early 1950s, Lambert switched from trumpet to the bass.

"We had a guy in the band out of the Carolina Cotton Pickers called Lou Williams," said Lambert. "That band was in the caliber of Cab Calloway. Lou got stranded in Little Rock and needed a job. Hosea bailed him out and hired him to play bass and do arrangements for our band. After awhile, Lou stayed in Thibodaux to just write and do arrangements, so we needed a new bass player when we were on the road. I knew a little bit about the bass because I played the guitar and the bottom four strings on the guitar are tuned the same as a bass. I told Lou, 'I'll try playing bass if you keep coming up with the new arrangements'."

Around this time, the Serenader's made the complete transition to R&B.

"At the time the money was in rhythm and blues," said Lambert. "That's what the public wanted to hear. Naturally a musician had to keep up with the different styles if he wanted to survive. It wasn't hard for a musician from here to make the switch because New Orleans guys came to Thibodaux playing different styles of music."

In May 1953, the Serenaders were booked into New Orleans' Dew Drop Inn for the entire month with comedian Lolly Pop and emcee Sporty Johnson. During the band's tenure at the club, the members were required to join the #496 chapter of the Musicians Mutual Protection Union. Because Hill didn't play an instrument, the Union required that the band change it's name. The Serenaders then became known as the Lloyd Lambert Orchestra. At that time the group consisted of Lambert on bass, Lawrence Cotton on piano, Joe Tillman, Gus Fontennette, and Clarence Ford on saxophones, Oscar Moore on drums, and John Gerald on trumpet.

During their engagement in New Orleans, the Dew Drop's owner, Frank Painia, introduced the band to a piano player who recently hit town from Dallas, Ray Charles, and a colorful character from Mississippi, Eddie Lee Jones, a.k.a. Guitar Slim. Lambert would briefly tour and record with Charles, but Slim and Lambert formed an unforgettable musical partnership.

"Slim had been playing with bands Frank Painia [and even earlier Percy Stovall] had put together," said Lambert. "Slim didn't impress me as a musician, but as an entertainer, he could tear up a house. Hosea liked Slim, so he and Frank worked out a proposition. We backed Slim and Hosea booked us."

Slim moved to Thibodaux and stayed at the Sugar Bowl to be close to the band. Originally, Hill booked Slim locally, but when he got hot, he began booking him all over the United States.

"Playing with Slim wasn't easy because his timing was terrible," said Lambert. "But we got to the point where we could anticipate when Slim was going to jump time and we played along with him. It was impossible to write a song with Slim. Like on 'Any Time At All,' Slim played a riff and we fell in behind. Most songs went like that."

Guitar Slim blew the charts wide open in 1954 with his Specialty Records debut, "The Things I Used To Do," which put him and Lambert and his band on the road for the next three years. In listening closely to Slim's "The Things I Used To Do," Lambert doesn't follow the horn line, the way bass players that came after him would on covers of the song. Instead he provides a foundation for the distinctive horns and Slim's out of control guitar.

One night Lambert was backing Slim of a double bill in Florida with B.B. King. One of the members of King's band came on stage with a four stringed instrument shaped like a Fender Telecaster guitar and plugged it into a large tweed covered amplifier. It was the first electric bass that Slim and Lambert had ever seen or heard. Slim insisted Lambert get one immediately.

"When we got back to New Orleans, I bought the first electric bass that Werlein's [a Canal Street music store] had. I was the first guy in Louisiana that played one. The bass I played though was made by Gibson [an EB-1]. It was shaped like a violin."

Lambert's electric bass was portable and added a new dimension to the band, but it also produced annoying problems.

"I had a hard time finding an amplifier that would hold that bass down," said Lambert. "I bought a Gibson amplifier that came with the bass. It had six eight-inch speakers in it, but I'd always blow one or two out when we got in a big hall and I had to play loud."

Luckily, Lambert's oldest brother Adam, who worked for Chicago's National Guitar Company, was able to solve his problem.

"Adam got me an amp with just one big speaker," said Lambert. "It was covered with leopard skin and had a big handlebar on it so you could haul it. When I got the sound straight, I just led the band with the electric bass."

Lambert worked on all of Slim's Specialty recordings, and in 1955 cut his own instrumental single, "Heavy Sugar"/"King Cotton," which did well in South Louisiana. He also backed Little Richard and other Specialty artists when they recorded in New Orleans.

When Atlantic/Atco signed Slim in 1956, Lambert and band continued to provide accompaniment. However, the three singles Slim cut for the label did little and the colorful guitarist died unexpectedly in New York in 1959.

Lambert kept the band together and Hill booked dates with them supporting Nappy Brown in the Southwest. In 1959, Brown and Lambert had a disagreement in Texas and the tour abruptly ended. Rather than return to Thibodaux, Lambert decided to stick around Houston where he found studio work at Duke Records, and began an eight year stint with Arnett Cobb's jazz band.

"I got to know the Houston Symphony director Andre Previn," said Lambert. "He was also a great pianist and he had a small jazz group that played around town. He lent me an upright so I could get my chops back. I had to get my hands back in shape because the upright is a lot harder to play than an electric bass. I worked a lot of private parties with Andre like the lift-off parties at N.A.S.A."

By 1973, Duke had folded and work was becoming scarce around Houston. Lambert's brother Phamous, a Dixieland pianist, convinced him to move back to New Orleans where there was plenty of employment for a steady bassist.

"There was a lot of work opening up on Bourbon Street," said Lambert. "The guy who opened the Stage Door was putting a band together and needed a bass player. He gave me the arrangement book and I looked it over. I played one rehearsal and they hired me."

Lambert went on to play with Snookum Russell and Thomas Jefferson before landing a job as bandleader at the Maison Bourbon in 1981. He played Dixieland there in the afternoons for over a decade, and often filled in with other bands when needed.

In 1988, Lambert briefly returned to playing rhythm and blues after he helped rediscover James "Thunderbird" Davis, a blues singer who had opened shows for Guitar Slim and recorded for Duke. Lambert accompanied Davis on his acclaimed Black Top release, *Check Out Time,* and he also recorded with Snooks Eaglin.

"I like good music," concluded Lambert. "I like to hit good notes behind great soloists and singers. I just enjoy playing good notes."

Lambert died of cancer October 31, 1995. He was buried in Thibodaux's Moses Cemetery, not far from his good friend Guitar Slim.

CHAPTER TWENTY
~ Irving Banister: Behind the Best ~

Being a backup musician is a lot like being an offensive lineman on a football team. There are always people behind you getting more money and recognition, but there is a sense of pride in knowing that without your hard work, they couldn't pass or run the ball successfully.

If guitarist Irving Banister sees himself in that role, then his resume would certainly rank him as an "All Pro." In a career spanning nearly five decades, Banister has backed numerous New Orleans R&B vocalists on live dates as well as on recording sessions.

Over the years, Banister has developed a style that is quite different from New Orleans guitarists like Justin Adams, Edgar Blanchard, Ernest McLean, and Roy Montrell. Banister has no background in playing Dixieland music or contemporary jazz, as his influences are strictly blues and rhythm and blues. His signature is injecting sharp clusters of treble notes that contrast with his rock steady rhythm playing. This gives listener the illusion they are listening to two guitarists rather than one (Banister's playing on Danny White's "Loan Me Your Handkerchief" and "Kiss Tomorrow Goodbye" are examples of this technique). His current preference of a vintage Fender Telecaster guitar and a Fender Twin Reverb amplifier add to his bite.

Born in New Orleans on February 16, 1933, Banister became a guitar player by accident.

"I was playing the trumpet until I was 17, but I got my front teeth knocked out," said Banister. "I couldn't hit the high notes anymore. There weren't any guitar players in the band, so I bought a big hollow body Epiphone, a pickup, and amplifier from a music store on South Broad Street for $100."

At the time, Banister was playing with some neighborhood pals in a group called the Chapaka Sha-Wees, which included James "Sugar Boy" Crawford and Warren "Big Boy" Myles. In 1952, the group came to the attention of Dr. Daddy-O who invited them to play on his Saturday morning WMRY show. Radio exposure led to recording dates with Aladdin and Chess, but Banister laughed when recalling how limited a musician he was at the time.

"Every song was in B flat. I tuned the top three strings to a B flat chord and the bottom three strings regular. I'd just play the B flat chord open, and then go to the four and the five chords. I'd just lay my finger across the strings at the third and fourth fret. We didn't have a bass player, so I'd play the bass patterns on the bottom strings. I wasn't good enough to solo then."

Banister was drafted into the Army during his stint with Sugar Boy—missing out on playing on the Carnival classic "Jockamo," but was adequately relieved by Snooks Eaglin—and was stationed in El Paso, Texas.

"When I got there a Mexican guy gave me lessons," said Banister. "He listened to me play in the B flat tuning and said, 'You can't play anything with the guitar tuned like that.' He showed me how to tune the guitar properly. I could read music from playing the trumpet, so once I learned the fret board, I really improved. He also introduced me to solid body guitars with thin necks. You could really bend the strings on those. I never went back to the big hollow body guitars after that. T-Bone Walker and Gatemouth Brown were popular in Texas then and I picked up a lot of their style. T-Bone was a real showman and from him I learned how to do the splits on stage and how to play the guitar behind my head [Bannister still holds a guitar "Texas style," slung over his right shoulder, rather than putting the guitar strap over his head]. In El Paso, I played at the Black and Tan Club and sometimes over the border in Juarez."

After Banister got out of the service, he returned to New Orleans and got his old job back with Crawford. At the time, the band was almost exclusively playing clubs run by alleged mobsters, Pascal "Pops" Perez and Pete Marcello.

"We played the Joy Tavern on the West Bank and a bunch of gambling joints on Jefferson Highway," said Banister. "We even played a place on an island that didn't have anything but a bandstand and a roulette wheel. All our work was white clubs— that's why I left Sugar Boy around 1956. We couldn't eat, drink or sit down in these places. We couldn't even use the bathroom. I got a job with Eddie Bo who was on the road doing all black clubs. We had to sleep six to a room in boarding houses sometimes, but at least we didn't have to worry about going to jail most of the time."

Banister played on several of Bo's early recordings including "I'm Wise" and "Hey Bo," released on Apollo. Featuring Walter Lastie on drums, and David Lastie on saxophone, Banister considers Bo's mid-1950s band among the best to have ever come out of New Orleans. Banister was then studying other guitarists and listening to records that Mickey Baker, Pete Lewis, and Wayne Bennett played on. He incorporated portions of their style to make himself an even more skilled musician.

"Shaw was booking us [Eddie Bo] out of New York and put us on

packages with Charles Brown and Amos Milburn," recalled Banister. "We
stayed real busy for a couple of years. But it seemed like when they
teamed us up with Amos Milburn things slowed up. Amos [who was living at the Dew Drop at the time] insisted on using our band on the road.
But by the late 1950s, his records had stopped selling, he didn't get a lot
of gigs, so we didn't work as much."

After work with Bo began to slow, in 1959 Banister hooked up with
Danny White and the Cavaliers.

"Pete Marcello had a club on Jefferson Highway and the band there
worked six nights a week," said Banister. "He said they needed a guitar
player. I showed up one night not knowing who I was going to work with
but it turned out to be Danny. I fit in pretty good with the Cavaliers
because they were doing a lot of the same material that Bo was doing."

Banister would immediately became a cornerstone of the Cavaliers
sound and he would appear on most of White's Frisco singles.

"Our bass player, Curtis Mitchell, deserves credit for those Danny
White arrangements," contended Banister. "He wrote charts on those sessions for every instrument. He even wrote out my solos. Danny's records
could have been bigger if he was on a national label and we could have
toured. We had hits in New Orleans, but in Shreveport, they never heard
them. We only worked around New Orleans, and like Sugar Boy, we only
played at white clubs. We played a lot of Tulane frat gigs and clubs like
the Safari, the Sands and the Dream Room."

The early Sunday morning set at the Dream Room on Bourbon Street
was the Cavaliers' marquee gig.

"Every night the place was packed," said Banister. "We usually had a
job before we played the Dream Room and a lot of people would follow
us there. Sam Butera used to come in the Dream Room and steal Danny's
stage routine. I know, because I saw him in Las Vegas and he had Danny's
stuff down pat. Mac Rebennack used to come in there a lot and watch me
play. I used to sing on the first set back then but I sounded like Mac does
now so I quit. Mac was doing some producing then. He used me on some
sessions but I don't remember the artists. I do remember playing on some
country sessions, which blew some minds, but I learned to play that stuff
in Texas."

White eventually left New Orleans and the Cavaliers disbanded.
Banister returned to play with Sugar Boy Crawford. In 1963, Banister was
traveling to Monroe, Louisiana, with Crawford and the band when they
were stopped by the police. Crawford and a state trooper got in an alter-
cation, and Crawford was pistol whipped by the arresting officer.

"Sugar Boy was in the hospital for nearly a year," said Banister.

"That's when I started Irving Banister and the All Stars. I took some of the guys from Sugar Boy's band. For a while I had Smokey Johnson on drums and George Porter on bass, but George took a job with Art Neville who had a job playing at La Ray's on Dryades Street. When Sugar Boy got out of the hospital, we started playing with him again but that beating affected his mind. He couldn't sing the fast numbers anymore so he retired. I went back to my band and picked up freelance gigs with other bands when the All Stars weren't working. I'm still doing that. I've worked with local artists like Johnny Adams, Irma Thomas, Ernie K-Doe, and touring acts like Solomon Burke."

In 1992, Banister contributed to Dr. John's *Goin Back To New Orleans* CD. Banister and the All Star's also found a cozy gig at Margaritaville in the French Quarter doing what he does best—playing rhythm and blues.

"I've always considered myself an R&B musician," said Banister. "I never got into jazz because it was too complicated and I don't feel it. But R&B, that's my kind of music."

Jack Dupree w/stepsister and the author - 1990

Ad courtesy of Dave Booth

Photo courtesy of Janis Johnson

Clarence Samuels and Dave Bartholomew - 1999

Fats Domino

Fats' mid-1980s
business card

Tommy Ridgley - 1960

Chuck Carbo, Joe Turner, Frank Painia, unknown
inside the Dew Drop - circa 1960

Eddie Bo onstage - 1961

Ray Charles - circa 1956

The "Frogman" - 1957

Lil Millet (bass) and the Creoles - early 1960s

Al Johnson - 2001

Frank Mitchell
- circa 1955

Introducing Those Fabulous, Zany, Torrid and Entertaining Gondoliers

ONE OF AMERICA'S MOST VERSATILE SEXTETS, POUVEROURYES OF POP, MODERN JAZZ, MUSIC FOR DANCING, LATIN AMERICAN, FOLK, DIXIELAND, ROCK AND ROLL AND LOADS OF FRESH COMEDY.

TRULY AN ORGANIZATION DEDICATED TO TOP NOTCH ENTERTAINMENT

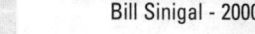

Bill Sinigal - 2000

PLACE

DATE

Time   Admission

SHOW & DANCE
Featuring In Person
Johnnie Baker
Along With Sensational Recording Artist
★ **Sonny Boy Williamson**
"Wake Up Baby"   "Don't Start Me Talking"
Plus **Irving Bannister**
& The All Stars
WITH
SWEET LORRAINE

Lloyd Lambert - 1955

Part III

Clubs and R&B Culture

This abbreviated, but important chapter, collects discourses and profiles that might not seem entirely related and don't fit cohesively as the other chapters of this book do. This can't really be helped, but the understanding reader will realize that these essays document a fascinating culture and lifestyle, one that was shaped by rhythm and blues music.

New Orleans has always had a reputation for being an important music and entertainment center. The city's mark on the field of entertainment was in many ways struck by it's live music venues. These clubs, parks, social clubs, auditoriums and dance halls served as a breeding ground for New Orleans R&B. There have been hundreds of R&B venues in New Orleans including The Gypsy Tea Room, Club Desire, the Hide Away, Lincoln Beach, Rip's Playhouse, the Nite Cap, the Golden Cadillac, the Dream Room, Club Tiajuana, Natale's, the Brass Rail, Prout's Club Alhambra, Mason's Las Vegas Strip, the Safari Room and the F&M Patio, just to name a few. It was at these locations that the genre took shape and thrived. Along with the music, the audience, the club owners, and promoters would create a unique culture and history. It is something New Orleans should be extremely proud of.

CHAPTER TWENTY ONE
~ The Dew Drop Inn: The South's Swankest Night Spot ~

The club that rekindles the fondest memories and stories with rhythm and blues performers in New Orleans is the infamous Dew Drop Inn located at 2836 LaSalle Street. For 25 years, the Dew Drop lived up to its boast of being "The South's swankest night spot." From 1945 to the late 1960s, the Dew Drop was synonymous with top flight black entertainment, drawing singers, dancers, comedians, and female impersonators like a magnet.

"The Dew Drop was it," said the late Joseph August, better known as "Mr. Google Eyes," who often worked at the club as a singer and emcee. "It was the foundation for musicians in New Orleans. Whether you were from out of town or the city, your goal was the Dew Drop. If you couldn't get a job at the Dew Drop, you weren't about nothing."

Even thought the club would embrace the lives and careers of hundreds of people, the Dew Drop's story constantly returns to one man, Frank Painia.

Born in Plaquemine, Louisiana, June 3, 1907, Painia moved to New Orleans with his wife Freddie and two young children in 1934. A barber by trade who had gone only as far as the seventh grade, he left Plaquemine to escape the depression-weary rural Louisiana. Upon arrival in New Orleans, the Painias moved in with his sister and he became a partner in a barber shop on LaSalle Street. When the shop was razed to make way for the Magnolia Housing Project, Painia opened his own shop across the street on the corner of LaSalle and Sixth.

One who could spot and take advantage of a good business opportunity, Painia bought out an Asian merchant who owned a bar and grocery just two doors away on LaSalle. He renovated the building to accommodate his barber shop and a restaurant was added to the building. To help him operate the business, brothers Paul, an excellent cook, and Easton, a bartender, moved to New Orleans from Plaquemine. Dubbed the Dew Drop Inn, the establishment opened in April of 1939.

Business was slow in the beginning but Painia persevered.

"Daddy had a mind for business," said his daughter Laura Jackson, who worked at the Dew Drop as cashier and bookkeeper. "He was a real go-getter. He was always expanding and moving things around. He had a chance to buy the building next door and saw a way to turn a profit. The war was on so there was a lot of people in transit. A hotel was going to do well because there wasn't a quality place for blacks to stay then. The Dew Drop is actually two buildings."

Although Painia's daughter pointed out, "The place was really jumping during the War," the Dew Drop hadn't yet begun to feature live entertainment. However, another business venture for Painia surfaced. He began booking national acts like Louis Jordan and Jimmie Lunceford at the Booker T. Washington Auditorium and the Coliseum Arena. More often than not, Painia's shows drew large audiences and he made handsome profits.

Since many entertainers already ate and slept at his establishment, and he could avoid paying rent and taxes on other venues, Painia decided to utilize his own space. Presenting shows at the Dew Drop was a logical progression.

Painia began experimenting with local talent in his barroom and found they could draw people to his establishment. As the war in the Pacific was concluding, workmen were putting the finishing touches on the latest addition to the Dew Drop, a club destined to be New Orleans' best known night spot.

"Ssh,ssh," whispered a headline in the August 14, 1945 issue of *The Louisiana Weekly*. "Don't tell anyone, but the Dew Drop Inn is really coming up with that Northern stuff in the next week or three. Mr. Frank Painia, one of the city's better Negro business men, will see to it that there will be a decent dance hall for his people."

Referred to as the "Groove Room," by October 1945 *The Louisiana Weekly* was already calling the Dew Drop's dance hall, "New Orleans' swankest nightclub." Featuring two shows nightly on weekends and amateur contests on Monday evenings, the Dew Drop booked the kind of entertainment that backed up its reputation.

A typical show, advertised in the December 22, 1945 *Louisiana Weekly*, listed Joe Turner—"King of the blues who will be back with a new sack of songs for Christmas, along with a brand new show;" Bobby Grant—"Just back from St. Louis, nationally known female impersonator;" Iron Jaw Harris—"Dancing with three tables in his mouth;" Virginia Plummer—"Exotic dancer;" and Decoy—"Now you see him now you don't." Admission was 75 cents. If reservations were required, they could be acquired by dialing JA-7605.

"You always got a full floor show," said Naomi Swan, Painia's niece who worked behind the bar at the Dew Drop for 25 years. "Frank always had an emcee and a comedian that would loosen up the audience. Then you had your shake dancers and female impersonators that came on before the star attraction. The Dew Drop always had a house band. Back in the

1940s, it was either Dave Bartholomew or Edgar Blanchard and the Gondoliers.

"I guess by today's standards the club wasn't much. It held only 200 to 300 people. It had plain wooden tables and chairs, but they were always covered with clean white tablecloths, and everyone that worked there had a fresh uniform on. The Dew Drop always had a reputation for being a good clean club where you came to have a good time. Frank didn't stand for narcotics, prostitution or fighting. He liked to have a good time like anybody else, but he was a family man. Eventually he brought his whole family from Plaquemine and he gave them jobs at the Dew Drop. I was just a little thing working in the bar, but I felt protected because I had nothing but family around me. If someone would ever get smart with me, Frank would cut them off and say, 'Do you know you're talking to my niece?'"

Many black entertainers passed through the doors of the Dew Drop. Early national attractions included Amos Milburn, Ivory Joe Hunter, the Ravens, Clarence "Gatemouth" Brown, Chubby Newsome and Calvin Frazier.

Painia had an eye for talent, and many artists credit him with their early success. According to Swan, Painia was instrumental in getting Larry Darnell's career off the ground among others.

"Frank picked Larry out of a revue called the Brown Skinned Models in 1949. He gave him a job singing in the front bar. Larry had a boyish look and when he sang he drove the women wild [ironically Darnell preferred men]. He did so well that people left the the nightclub to see him in the front bar. Frank had a lot of connections in the business and arranged for Larry to make his first record, 'I'll Get Along Somehow.' That made Larry a star."

Painia saw another way to take advantage of the abundance of local talent. In April of 1949, he opened the Dew Drop Inn Booking Agency.

"Sometimes we'd have four bands out on the road on one night," said Gerald Painia, Frank's son who helped run the booking agency. "Whoever came up with a big record in town, Dad would book. He had a circuit that stretched from Texas to Alabama that included everything from colleges to roadhouses. We booked Earl King, Guitar Slim, Shirley & Lee, Smiley Lewis and Chris Kenner. We had some great musicians in the bands too— Lee Allen, Huey Smith, Roland Cook and Allen Toussaint."

Normally a man of few words, Toussaint drops his reserve when discussing Frank Painia and the Dew Drop.

"I wish you could have seen it in its heyday," said Toussaint. "If you were a musician, at some point in the day you were going to go by the

Dew Drop. It was a musicians' haven. When bands got ready to go to Houma or Vacherie, they met at the Dew Drop. When they came back at 2 a.m., they'd go inside the club and jam. There were musicians around the Dew Drop 24 hours a day. Frank was the kind of guy people looked to for answers. He walked around with his chest poked out, but it wasn't a put-on. He had strong features and walked with a lot of grace. When he showed up, everybody got shook up. He gave the orders and everybody listened. Whoever dropped the glass cleaned it up real quick, and the guy with the mop started mopping real good."

A highly respected man in the black community, Painia was a pioneer in the civil rights movement in New Orleans. In a nationally publicized incident, Painia, along with white film star Zarchary Scott, was arrested in November 1952 and charged with disturbing the peace and "mixing." Scott, on location in New Orleans, came to the Dew Drop to see "Papa" Lightfoot and emcee Patsy Valdalia. According to *The Louisiana Weekly*, the New Orleans Police Department received a complaint that "Negroes and whites were being served together," and sent several squad cars to the club to investigate.

"I remember that night like it was yesterday," said Laura Jackson. "Father decided to make a stand and went to jail. Whites had always come into the Dew Drop—in fact a lot of policeman visited the place. The ongoing joke was that if you needed a cop for something, you had to call the Dew Drop. They [the New Orleans Police Department] just wanted to make an example of someone. They threw the charges out the next day, but my father wasn't afraid to go to jail. In fact he went a number of times. But he had a purpose. He continually lobbied the city council to eliminate segregation laws."

The Dew Drop flourished during the 1950s. When the public's taste in music gradually changed, Painia adapted, continuing to offer the best entertainment in New Orleans. At one time or another, Ray Charles, Christine Kittrell, James Brown, Little Richard, Milt Jackson, Amos Milburn, and Charles Brown were familiar faces on LaSalle Street. In fact many of the previously mentioned artists listed the Dew Drop Hotel as their address on their recording contracts.

Another figure associated with the Dew Drop for nearly two decades was Patsy Valdalia, a transvestite singer and emcee.

"Patsy was something else," laughed Swan. "She was as gay as they came and didn't care who knew. She made herself queen of the Dew Drop. Patsy was so funny on stage because she used expressions she knew nothing about. She'd throw her arms out and sing, 'Truss in me!' Patsy didn't want anyone looking better than her either. When the new female impersonators came to town she'd check them out. Once one came from Los Angeles and I couldn't believe she was a man. She was so tiny and so pretty. That night Patsy called to get our opinion of the new impersonator. Paul Painia told me to tell Patsy, 'Don't bother coming into work tonight.' That made Patsy mad as hell and she was at the Dew Drop in five minutes."

Patsy also hosted the Dew Drop's legendary after-hours jam sessions.

"Frank would find out which entertainers were in the club and tell Patsy," said Tommy Ridgley. "You see even artists that weren't playing at the club stayed at the Dew Drop because it was the best black hotel in the area. Also a lot of the bands Frank sent out of town came back to the Dew Drop after driving back from their gig. Patsy would point out who was in the audience and make a big fuss over what a big star they were then call them up to the bandstand. One night, I remember being on stage with Bobby Bland, Little Willie John and about 15 other musicians. Sometimes you wouldn't get out of the Dew Drop until 9:00 a.m."

The early 1960s continued to be heady years for the Dew Drop as Painia varied his shows to keep up with the public's taste. When soul became popular, the Dew Drop often featured Joe Tex, Sam Cooke, Al "TNT" Braggs, Otis Redding, and the Ike & Tina Turner Revue.

The "King of Rock and Soul," Solomon Burke, has nothing but praise for the man he first met in 1961.

"A musician had no better friend than Frank Painia," declared Burke. "Everyone that was out there at the time knew that if you got in a jam, if you could get to New Orleans, Frank Painia would help you out. He would feed you [Burke, and numerous others, recalled the Dew Drop served the best plate of red beans and rice you ever tasted] and put a roof over your head until you got back on your feet. Frank had a room in the back of the hotel that was filled with clothes people left at the hotel and he'd let you wear them if you needed to. If he couldn't use you at the Dew Drop, he'd get on the phone and try and get you some work somewhere."

B.B. King echoed Burke's sentiments.

"I don't think there was a successful black entertainer or musician from my generation that didn't know Frank Painia. He was a friend and a guy that helped a lot of artists' careers. He was very good to me. I played at the Dew Drop several times, but what I remember best was the fabulous late night jam sessions."

However by the mid-1960s, the Dew Drop's luster had begun to fade.

"I think integration really hurt the Dew Drop," explained Jackson. "All of a sudden blacks could go to places they were weren't allowed at before like Bourbon Street. That was new to them. It meant a lot of our customers left and never came back.

"Also my father got sick in 1965 and he was continually in and out of the hospital. He had always been at the Dew Drop six or seven days a week. The only time he took a day off was to take the family fishing. When he couldn't be there every day, things started to slip."

"Being sick meant he couldn't concentrate on business," added Swan. "I think Frank began to think he could present any type of show and people would just show up like they did before. He was the type of man who always wanted things done his way. He didn't take advice too well even if it was good."

By the late 1960s, the Groove Room was closed, and the more profitable hotel portion of the business was expanded in its place. Live music continued in the front bar—the Dew Drop Cafe—but the impressive floor shows were no more. The bold ads that once appeared in *The Louisiana Weekly* (which often contained a photo of Painia) had shrunk and appeared irregularly. Still, they recalled the better days when they boasted "Blazing Action—Boss Entertainment." Mostly local stars like Diamond Joe, Li'l Booker (a.k.a. James Booker, who was busted outside the Dew Drop for possession of narcotics and sent to state prison) Johnny Adams and Irma Thomas performed. As late as the summer of 1967, "the Boss of the Blues," Big Joe Turner was still a Dew Drop attraction.

"Even though he was still doing well with the bar and hotel, I know it had to hurt him when the nightclub closed," said Swan. "That was his baby. He liked nothing better than getting a bottle out when an entertainer came to town and having a few drinks with them. That was his life. By the time I stopped working there in 1969, they had stopped having live entertainment altogether. Frank was really sick and there was nobody to take his place."

Painia eventually succumbed to cancer in July of 1972. He was eulogized on the front page of *The Louisiana Weekly*, which stated, "Painia was always at the front of any movement to make Black people push forward." After his death the barbershop, restaurant, and bar were leased out to new occupants, while Painia's wife struggled to keep the hotel operating. By the mid-1970s, the building had fallen into disrepair and on more than one occasion was listed for sale.

Today the Dew Drop still sits quietly on LaSalle Street, its stucco facade covered with weathered aluminum siding, looking forlorn and in need of a facelift. But the building is still in the Painia family. Frank's grandson, Kenneth Jackson, who once ran a snowball stand for his grandfather, runs the hotel and cuts hair in the barber shop.

"I couldn't stand to see the family lose this place," said Jackson. "It's just too close to me. Besides I think my grandfather would turn over in his grave if it was lost.

"I was really close to my grandfather and he used to give me little projects to do and let me run errands for him. People still come by here and talk about the days when the Dew Drop was really jumping. Sometimes when people come by here I can see on their faces they're thinking about the good times this place once held. It never fails that at every Mardi Gras, someone from out of town asks for Frank Painia. You can see that they're disappointed because he's dead and because the place isn't like it used to be.

"Right now I'm trying to get the business back on its feet and pay off the mortgage. I'm doing repairs to bring some of the class back to the place. Sooner or later I'm going to renovate the bar and maybe add a restaurant and live music again. Who knows, maybe some day I'll light up LaSalle Street just like my grandfather did."

CHAPTER TWENTY TWO
~ Patsy Valdalia: The Toast of New Orleans ~

New Orleans has had an obvious abundance of colorful entertainers over the years. However, perhaps none were as flamboyant as Patsy Valdalia. For nearly two decades, Patsy—who was also referred to as "Toast"—as in "The Toast of New Orleans"—was the female impersonator/singer/emcee at the Dew Drop Inn, the city's premier black night spot for a quarter of a century.

"In New Orleans, if you were any kind of musician or entertainer, you worked the Dew Drop," said the late Tommy Ridgley. "When you got to the Dew Drop you got Patsy. Patsy sang, told jokes, introduced the performers and acted as hostess. Patsy also organized those great after-hours jam sessions the Dew Drop was known for."

Patsy's given name was Irving Ale and he was born at Vacherie, Louisiana, in 1921. Patsy was quite young when his father Willie died and shortly after, he accompanied his mother Orelia to New Orleans. For several years the family lived in a small shotgun near the corner of Maple and Hillary Street. Bassist Chuck Badie recalls Irving attended McDonogh 24 on Burdette Street and that he often played football on the nearby levee. Orelia, a registered nurse, later bought a house on South Liberty Street and watched her youngest son grow up to be quick-witted, religious, extremely intelligent, athletic and gay. Irving was fascinated by the female impersonators who entertained in the clubs and theaters around New Orleans, especially one billed as "Caldonia." He admired their flashy wardrobes, the attention they received and their opulent lifestyle. Irving had found his life's calling.

"In the culture that Patsy grew up in it was especially rough being a homosexual," said Harold Battiste. "I think Patsy saw that being an entertainer, and Patsy was a natural entertainer, would allow him to express his sexuality and to a degree skirt the stigma of being gay."

Irving chose the professional name Patsy Valdalia, an adaptation of Vidalia, Louisiana's sweet onion. The imagery of sweetness might be something a female impersonator would strive to portray, but the appellation might have been a double-entendre. Cosimo Matassa recalls that when he grew up in the French Quarter, "Vidalia," was the slang term for men who solicited prostitutes. When taxi drivers picked up "Johns" on Bourbon Street, they referred to it as a "Vidalia run."

In 1947, Patsy was mentioned several times in *The Louisiana Weekly* which reported appearances at the Gypsy Tea Room, as well several other clubs around New Orleans. Patsy was discovered by the Dew Drop's owner Frank Painia at the Club Desire when he was part of a group female impersonators called the Valdalia Sisters. Painia was so convinced Patsy was a woman that he lost a wager on it with a companion. Painia lost the bet, but was so impressed with Patsy's performance that he hired him to perform at his club. Over the next two decades, Patsy Valdalia would become synonymous with the Dew Drop.

The relationship between Painia and Patsy was professional, friendly and more often than not hilarious. Numerous times Painia had to bolster Patsy's self-confidence because he was jealous of other female impersonators booked at the Dew Drop. However, Patsy also made Painia aware that the only reason he was making money in his nightclub was because the patrons were coming to see "Toast.".

Painia gave Patsy a room upstairs at the Dew Drop Hotel that was used for wardrobe changes, relaxing, entertaining and sexual encounters. The late Bobby Marchan, who mirrored Patsy's role at the rival Club Tiajuana, and resided at the Dew Drop, recalled Painia paid Patsy $12 a night at the Dew Drop during the 1950s. Painia also supplied Patsy with a fifth of Cutty Sark most nights..

"Patsy's theme was 'Hip Shakin' Mama,'" said Irma Thomas. "The house band played that every night. He'd be dressed in a beautiful gown with a shoulder length wig. Patsy was six feet tall and had an athletic build, but not in a macho way. When Patsy was in drag it was hard to tell that he wasn't a woman. Patsy would tell a few jokes—he especially loved to poke fun at himself—and then introduce the first act. Then he'd run up to his room, change costumes and bring on the next entertainer.

"Nobody [in the audience] dared mess with Patsy. If they did, Patsy made them look like a fool. He was also helpful to other entertainers, especially me. I appreciated it because I was young and inexperienced. He gave me tips on how to wear makeup, what clothes to wear, how to move on stage and how to get off and on the bandstand. I got 'Hip Shakin' Mama' from Patsy and I've done that song my entire career."

Patsy also wore fabulous costumes many which he ingeniously embellished. According to Warren Lee, Patsy would collect the colorful glass beads tossed from floats during Mardi Gras parades. He'd then hammer them into fragments and use contact glue to attach them to stylish women's shoes. When Patsy wore them at the Dew Drop, the lights reflected off the shoes in brilliant colors. Many women in the audience would subsequently search for a similar pair on Dryades and Canal Street, but off course with no luck.

Patsy also organized and emceed the spectacular Halloween Gay Ball that was held annually at the Dew Drop.

"That was the biggest show of the year at the Dew Drop," confirmed Marchan. "All of your best female impersonators were there because there were prizes for the most outstanding costumes. It was hard to get into that show because all of the Dew Drop regulars were there, and a lot of white people from the French Quarter who heard about the show."

Apparently the Gay Ball stirred up a lot of jealousy between Patsy and other contestants. Earl King recalled that Patsy got so upset when he didn't win the contest once that he demanded (unsuccessfully) that Painia eject the winner from the club and award him first prize instead.

A *Billboard* article dated July 18, 1953, noted that "Pat Valadear" was signed by Mercury Record's Dee Kilpatrick along with several other New Orleans artists. Patsy traveled to Los Angeles to record with transplanted New Orleans bandleader Plas Johnson. Credited to "Pat Valdelar," he recorded two songs for Mercury that were part of his Dew Drop repertoire, "Rock Me Baby," a jump blues, and "Put Your Hand Over Your Heart," earlier a hit for Atlanta female impersonator Billy Wright. According to Earl King, when Patsy performed "Put Your Hand Over Your Heart," he would instruct the men in the audience to put their hand over their crotch. The single, which proved to be Patsy's entire recorded legacy, bombed.

"Maybe the record companies didn't think Patsy was qualified," speculated Marchan. "Patsy couldn't sing as well as Larry Darnell [a very successful recording artist and once Patsy's par amour] so he didn't pursue recording. Now I was a female impersonator but I could sing."

Cosimo Matassa had another theory:

"It's hard to believe Patsy didn't record more because 99 out of 100 A&R guys that came to town went to the Dew Drop. You'd thing that more than one of them would take a chance on Patsy only because he was different. Perhaps they didn't look at him as a singer. Being an emcee, he'd often cut a song short, ad lib, announce who was in the house, and tell jokes. Patsy came by the studio with other artists, but I never recorded him and he never showed up at auditions."

Possibly, Patsy was satisfied with the security the Dew Drop offered. He lived with his mother and they were very close. Being a recording artist would bring with it complications like putting a band together, coming up with new material and tours that would take him away from New Orleans. Patsy saw plenty of one-hit, and no-hit wonders around the Dew Drop, and wasn't interested in that fate.

"Patsy would wait tables at the Dew Drop around Christmas and Carnival when it got real busy," recalled Earl King. "One night there was a table full of people from out of town that ordered a set up, that was a half-pint, ice and some Cokes. The Dew Drop charged $5 for that. But Patsy asked the people for $15 and pocketed the difference. They later ordered another set up but Patsy was in the kitchen and they had to order it from another waitress. The girl charged them the regular $5. The people got mad and told Frank what Patsy did. Frank went into the kitchen and told Patsy, 'Get your ass back on stage and forget about waiting tables. You're making more money around here than I am!'"

Patsy was still working at the Dew Drop in the mid-1960s when dwindling business and poor health forced Painia to eliminate live entertainment at the club. Patsy spent the 1970s caring for his mother, volunteering at neighborhood playgrounds, and stopping at the Dew Drop to drink to recall the days when he was "The Toast of New Orleans."

Patsy's last public appearance was Halloween night 1980, when he hosted a Gay Ball at the Sportland (the old Blue Eagle on Felicity Street) which featured Earl King and B.B. Daddy (Dell Stewart). On the same evening, across town at Club Alhambra, Bobby Marchan was also hosting a Gay Ball.

When Jon Foose interviewed him in March 1981, Patsy was a shadow of his former flamboyant self.

"It was kind of a rambling interview and he was pretty out of it," recalled Foose. "His mother was there but she was pretty ancient. Patsy was weak and obviously pretty ill. He was in hospital greens and I got the idea he was learning to be a nurse's aid."

Around this time, Patsy fell in a grocery store sustaining minor injuries. He tried to sue the store for compensation but was unsuccessful. Patsy eventually died at home August 29, 1982. His *Times-Picayune* obituary noted: "He was a female impersonator at the now defunct Dew Drop Inn on LaSalle Street until his retirement in 1979. His stage name was Patsy Vidalia." Patsy Valdalia is buried in an unmarked grave in the Carrollton Cemetery.

"Patsy lived for a good time," said Marchan. "He loved to eat good food and drink. He was a fabulous entertainer. Movie stars from Hollywood came to the Dew Drop just to see Patsy Valdalia. We were rivals, but he was my very good friend."

CHAPTER TWENTY THREE
~ The Sugar Bowl: Hosea's Place ~

Sixty-five miles southwest of New Orleans lies the peaceful country town of Thibodaux, Louisiana. Nestled on peaceful Bayou Lafourche, for many years it was a center for sugar refining and the oil field supply business. However, with those industries in steady decline, many of Thibodaux's residents struggle to make ends meet and the town looks a little frayed around the edges. Of late, the busiest section of the town is Highway 1, the route to Baton Rouge, Houma, Avondale and New Orleans, where the majority of the population of the town is employed.

While at first glance Thibodaux and New Orleans appear to be significantly different, they share a common thread—music. Over the past century there has been a constant interaction of musicians between the two centers. During the classic period of New Orleans rhythm and blues, the 1950s and 1960s, the tie that bound the two cities was especially strong primarily because of the renown Sugar Bowl night spot. The club was somewhat of a satellite of New Orleans' Dew Drop Inn, as it featured many New Orleans artists and the same national acts that played on La Salle Street.

The Sugar Bowl was owned by the late Hosea Hill, a shrewd and successful business man who enjoyed stylish clothes, a drink with friends, gambling, baseball, the company of beautiful women, and good music.

"Anything worthwhile that came to Thibodaux Hosea Hill brought it here," declared his son Thurston Hill, who worked for his father for many years and still lives in Thibodaux. "He was the most important and respected black man in Thibodaux. If you needed a favor, a loan, or a job—you came to see my daddy."

Hosea Hill was born in 1907 at Chackbay, six miles south of Thibodaux. Hill's family owned a parcel of land and farmed sugar cane. Hill's mother was an entrepreneur who used some of the profits from the harvest to open a cafe in Thibodaux that was located on the corner of 10th and Narrow Street.

"People called it the Bucket of Blood," laughed Thurston. "Somebody was always getting cut in there or there was a fight. But it was a popular place and my grandmother made a lot of money there. She set my daddy up in business."

In 1932, Hosea Hill rented a building near his mother's cafe and opened a bar appropriately called the Sugar Bowl. Open 24 hours a day, the bar catered to cane scrapers and roughnecks in search of a drink, a good time, and perhaps a crap game. After surviving the depression and World War II, the Sugar Bowl thrived in the Post-War economy. In addition to offering games of chance and liquor, Hill added music to Sugar Bowl's list of attractions.

Although he could neither sing nor play an instrument, Hill formed a band called Hosea Hill's Serenaders which acted as the Sugar Bowl's house band. A crack group that featured Thibodaux's top musicians, Hill also began booking the Serenaders into the surrounding towns when they weren't playing the Sugar Bowl. He also began hiring New Orleans acts like Fats Domino, Tommy Ridgley, and Lloyd Price which proved to be very good for business.

Around 1952, Hill saw that he could make more money by moving to a larger location that would hold more people and attract R&B artists of higher stature.

"The building on Narrow had got too small," said Thurston Hill. "It could only hold a couple of hundred people. Hosea bought an apartment building on Lagarde Street and tore the downstairs out. He built a bar, cafe, kitchen and dance hall. The dance hall had two balconies and could hold 800 to 900 people. He had entertainment every weekend and the place stayed packed."

Because of their similar businesses, Hill became acquainted with Frank Painia, the owner of New Orleans' Dew Drop Inn.

"Frank and Hosea were best friends and business partners," said Beatrice Hill, Thurston's wife, who worked at the Sugar Bowl behind the bar. "The Sugar Bowl didn't have the big floor shows with the dancers and female impersonators like the Dew Drop, but Hosea booked a lot of the same singers and musicians. We'd visit the Dew Drop a lot and Frank treated us like we owned the place."

Hill and Painia often booked acts together. By offering an artist a guarantee of multiple nights of work, they could get a lower per night price. When an artist wasn't appearing at the Dew Drop or the Sugar Bowl, Painia and Hill would book them into other clubs and halls in the surrounding area.

Together Hill and Painia put a lot of New Orleans artists on the road, perhaps the most famous being Guitar Slim.

"Frank introduced Slim to Hosea," said Beatrice. "I think Frank was going to lose his booking license and he asked Hosea to take Slim over. Slim moved to Thibodaux and stayed at the Sugar Bowl [Hill had apartments above the club and also purchased an adjacent apartment building on Lagarde Street where many musicians stayed]. The first time I saw Guitar Slim I was in high school and living in Labadieville [a town just north of Thibodaux]. I had a girlfriend that lived in nearby Freetown and I walked seven miles to go visit her. She was the niece of man who owned a club there and Slim just loved her. When I got to her house, Slim was up in a tree outside her house plucking on his guitar trying to impress her. He stayed up there all day."

Hill had his hands full with the alcohol-fueled guitarist but he made a great deal of money with Slim, especially after "The Things I Used to Do" became a hit in 1954.

"Slim went around the country for three years behind 'The Things I Used To Do' and every date was booked out of Thibodaux," said Thurston. "If Slim would have cut more records, I think he would have stayed popular longer. Slim was a guy who never took care of himself. He would get his uniform [stage clothes] ringing wet and then go outside in the cold. That's how he got sick. Pneumonia and port wine killed Slim."

When Slim died unexpectedly in 1959, Hill covered the expenses of the funeral and burial. Slim's death deeply affected Hill, who came to regard Slim as part of his family. Nevertheless, at the funeral Hill provided a moment of unexpected humor.

"In the front pews of the church were five or six of women and a bunch of kids," said Thurston. "They were all fussing. All the women claimed Slim was their husband and the daddy of their children. Hosea called the women to the back of the church and said, 'Ladies, the undertaker hasn't been paid yet and he needs some money from Slim's wife or he can't bury him.' At that point it got real quite and none of the women claimed Slim as their husband."

During the early 1960s the Sugar Bowl flourished, presenting Carol Fran, James Davis, Lee Dorsey, Nappy Brown, Ike and Tina Turner, Hank Ballard and others. When a big act like Lloyd Price or James Brown came to town, Hill booked them at Thibodaux's baseball park, Stark Field, thus producing the area's first racially integrated events. He also booked Sam Cooke into the Morgan City Auditorium. For the Cooke date he had to change the advertising placards to read "concert" rather "dance," because the city officials didn't want blacks and whites twisting the night away together.

Beatrice maintained that the most popular attraction at the Sugar Bowl during this era was Ray Charles.

"Ray Charles played the Sugar Bowl four times a year. I remember the first time he played we had a flood and there was water in the Sugar Bowl. The bar maids were trying to sweep the water out to get the place ready when people started arriving. The people coming in were so anxious to see Ray Charles that some of them grabbed mops and brooms to help us out."

She also recalls that Bobby Marchan's revue, then based in Pritchard, Alabama, got stranded in the area and Hill put them up for three months at the hotel until they could raise the money to get back home.

"Hosea was always helping out musicians," continued Beatrice. "If they needed clothes, money or an instrument, they could come to Hosea. A lot of musicians will tell you they might not have made it if Hosea hadn't been there to help out."

By the late 1960s Hill had taken on other business ventures, including owning and driving school buses. This meant he no longer had the time to be the hands on owner of the Sugar Bowl.

"It had got run down and police told Hosea to clean the place up," said Beatrice. "Hosea got me and Thurston to turn it around. We worked there a year cleaning and fixing the place up. We ran off the deadbeats and the business started running pretty good again. Then Hosea's second wife decided she wanted to take it over. She got rid of us and it started going down again. The place burnt down around 1969 because of faulty wiring. Hosea always had his friends do jack-leg repairs around the place and it caught fire one night."

Hill didn't miss a beat though as he set up a temporary club inside his apartment building next to the Sugar Bowl.

"Hosea rebuilt the club in about six months," said Beatrice. "But he had to borrow money to build it. He didn't have insurance on the old building and he lost everything."

Unfortunately, the new version of the Sugar Bowl couldn't replace the old one. It didn't help that Hill was diagnosed with cancer and that his second wife, a school teacher, had no idea how to run a club. Hill continued to book bands however, even from his hospital bed.

"Daddy booked the first show at the Thibodaux Civic Center in 1973," said Thurston. "Bobby Bland appeared there the day we buried my daddy. Bobby didn't know until after the show and he got real choked up because he was real close with Hosea. Bobby's never been back to Thibodaux since that night."

Hill's second wife inherited the Sugar Bowl and the bank liens on the building. Thurston and his brother Harvey were interested in buying the business but neither could raise the necessary funds. Hill's widow continued to let others run the Sugar Bowl which no longer provided entertainment. Eventually, it became an eyesore as well as haven for winos and drug users. The Sugar Bowl closed in the early 1980s and a few years later, it burned to the ground. In 1996, the Habitat for Humanity Foundation purchased the property and three newly built houses now stand where the Sugar Bowl once did.

Both Thurston and Beatrice concur that Thibodaux's luster dulled after Hosea Hill's death and the demise of the Sugar Bowl.

"As far as entertainment was concerned Hosea Hill put Thibodaux on the map," said Beatrice. "There was a time when all the big entertainers knew about Thibodaux and Hosea Hill. Today hardly anybody knows about Thibodaux."

CHAPTER TWENTY FOUR
~ Percy Stovall: The Rural Bandit ~

Between 1948 and 1977, the late Percy Stovall was the premier source for live rhythm and blues music in New Orleans and the Deep South. Every important New Orleans R&B musician worked for Stovall at one time or another, as did many national touring artists with hit records that came through the area.

His approach to business was novel but extremely successful. Considered strict —he fined bands for being late, sloppy in appearance, as well as for drinking or smoking on the bandstand—musicians knew that if they wanted to work and make money, they'd better get tied in with Stovall.

Born in New Orleans February 17, 1906, Stovall was an intelligent humorous man of delicate stature with a sharp mind for the entertainment business.

"I started booking musicians to get some extra income," said Stovall in 1982. "At the time [1948] I owned the Pelican Lounge on South Rampart Street. I had Edgar Blanchard's band the Gondoliers working for me. He had Otis Ducker [saxophone] and June Gardner [drums] with him.

"This was the time Paul Gayten and Annie Laurie had big records out ["True" and "Since I Fell For You"]. Larry Darnell too ["For You My Love"]. They needed a band and some places to play outside of New Orleans. I wound up selling the club and started booking these artists into the towns between Houston and Pensacola."

Stovall's stable of artists gradually grew and he began booking Chubby Newsome and Roy Brown.

"Edgar and the group worked for a long time at Don Robey's Bronze Peacock club in Houston," said Stovall. "But the war in Korea started and it took away a lot of musicians. Bookings got slow, so I took the Civil Service exam and got a job in the Post Office. I forgot about booking musicians."

After working at the Post Office for a couple of years, Stovall came home one evening and found Eddie Jones, a. k. a. Guitar Slim, sitting on his porch.

"Slim said he heard about me booking musicians," said Stovall. "I wasn't really that interested at first but he said, 'Stove, you can make as much money in one night booking me as you do in a week now.' After a couple weeks of hearing this every night, I bought his bill of goods. I went back to booking musicians and quit the Post Office."

Stovall played an important role in getting Slim's career off the ground. In the early 1950s Slim hadn't yet cut a successful record so Stovall had to book him into small towns for very little money. However, Slim always sent the audience home raving about his spectacular performances. A month or two later, Stovall would book Slim back at the same club for much more money, knowing people that saw the initial show were still talking about the last engagement and that club owners were listening. In 1952, Stovall arranged a Nashville recording session for the JB label where Slim recorded "Feeling Sad"/"Certainly All," a sizable regional hit.

While booking Guitar Slim, Stovall set up the Continental Booking Agency which began handling other R&B and blues entertainers who wanted to work in the South. By the mid-1950s, Stovall's agency was one of the busiest in the nation, routing bands from Mexico to the Carolinas.

"I had this boy staying with me from Moss Point, Mississippi," said Stovall. "He got the World Almanac out and found the populations of all the towns and cities in the South. We called information in each town and asked the operator for the black taxi company there. Then we called the taxi company and asked them for the name of the biggest black night club in the area. After we found out that information it was easy.

"When somebody wanted to work down here I wouldn't buy them for just one show—I'd buy a dozen. I could always get a good price that way. Most entertainers would jump a the chance to work 12 straight nights. Then I'd get on the phone and call up the joints and tell them, 'Look I've got Jimmy Reed, Little Walter or Big Joe Turner, and this is the price.' I could book a dozen jobs in two hours that way. You might lose money on one or two dates, but by booking 12, you'd always make back your money plus a whole lot more.

"I got to know who and when to book in certain towns. I'd always book blues up in those Mississippi towns like Greenwood, Leland, and Clarksdale around cotton picking time. That's when the people there had money. They liked that lowdown guitar and harmonica so we'd go through there with Little Walter or Jimmy Reed and clean up. I'd also book shows into Georgia when they picked peanuts and peaches, and the Carolinas when they harvested tobacco. When they harvested oranges in Florida, that's where you went."

Stovall also booked several dates for Fats Domino in the early 1950s. After Domino's manager Melvin Cade died in 1952, Domino asked Stovall if he was interested in taking him on full-time. Stovall had to decline because he already had his hands full with Guitar Slim. Later though he would manage New Orleans artists like Ernie K-Doe, Barbara George, Irma Thomas, Eddie Bo, Johnny Adams, and Earl King.

"Stovall was a rural bandit," laughed King, who was booked by Stovall for nearly two decades. "He was the sharpest promoter they ever had around New Orleans. Stovall kept two phones in his house. One phone had a number that he gave out to his friends and to musicians. The other phone had a number he only gave out to club owners and talent agencies. One day Stovall told me, 'Earl you see that phone? Every time it rings it's money. That means it's somebody calling to book someone.'

"He'd book big acts in small towns out in the country with his band and Stovall kept a good band at all times. Usually he had Robert Parker or James Rivers on saxophone and they could play with anybody. After the gig, they'd all come right back to his house at 1731 Third Street.

"Stovall also promoted a lot of gigs himself. For instance he might take a band to a hotel in Pensacola. That would be their home base for a week. Then the band would work all the little towns around there. After the gig, everybody would head back to the hotel.

"I was on the road once with Johnny Adams, Tommy Ridgley, Irma Thomas, and Robert Parker. Stovall was taking a terrible beating. Then on a Tuesday night we got to Florence, South Carolina. We pulled up to building as big as Schwegmann's [a grocery store] in the middle of nowhere. I thought to myself, 'Lord nobody's gonna come out here again tonight,' but once it got dark the cars kept coming and coming.

"Stovall had signals he flashed at the band from the door. If he pointed a flash light at the band or held a lit cigarette lighter up, that meant keep playing and don't take no intermission—he hadn't made enough money at the door and he wanted to keep attracting people from outside. Once he lit his cigar though, he'd made enough money and it was okay to take a break.

"On this particular evening the place was packed. There were as many people outside the place as inside and that hurt Stovall to his heart. The Fire Marshal was there and he wouldn't let anymore people in the building. Stovall took the bass player aside and he said, 'Walter, why don't you sneak some of those winos from the parking lot in here so they can start a fight.' He wanted to clear some of the crowd out of the building so he could sell tickets to the people waiting to get in. He wasn't able to, but Stovall made up enough money to cover those gigs he lost money on."

In New Orleans Stovall booked shows at the Dew Drop Inn, Municipal Auditorium, Lincoln Beach, the I.L.A. Hall, the Harlem Gym and Booker T. Washington High School. He was also the first black promoter in the area to book R&B acts at white college fraternities and C.Y.O dances. However, Stovall's favorite venue was the Blue Eagle on Felicity Street.

"The Blue Eagle wasn't anything but a hole in the wall," laughed Stovall. "But if B.B. King, Bobby Bland, Little Walter or Junior Parker played, there would be line to get in two blocks long."

For local dates, Stovall printed placards advertising the shows, paid for radio spots, and let the touring artists stay at his house. Stovall, who successfully promoted R&B acts this way for nearly three decades admitted though that he did have one problem.

"It was tough drawing a crowd for a female performer. A lot of wives didn't want their husband to go see them because they were jealous. But if Sam Cooke or Bobby Bland were performing somewhere, they wouldn't let up on their husband until they got to go. They wouldn't do that for a woman.."

Stovall did have one exception though and that was Irma Thomas. Stovall booked Thomas all over the South until 1964, when her national hits attracted engagements beyond Stovall's network of contacts.

Throughout the 1960s, Stovall continued to work with New Orleans artists and national hit makers like Joe Simon, Little Johnny Taylor, Solomon Burke, Ike & Tina Turner, Wilson Pickett, Jimmy Hughes, and Joe Tex.

Stovall booked shows until 1977, when cataracts forced him to retire. However, several artists had developed such a strong allegiance with Stovall that they continued to pay him a commission on New Orleans dates long after he shut the doors at the Continental Booking Agency.

Percy Stovall died of natural causes in February of 1984.

CHAPTER TWENTY FIVE
~ The Popeye: Strong to the Finish ~

A dance inspired by the legendary spinach chomping, fist-swinging, Olive Oil protecting cartoon character, the Popeye was New Orleans' answer to the Twist. Not only was the Popeye the rage at most of the city's sock hops and fraternity parties in 1962, it also inspired a rash of Popeye-related singles.

The Popeye was a shuffle-like dance that included several of the mannerisms the cartoon character had including, putting one hand over your forehead, bending forward, flexing your biceps, putting one hand on your shoulder and the other behind your back.

"It was the local black kids that started doing the Popeye first," said Deacon John Moore, who played guitar on a couple of Popeye records. "Then the college kids picked up on it and it got real popular with them. After awhile, the black kids started doing the Slop and the Pony, but the white kids kept doing the Popeye."

The record that sparked the Popeye craze was Chris Kenner's "Something You Got" released on Instant Records in the fall of 1961.

"'Something You Got' was a big record in New Orleans," recalled the late Joe Banashak, who headed up Instant. "I couldn't figure out why, because I couldn't even give the record away in Baton Rouge. I asked K-Doe and Benny Spellman why the record was selling? They said, 'Don't you know man? The kids are learning the Popeye to 'Something You Got.' I'll tell you how dances affect the record business. We sold 30,000 'Something You Got' singles off the Popeye just in New Orleans."

Two other popular early Popeye songs were Barbara George's "I Know," and the Hollywood Argyles "Alley-Opp." However, until early 1962, there wasn't an actual record on the market that had the word "Popeye" in the title.

The first song to use the cartoon sailor's name was "Pop-Eye," issued on Ace, and credited to Huey Smith and His Clowns. The label on the single claimed Huey Smith and the Clowns were "The Originators of the Popeye Dance." Of course they weren't, but the record certainly had the Popeye beat down pat. According to Ace president, the late Johnny Vincent, it was his idea to cut a Popeye record just as the dance was taking off.

"I had an unfinished track on Huey that I really liked," said Vincent.

"I'd seen this dance that the kids were doing and it was really taking off. I wanted to get a record out that told people how to do the Popeye. I got Huey's track out and brought two brothers from Jackson in the studio, Cliff and Ed Thomas, to overdub vocals. I really put the song together, but I put Huey's name on it because I felt that was the right thing to do."

"I'd left Ace and was recording for Dave Bartholomew at Imperial," said Smith. "One day I was at the studio and ran into Gerri Hall and Jesse Thomas [members of the Clowns]. They told me they were going to finish a track I'd recorded back when I was still with Ace. I didn't know it was a Popeye record. When it came out with my name on it, somebody went to Dave and said I was working for Johnny again. Dave got mad and said I broke my contract. I didn't, but he never recorded me again. 'Pop-Eye' turned into a pretty big hit though and I toured quite a bit off of it."

Vincent claimed he flew to New York and struck a deal with King's Features, who syndicated the Popeye cartoon, and paid them $420 for the exclusive rights to use the name Popeye on the single.

Another early Popeye record was Eddie Bo's vibrant "Check Mr. Popeye" which appeared on Ric. Bo's label mate, the late Tommy Ridgley, recalled being in the studio when Bo came up with an idea for a Popeye record.

"Eddie said, 'I got this idea for a dance and I want to see what you think.' So he ran it down about putting your right hand behind your back and your left behind your head. Well the record came out [with Bo's wife credited as composer] and it was a hit from day one. Every radio station in New Orleans played it. We did a show at Lincoln Beach and Eddie had a Popeye line longer than your eyes could see. The next thing you know, everybody had a Popeye record out."

Several New Orleans-based labels had Popeye singles out early in 1962. Minit had Ernie K-Doe's "Popeye Joe," Imperial had Wardell and the Sultans's instrumental, "The Original Popeye"; AFO/Sue had the Senors' "Searchin' For Olive Oil," and Ace tried again with Scotty McKay's "Olive Learned To Popeye." Other local Popeye related records included Blazer Boy's Imperial release, "New Orleans Twist" and Chris Kenner's fabulous Instant hit "Land of 1,000 Dances."

The Popeye dance craze caused enough of a stir in New Orleans to warrant a story in *Billboard*, "N.O. Twist Gives Way To Popeye Muscles."

"It was the Popeye, head and shoulders over the Twist here last week, as a new dance craze hit town just prior to the city's Mardi Gras," reported the magazine. "The record that was the big breakout was, 'Pop-Eye' by Huey Smith and the Clowns on Ace, though New Orleans radio stations were playing at least two other Popeye versions which were destined to be in the hands of retailers in a matter of days or even hours. Stores through-out town were getting calls for 'Check Mr. Popeye' by Eddy Bo on the Ric label and 'Popeye Joe' by Ernie K-Doe. Since the stores had Huey Smith's 'Pop-Eye,' they were selling it in no uncertain terms as youngster were dancing the Popeye."

As the Popeye got more popular in New Orleans, it spread to other cities. In Philadelphia, Chubby Checker cut "Popeye the Hitchhiker" on Parkway and the Sherrys had "Pop Pop Pop-pie" on Guyden. In Memphis, The Mar-Keys waxed "The Popeye Stroll" on Stax and Earl Forrest (with James Booker on organ) had "The Beale Street Popeye" on Duke. In New York Leroy Anderson covered Eddie Bo's "Check Mr. Popeye" on Hit. Solomon Burke's "Down In the Valley" on Atlantic also became a popu-lar Popeye record.

Closer to New Orleans, Baton Rouge's Tabby Thomas countered with "The Popeye Train" on Excello, while Lake Charles' Cookie and the Cupcakes cut the rocking, "Mary Lou Doing the Popeye."

However, most of the non-New Orleans Popeye records didn't have the lazy back beat that inspired dancers in the Crescent City. Eventually, it was Huey Smith's "Pop-Eye" that sold the most Popeye singles and it reached number 51 in *Billboard's* Hot 100. Eddie Bo's "Check Mr. Popeye" sold well, but it may have been hamstrung by King's Features which weren't offered a piece of the record. Most of the other Popeye sin-gles did quite well in New Orleans.

"A lot of record companies thought the Popeye was going make them rich and become as big as the Twist," said Moore. "They sunk a lot of money into making and promoting Popeye records. But the Northern kids couldn't relate to that extra syncopated New Orleans beat, so the Popeye never really left the city. Eventually people forgot about the Popeye and started doing other dances."

Part IV

The Record Labels

The success that out-of-town record companies—Deluxe, Imperial, Aladdin, Specialty, Mercury, Ember, Chess and Atlantic—had exploiting New Orleans rhythm and blues during the 1950s eventually spawned a plethora of local labels. Since the music industry was then fueled by the sales of singles, anyone with the dream of cutting a hit record and a few hundred dollars in venture capital could immediately get into the record business. By the early 1960s, the city was teaming with competitive, hustling New Orleanians looking to make their fortune in the record business.

Some of these small label owners including, Al Scramuzza, Connie LaRocca, Lionel Worthy and Larry McKinley, got into the business as sideline to their primary enterprises—seafood retailing, a restaurant, repairing cars and radio broadcasting. Many labels were also extensions of record wholesalers—Ace, Minit, Instant, Watch— record stores— Wonder, Cinderella, Wurley Burley—or nightclubs—Dew Drop and Rip. Some labels were run by experienced record men. Ex-Specialty producer founded AFO, one time Imperial producer Dave Bartholomew ran Broadmoor and Trumpet, while studio owner Cosimo Matassa was involved in several labels including Rex, White Cliffs and Dover. Several musicians also took matters into their own hands. Willie Tee formed Gator, Earl King had Kansu and King Walk, Frankie Ford co-owned Spinnet, Red Tyler had a hand in AFO and Par-Lo, while Eddie Bo made several records on Bo-Sound.

Unfortunately for many New Orleans labels, they came along at a time when British rock music, as well as Motown and Memphis soul was beginning to dominate the airwaves. Still dozens of local entrepreneurs were ready to throw the dice. Many New Orleans labels lost the gamble however and disappeared quickly with only scant local success and a handful of singles. While regional success could sustain a label—at least until the dry spell which inevitably happened—the goal of the New Orleans record label owners was obviously to secure a national hit. Some like Minit, Instant, NOLA, Par-Lo and AFO did, but that didn't necessarily secure success. In fact in the case of Par-Lo, AFO and NOLA it lead to disaster.

To reach the national market, New Orleans labels had two choices. They could lease their records or productions to major companies in New York, Philadelphia, Chicago or Los Angeles—some which occasionally were lazy and/or dishonest. The other alternative was to rely on a fragmented network of regional distributors—many who weren't always inclined to pay their suppliers for the records they sold. Either way they were at a disadvantage.

By 1970, New Orleans' record men and women began to see that their industry was sputtering. However, the decline of Independent record labels was an industry-wide trend. As major labels got more involved in recording jazz, soul, country and R&B, the smaller labels who cultivated regional styles of music found it nearly impossible to be successful at any level. This trend would eventually signal the death of regional styles of R&B (as well as other genres) as the majors would develop a homogenized and predictable style of black music. At the time, New Orleans could support only one major independent distribution company, All South, but it couldn't have stayed afloat as long as it did had it not also carried major independent labels like Motown, Chess, Duke, Atlantic and select lines the major labels offered them. Of the few New Orleans labels left to fight the struggle, Sansu, Soulin' and Hep' Me saw that the only way to stay afloat was to lease material to major labels. But that only sustained them temporarily. By the end of the decade, not only had public's taste in music continued to change (by then most listeners referred to New Orleans R&B as "oldies") but New Orleans radio abandoned the genre once the local labels could no longer meet the escalating monetary demands program directors and deejays demanded. Instead they embraced music released by major labels with deeper promotional pockets.

Ironically, by the early 1980s, the time when renaissance of New Orleans music had begun, almost none of the old line players were left standing. All South folded and the remaining New Orleans labels releasing R&B music had closed their doors. New Orleans-based Black Top and Orleans came along to take advantage of the trend towards LPs and later CDs, but for the most part, the destiny on the New Orleans recording industry was back in the hands of the majors and out-of-town record labels.

Regardless of their success or lack of success, these feisty local labels—close to 200—helped to create, shape and nurture the New Orleans sound that would eventually reverberate around the world. The abundance of New Orleans rhythm and blues, soul and rock and roll CD reissues currently available are evidence of that.

CHAPTER TWENTY SIX
~ Lew Chudd: Imperial Records ~

One of the unsung pioneers of New Orleans rhythm and blues was the late Lew Chudd, the founder of Imperial Records. Although his label was based in California, it would launch the careers of numerous New Orleans artists, as Chudd was one of the first to promote and commercialize the city's sound nationally.

Lewis R. Chudd was born in New York on July 1, 1912. Tall and slender, he played minor league baseball in the St. Louis Cardinals farm system. (In the 1950s, he told several people that one day he intended to buy the New York Yankees.) He was later an NBC radio executive, and during WW II he served in the Office of War Information.

After his discharge in 1945, Chudd founded Crown Records. After less than 12 months, he sold the company to Irving Feld, who later managed Madison Square Gardens. The following year, Chudd moved to California and formed a new label, Imperial with a $10,000 investment. After just one year of operation, Imperial grossed a not too shabby $90,000.

"Lew was a smart, hard-nosed business man," stressed Cosimo Matassa, who engineered and recorded all of Chudd's New Orleans sessions. "He didn't compete with the majors. He found his own niche in the marketplace and exploited it."

"He started out recording Spanish versions of popular American hits. That's why he named his company Imperial. His largest market was in California's Imperial Valley where a lot of Latinos live. Later he got into black music. The majors weren't recording or promoting it and he saw that there was a market for jazz and rhythm and blues records."

"Lew was the kind of guy who would have been successful in any kind of business," added Eddie Ray, who worked for Chudd as a marketing man for eight years. "He would have been successful selling hardware, but it just so happened he was in the record business. He didn't make too many creative decisions—he pretty much left that up to Dave Bartholomew."

In 1947, Chudd began recording several West Coast jazz and swing bands, but by then those styles of music were waning in popularity. Imperial wouldn't make significant inroads into black music until two years later when Chudd introduced himself to bandleader Dave

Bartholomew while on the road promoting records.

"I was working at a club in Houston, the Bronze Peacock, when this guy comes in and introduces himself as Lew Chudd from Imperial Records," recalled Bartholomew. "He was in Texas selling records to Mexicans. He told me he was interested in selling rhythm and blues records, and that he was going to be in New Orleans in a couple of weeks. I forgot about him, but one day he showed up at my door and we drew up the papers. If you were in a room with Lew, you wouldn't pay much attention to him. He was the kind of guy that sat in the corner and took notes while you were playing. Afterwards, he'd come up to you with his notebook and ask you about your material."

Chudd and Bartholomew's initial collaboration was Jewel King's "3 X 7 = 21" and Tommy Ridgley's "Shrewesbury Blues." Both did well in New Orleans, but it was the signing of Fats Domino that put Imperial in the national spotlight.

One evening in November or December of 1949, Chudd, Bartholomew, and Al Young (who sold Imperial discs at the Bop Shop on South Rampart Street) took a taxi to the Hide Away Inn to hear the young piano player the public was raving about. Young and Chudd—both white men—had to lay on the floor of the taxi during the ride to avoid being seen by the police, who might well arrest the men for mixing with blacks.

"The first time I heard Fats it knocked me out," recalled Chudd in a 1957 *Cash Box* article. "The club was packed and noisy. But the noise changed to a mountain of hand clapping. If ever there was a singer who reached to listeners' sense of rhythm it was Fats."

Chudd got Domino's signature on an Imperial contract and a few days later the 21-year-old boogie woogie pianist entered the J&M Studio to record "The Fat Man." A landmark recording, "The Fat Man" would sell over one million singles and expose New Orleans' rhythm and blues style to the rest of the country. It also marked the beginning of an awesome run for Imperial which became one of the most successful rhythm and blues labels of the 1950s.

As good as many Imperial discs were, Chudd worked his product hard. His 12 to 16 hour days consisted of calling an extended network of salesmen, distributors, deejays, radio programmers and jukebox operators. He also looked after pressing records, placing ads in the trade magazines, booking studio time, paying bills, shipping orders and running four publishing companies. Like all successful independent record entrepreneurs of the era, he also spent a great deal of time on the road hustling records and keeping an eye out for talent.

"You never get a second chance at the record buyer," Chudd told

Cash Box. "The record must be in the store when the buyer wants it, and not next week. With the amount of merchandise in record shops today, the buyer can easily settle for a second or third choice if the first is not available."

In talking with disc jockeys and regional distributors, Chudd would find out what local records were hot. Often he would attempt to lease regional hits from smaller labels if he thought he could profit from the transaction. Matassa recalled Chudd especially enjoyed telling the story of how he once purchased a master to a square dance record for $50 and sold 100,000 copies of it on Imperial in just four months. When Chudd couldn't buy or lease a master, he sometimes got one of his artists to cover the song he'd been after and have the Imperial version in the marketplace in a matter of days, thus cutting into the original's sales and adding to Imperial's coffers.

Chudd gave Bartholomew a free rein to pursue and sign talent, and he also sent West Coast artists T-Bone Walker and Pee Wee Crayton to New Orleans to record. Domino of course became Imperial's cornerstone, but in the early 1950s the label also signed New Orleans artists like Smiley Lewis, The Spiders, Billy Tate, Archibald, Little Sonny Jones, The Hawks, Jesse Allen, as well as Bobby Mitchell and the Toppers.

Perhaps Chudd's only less than shrewd move was to alienate Bartholomew in 1951. In a squabble over a bonus, Bartholomew left Imperial and began recording and producing sessions for Decca, King, Aladdin and Specialty. As a result, there was a marked drop in the quality of Imperial's New Orleans releases and sales began to plummet. It wasn't until Chudd heard Bartholomew's superlative arrangement of Lloyd Price's 1952 Specialty debut, "Lawdy Miss Clawdy," that he realized he'd taken Batholomew's contributions for granted. Shortly after Chudd heard Price's hit, he flew to New Orleans and patched up his rift with Bartholomew. They negotiated a new contract and together they ensured Imperial's continued success.

Chudd proved to be one of the most innovative and intelligent record men of his era. To get more of his material programmed on the radio and jukeboxes, as well as exercise his publishing catalog, he formed the subsidiary labels Bayou, Post, Knight, and Colony. He also contacted motion picture companies and got his material included in several films. Imperial was also one of the first labels to print color picture sleeves on 45s and issue EPs—extended play four-song 45 rpms. The label was also one of the first independents to get into the expanding album market.

"Lew Chudd could sell more records than anybody else in the world if he wanted to," claimed Bartholomew.

Nevertheless, Chudd also had an abrasive side according to Cosimo Matassa:

"Back then [the mid 1950s] I charged $15 an hour. That included studio tape and my time. I used to get letters from Chudd complaining that I charged too much, but I was just barely getting by. Lew Chudd wasn't exactly famous for helping anybody either. When Lew was hot, he strong-armed distributors into taking more records than they really needed. That eventually alienated them. Later when Imperial wasn't doing so well, the distributors turned on him. They wouldn't take a chance on his records when they might have been able to help him and make a sale."

As much as Chudd relied on Bartholomew's expertise and artistic choices—Bartholomew became a vice-president with the company in the mid-1950s—they still didn't see always see eye-to-eye.

"Lew used to make Dave mad as hell sometimes," continued Matassa. "Sometimes he'd issue the wrong take that Dave sent or promote the wrong song. Lew left most of the musical decisions up to Dave, but there were some artists Dave believed in that Lew rejected."

As the decade progressed, Chudd continued to diversify his label by signing country favorite Slim Whitman, as well as teen idol, Ricky Nelson. Both artists would become Imperial best sellers. By 1957, Imperial was grossing $7,000,000 a year, keeping seven pressing plants busy, and had opened a New York office. On the New Orleans front, Bartholomew signed Roy Brown, James "Sugar Boy" Crawford, Al Reed, and Chris Kenner, who accounted for national and local best sellers .

However, at the end of the decade, Domino and Bobby Charles were the only New Orleans artists left on Imperial, as Chudd purged his R&B roster and began concentrating on the pop market. In 1960, Chudd became partners in Minit Records, a label formed by Joe Banashak who distributed Imperial in New Orleans through his company A-1. Chudd got Minit releases into his national network of regional distributors and the label flourished. By the end of year, Minit had supplanted Imperial as New Orleans' hottest record company, spinning out hits by Ernie K-Doe, Jessie Hill, Aaron Neville, and Benny Spellman. Chudd enjoyed the profits from wholesaling Minit's releases, but he was perturbed by Imperial's slide in the marketplace, and more than slightly jealous of Banashak's good fortune.

Minit's success rekindled Chudd's commitment to New Orleans. Under Bartholomew's supervision, Earl King, Snooks "Ford" Eaglin, Berna Dean Washington, Wardell and the Sultans, Frankie Ford, Al Robinson, Shirley and Lee, Robert Parker, and Huey Smith were then signed to Imperial. In addition, Bobby Mitchell and Smiley Lewis cut new material. Chudd also purchased the Aladdin catalog, an important early source of New Orleans rhythm and blues. However, of his New Orleans artists, only the dependable Fats Domino was still a consistent hit maker, but even his appeal was steadily eroding.

By 1963, the ever astute Chudd sensed a growing change in the record business. Imperial's sales were steadily plummeting, as the major labels were steadily squeezing the independent labels out of the marketplace. Once Domino and Nelson were lured away by larger labels, Chudd realized it was time to cash in his chips. Without warning, he sold all his labels to Liberty Records.

"I had no inclination Lew was going to sell out," said Bartholomew. "He just called one day and said, 'Dave, box up all the tapes and ship them to California. I just sold the label.' I thought he was premature, but what could I do? It was his label. I can't really complain. I think Lew was honest and I was paid in full."

Imperial's departure from New Orleans precipitated a rapid downturn in the city's music industry. While several other factors came into play— certainly the changing tastes in popular music—the city wouldn't recover from the shock for over two decades

Chudd took his profits from the sale of his music holdings and purchased several radio stations on the West Coast. He lived out his life in comfort and died of heart failure at Los Angeles June, 15, 1998.

CHAPTER TWENTY SEVEN
~ Ric & Ron Records: Records With Class ~

Between 1958 and 1962, the Ric and Ron labels were an important force in New Orleans rhythm and blues. Together they provided Johnny Adams, Irma Thomas, Martha Carter, Robert Parker,Warren Lee, and Al Johnson their first opportunity to record. They also extend the careers of Eddie Bo, Bobby Mitchell, Tommy Ridgley, and Professor Longhair.

The punchy Ric and Ron sound was unique, even when compared to Minit, Instant, Ace, Frisco, and Imperial, labels active in New Orleans during that same period. This was due largely to the ambitious owner Joe Ruffino, whose aspiration was to create a label different from the competition.

Joseph Ruffino was born in New Orleans in 1922 and raised in the French Quarter on the 600 block of St. Philip Street. Ruffino's father owned a bakery that catered to other Italian immigrants in the immediate neighborhood. Eventually the business was expanded to include a bar, restaurant and parking lot.

After Ruffino returned from WW II, he worked in all of the family businesses and collected insurance payments. By the mid-1950s, the entrepreneurial Ruffino opened a theater and a popular record shop near the corner of St. Philip and North Rampart Street. Through the record shop he met Johnny Vincent, who owned the Ace label and ran Record Sales, a distribution company located on St. Charles Avenue. Vincent saw that Ruffino was a hustler and hired him as a salesman. However, once Ruffino started working at Record Sales, he realized that the real money in the record business wasn't in retailing or wholesaling— it was in manufacturing. In 1958, Ruffino took the next step and formed his own label, Ric, named after his oldest son.

Ruffino went into the business with Vincent's blessings who went as far as supplying masters by Edgar Blanchard and Mercy Baby for Ric's initial releases. However, Ruffino was interested in developing a label with it's own identity, so he began recruiting New Orleans artists with a unique style. Ruffino put his early sessions in the hands of arranger Edgar Blanchard and enlisted songwriter Dorothy La Bostrie, the composer of Johnny Adam's "I Won't Cry," and Irma Thomas "Don't Mess With My Man."

The initial batch of Ric 45s and 78s were well received in New

Orleans. The original Ric singles were issued on drab blue and white labels, but later Ric releases were redesigned in an eye-catching yellow, black and white.

In early 1959, Ruffino formed Ron Records named after another son. Initially Ron was an outlet for masters Ruffino leased or purchased from other labels or producers, but that changed when he began signing more and more local talent. Early Ron artists included Professor Longhair, Robert Parker, Irma Thomas, Chris Kenner, and Eddie Lang. Along with Al Johnson, Tommy Ridgley, Johnny Adams, and Eddie Bo on Ric, by 1960 Ruffino had a very impressive roster of New Orleans talent divided between his two labels.

Initially Ric and Ron operated out of Ruffino's Lakewood Street home. Later the business briefly moved into the back room of One Stop Records on South Rampart, before finally relocating to 630 1/2 Baronne Street, then in the heart of New Orleans record row. Besides the standard methods of promoting records, Ruffino had a novel, semi-legitimate way of pushing records locally. Occasionally he would include the name of an important deejay in the writer credits on a new release, thus assuring it would get air play on at least one New Orleans station.

Ruffino's first brush with success outside New Orleans was with Adams' debut, "I Won't Cry," which broke in the Southeast and was leased to Ember for national distribution. Next came Thomas' debut, "Don't Mess With My Man" which entered the R&B charts in the spring of 1960. However, most of Ric and Ron's releases—including Lenny Capello's "Cotton Candy," Ridgley's "Is It True,' Longhair's "Go To The Mardi Gras," Bo's "Tell It Like It Is," and Johnson's "Carnival Time"— were strictly local bestsellers.

Ruffino's best shot at a big national hit occurred in the fall of 1960 with Joe Jones' "You Talk Too Much." Jones was a veteran New Orleans' bandleader who had previously recorded for Flame, Capital, and Roulette. "You Talk Too Much" was written by Reggie Hall for his brother-in-law Fats Domino, but Domino wasn't interested in the song. It was then passed on to Jones who recorded it twice—initially for Roulette in 1958 and later for Ric. Roulette never issued their version but the Ric rendition, recorded in June of 1960, took off immediately.

Once Jones' Ric single started climbing the pop charts, Roulette sued Ruffino over the publishing and ownership of the master of "You Talk Too Much." A federal judge temporary halted the sale of the record, (In the interim, Frankie Ford covered the tune for Imperial) but eventually Ruffino was forced to settle with Roulette in order to avoid a costly legal battle. Losing "You Talk Too Much" took it's toll on Ruffino and made him a bitter man according to those around him. Denied the chance of establishing his label as a national hit maker, Ruffino retaliated by having Martha Nelson (a. k. a. Martha Carter) cut "I Don't Talk Too Much," but it remained a local novelty.

By 1961, Ric's roster was trimmed down to three artists: Eddie Bo, Johnny Adams, and Tommy Ridgley. Ron, however, exercised more on a revolving door policy as Warren Lee, Bobby Mitchell, and the Party Boys had releases. Ruffino also started the short-lived Vibra and Soundex labels, the later which had local success with Ronnie Barron's "The Hip Parade" and Warren Lee's "Anna (Stay With Me)."

Blanchard's dated arrangements had given way to those by Harold Battiste, Eddie Bo and Mac Rebennack, younger musicians with an ear for changing trends in music. Ric had tremendous local hits with Bo's "Check Mr. Popeye," and "Every Dog Got A Day," as well as Ridgley's "In The Same Old Way" and "My Ordinary Girl." However, it was Adams' "Losing Battle" that sold the most singles for Ruffino, reaching reaching number 27 in the R&B charts in the spring of 1962.

Not long after, Ruffino suffered a heart attack, an event which slowed Ric and Ron's ambitious release schedule. Unfortunately, he returned to work before completely recovering and succumbed to a second coronary late in 1962, effectively shutting down the labels. Two Johnny Adams singles appeared on Ric in 1964 and 1965, but they were left over masters Ruffino's brother-in-law Joe Assunto released and sold out of his One Stop Record Shop.

Ric and Ron folded with a combined total of 70 singles and one album. While Robert Parker, Irma Thomas, Eddie Bo, Professor Longhair, Tommy Ridgley, and Johnny Adams went on to record for other labels, and achieved the international success Ruffino feverishly sought, in retrospect, only a few surpassed the mastery and imagination of their Ric and Ron sides.

"Those records [Ric and Ron] were professional by anyone's standards,' emphasized the late Tommy Ridgley. "Ruffino was stubborn and had his own ways of doing things, but he could recognize talent when he saw it. He never cut corners in the studio like a lot of other guys, and he worked his tail off when your record came out. It was a small company but it was very professional. All of our records were great."

CHAPTER TWENTY EIGHT
~ AFO: All For One ~

Besides being one of the labels which broke up the monopoly out-of-town companies had on New Orleans talent, AFO (All For One) was after Motown, one of the first exclusively black owned record labels and publishing companies in America.

AFO, and the At Last Publishing Company, was headed up by ex-Specialty producer and arranger, Harold Battiste. The corporation executives included Alvin "Red" Tyler, Melvin Lastie, Roy Montrell, Chuck Badie and John Boudreaux, all veteran New Orleans jazz and rhythm and blues musicians. Together they pooled their limited resources and opened an office at 712 North Clairborne Avenue.

The July 10, 1961 issue of *The Louisiana Weekly* announced the launch of AFO. In the story they reported:

"'Negroes create and write the music,' the AFO officers said. 'Negroes sing and perform, but never reap the financial benefits of the industry. We have been thinking about this venture for quite some time, and have finally gone into business.'"

AFO's initial releases were by Lawrence Nelson, a .k. a. Prince La La, and Barbara George. Both artists were brought to AFO by Jessie Hill. They completed a split session. La-La accounted for "She Put The Hurt On Me," George recorded "I Know."

Based on the spiritual, "Just A Closer Walk With Thee," "I Know" featured what would become a most influential trumpet solo by Melvin Lastie, an oddity at the time because most New Orleans R&B records up to that point had piano or saxophone solos. Around this time, Battiste was approached by Sue Records, a New York-based label owned by a black executive, Juggy Murray.

"It seemed like a perfect match for us," said Battiste. "We were a black company and now we had a black guy handling our national distribution. I thought we'd completed the circle. At first Juggy was, 'Brother this and brother that.' That's what we wanted to hear. Then 'I Know' took off and everything looked great. I didn't know Juggy had alliterative motives."

"I Know" soared to number three in the pop charts, after La-La's record climbed to a respectable number 28 in the R&B charts. George's second single, "You Talk About Love", topped out at number 46 in the pop charts and it seemed that AFO was on the way to success in a big way. Sadly they would soon have the rug pulled from underneath them by their Big Apple benefactor, Juggy Murray

After distributing six AFO singles nationally, Sue terminated their agreement with AFO, on the pretext that without Murray's authorization, Battiste and the AFO Combo played on the Lee Dorsey's Fury session which produced the hit, "Ya Ya." However, what Murray really was after was Barbara George and he eventually convinced her to buy out her AFO contract and sign directly with Sue. Once she did her career floundered and supposedly wound up in St. Gabriel penitentiary on an armed robbery rap.

"There wasn't anything we could do then," said Battiste. "We weren't in the position to fight fur coats and new Cadillacs."

AFO persevered though, as Battiste set about producing some great local recordings. Battiste would discover lots of new talent including Willie Tee, Tami Lynn, Oliver "Nookie Boy" Morgan, Wallace Johnson, Shirley Raymond and the Blenders. Another of his discoveries Jimmy "Pistol" Jules had an a great AFO produced single, "Talk About You"/ "Take It Like It Is," leased to Atlantic. The much traveled Eddie Bo had a couple of great singles on At Last, the best being "Tee Na Na Na Na Na Nay." So did Mac Rebennack and Ronnie Barron (as Drits and Dravey), who recorded, "Talk That Talk"/"My Key Don't Fit."

Since all of the AFO executives had a background in jazz, naturally they recorded it in the studio. The AFO Combo recorded an album, *A Compendium*, featuring vocalist Tami Lynn, and *Monkey Puzzle*, which featured Ellis Marsalis on piano. However, without a national hit, and only sporadic local sales, AFO had a hard time staying afloat and collapsed in 1963.

Almost all of the AFO executives immediately headed West and began working with Sam Cooke at SAR Records. Most had returned though by the time Cooke died in 1964. However, Battiste stayed and would strike gold when he produced Sonny and Cher's, "I Got You Babe."

Battiste finally returned home in 1992, accepting a teaching position at the University of New Orleans. Soon after he reactivated AFO, supervising new jazz recordings and getting a lot of his original AFO masters reissued.

CHAPTER TWENTY NINE
~ Connie LaRocca: Frisco Records ~

Frisco Records was one of dozens of small New Orleans labels in the early 1960s hoping to record the next million-seller like "Mother-In-Law," "I Like It Like That" or "I Know." Owned by WYLD disc jockey Hal Atkins, and the energetic, and entrepreneurial Connie (Sculco) LaRocca, they nearly did.

"I was born in San Francisco," recalled LaRocca. "That's how I named the company. In fact the original label had a drawing of the Golden Gate Bridge on it. I came to New Orleans at Mardi Gras in 1947 and I met my husband Pete. We got married the following December.

"I didn't really like New Orleans at first. I had a good job working in San Francisco as a teletypist for Standard Oil. I didn't like roaches or hot weather, and I'd never experienced segregation before. I'd always go home every summer in order to keep my sanity. My first job in New Orleans was dress buyer for D.H. Holmes. I made $25 a week. That was considered good money here then but in California that was nothing."

LaRocca's husband owned and managed Jim's Fried Chicken on South Carrollton Avenue. LaRocca eventually joined her husband at the popular family owned restaurant that was open 24 hours a day.

"I was a cook, a waitress, a cashier, a dish washer—whatever was needed," said LaRocca. "It was a pretty stressful job. People yelled at you and you had to run around with a smile on your face all day. To unwind, I'd go listen to music a couple nights a week. I'd put the kids to bed [three boys] and leave them with my husband and go out with my girl friend from Ireland. We often went to the Safari on Chef Menteur Highway. We loved rock and roll and rhythm and blues. To me that was really exciting music."

"I always told my husband where I was going and we never had any problems because we trusted each other. My girlfriend who was single would dance but I never would. I didn't want people talking about me. Besides, I just enjoyed sitting and listening to the music. I'd stay out until midnight, but be back at the restaurant the next day at 7:00 a.m."

From frequenting the Safari, as well as clubs like the Sabu and the Court of the Two Sisters, LaRocca got to know Tommy Ridgley, Clarence Henry, Danny White, and Irma Thomas. She wanted to get into the music business and Ridgley encouraged her to start a booking agency so he could more readily be hired to play the better paying white dances. LaRocca eventually rented an office at 1140 North Claiborne and started booking Ridgley and other local bands in the afternoon after she left the restaurant.

"I called my office Park Avenue because back then Claiborne had oak trees on the neutral ground," said LaRocca. "The place became a popular hang out for musicians and bands started rehearsing there."

Through the booking agency, LaRocca became acquainted with WYLD disc jockey Harold Atkins. Atkins, who in addition to his on-air duties was also a performer and well connected in the entertainment business. He helped LaRocca book national acts like Solomon Burke and Big Al Sears into Municipal Auditorium. He also harbored aspirations of being involved in owning a record label. Together Atkins and LaRocca started Frisco Records in June 1962. Atkins scheduled sessions and took care of the promotion of new releases. LaRocca manned the phone and made sure distributor orders were filled.

"It was a man's world back then and a lot of people resented a woman being in the record business," said LaRocca. "There where a lot of doors closed to me that would have been open if I were a man. But Harold helped me and he knew everybody in the business. When we went to New York on business, he knew all the key disc jockeys to visit and a lot of the stars—people like Della Reese and Nancy Wilson."

Frisco got started by leasing two masters from Rip Roberts' Rip label—"Stubborn Old Me" and "Big Ben" by Atkins, as well as Deacon John's "Preacher Man" and "When I'm With You." (The Deacon John sides were never issued.) Atkins' master was issued under the alias Al Adams, as not to jeopardize his position at WYLD. "Stubborn Old Me" (penned by Earl King) did well locally so LaRocca and Atkins decided to cut their own follow up.

"Going to Cosimo's Studio and watching the sessions was really exciting," said Larocca. "Everything was done really professionally. I didn't pick the musicians, Harold did that. He'd get Porky Jones or Wardell Quezerque to arrange the sessions. We always used the best musicians when we did our records."

Clearly Frisco did use great New Orleans musicians as Art Neville, Clarence Ford, Mac Rebennack and Nat Perrillat among others played on their sessions.

Adams' second release didn't show much promise, nor did a Porky Jones instrumental coupling. However, Frisco's fourth release, Danny White's "Kiss Tomorrow Goodbye" provided the label with its first hit.

"I got to know Danny at the Safari," said LaRocca. "He was a fabulous entertainer. He was probably the most popular entertainer in town even though he didn't have a record out. I approached him about recording and one day he came by Park Avenue to listen to material. Al Reed had wrote "Kiss Tomorrow Goodbye" which Danny liked and we recorded it."

Atkins played the demo on WYLD and the exceptional ballad became an immediate hit in New Orleans. It would go on to sell 100,000 singles.

"All South Records was our distributor here," said LaRocca. "'Kiss Tomorrow Goodbye' got so big we couldn't keep up with the orders. Finally, I leased it to Arleen Records out of Philadelphia. They promised to do big things with it, but I don't think they promoted it very much. They just coasted on our hard work. Everybody thought we made big money on that record, but after we paid all the bills, in the end we just barely broke even."

"'Kiss Tomorrow Goodbye' might well have even done better if the invasion of British rock music hadn't come along. I didn't realize it at the time, but the Beatles were killing the labels like mine that made rhythm and blues, and rock and roll records."

The next batch of Frisco releases by Willie West, the Rouzan Sisters and White boasted fine production, but their popularity was limited to New Orleans. Frisco wouldn't reach the bright lights again until White's unforgettable fourth single, "Loan Me Your Handkerchief," (another Earl King composition) that came out in the summer of 1963.

"'Loan Me Your Handkerchief' got real big, so Harold and I went up to New York to talk to the people at ABC-Paramount," said LaRocca. "They painted a nice picture and we leased them the single, we made a deal where we'd produce Danny's records and they'd put them out. Like Arleen though I don't think they did much in the way of promotion."

In 1964, Atkins left New Orleans and took a job at WDIA in Memphis. At that point, White's sessions were moved to the Stax Studio where he was produced by Isaac Hayes and David Porter. White cut some great records in Memphis, but never had another hit.

Frisco's last hurrah was provided by the Rouzan Sisters, whose timely "Man of War" was number one in 1965 on WNOE for three weeks. However, a year later LaRocca decided to pull the plug on Frisco after Atkins died unexpectedly.

LaRocca stored all of her files and master tapes in a closet where they remained for over three decades. She went back to work at Jim's and only occasionally thought about the record business. In the early 1970s, she got Earl King to see if he could lease the masters to an interested label but he had no luck. However, by the mid-1990s, LaRocca started getting inquires about reissuing the Frisco tapes and in 1998 the first volume of *The Frisco*

Records Story was issued on the British Ace label.

"I'm glad it finally came out," said LaRocca. "I just feel bad that it didn't come out before Danny died [January 1996] because he begged me to get somebody to put his stuff out. Danny would have loved to have seen it."

CHAPTER THIRTY
~ Scram Records: Seafood Platters ~

One of the more colorful individuals to get involved in the local record business was Al Scramuzza who started the Scram and Power labels. A successful Italian-American businessman, Scramuzza owned the popular Seafood City store, once a North Broad Street landmark. He entered the record business in 1962, bringing with him the same energy and enthusiasm he had for the seafood business.

"The record business was really a pet thing for me," recalled Scramuzza in 1983. "At first I didn't know anything about making records, but I used to sponsor Poppa Stoppa's show on WJMR. So by being around deejays, I got interested in the record business. Since I came up playing music, I was curious about recording it. I got to listen to a lot of records around the stations and I got to know what the deejays would play. I picked up a few good tunes and a some people asked me if I'd produce them. Finally I said, 'Okay, lets try and cut something.' We bought studio time at Cosimo's when we could get it cheap. Later we used Traci Borges' studio in Metairie and we did some sessions in Ruston, Louisiana.

In addition to starting Scram, Scramuzza also set up the Uzza Publishing Company. Scram's initial release was Ritchie Matta's "Time Out," an attractive single that was produced and written by Allen Toussaint. Not surprisingly it had a sparkling Minit/Instant feel to it and it got played on several local stations.

"I had good hopes for Ritchie because he was very talented," said Scramuzza. "I cut 18 sides on him before he went in the Marines. When he got out he kind of shied away from recording though."

Some of Scram's initial releases did well locally including "Street Jam," by the Sphinxes which received heavy air play on all of the local black station in 1963. Scramuzza explained how he marketed his early releases:

"Since I used to advertise my seafood business a lot on the radio, I'd try and get the deejays to give my stuff a complimentary spin. We also bought space in the radio and record store survey sheets. I thought he public was the best judge so I'd take a consensus on a record's potential. I'd play a record for several people, but If they said no more than yes, we'd drop it and try another."

This release practice was used on probably Scramuzza's most off the wall tunes, "Doin' The Crawfish."

"I wrote that and it came out a couple of times," laughed Scramuzza. "Eddie Bo and Ray Bracken both cut it. I had 1,000 copies pressed and gave 200 away as promos. It never did anything, so I gave the other 800 to customers in my store. Now they're collectors items."

Scramuzza found that the record business wasn't successful enough to warrant sacrificing time from his busy seafood business, so in 1965, he temporally shut Scram down .

The North Broad Street seafood king did pick up the music bug again though after running into Eddie Bo who lived down the street from his store. Always looking for an opportunity to produce and record, Bo became Scramuzza's A&R man and the entrepreneurial Scramuzza reactivated Scram.

"I got back into the business in 1968," said Scramuzza. "We had a few little things [including Little Sonny Jones' "Seven Days" and Walter Washington's "Pony Express"] and then we leased Mary Jane Hooper's [her singles came out on Power] 'That's How Strong My Love Is' to World Pacific. It was great record but they let it die.

"Then we had Eddie's, 'Hook and Sling.' It went as far as a record can go locally in the R&B charts— number one. I knew that record had it. I used to tell guys around the store who unloaded the crawfish, 'Hook it, sling it.' So Bo and I got together and cut it at Borges' studio. We got a great sound out of there. The record took off immediately. We did something like 2,000 the first week and it went top 10 locally. Atlantic was interested in leasing it but I thought I'd try to distribute it myself. I had 50,000 pressed and was sending it to distributors all over the United States. We even got radio play all over the country on our own. We weren't making much money though because all our bread was tied up with the distributors. One guy in St. Louis order 2,000 one week, 3,000 the next, and then another 2,000 without paying us a cent. We did close to 100,000 before Scepter picked it up. Sam Garth [Scepter's president] called me from New York and he was head over heels over the record. The next day he flew down here to sign the papers."

In return for the rights to "Hook and Sling," Scepter paid Scramuzza an advance and picked up all of Scram's accounts receivable on the single. In the end, "Hook and Sling" was a national hit, rising to number nine in *Billboard's* R&B chart, and number 73 in the pop chart, during the summer of 1969.

Scramuzza blames himself with the eventually demise of Scram, which also had good releases by New Orleans veterans Benny Spellman and Curley Moore.

"I got too greedy," he admitted. "I had another good record with Mary Jane Hooper, 'Teach Me.' Scepter was interested, but I felt they didn't offer enough money. I tried to push it myself but nothing happened. Eddie and I played too hard to get, and that was bad because things didn't go right after that. Who knows, I might still be in the business if I'd have went for the deal."

Scramuzza tried a few more releases, but met with only sparse local success. Tastes in black music were changing by 1970, and Eddie Bo's arrangements were being to sound alike. By 1971, Scramuzza shut Scram and Power down in order to concentrated on what he knew best—the seafood business. However, he still had an interest in entertaining and for the next two decades, his hilarious self-produced commercials were a highlight of late night New Orleans television.

"We pressed about thirty records," said Scramuzza, summing up his involvement in the record business. "But I'd only consider around eight of them actual releases because they went in the record shops. I enjoyed the record business because you met a lot of interesting people and you got a lot of different ideas in the studio. Sometimes I felt that mixing a record was just as important as recording it. Really, the record business was lot of smoke and no fire. In the end I don't think I made five cents. I fronted my artists money all the time. As quick as money came in we spent it on recording new stuff. I was more of a friend than a manager. When Mary Jane had her baby I paid the hospital bill. Hell, the record business was as addictive as gambling or drinking."

CHAPTER THIRTY ONE
~ Hep' Me Records: Senator Jones ~

One of the last maverick independent New Orleans R&B producers/record label owners was the no-nonsense Senator Jones. Between the late 1960s and the early 1980s, Jones recorded an enormous amount of great New Orleans talent and ran several labels under the Erica Productions umbrella from a cramped office in the Masonic Building on St. Bernard Avenue. Artists like Johnny Adams, Barbara George, Tommy Ridgley, Chris Kenner, James Rivers, Walter Washington, Charles Brimmer, Bobby Powell and Eddie Lang among several others recorded for "the Senator" during their careers.

A street-smart hustler who knew the New Orleans radio and the independent record business backwards and forwards, Jones was able to keep his labels going while others failed. In doing so, he discovered a lot of New Orleans talent and extended the careers of many artists in an era when the local R&B record industry was otherwise stagnant.

Senator Nolan Jones was born November 9, 1934, at Jackson, Mississippi. His family moved to New Orleans in 1951, but returned to Mississippi after just a few months. Jones however stayed and in 1953 was drafted and stationed at Fort Benning, Georgia. While in the army, Jones sang with the Desperados, a vocal group that also included Jo Jo Benson and Oscar Toney, Jr. Jones recalls the group playing shows with the Five Royals, as well as Hank Ballard and the Midnighters when they performed near the base.

Jones returned to New Orleans in 1957 and began sitting in with groups around town. He befriended Al Johnson and helped compose "You Done Me Wrong" which Johnson recorded in 1958. In the early 1960s, Jones began frequenting One Stop Records on South Rampart Street, a popular haven for musicians, writers and singers.

One of the sales clerks at One Stop was Beryl "Whurley Burley" Eugene, who decided he might profit from starting his own record label. In 1963, the Whurley Burley label debuted with Jones' "Call the Sheriff"/"Let Yourself Go," a totally dreadful record.

The following year, Jones cut "Sugar Dee" for Watch, and "The Sheriff" for International City. Jones claims the latter got played on local radio and he picked up live gigs as a result. Another session produced "Mini Skirt Dance," which International City leased to Bell Records.

However, after four tries, Jones realized he wasn't going to make it big as a recording artist. Bitten by the record bug though, he decided to start working on the other side of the studio board.

"I could see that local acts weren't getting recorded as much as they should," said Jones. "I saw New Orleans artists steal the show from national acts with hit records. That's when I started thinking about producing."

In 1968, Jones formed his first label, Black Patch (at the time Jones wore an eye patch) and he recorded guitarist Rocky Charles' debut "Mr. Rickashay." When the single didn't sell, he folded Black Patch and started the Shagg label.

"I recorded 'Kid Stuff' by the Barons," recalled Jones. "I put that record out on Shagg 711—Shagg was a nickname a lot of artists called me. 'Kid Stuff' did pretty well. Cosimo Matassa leased it to Dover [Matassa's distribution company] during the session. He paid me $800, which paid off Wardell Quezergue [the arranger] and the musicians."

Initially, Jones needed capital to get his label going and he relied on club and motel owner Ferdinand Prout, as well as record salesmen Elmo Sonnier and Whitney Picou, to bankroll his early productions. The second Shagg recording was by Guitar Ray, who had earlier recorded for Hot Line and was a cousin of Earl King. The coupling of the intense "I'm Never Gonna Break His Rules"/"You're Gonna Wreck My Life" was one of the better New Orleans blues releases of the late 1960s.

"I was working in a record shop back then on the corner of North Galvez and London Avenue," said Jones. "Ray brought his guitar by and told me he had some songs. He had a nervous breakdown and just got out of the hospital. He sounded good so I got some studio time at Cosimo's after he moved to Camp Street. The record didn't do too much, but I used to get letters from Europe asking me about it."

After just two issues on Shagg, Jones decided to shelf it and start the Superdome, Jenmark, JB's and Hep' Me labels.

"As I got more artists, I didn't want to go to the radio station with seven records on the same label," said Jones. "I know the deejays would say, 'I can't play all of those records, they're on the same label.' So I started new labels and I switched colors on the record labels to make them look different.

Eventually though, most of Jones releases came out on Hep' Me, a label that got it's name in a curious manner.

"When John McKeithen was running for governor [1967] he would get on T.V. and say, 'Won't you please hep' me.' Well, that got him elected. I figured if it was good enough for him, it was good enough for me."

Ray J. had the first release on Hep' Me in 1973 with a cover of Dr. John's "Right Place, Wrong Time," which sold decently around New Orleans. Ray J., a k.a. Raymond Jones, was a music teacher at Xavier Preparatory High School and a veteran R&B keyboardist. He also began arranging sessions for Jones including "Second Line Pt. 1 & 2" by Stop Inc. in 1974.

"That group was led by two brothers, Clyde and Brian Tolivar," said Jones. "I did about six or seven records with them, but they were too hard to control in the studio. Bill Sinigal had recorded the original 'Second Line' on White Cliffs. The master had been lost and they couldn't press any more records. But it was still a popular Carnival song even though nobody could buy it. I asked Bill if it was okay to record it again and he said, 'Sure.' That's Alvin Thomas playing tenor sax on my record. He played because no one in the group could get that second line feeling."

Jones also had success with Eddie Lang's topical "Food Stamp Blues" on Superdome. Lang was a very good local blues singer and guitarist who had recorded in the 1950s for RPM and Ron. "Food Stamps Blues " was leased by Jewel Records who turned it into a modest Southern hit.

Also in 1974, Charles Brimmer's smoldering "Afflicted" was a local chart topper for Hep' Me. The following year, Jones produced Brimmer's biggest record, "The New God Blessed Our Love" which was leased to Chelsea. Chelsea later picked up several other singles and two albums worth of material Brimmer recorded for Jones.

With his labels beginning to get a foothold in the local R&B market, Jones cut a deal with Marshall Sehorn. In return for unlimited access to SeaSaint Studio, Jones turned over a percentage of his profits to Sehorn and gave him the licensing rights to the material he recorded.

The most successful artist Jones signed was Johnny Adams, who cut scores of remarkable sides on a number of Jones' labels beginning in 1977. Adams hadn't recorded in two years since his run with SSS and he needed a single to help him get work in clubs. Jones was certainly willing to accommodate and he would record Adams often.

"Johnny was by far the greatest singer I've ever heard," said Jones. "I must have asked him 90 times to make a record before he agreed. The first time I booked the studio he didn't show up which made me mad as hell. I didn't think he'd show up the second time, so when he did, we just pulled tunes out of the air. That's how that first single "Stand By Me" and the *Stand By Me* album came about. Marshall then made a deal with Chelsea Records to release it."

While *Stand By Me,* and Adams' initial JB's singles, consisted of reworkings of soul classics, Adams later releases were far more imaginative. Jones' first hit with Adams was with their interpretation of the Conway Twitty's "After All the Good Is Gone." Originally released on Hep' Me in 1978, the single became a strong regional mover. Ariola leased it for national distribution and also contracted Jones and Adams to do an album, *After all the Good Is Gone*, arguably the best of the late singer's career.

Adams continued to record excellent Hep' Me singles which sold well in New Orleans, including "Hell Yes I Cheated," "Spanish Harlem," "I Live My Whole Life At Night," and "Love Me Now," an extraordinary Paul Kelly ballad that was leased by PAID records. Adams remained a mainstay at Hep' Me until 1983, when he signed with Rounder, a move that Jones didn't take well.

"I guess Johnny didn't remember all the hard work I put into his records," fumed Jones at the time. "He never made any better records than the ones he did for me."

Another consistent artist for Jones was Baton Rouge's Bobby Powell, who began recording for Hep' Me in 1978. Powell, who had a national hit in 1965 with "C.C. Rider" on Whit, recorded blues, spirituals and soul for Jones.

"Bobby is a sweet artist," confirmed Jones. "He can deliver whatever you ask him to. I recorded him mostly in New Orleans, but I did a live gospel album with him in Baton Rouge. He does blues, but he also leads a choir at his church. We had a number of good records. I'm speaking of "The Glory of Love," "Sweet Sixteen" and "I'm A Fool For You."

Jones recorded other R&B veterans like Tommy Ridgley, Barbara George, Chuck Carbo and Chris Kenner, but he also gave younger artists like the Las Vegas Connection, Walter Washington and Clem Easterling a chance to record.

However, by 1985 many New Orleans area radio stations were under the control of out-of-state owners and corporations. As a result, Jones lost a lot of his old contacts and was having a great deal of difficulty getting his records played. When the stations stopped programming his new releases, he had a hard time getting shops and distributors to buy them. Once that happened, Jones obviously could no longer afford to make records.

"The stations in New Orleans forgot about us small companies," reflected Jones. "It got to be impossible to make a profit from a local record."

Jones eventually threw in the towel—other than recording himself infrequently–and began managing a motel and club on the West Bank. By the early 1990s, he'd moved back to Jackson, Mississippi, and began doing radio promotion for Malaco Records, a job he kept for two years. Briefly, he was partners with the late Johnny Vincent, who had reactivated the Ace label, but their personalities clashed and eventually they split. Today Jones still lives in Mississippi and works as a deejay on a small AM station. He occasionally does independent record promotion, and like many ex-producers, says he still wants to get back in the studio and make records again.

Part V

Blue Eyed
Rhythm and Blues

Without posting a lengthy roster of singers, musicians and bands, New Orleans, and the rest of Louisiana, is definitely the birthplace of blue eyed rhythm and blues. It was the first place white musicians played R&B and New Orleans was the first city where black and white musicians played the style together in a recording studio. Amazingly, this process took place in a segregated environment, one where schools and businesses weren't integrated, and in a city that had two separate unions for black and white musicians.

However, even though black and white children couldn't share the same classrooms, the close proximity of white and black neighborhoods meant that kids often played in the same playgrounds, and on the same street corners. Being that music is such a major ingredient in New Orleans culture, many children learned to play an instrument. Naturally they'd jam with other kids in the neighborhood (often oblivious to each others race) and exchange musical ideas. This would provide the ingredients for a unique style of R&B music, one that borrowed the black elements of Dixieland, parade music and swing, as well as contain elements of French, British, German and Italian music. Later country, pop and cajun music would also affect it's development.

R&B music was also accessible to whites via live performances. Although New Orleans clubs were segregated, many black rhythm and blues artists played white clubs and dance halls, and appeared at venues like the Municipal Auditorium and Ponchartrain Beach on rock and roll shows. Fraternities and sororities at white colleges like LSU, Nichols State, Tulane, USM, USL, Ole Miss and the University of Alabama, often booked New Orleans R&B bands for dances. In fact, many New Orleans R&B artists had a much stronger appeal to white listeners and record buyers than black listeners.

White teenagers also had unlimited access to R&B via the radio. Not only could they listen to Smiley Lewis, Fats Domino and Lloyd Price records played by black disc jockeys like Ernie the Whip, Okey Dookey and Larry McKinley, they could tune into white stations and hear the same records played by Poppa Stoppa, Jack the Cat and Herb Holiday. A glance at WNOE and WTIX (white stations) play lists from the late 1950s and early 1960s revel that their programming was usually split equally between white pop and rock and black R&B. Combine that with what the black stations were playing, and you realize that R&B music was at one time more accessible on New Orleans radio than white music.

Although it was located in far away Nashville, the importance of radio station WLAC, 50,000 watts of clear channel rhythm and blues, can not be underemphasized in the development of Blue Eyed Rhythm and Blues. When the smaller am stations went off the air at night, many radio dials switched to 1600, where John R, Gene Nobel, and Bill "Hossman" Allen played a steady a diet of rhythm and blues, plenty of it which originated in New Orleans, into the wee hours of the morning. Although the station could be heard from Canada to the Caribbean, it's target audience was in the South and many teenagers in Louisiana went to sleep at night listening to the station.

It should be no surprised that many white teenagers wanted to become R&B/rock and roll musicians and some became just as good as their black counterpart. In fact some white artists were so into the sound that many listeners assumed they were black upon listening to their records.

CHAPTER THIRTY TWO
~ Mac Rebennack: Dr. John ~

No other New Orleans artist has worn more musical jackets than Mac Rebennack, a. k. a. Dr. John. During a career that spans more than four decades, he has served as a greasy-kid stuff rock and roller, producer, writer, sideman, psychedelic icon, jingle creator, blues and contemporary jazz musician, as well as an all around torch bearer of New Orleans music. As he has aptly stated, "I did whatever I had to do to get the job did."

Although Dr. John isn't a physician, the magic his music has created is medicinal. It was he who first added the physical and visual aspect to New Orleans music. In the late 1960s psychedelic era, his outlandish shows were a celebration of New Orleans. Tossing glitter, wearing grease-paint, feathers, snake skin and bright colors, as Dr. John, Rebennack brought the flavor of Mardi Gras, as well as the sounds and mysteries of New Orleans to stages around the world.

Rebennack may have long ago toned down his stage act, but his music is still vibrant and progressive, yet true to the New Orleans tradition. His two Grammy awards—the most recent, 1993's Best Traditional Blues Album, for *Goin' Back to New Orleans*—only underline his ongoing contribution to popular music. He has created an enduring musical personality all his own, yet one that pays tribute to his home town.

Born Malcolm John Rebennack Jr., November 21, 1940, he was raised in New Orleans' middle-class Third Ward. A cherub as an infant, he was just nine months old when his photograph appeared on the front panel of Ivory Snow laundry detergent boxes. At the age of three, he developed an interest in music and was singing and picking out songs on the family's baby grand piano.

Rebennack's family was supportive and nurtured his interest in music. His Uncle John played the piano as did hip Aunt Andre who taught him "Pinetop's Boogie Woogie." Mac Sr. let his son listen to hillbilly and blues 78s that he brought home from his appliance store. His mother even wrote songs with him when she was learning how to type. The Rebennacks often hosted what amounted to family jam sessions in their living room, with aunts, uncles and grandparents contributing. In grade school, he took piano lessons, but he grew bored because he could already outplay the nun who taught him.

At the age of 12, Rebennack's mother took him to Werlein's music store on Canal Street and bought him his first guitar. Originally, he disdained music lessons, preferring to copy what he heard on Lightnin' Slim and Lightnin' Hopkins 78s. Eventually he did consent to lessons and one evening Rebennack's first guitar teacher, Mr. Guma, stopped by his student's house and heard music coming from the back room. Guma told Mrs. Rebennack he thought it was great that Mac was listening to recorded music. Mrs. Rebennack laughed and pointed out that her son wasn't listening to records or the radio, he was playing the guitar.

In his spare time, Rebennack accompanied his father—who augmented his income repairing televisions, radios, amplifiers and public address systems. One Saturday afternoon, father and son took the ferry across the Mississippi to Gretna's Pepper Pot where their P. A. system was acting up. The band playing at the Pepper Pot was led by Professor Longhair. The younger Rebennack wasn't allowed inside the club, but he pulled up a log next to the window so he could watch the band. Mac was immediately mesmerized by Longhair's dexterity at the piano and his quirky rhythm. He'd stumbled upon his musical mentor. On another repair call, the Rebennacks went to the Golden Cadillac on Poland Avenue, where Fats Domino's band was playing—sans Domino. It was here Rebennack first encountered Walter "Papoose" Nelson, who became his guitar tutor.

"Papoose was showing me T-Bone Walker, Mickey Baker and other guitarists like that," recalled Rebennack. "When I started taking lessons, I was listening to people like Lightnin' Hopkins. Papoose said, 'You can't get in no bands playing like that. You got to learn stuff by this guy and that guy.' He wouldn't let me play any leads. I would sit with him for hours and he would just have me strum chords behind him. That made an impression on me."

Rebennack's father was also a friend of studio owner Cosimo Matassa. Matassa let Rebennack watch sessions from the booth and act as a go-for. The inquisitive youngster often asked musicians how to play certain songs and Matassa periodically had to run him off when became too much of a nuisance. Nevertheless, Rebennack kept returning and eventually befriended most of the musicians who entered the studio.

"I remember walking in there when Dave Bartholomew was doing something," said Rebennack. "They were on a break and I walked over and touched Earl Palmer's drums. The next thing I knew, I got thrown out. It was just because they were Earl Palmer's drums that I wanted to touch them—I loved the way Earl played. Dave was like, 'Get this kid out of here before he breaks something!'"

"I can't remember Mac not being around the studio," recalled the late

Johnny Vincent, the owner of Ace Records who hired Rebennack as an A&R man. "He used to hang around and ask questions all the time. But he was one of the greatest little prospects as a producer and writer, even at the age of 16."

By the time he was in his teens, Rebennack was totally immersed in his hometown's R&B tradition. Not only did he listen to all of the local R&B stations, he also scoured record shops in search of the sounds he heard Jack the Cat, Okey Dooky, Dr. Daddy-O and Poppa Stoppa play on the radio. He continually played records over and over at home until he learned particular riffs on the piano or guitar.

In 1954, Rebennack enrolled at Jesuit, a prestigious Catholic high school on North Carrollton Avenue known for its academic and athletic excellence. However, during the mid-1950s, like every other high school in America, Jesuit was caught up in a rock and roll fervor. At Jesuit, word got around that Rebennack hung out at Cosimo's where Lloyd Price, Smiley Lewis, and Fats Domino recorded. He became Jesuit's resident rock and roll expert, entertaining fellow students with the latest Chuck Berry licks, fielding questions about rock and roll and reporting on who was at Cosimo's making records.

Rebennack formed a band with some other Jesuit students, the Dominoes, who wore black jackets emblazoned with dominoes. At the annual Jesuit talent show, the group performed several Fats Domino songs. While the student body was appreciative, the Jesuit priests in attendance were anything but impressed by what they heard. From then on the priests kept a sharp eye on the rock and roller. Rebennack eventually dropped out Jesuit during the 11th grade in order to play music. A distracted, but not poor student, Rebennack signed up for correspondence school and would eventually earn a high school diploma. As events transpired, Rebennack didn't really need school, as Cosimo's, and the clubs which blared R&B were his classrooms.

When he was 17, Rebennack's new band, usually called the Skyliners, consisted of drummer Paul Stahle, saxophonist Leonard James, trumpeter Warren Leoning, bassist Earl Stanley, and Rebennack, who played guitar and occasionally piano. The band often changed names to accommodate the vocalists they backed (Paul Marvin, Frankie Ford or Jerry Byrne) or the club owner who booked them. Stahle had several fronts for his bass drum with different band names that he changed in order to fit the occasion. The group usually stayed busy working everything from French Quarter B-drinking joints to high school proms.

"We had a lot of different names because we could hustle more gigs that way," claimed Rebennack. We'd tell the club owner, 'Well we can get you this band. But if you don't like that group, we can get you this other band.' It was really the same group, it was just a question who was the leader and what we decided to call the band. Once we won a battle of the bands contest, but were disqualified after the judges figured out that we played one set dressed one way, and the second set dressed another way. Leonard James lived across the street from me and my parents trusted him. They would let me go work in strip joints with him. This guy really knew how to hustle gigs. He'd walk in a club and go talk to somebody. The next thing I knew we were working there that night."

Rebennack's first recording session, around 1957, came via Papoose at an abbreviated guitar lesson.

"I went for my lesson and the next thing I knew I was heading to Cosimo's to be on a session," said Rebennack. "Papoose sent me to sub for him. He just didn't want to go down there that day. I'm not sure who the session was with, but it might have been Eddie Bo. I get to the studio and who am I working for but Paul Gayten. Paul knows me from hanging in front of the Brass Rail [where Gayten's band performed] when I wasn't old enough to get in. Right away he jumps in my shit with both feet. 'What the hell is going on!?! I thought I had Papoose?' I'm thinking, 'Oh my God, I know he'd like to have Edgar Blanchard or somebody else here. I wish I had his phone number so I could just call him.' But he used me. I remember Paul hung a jacket that stuck on me for a long time. Gayten was really hip that I was copping T-Bone Walker. He hung this jacket on me that said 'Little T-Bone.' It stuck with me a long time."

Word got around that Rebennack had pretty good guitar chops, even for a young white kid. Eventually he started getting calls from producers when studio regulars like Papoose, Ernest McClain, Blanchard, Roy Montrell or Justin Adams weren't available.

"Me, James Booker, and Leonard James would hang around the studio just hoping that somebody wouldn't show up," said Rebennack. "Maybe somebody would give us a shot. We weren't even in the Union or anything—we just loved to hear music. Me and Booker would be listening to Huey Smith or Edward Frank, and we enjoyed that."

Rebennack was also composing songs as a teenager. His first success, "Lights Out," was a Little Richard-inspired rocker recorded by Jerry Byrne for Specialty Records in 1957. Rebennack had brought Byrne and the song to Harold Battiste, who was Specialty's New Orleans A&R man. "Lights Out" was a successful regional record as was it's flip, "Carry On." Unfortunately, Specialty was winding down their New Orleans operation around the time Rebennack arrived and they offered limited opportunities to record. But as luck would have it though, Rebennack's and Battiste's paths would later cross several times.

"You have to give Mac a lot of credit," said Battiste. "He was dedicated. He followed guys like Papoose and Roy Montrell [who replaced Papoose in Domino's band and tutored Rebennack] to learn from the source. I never thought it was odd that he hung around black musicians. Elvis was coping the black sound— why not Mac? Everybody liked Mac. The only problem though was once he started picking up checks at the black musicians' union, some guys resented that. "

"Nobody really gave any thought about Mac being white," said the late Johnny Adams, who was often produced by Rebennack and recorded several of his songs. "He was just one of the guys and real good around the studio."

In 1957, Rebennack and the Skyliners won a battle of the band contest sponsored by Werlein's, beating out over 100 bands. First prize included a Decca recording contract and the group cut an instrumental album, *Boppin' and Strollin'*, issued under Leonard James' name

Before the end of the decade, Rebennack was hired for $60 a week to be an A&R man by Johnny Vincent to work with Ace and he would play a very important role in the development of the label.

"I think Johnny Vincent hired me because I wrote songs and hung around the studio all the time," said Rebennack. "I was what they called an A&R man. Now they call it a producer. It was my job to get the artists material for the date, hire the musicians and put the session together. If I needed to hire an arranger—which was very rare—that was also my end. I made sure that the artists got good production. It was also my job to scout talent and find their repertoire. I got songs arranged and made records out of them. I did some of the Huey Smith and the Clowns things, Jimmy Clanton, and Frankie Ford too. I did a bunch of unknown artist out of here that were never heard of—Guitar Ray, Al Reed, Luther Reeves, and Chuck Carbo that was with the Spiders group. From working at Ace, I got the knowledge to work with the studio band on a real tight basis. My cues for what I was suppose to be doing I learned from watching guys like Huey Smith, Allen Toussaint, Dave Bartholomew and Paul Gayten."

One of first records Rebennack produced and played on for Vincent was the memorable "Morgus the Magnificent," credited to Morgus and the Ghouls. On it he takes a memorable guitar break ala Guitar Slim. The single appeared on the Ace subsidiary Vin in 1959.

"We cut that at a radio station [WWEZ]. Ken Elliot's [deejay "Jack the Cat"] son wrote that. He sings on it with Frankie Ford and Jerry Byrne. Morgus was a real popular TV show host back then in New Orleans showing monster movies."

The first single credited to Rebennack, "Storm Warning" came out on Matassa's Rex label which Ace distributed. His second single, "Sahara," came out on Ace.

"I cut those for Coz [likely in 1959]," said Rebennack. "They were supposed to part of an instrumental album—one side guitar, one side piano—but it didn't come out. 'Storm Warning' was kind of a Bo Diddley guitar instrumental thing. A lot of the studio guys that was around then are on there— Lee Allen, Red Tyler, Frank Fields, Melvin Lastie and Hungry Williams. On "Sahara," I'm playing organ with those guys."

In 1960, Rebennack had the first of several falling-outs with Vincent over money, ethics, talent, music, and whatever else producers and label owners disagree over. Rebennack had already been doing some random session work for Ric and Ron Records and he was hired to A & R by label's owner Joe Ruffino. At Ric and Ron, Rebennack worked on Eddie Lang's "Troubles, Troubles," Johnny Adams' "I Won't Cry," Irma Thomas' "Don't Mess With My Man," and Professor Longhair's immortal "Go To the Mardi Gras."

"Joe had a small operation but looking back on it he had some great artists," recalled Rebennack. "Joe was going to give me a piece of the label and make me co-president, but he died before we could sign the papers."

Gig-wise, Rebennack stayed very busy. Besides the local clubs and dances, Rebennack was called upon to put accompaniment behind the touring acts that appeared at the Ponchartrain Beach Amusement Park and the Municipal Auditorium.

"I'd put a band together to back those big rock and roll and rhythm and blues shows that would come to New Orleans," said Rebennack. "The shows had contracts that stipulated that you had to have like a 17-piece band for some of the shows. My band could cut it—I just hired extra musicians. We got to work with Jerry Lee Lewis, Fabian, and Bobby Darrin— whoever had a hit record out. In those days they had segregation, so at the Auditorium, they'd have Tommy Ridgley's band work the black show and my band would work the white show."

Rebennack and his group also toured and sometimes spent several weeks on the road. In 1962, while in Jacksonville, Florida, with a what he referred to as a "Twist band," Rebennack got involved in an incident that nearly ended his career and life. Rebennack interceded in a scuffle between a motel manger and his singer/keyboard player, Ronnie Barron. The manager pulled a pistol and in the ensuing struggle, the gun fired and a bullet struck Rebennack's left index finger. A doctor saved the finger, but the bullet severed several muscles and arteries.

"I couldn't play guitar no more," explained Rebennack. "The finger that got hit was the one you use to bend strings and fret with. I got real depressed after that."

Rebennack's injury partially lead to an increased reliance on narcotics, an addiction which began in the mid-1950s.

"I took a job playing bass in a Dixieland band on Bourbon Street," said Rebennack. "It was weird because I didn't even own a bass. At first I borrowed an upright bass and then I got a Fender [electric] bass. It was horrible. Some nights there would be blood all over the bass and I just didn't dig what I was playing. Then I started hustling around and started playing a little drums. Then James Booker got me a job playing keyboards. He was playing down the block and said, 'Look Mac, I'll show you the [Hammond B-3] organ.'

"At that time, Jimmy Smith had just come out with 'Chicken Shack.' Booker convinced the guys that he worked for [the Conforto family who owned several French Quarter clubs] to sell the pianos they had and buy organs for all their places. Booker taught me just enough organ so I could audition for the gig which I got. Actually, I wound with three or four gigs. Eventually, I put a little band together to play behind the organ. We backed up strippers from 10 p.m. until 2 a.m. Then we played dance music from 2 a.m. until 6 a.m. After that we played a jam session for the street people that lasted until 10 a.m. We'd play 12 hours straight with no break. All around you there were shootings, stabbings, and people hitting each other over the head with bottles. That was everyday. It's not like there were days off either—there was no such thing."

Despite his hectic Bourbon Street schedule, Rebennack was still a familiar face at Cosimo's. In addition to his A&R duties at Ric/Ron and Ace, he also produced sessions for Montel, Tribe and drew-Blan. He also was part of AFO Records where he cut a great duet with Ronnie Barron, "Talk That Talk," which appeared on Another, as by Drits and Dravey. In 1962, Rebennack had his first taste of chart success when Johnny Adams' "Losing Battle," a song he wrote and produced for Ric, reached number 27 in the R&B charts.

As brightly as the future looked for the New Orleans music industry in 1962, fortunes reversed the following year. Commercially, national hits were no longer coming from New Orleans as the city's sound was replaced in the charts by releases coming out of Memphis, Detroit, Los Angeles, and especially England. Several of the larger inde labels (Imperial, Ric, Ron, Chess, Minit, AFO and Ace) folded or pulled up their New Orleans stakes by the end of 1963.

Besides losing session work, many musicians forfeited the income generated from playing live music. In an effort to reduce prostitution and B-drinking, New Orleans' District Attorney, Jim Garrison, began busting French Quarter clubs that featured live music on the premises they attracted narcotics traffickers. Garrison eventually shut many clubs down, several which employed Rebennack. Just when things looked like they couldn't get worse, Rebennack got busted for possessing heroin and wound up doing two years in a federal prison in Forth Worth, Texas. Upon his release, he headed to Los Angeles.

"There was no work left in New Orleans then," said Rebennack. "If I wanted to keep playing music, I had to go to the West Coast."

Luckily for Rebennack, he followed a path already worn by several New Orleans musicians. Upon his arrival, he fell in with a clique of musicians led by his old friend and mentor Harold Battiste. Battiste, who was then producing Sonny and Cher, arranged for Rebennack to join the pop duo's band and recommended him to other producers.

"I did sessions with Johnny Watson, the Simms Twins, King Floyd, and the O'Jays," said Rebennack. "I also did some work for Phil Spector. But jeezz, I went from doing sessions with Professor Longhair and Irma Thomas, to working with the Electric Alarm Clock [sic] and Iron Butterfly. I didn't know what I was walking into. I remember at one session being told by a producer to play 'smiles' on a track. That stuff New Orleans players were laying down was just too real. They wanted dragon and butterfly stuff. I liked it though that they used a lot of New Orleans cats to get some funk. But when I first saw producers use six piano players and five guitar players on a session, I thought they were padding the payroll. They weren't though, they were looking for a sound."

Battiste would become instrumental in Rebennack's transformation into the Dr. John character. The original Dr. John who claimed to be a West Indian Prince was a freed slave who lived in New Orleans prior to the Civil War. He told fortunes, sold gris-gris, cast spells, held seances, taught magic tricks and oversaw voodoo ceremonies. Rebennack had nurtured a fascination for voodoo, beginning when his sister brought home several books on Haitian voodoo from a French Quarter antique shop where she worked. Several musicians Rebennack hung with (especially Jessie Hill) shared his interest, and they often visited the Cracker Jack curio shop on South Rampart Street.

Battiste had some prepaid studio time available after a Sonny and Cher session in the fall of 1967, so he and Rebennack began to experiment. Both men had been impressed by an unreleased 1962 AFO track by Price La La, "Need You," that contained a unique Afro/New Orleans feel. They decided to follow that same direction. Rebennack and Battiste went into the Gold Star Studio with several New Orleans expatriates (including Hill, Plas Johnson, Shirley Goodman, Dave Dixon, and Tami Lynn) to record several offbeat—as far as main stream rock and roll at the time was concerned—tracks. Sonny Bono heard the session and talked his label, Atlantic, into releasing them. *Gris-Gris*, which was credited to "Dr. John the Night Tripper" was released with trepidation early in 1968.

"I wanted to do the Dr. John concept with Ronnie Barron but he had a contract with another label and couldn't do it," related Rebennack. "So I did it myself. The music on *Gris-Gris* was intended for people that had never been to New Orleans. I knew Ahmet Ertegun [Atlantic's president] was upset about the record because I was sitting in the studio doing a session with Bobby Darrin [before *Gris-Gris* was released] and he came in and said, 'What the hell is this record you gave me?' He ate up a lot of Bobby Darrin's studio time yelling at me. He thought he was stuck with another record he didn't know what to do with. It wasn't exactly something you could put in a slot. You couldn't put your finger on the what the hell it was. Gris gris is the New Orleans word for voodoo and it was voodoo music. But there's not exactly a calling for that in the marketplace. Luckily it just happened to fit into the psychedelic movement."

Despite Ertegun's misgivings, *Gris-Gris* found a home on alternative FM radio. The album became an underground hit, doing well enough sales wise to keep Atlantic interested in a follow up, even though all parties had considered *Gris-Gris* a one shot deal. The record was promoted by Rebennack who took the Dr. John show on the road. After being assured by New Orleans voodoo experts that he wasn't disturbing the spirits, he created an unfathomable show to accompany his music,

"It was a show in the New Orleans tradition," emphasized Rebennack. "We were lucky with it because all those love-ins, freak-ins, and be-ins were happening at the time. I got Chicken Man and some other guys that did real voodoo shows. That was too much for some people, so I toned it down and did a smaller version of the show. The lineup kept getting smaller, because a lot of people didn't want to go on the road. All the musicians were sitting pretty doing session work. They had no reason to travel."

1968's *Babylon* continued in the direction of voodoo rock, but *Remedies*, from 1970, contained a more traditional New Orleans R&B sound. In between the two albums, Rebennack had a falling out with Battiste and signed a deal with Charlie Greene and Brian Stone, powerful rock managers who boasted Sonny & Cher, and the Buffalo Springfield as their clients. However, shortly after signing, Rebennack, discharged the duo after he found out Greene was was trying to take too much control of his music and business affairs. Inconveniently, this happened on the eve of his fourth album which was recorded in England.

With the aid of Eric Clapton and Mick Jaggar, Rebennack recorded dozens of tracks for *The Sun, Moon & Herbs*, a projected three-LP set. However, when Rebennack returned Stateside, he found most of the tapes were missing or unusable. Rebennack suspected Greene sabotaged the project. Eventually he and Atlantic's engineer Tom Dowd rescued part of the project, remixing several tracks and adding overdubs. Eventually, *The Sun, Moon & Herbs*, was released as a single album in 1972.

At the time, Rebennack found himself sinking into debt. His records were selling reasonably, but not in sufficient quantities to cover studio costs (particularly those incurred on *The Sun, Moon & Herbs*) and the advances his label allocated him. Luckily, Atlantic co-president Jerry Wexler helped Rebennack straighten out his finances and initiated a redirection in Rebennack's career. Wexler, who was instrumental in recording several other New Orleans artists, including Professor Longhair, Jack Dupree, Tommy Ridgley, and Guitar Slim, suggested Rebennack return to his roots. At the end of a Leon Russell session, Wexler, Russell and Rebennack lingered in the studio having a few drinks. Wexler and Russell started calling out old New Orleans songs which Rebennack handled on the piano. At the end of the night, Wexler suggested Rebennack get back in touch with Battiste and record an album of New Orleans R&B standards. The resulting 1972 album, *Gumbo*, turned out to be a landmark. Here's what Rebennack said about the album in the liner notes:

"It's like a picture of the music New Orleans people listen to, a combination of Dixieland, rock 'n' roll and funk. The origin of funk is in New Orleans coming out of Mardi Gras music: your basic 2/4 beat with compounded rhythms and syncopation added on. This album is basic good-time New Orleans blues and stomp music with a little Dixieland jazz and some Spanish rumba blues: There isn't any what you might call voodoo rock or gris-gris, because my producers and I thought that the people might enjoy the root music from New Orleans which was maybe the chief ingredient in what we know today as rock & roll."

Gumbo brought a great deal of attention to the New Orleans rhythm and blues tradition and concluded the gris-gris/voodoo rock period of Rebennack's career. Lauded by critics and a strong seller, *Gumbo* was followed by the extraordinary *In the Right Place*, an album produced by Allen Toussaint and featured the Meters as the backup group. The album featured two hit singles, "Such A Night" (number 42 pop) and "Right Place Wrong Time" (number nine pop).

"'Right Place Wrong Time' was written and put together in the studio," recalled Rebennack. "It was a thing I'd been fooling around with the Meters but I never finished writing the words. We got in the studio and began throwing ideas for lyrics around at each other. We got a good groove going and we got a nice little arrangement on it. It fit right in with what was going on at the time."

1973 was a busy year for Rebennack. With *In the Right Place* in the charts, Rebennack made several national television appearances and toured Europe with Professor Longhair and the Meters. In the fall, he was back in the studio to record the *Desitively Bonnaroo* album. While the formula was similar to *In the Right Place*, and it contained several great songs, sales wise the album didn't live up to Atlantic's expectations.

"After doing five records for Atlantic I finally made one that really sells," said Rebennack. "All of a sudden they wanted me to do something really commercial. We made *Desitively Bonnaroo* which I thought was pretty good, but it wasn't super commercial. Then Atlantic wanted me to cut an album with the Average White Band. I asked them, 'Why should I make a record with the Average White Band when I'm touring with the Meters?' Finally I started making money for Atlantic, but I wound up getting dropped. It didn't make sense."

After Atlantic, Rebennack recorded an album for Columbia, *Triumvirate*—a collaboration with Mike Bloomfield and John Hammond—before moving to United Artists where he cut *Hollywood Be Thy Name*, an inconsistent effort that featured live and studio tracks. When Rebennack wasn't touring or cutting his own material, he continued to pick up studio credits. During the 1970s, he worked with Buddy Guy and Junior Wells, Johnny Winter, Luther Allison, The Allman Brothers, Maria Muldar, Aretha Franklin, James Taylor, Kate Smith, Levon Helm, and Van Morrison among others. In 1977, he appeared in the Band's farewell concert and film *The Last Waltz* performing "Such A Night."

In 1979, Rebennack recorded *City Lights* for Horizon, an A&M subsidiary. Produced by Tommy LiPuma and Hugh McCracken, the album was a departure from his previous work and signaled a maturation of Rebennack's style, and a graduation from the rock scene.

"I wanted to do another record like *Gris-Gris*," said Rebennack "That turned out to be *City Lights*. It included songs me and Doc Pomus wrote, and songs that me and Billy Charles wrote. From that experience, I came in contact with Hugh McCracken, Steve Gadd, Richard Tee and other New York dudes. I really dug that record. The songs on it opened up a lot of spaces for me. I fell into slots I hadn't fallen into before—jazz slots and things. Jazz stations in New York and L.A. were playing cuts from *City Lights*. I mean I took a band on the road that had David Sanborn and Steve

Gadd in it. It was a whole different thing that I wasn't used to.

Rebennack's next album, *Tango Palace*, was stylistic close to *City Lights* and was also produced by LiPuma for Horizon.

"That was supposed to be called *I Thought I Heard New Orleans Say*," said Rebennack. "I wasn't aware of it at the time, but halfway into the record, A&M was getting ready to dump Horizon. The record turned from *I Thought I Heard New Orleans Say* to something else. It was going to be the musical story of some guys from New Orleans who get stranded in New York and work in the tango palaces and rum-rum joints so they can make enough money to get back home. I cut all these songs telling this story and then one other to appease the record company. Then they asked for another, and then another. By the time we were through, everything was sidetracked. The day the record came out—Horizon went under. The record got played on the radio, but nobody could buy it."

By the early 1980s, Rebennack's career continued to expand. He had moved to New York, which helped two of his newest ventures—working on movie soundtracks, as well as radio and television commercials.

"I made more money doing Scott tissue, Oreo cookie, and Popeye's chicken jingles than the last seven records I had did," laughed Rebennack. "I've been doing jingles since the 1950s, but back then you didn't get any residuals."

Rebennack also continued to write new material with Doc Pomus and several of their best compositions were recorded on B.B. King's *Got to Be A Better World Somewhere*, a fine album Rebennack also played on. Unsigned by a major label, in 1981 Rebennack recorded two albums for the Baltimore-based inde Clean Cut—*Dr. John Plays Mac Rebennack* and *The Brightest Smile In Town*.

"Those records were both cut at one session," said Rebennack. "They were easy to make because it was just me and the piano. I recorded a lot of stuff I normally like to play when I sit down at the piano alone."

The decade found Rebennack spending more time abroad, working in Europe, Australia and the Far East. He continued to build an international following, especially after many of his out-of-print recordings were reissued in England and Japan. In America, a number of mysterious albums containing Rebennack out takes, demos, and live material also began appearing. However, the first legitimate reissues of his work—*Gris-Gris* and *Gumbo*—didn't appear in the United States until Alligator reissued them in 1987.

In 1988, Rebennack was involved in a car wreck and had several ribs broken. However, he bounced back in a couple of months, writing, recording soundtracks, touring, taping jingles and appearing in the film *Candy*

Mountain. As busy as he was, Rebennack didn't do another new album until 1989. (Two great concert sets *Such A Night: Live In London* and *Mardi Gras At The Marquis*, did appear in Europe.) Despite his track record and his reputation as a great musician, Rebennack had a hard time getting a satisfactory record deal until Warner Brothers entered the picture.

"I really trusted Tommy Lipuma and he's the reason I signed with Warner Brothers," said Rebennack. "I had been talking to Ahmet Ertegun about resigning with Atlantic, but he was driving me crazy about a single. We never could get eye-to-eye on it. Tommy had called me five years before [signing with Warner Brothers] but the people at Blue Note said, 'No, don't make a record with him. We want to make the definitive Dr. John record.' Then Blue Note started talking about doing another solo record, which I didn't think made any sense because I'd already done that. I'd being going back and forth with Blue Note about what we were going to do, but after five years, there still was no record. Finally, Tommy called again and said, 'Look, lets just do a good album. Don't worry about a hit single. Let's just do it.' Naturally I jumped in with both feet."

"I always stayed in touch with Mac over the years," said Lipuma, who had worked with Rebennack as early as the mid-1960s in Los Angeles. "When I moved to New York, I used to see him at the Lone Star. One day Bob Merlis, who does PR for Warner Brothers, gave me a copy of *Dr. John Plays Mac Rebennack*. Mac did a couple of standards on it. When I heard them, a light bulb went off. I had this idea of doing an album like Ray Charles' *Genius + Soul = Jazz*. I called Mac about the idea, and he was all for it. I don't think the public wanted just another Dr. John album—they wanted something different."

The Rebennack/Lipuma collaboration produced *In A Sentimental Mood*, an album considered a comeback by Warner Brothers—but not Rebennack. He and Lipuma went through nearly 100 songs before deciding on the nine that went on the album.

"Tommy had the idea of doing old songs," says Rebennack. "I dug it from jump city. Originally, we were going to just cut Louis Jordan tunes, but after a feeling out procedure, we shifted gears and took another direction. We went through a stack of old material, stopping when it felt right and cutting most of it as live as we could. All of those songs I played behind other acts at one time or another. We used to do those Tin Pan Alley tunes on our after-hours gigs, and it was kind of a tribute to that kind of thing and also a tribute to Ray Charles and Charles Brown. I always liked the way they both took those popular kind of songs and turned them into R&B rather than pop."

Many listeners aptly compared *In A Sentimental Mood* to the Ray Charles classic 1961 album, *Modern Sounds In Country and Western*.

"I didn't know it at the time but my arranger, Marty Paich, was Ray Charles arranger back in the early 1960s," said Rebennack. "I was trying to go for a Louis Jordan sound and get away from Ray's sound, but Marty's arrangements were so distinct it made it impossible."

"That was incidental," claimed Lipuma. "When I asked Marty to arrange the album, I had no idea he had worked with Ray Charles. It's kind of cosmic, but he really gave the album a touch of class."

In a Sentimental Mood earned flattering reviews and earned a Rebennack his first Grammy Award for his duet with Rickie Lee Jones on "Makin' Whoopie." The success of the album created an avalanche of work for Rebennack. As far as live dates, he could pretty much pick and chose. Television and radio commercial work continued to pour in, as it became virtually impossible to listen to either medium for much longer than an hour without hearing Rebennack sing or play on an advertisement. He also continued to pile up session work, including Johnny Adams' *The Real Me*, which contained several songs co-authored by Rebennack and Doc Pomus.

His next outing, *Going Back To New Orleans*, from 1992, had the Neville Brothers, Al Hirt, Danny Barker, and Pete Fountain on-board. Many listeners consider it his best work.

"I had the idea to do something like this [*Going Back To New Orleans*] for a long time," he said. "It mostly was just street stuff but it was a lot of material to try and narrow down, especially when you're looking at more than 100 years of music. I tried to get people involved that meant a lot to me and people that wrote songs that meant a lot to me. All the people I come under."

Although the album won Rebennack's second Grammy, he and the Warner Brothers parted company when he and the label couldn't come up with a concept for another CD. Rebennack wound up signing with MCA and in 1994 cut *Television*. That same year, his biography, *Under A HooDoo Moon*, was published by St. Martin's Press.

"I think it [the book] would have been better if I hadn't been under the influence of lithium poisoning," said Rebennack. "My head was real splattered then because I was coming out of rehab, but I'm glad I did it and didn't wait any longer. I never read the thing, but I got a lot of crap and flak about the stuff that was in it."

In 1997, *Trippin' Live*, recorded at Ronnie Scott's Club was nominated for a Grammy. Not unexpectedly, it included New Orleans material he normally featured on his shows. The following year he switched to

EMI and recorded, *Another Zone*, produced by John Lemke and included several English musicians.

"British guys are into their own bag," related Rebennack. "They do their thing, just like we do our thing. New Orleans guys might show up late for a session, but when they get there, it's business. British guys get there on time, but they fart around in the studio and they take a lot of time."

Rebennack doesn't plan on slowing down in the new millennium, continuing drawing on the past to create the future. He promises he won't, and can't possibly, stray far from the New Orleans sound that is his foundation.

"It's part of whatever I'm about," said Rebennack. "The importance of it is beyond anything I do."

CHAPTER THIRTY THREE
~ Roland Stone: Just A Moment ~

Aaron Neville referred to the late Roland Stone as, "The singingest white dude I've ever heard." Pretty fair praise from somebody who knows a little bit about singing.

In New Orleans, Roland Stone is best remembered for his 1961 hit "Just A Moment." However, he was more than just a local one hit wonder. Roland Stone was a terrific entertainer who possessed a confident voice, well suited to rock and roll, as well as rhythm and blues. He was also a member of two important early New Orleans rock and roll bands, the Jokers and the Skyliners.

Roland Stone was born Roland LeBlanc, August 12, 1941. His parents lived on St. Ann Street between North Rocheblave and North Tonti Streets.

"I grew up listening to country music—Hank Williams, Red Foley, and Ernest Tubb," said LeBlanc in 1999. "Then in the mid-1950s, I started listening to rhythm and blues on the Dr. Daddy-O, and Larry McKinley shows on WMRY. I started to love that music. In 1957, I was a freshman at Warren Easton when I joined a band that was just starting up called the Jokers. I played guitar. We did a lot of the popular R&B and rock and roll hits of the era. Originally there were five guys in the band, but we fired the singer so the rest of us could make more money. That's how I started singing. We got real popular and played all the Catholic junior high and high school dances in New Orleans."

In 1959, the Jokers were playing a St. Anthony's C.Y.O. dance on Canal Street when fate walked in the door.

"Mac [Rebennack] came up to me during the break and said he needed a new singer for his group," said LeBlanc. "Mac had a band called the Skyliners and was doing A&R for Ace. He said, 'Join my band and I can get you a record deal with Ace.' Ace was really poppin' then—they had big hits by Jimmy Clanton, Frankie Ford, and Huey Smith. Up until then it seemed inconceivable that I could make a record, so I said, 'Certainly.'

"The guys in the Jokers were pretty mad when I quit. They came over to my house and made me give back all the Battle of the Bands trophies we'd won. When I joined Mac's band, I switched to piano because Mac was on guitar. Mac introduced me to a lot of the harder R&B I didn't hear with the Jokers—like Ray Charles, Roy Brown, and Guitar Slim."

As events transpired, LeBlanc's recording debut came out on a small local label rather than the powerhouse Ace.

"I was with Mac's band about a month when one night we went by radio station WJBW," said LeBlanc. "Huey Smith was cutting a session but it turned into a disaster and most of the musicians left early. There was some studio time left so Mac said, 'Let's cut 'Junco Partner.'' I'd never heard the song before I met Mac. He had this great 45 collection and he had played the original [by James Wayne] for me."

"I'd never recorded before and Mac wanted to hear what my voice sounded like on tape. After we finished, Joe Caronna, who was in the studio said, 'Man this is great. Let me ask Johnny [Vincent] if I can put this out after we change the words a little bit.' Joe was a sales guy for Johnny who also managed Frankie Ford. He also had label called Spinett that he was partners in with Frankie. Joe had to get permission from Johnny because I already signed a contract with Ace. Joe told Johnny he'd put out the record on Spinett under a different name and not use Roland LeBlanc. Johnny said, 'Sure go ahead.'"

"Joe started thinking about another name for me. He came up with Roland Wheels, Roland Along, Roland Dice—but I didn't like any of those names. Finally he came up with Roland Stone. I thought it would be just a one shot thing so I agreed. I never thought the name would stick."

"We went back in the studio and overdubbed the song's vocals without the dope references. We called it 'Preacher's Daughter' and Mac added a hell of a piano part. 'Preacher's Daughter' got popular around New Orleans right away but nobody knew who Roland Stone was. Finally, word got around that Roland Stone was really Roland LeBlanc, the same guy that used to have the Jokers band. People started calling the radio stations and they started playing it, and playing it, and playing it. Nobody heard the record beyond Slidell, but around New Orleans it was pretty big. At first I used to like that song, but after we started playing it six or seven times a night, it started driving me nuts. We drew a tough crowd and all night long we'd get hoods coming up to the bandstand and yell at us, 'Play 'Junco Partner' again man!'"

An astute businessman, Vincent purchased the "Roland Stone" Spinett session from Caronna who in the interim had become LeBlanc's manager. Despite LeBlanc's objections, Vincent decided to keep the Roland Stone moniker on his subsequent Ace releases. Vincent didn't release 'Preacher's Daughter' on an Ace single, but later he included it on the *Just A Moment* album.

"Mac had this thing about 'Junco Partner,'" explained LeBlanc. "He thought there was just something in that damn song that was going to make it a hit. He wasn't sure what it was, but he was determined to find out. We even went to Cosimo's and cut it again for the *Just A Moment* album. Mac just wouldn't give up on that song. [Rebennack later cut it again as Dr. John on the the *Gumbo* album in 1972 and it's usually still often part of his live set.] We must have cut 'Junco Partner' 85 different ways.

"The other side [of the Spinett single] 'My Baby's Gone' was the only song I ever wrote. The break on it I stole from Ray Charles' 'Sinner's Prayer.' We used to kill the audience with 'Sinner's Prayer' every night. Earl Stanley played bass on that and the great John Boudreaux was on drums."

The first Roland Stone single on Ace, "Something Special"/"Desert Winds," was released early in 1960.

"Mac wrote both those tunes," said LeBlanc. "They were slanted towards pop because that was the market we were going after. Mac played guitar on both sides. Allen Toussaint arranged them and played the piano." 'Something Special' did well around New Orleans and in pockets along the East Coast. I did some record hops in Philadelphia to promote the single. Mac and I also joined a rock and roll caravan show with the Turbans and the Spaniels that toured the Gulf Coast for a couple of weeks.

The A-side of his his next single, "Just A Moment," was a memorable swamp pop ballad that reached number one on the WNOE and WTIX charts in New Orleans.

"There was a group from San Antonio, Sunny and Sun-Glos, that originally recorded 'Just A Moment'," pointed out LeBlanc. "Huey Meaux owned the publishing on the song and he sent the record to Joe Caronna hoping Jimmy Clanton would cover it. [Coronna occasionally supervised Clanton's recordings.] Jimmy said he didn't like it, but I thought it was great song. I told Joe, 'Let me cut it if Jimmy doesn't want to.'"

"I recorded 'Just A Moment' at a studio on the Gulf Coast [Singing River Studio in Long Beach, Mississippi]. We came back and did overdubs at Cosimo's. They brought in three black girls who looked about 12-years-old to sing background. One girl was so small she had to stand on a Coke box to reach the microphone. I had just gotten in a fight and had a fat lip, but I went in and redid the vocals swollen lip and all.

"Once the record came out it started to hit. All of a sudden, Jimmy Clanton had second thoughts about 'Just A Moment.' He went to Johnny and said he wanted to record it. Johnny had to keep Jimmy happy because he was Ace's best selling artist. So Johnny sat on my record and he didn't release it nationally. After it did about 100,000 in the South it died. Then they released Jimmy Clanton's version—my track with him singing on it.

Well guess what? That was one of Johnny's brilliant ideas that didn't work. Jimmy Clanton's record didn't do anything."

Clanton also covered LeBlanc's "Because I Do," another Mac Rebennack composition, that was contained on the *Just A Moment* LP. Clanton's version appeared on the *Venus In Blues Jeans* album.

The flip side of "Just A Moment" was "I Can't Help It," a Hank Williams song that featured Rebennack playing a Wurlitzer electric piano.

"That was around the time Ray Charles was having success with country material," said LeBlanc. "Johnny thought he might sell some records if I did country so we tried it."

LeBlanc's next single also included another Hank Williams cover, "Everybody's Lonesome For Somebody Else."

"The other side was 'I Was A Fool,'" said LeBlanc. "That had earlier been done by a guy from Baton Rouge, Johnny Fairchild, who also record-ed for Ace. I thought Johnny Fairchild did a great version of the song but Johnny Vincent wanted me to cover it. He had the publishing and thought the song might sell if someone else did it."

Late in 1961, Vincent issued the *Just A Moment* album which includ-ed to that point all three of his Ace singles, "Preacher's Daughter," and some great material that never was released on singles.

"Mac wrote 'I Wanna Wanna,' 'Symphony Two,' and 'Remember Me' that were on the album," said LeBlanc. "I didn't have a lot of input on my sessions because I was kind of intimidated by the great musicians that were in the studio. I mean who was I to offer suggestions to Red Tyler, Allen Toussaint or even Mac? When Mac had material that he thought was suitable for me, he'd call me and I'd go over to his house and listen to it. When Johnny would call a session, we'd get to the studio about an hour early, rehearse the material, and then we'd cut. Sessions never took longer than a two or three hours."

LeBlanc also recorded several sides at Ace that he wasn't credited for.

"'Kissin' Game,' 'Somebody Nobody Wants,' and 'Back To School Blues' were on Jimmy Clanton's *Teenage Millionaire* soundtrack album," said LeBlanc. "Dion sang them in the movie, but Johnny didn't want to lease material from another label. He had me recut those songs. That par-ticular session was a breeze. Mac just listened to the originals and wrote the charts out for all the instruments. I remember we had a big horn sec-tion in the studio. Big Boy Myles played trombone and John Boudreaux was on drums."

Another Ace recording that LeBlanc didn't get credit for was "Roll On Big Wheel," a fine Earl King composition, released under Benny (Mother-In-Law) Spellman's name.

"That was another one of Johnny's ideas," fumed LeBlanc. "Benny had just cut 'Mother-In-Law' with Ernie K-Doe. Johnny wanted to use Benny on something so he got him to do that "r-r-o-o-o-l-l on" part on the tune. When the record came out though, it had Benny's name on it—Roland got pushed aside."

The last Roland Stone single on Ace, "My Mother's Eyes"/"Someday Sweetheart," came out in the spring of 1962.

"Me and Mac were waiting in a lounge one night for Joe Caronna and we began fooling around at the piano," said LeBlanc. "Joe heard us do 'My Mother's Eyes' (a Frank Sinatra standby) and he thought that it would be a good song to record. The other side, 'Someday Soon,' was another one of Mac's songs."

Not long after the single was released, LeBlanc split with Ace, Rebennack, and the Skyliners.

"It was time for me to get out of the music business," said LeBlanc. "Everybody in the band was getting into drugs and we were all on an emotional roller coaster."

Nevertheless, in 1964 LeBlanc was playing music again at the House of Zin in the French Quarter. One evening Cosimo Matassa dropped by the club and suggested they get together and do some recording. "Remember That"/"Don't Believe Him Donna," was released on White Cliffs, but it didn't do much. Two years later, LeBlanc decided working at an uncle's dry cleaning shop beat hustling for gigs and keeping a band together. However, after two years he changed his mind and gave music another try.

"I moved to Texas in 1969 and started playing again," said LeBlanc. "I was Roland LeBlanc there, not Roland Stone and it was great. I didn't have to put up with people coming up to the bandstand all the time asking me to do 'Junco Partner,' I played R&B, had long hair, and wore platform shoes. They'd never seen anything like me in Houston before."

In 1983, LeBlanc was back in New Orleans running his uncle's business again with his past success as a local rock and roll icon was becoming a distant memory. However, in 1991 Orleans Records producer Carlo Ditta contacted him after reading a story about LeBlanc in the *Times-Picayune*.

"Carlo had some of my old 45s and asked me if I was interested in recording again," said LeBlanc. "I said, 'Sure, what have I got to lose?' A couple weeks later he called and said he talked to Mac. Mac wanted to do the session with me but was on a tight schedule. We only had one night to record. Earl Stanley played bass and Johnny Vidacovich was on drums. We called the CD *Remember Me* after one of my old tunes."

Remember Me revived a lot of great New Orleans music and LeBlanc's music career. While he continued to support his family with a day job, LeBlanc also began playing festivals, reunions, parties and local clubs.

In 1997, LeBlanc recorded a follow up live CD for Orleans which again displayed his New Orleans roots.

"I guess music is in my blood," said LeBlanc. "I just played at the Montreal International Jazz Festival [July 1999]. I had hundreds of people dancing to New Orleans rhythm and blues and they couldn't even understand the damn lyrics. But that's what good music can do."

Sadly, the Montreal date would be his last. LeBlanc died unexpectedly December 22, 1999, from complications after a routine hernia operation.

CHAPTER THIRTY FOUR
~ Ronnie Barron: Bad Neighborhood ~

It's an unfortunate truism that New Orleans musicians are often held in higher esteem elsewhere than in their own home town. Certainly the late pianist/vocalist Ronnie Barron fell into that category. Revered internationally, his death on March 20, 1997, barely caused a stir in New Orleans.

Barron's given name was Ronald Raymond Barrosse. He was born October 9, 1943, and grew up in a blue-collar neighborhood on Brooklyn Street in Algiers, one block from the Mississippi River. At the age of 15, Barron was already singing and playing piano with the Fidelities, a group that performed at the Orchid Club, a West Bank bordello/gambling joint. Professor Longhair also performed at the Orchid Club and Barron would observe him whenever he could. Spellbound by his technique and quirky rhythms, Longhair became Barron's enduring musical influence.

By the late 1950s, Barron had began cutting classes in order to hang out at the Specialty Records branch office on North Claiborne Avenue, hoping he might get signed by producer Harold Battiste. There he met Mac Rebennack—three years his senior—who was already writing songs and arranging recording sessions for the label. Rebennack and Barron both shared a passion—rhythm and blues. Together they began hanging out at Cosimo's studio where they watched Huey Smith, Smiley Lewis, Earl King, and Fats Domino record. Besides picking up tips from other musicians, they both hoped that someone might miss a session and one of them might be asked to fill in. Barron's got his first chance substituting for Huey Smith, who during a session, was hauled off by the sheriff because he was in arrears on alimony payments.

After Specialty closed it's New Orleans office, Rebennack began doing A&R work for Ace Records. In 1962, Rebennack recommended Ace sign Barron who had replaced Roland Stone in his band, the Skyliners. Rebennack arranged and played on Barron's first single, "Bad Neighborhood"/"Keeps Dragging Me On." Credited to Ronnie and the Delinquents, the release appeared on the short-lived JC logo, an Ace subsidiary label ran by Joe Caronna (as in JC). "Bad Neighborhood," with it's clever overdub of a pool ball being shot into a side pocket, did reasonably well in New Orleans. Rebennack also used Barron on Ace sessions he produced with Jimmy Clanton and Sugar Boy Crawford.

Rebennack would produce Barron's next release, "Hip Parade," a catchy dance record which appeared on Soundex, a label associated with the Ric and Ron labels. Barron and Rebennack also teamed up as Drits & Dravey on the bouncy, "Talk That Talk," released on Another, a label part of the AFO group.

Barron made one more Rebennack-produced single, "Did She Mention My Name," released on the Michelle and Wheeler Dealer labels. Frustrated by the rapidly stagnating New Orleans music scene, in 1964 Barron relocated to Houston where he played in a black club that producer Huey Meaux had an interest in. However, after a year in Texas, he returned to New Orleans only to learn Rebennack had moved to Los Angeles. Barron bought his own ticket west in December 1965.

With Rebennack's assistance, Barron picked up session work and formed the Prime Ministers, a group signed by Don Costa at RCA in 1967. At the same time, Rebennack and Harold Battiste began working on the original Dr. John recording project. Rebennack wanted Barron to assume the Dr. John role, but Barron's RCA contract wouldn't allow him to. Rebennack of course became Dr. John, but in the meantime, the Prime Ministers disbanded before their debut album could be completed. Barron then started working at the Factory in Hollywood where he was spotted by fellow New Orleanian, Louis Prima. Prima hired Barron as his arranger and supporting act with his high energy group, then installed at the Sands Hotel in Las Vegas.

Barron played with Prima for three years. During his Vegas days, he created his own cosmic character, Reverend Ether. (Ether is found between air molecules and is connected to the nervous system.) In 1971, Barron cut an album for Decca, *Reverend Ether,* that was produced by Rebennack's manager, Charlie Greene. The LP contained "Eighteen Sixty Two," a track Little Richard considered one of the best rock and roll songs he'd ever heard. However, rather than going on the road to promote the release, Barron joined Dr. John's band on tours of Europe and North America. Atlantic's Jerry Wexler, Rebennack's producer, used Barron on several sessions and was interested in signing him as a solo artist. Barron cut some demos in Muscle Shoals, but a deal with Atlantic was never reached.

In 1972, the Band's manager, Albert Grossman, saw Barron open a Los Angles date for Dr. John and invited him to move to Woodstock, New York, to join Paul Butterfield's new group, Better Days. Barron made two albums on Bearsville with Butterfield and was a member of the group until the band dissolved in 1975. He had an album deal with Bearsville, but he and Grossman couldn't agree on who would produce it. At that point, Barron again hooked up with Rebennack and contributed to the *Hollywood Be Thy Name* album. Next he was approached by John Mayall, who hired him for a European tour and used him on the *Banquet of Blues* album.

A rock-steady R&B and blues pianist, he later joined Canned Heat for recordings and tours. Other artists he played or recorded with in the 1970s included Tom Waits, B.B. King, Ry Cooder, John Lee Hooker, and Big Joe Turner. In 1978, Barron was signed by Columbia/Japan and recorded *Smile of Life*, an album that included tracks recorded in Japan and in New Orleans with Rebennack and the Meters.

In 1980, Barron began a belated acting career, appearing in *Stoney Island, Angel, One From the Heart, Above the Law, Code of Silence* and *Comeback*. However, music was his foremost interest and he worked on several solo projects during the decade. *Blues Delicacies* appeared in 1981, on Sunrise/Vivid. Two years later he cut *Bon Ton Roulet*—a tribute to Specialty Records for Takoma. However, Takoma sat on the project too long and the album wound up being released on the British Ace label. Both titles captured a lot of the classic New Orleans sound Barron grew up listening to and playing. It got stellar reviews.

Barron stayed active until the early 1990s when his health began to deteriorate. He eventually underwent a heart transplant but never regained the strength to be able to perform in public again. Barron composed new songs during his illness, but wasn't able to record them before his untimely death. He is buried at St. Bartholomew Cemetery in Algiers.

CHAPTER THIRTY FIVE
~ Skip Easterling: The Blue Eyed Soul Brother ~

One of the pioneers of Blue Eyed rhythm and blues was Skip Easterling, whose subtle but authoritative voice, had listeners in the 1960s and early 1970s wondering if he was a black or white recording artist.

James Robert "Skip" Easterling was born in New Orleans July 1, 1945, and raised on the Northshore in Slidell.

"When I about eight I was staying with my grandmother," said Easterling. "We lived near a Pentecostal church that had a brand new upright piano. She sent me out in the field to collect cow patties for fertilizer, but instead I'd run over to the church, sneak in a window and get on the piano. I got to the point where I could accompany myself when I sang. My grandmother caught me doing it a couple of times and whipped my behind with a sweet gum branch. But that didn't make me stop wanting to play music."

In 1955, Easterling began listening to the Louisiana Hayride broadcasts over KWKH in Shreveport where he first heard Elvis Presley. Impressed by the Memphis rockabilly artist, Easterling talked his mother into driving 200 miles to Shreveport so he could watch Presley perform at the Hayride. At the age of 14, Easterling had been in and out of reform school and Eddie Lang's Blue Note Lounge.

"Eddie was a blues guitarist from New Orleans," said Easterling. "He got married and moved to Slidell. Eddie had the best band around town. Eddie played his own tunes like 'Come on Home,' but he also did the happening tunes of the day like Eddie Bo's 'Tell It Like It Is' and 'Every Dog Got A Day.' Eddie Lang became my mentor and he let me sit in and sing with his band. One night he turned to me and said, 'Skip, you know for a white boy you got a lot of soul.'"

Easterling's friendship with Lang led to a trip to Cosimo Matassa's studio in 1962. As James Easterling, he recorded "You Think You're Smart"/"Angel of Mine," the lone release on Reno, a label Lang started with Johnny Williams, Easterling's manager.

"They might have pressed 300 singles but we never got any air play," said Easterling. "What I remember most about that record was going by WNOE and WTIX. Johnny and I could walk in the front door of those stations. But because Eddie was black, he had to use the back door. I felt bad because Eddie was one of the finest people I ever met."

Still in his teens, as Skip Williams, Easterling began playing R&B in small clubs on the Northshore and occasionally in New Orleans. In 1963, he cut a demo of Junior Parker's "Next Time You See Me" at Skip Godwins' House of Music Studio, which Easterling and Williams hoped to shop to a label.

"Johnny opened the phone book and saw Joe Banashak's A-1 Distribution Company—Instant and Minit Records," said Easterling. "He called and talked to Joe's wife Bobbie. She said if we had a tape to bring it down to their office on Baronne Street. We went down there and Bobbie listened to some of the tape and she called Joe. He listened to it and said, 'Son, you and I are going to make a lot of money.' I signed a contract, but because I was under 18, I had to get my mother's permission."

Easterling was assigned to ALON Records, a sister label of Instant that released Allen Toussaint productions.

"At the time Allen was in the army but he left Joe a lot of rhythm tracks," said Easterling. "Two of them were 'Sugar Blocks' and 'Don't Let Him.' They had scratch vocals on them by Mary Lynn. Joe played me the tracks and asked me if I'd like to recut them? Of course I'd have said yes to anything he played so we went to Cosimo's and recut them. When the record came out, Jack the Cat at WNOE, and Skip Wilkerson at WTIX played the piss out of 'Don't Let Him.' It was probably some of the worst singing I've ever done in my life, but back then I couldn't hear enough of it. I used to go back to Slidell and drive around in my mom's Falcon. I'd push the buttons on the radio and I'd be all over it."

Banashak took a special interest in Easterling and hired him to work at his distribution company and invited him to live with his family in Algiers.

"We went back in the studio and cut 'Wishing Well' and 'You Sit and Cry Alone,'" said Easterling. "Chris Kenner was at the studio that night and he told me, 'Skip that's a hit.' Sure enough WTIX and WNOE made it a pick of the week, but all of a sudden the Beatles started to happen and a lot of the New Orleans stations stopped playing local artists. At that point Joe decided to market me as a rhythm and blues artist because he could still get his records played on the black stations. My first R&B record, 'Shiny Gold Ring,' was one of the worst songs I ever cut."

By the mid-1960s, Easterling was a regular at Papa Joe's on Bourbon Street, in a band with vocalist Joe Barry, guitarist Joey Long, saxophonist Johnny Penino, bassist Earl Stanley, and drummer "Little" Joe Lambert.

"We were doing Bobby Bland, Irma Thomas, Arthur Alexander, Danny White, and Art Neville tunes," recalled Easterling. "Back then, if you got a job playing on Bourbon Street you were really something. We played the 3:30 a.m. to 10 a.m. set and packed them in. Then we got a job across the street at the Dream Room playing the 9 p.m. to 2 a.m. set. We just rolled our amps back and forth across Bourbon Street after the gigs."

For about a year the group also included a singer from Texas who also waited on tables.

"Angelo [the owner of Papa Joe's] hired this guy he called 'Jose Martinez,'" laughed Easterling. "The first night he sang 'Holy One.' I remembered buying that record a few years before and I really liked it. When 'Jose' walked off the stage I said to him, 'I'm willing to bet your real name is Freddie Fender?' He laughed and said, 'Yes it is.' He couldn't use the name Freddie Fender at the time because of the terms of his parole. [Fender did a stretch in Angola after a marijuana bust outside the Carousel Club in Baton Rouge.] We wound up becoming very good friends."

Toussaint had been discharged by the army and had returned to New Orleans in 1966 when he wrote and produced the soulful, "Run Along To Mama" and "All For You" with Easterling.

"That session led to some friction between Joe and Allen," related Easterling. "Allen said that I sang flat. He and Joe got in an argument at the studio and not long after, they dissolved their partnership."

With Toussaint out of the picture, Banashak appointed Eddie Bo as his new in-house producer.

"Probably the best thing that happened for me was when Eddie came along," said Easterling. "He had a way of making you feel relaxed but he was still able to get the most out of you. The first session I did with Eddie was 'The Grass Looks Greener.' Joe was in the studio and he was making a fuss over the way he wanted me to sing. Eddie took me aside and he said, 'Skip forget about Joe. Don't sing the way someone else wants you to sing—sing from the heart and do it your way.' Well I took his advice and I have to say that probably was the best vocal performance of my life."

"The Grass Looks Greener" rapidly made it to the top of New Orleans R&B charts, primarily because WBOK's Shelly Pope wore the record out.

"That's when I first started working black clubs," said Easterling. "I was sort of a novelty, but I played the kind of music that audiences wanted to hear and I always got over."

Bo also produced the splendid 1967 ballad "Just One More Time," but soon after, he also had a falling out with Banashak. As a result, Easterling's late 1960s sessions were handled by a succession of producers and the results were often mediocre. By 1970, Banashak had folded ALON and transferred Easterling to Instant. He also paired him with Huey Smith who began doing Instant productions.

"Joe called me and said he wanted me to cover 'Hoochie Coochie Man,'" said Easterling. "I was familiar with the Muddy Waters version but I wasn't into that Delta blues style. I pleaded with Joe, 'Please don't make me do that song.' But he was adamant. He said, 'Huey's got a completely different arrangement of it.' Well I was greatly relieved when I got to the studio because Huey had copied the bass line from King Floyd's 'Groove Me.' I went into Jazz City Studio and they recorded my voice over the rhythm track. It was like singing along with the radio. Later they added the horns.

"I called my wife from the studio after the session to tell her I was on the way home. She asked me how things went and I said, 'Well I really wasn't that impressed.' She wanted to hear the song so Cosimo played the half-track recording of it over the phone. After she listened to it she said, 'Skip that's going to be the biggest record you've ever had because it's got that happening beat.' I laughed, but she was right. It took off on all the black stations in New Orleans and the Deep South, but the white stations wouldn't play it. ["Hoochie Coochie Man" was the number one record on New Orleans' WBOK when Jean Knight's "Mr. Big Stuff"—nationally a number one R&B single—was number two.]

"Booking agents like Percy Stovall and Cleon Floyd started calling to get me to play black clubs. I sold out the I.L.A. Hall in New Orleans. Then I started doing gigs in Alabama and Mississippi with William Bell, King Floyd, Jean Knight, and Barbara Lynn—people I felt I had no business being on the same stage with. I couldn't believe I was making $1,500 for a 40 minute show.

"We went back and cut 'Too Weak To Break the Chains' [produced by Smith and Tex Liuzza] which I thought was even better than 'Hoochie Coochie Man,' but we couldn't get any air play. I wound up back playing four-hour gigs at redneck bars in Bogalusa and Picayune for $100."

Easterling had several more more singles on Instant, including a great version of "Travelin' Mood," but the program directors largely ignored them. By 1972, Banashak had became a Jehovah Witness and pretty much got out of the record business leaving Easterling without a label. In 1975, after he returned home from a gig in Pearl River, he checked his answering machine.

"Freddie Fender called from Corpus Christie, Texas," said Easterling. "I called him back and he said he had just cut 'Before the Next Teardrop Falls' and that it was going to be a hit. He wanted me to get the band from Papa Joe's back together and meet him in Texas. I got in touch with Earl but he said, 'No thanks.' I called Johnny and he said, 'Not interested.' I couldn't get anybody to go. They didn't think Freddie was going anyplace.

But I'll tell you those boys regretted not going after 'Before the Next Teardrop Falls' became a hit."

Easterling got out of the music business for a year and began working for a pest control company. However a year later, Reuben Howell, an ex-Motown artist who was selling used cars in New Orleans, convinced him that they should form a band. Easterling played with Howell until 1978 when Fender called again.

"He said I had one hour to make up my mind," said Easterling. "I talked it over with my wife and she said, 'Go ahead—just behave yourself and do a good job.' I met Freddie in Las Vegas at the Silver Bird Casino. He was appearing with George 'Goober' Lindsey from the Mayberry television show. From Las Vegas we flew to Nova Scotia, Canada. I got to see the world with Freddie and he took good care of his band. But it got old after awhile and I missed my family."

Easterling stayed with Fender until 1981, not long after the tragic tour bus accident that killed Joe Lambert.

"That was the straw that broke the camel's back," reflected Easterling. "I knew it was time to come home. My family was growing up and I wanted to be around them."

Easterling worked briefly on a tug boat, but In 1985 he opened an eight-track studio where he cut his last single "Meat Rack Tavern." In 1996, Easterling became interested in shopping some of his original songs and have them recorded by other artists. He began taping demos at Slidell's Mohawk Studio, but what started out as way to sell songs turned into a Skip Easterling CD project. However, shortly after he began work on the CD, Easterling was hospitalized with emphysema. He recovered, but in a highly publicized crime, his granddaughter Lorin was kidnapped, raped and murdered.

"You can't possibly imagine what losing a child like that does to you and your family," said Easterling. "That little girl is the last thing I think of before I go to sleep at night and the first thing I think of when I wake up in the morning. I got to the point where I didn't care about finishing the CD anymore, but I went back in the studio and did 19 tunes. George Cureau [the engineer] wanted to put it out the way it was, but I realized that my heart wasn't in a lot of the vocals and that I was capable of doing better. Finally, after a year and a half, I picked myself back up out of the doldrums by the grace of God and Prozac. I wanted to make damn sure the CD is the best thing that I'd ever done so I started working on it again. I felt I owed it to Lorin and my family."

Easterling's CD, *What's The Story On You* was remixed and completed at Bogalusa's Studio In the Country in the summer of 2000.

Percy Stovall - 1981

Patsy - 1957

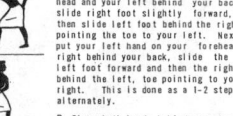

The ORIGINAL POPEYE

...AS DEMONSTRATED BY EDDIE BO

A. Put your right hand on your fore-head and your left behind your back, slide right foot slightly forward, then slide left foot behind the right, pointing the toe to your left. Next, put your left hand on your forehead, right behind your back, slide the left foot forward and then the right behind your back, slide the left, toe pointing to your right. This is done as a 1-2 step alternately.

B. Place both hands behind your back and slide feet in a 1-2 step as described above.

C. Place both hands together behind your head and continue to slide feet in a 1-2 motion.

D. Put your right hand on your shoulder and left behind your back, slide feet in a 1-2 motion again. Do the same alternating the hand and foot motions.

E. Put both hands on the hips, then slide beginning with the right foot & then the left as described above.

RIC RECORDS, INC.

630½ BARONNE ST.
NEW ORLEANS, LA.

AFO Executives - 1961   Top left to right: Red Tyler, John Boudreaux, Roy Montrell, Chuck Badie, Bottom: Melvin Lastie, Harold Battiste

Thurston and Beatrice Hill inside the Sugar Bowl - 1962

SUNDAY **DEC. 28** L. A. AUDITORIUM
2700 S. Claiborne Avenue
8:30 P. M. TILL ?
Adv. Tickets $1.50   At Door $2.00
With Giveaway Ticket $1.75

CHATMAN AND THE BUS DRIVERS present
A HOLIDAY SOUL FESTIVAL

FEATURING **OLIVER and the ROCKETS**
CHAS. BRIMMER
BEVERLY BROWN
CLEMON SMITH
ELECTRIC SOUL TRAIN
WILLIE WEST
DEACON JOHN
GEORGE VINNETT & "MR. G" - M. C's

Unknown, Fats Domino, Slim Whitman, Jayne Mansfield, Lew Chudd - circa 1957

South Rampart St. - 1982

Senator Jones - 1983

Roland Stone - 1960

Connie LaRocca - 1962

Skip Easterling - 1962

Al Scramuzza - 1980

Part VI

The Second Generation and Beyond

Many of the artists profiled in this section were inspired by the success New Orleans R&B artists had in the 1950s. Some graduated from being a sideman to a bandleader/recording artist, others started their career when the genre was at it's commercial peak in the 1960s, while many took the soul road when that style dominated the national charts. In addition, some pursued their dreams and eclectic vein of music as far as they could take it. Like "The Founders" chapter, many of the artists have become successful nationally, but others not nearly so.

By the early 1960s there was a discernible change in the sound of New Orleans's R&B. This modification was caused by several factors many which the artists profiled here helped to create. During the 1950s, most of New Orleans' R&B hits were produced by Dave Bartholomew and released on the California-based Imperial label. Aladdin, Specialty, Chess, Ember and Atlantic (also out-of-town labels) found success here as well, but more often than not, they reprised Bartholomew's proven formula.

By the 1960s, the New Orleans music industry was being rested away from out-of-town record labels by feisty local companies. These labels employed and encouraged new producers, writers, and arrangers like Allen Toussaint, George Davis, Earl King, Wardell Quezergue, Eddie Bo, Mac Rebennack, and Harold Battiste, all who brought innovative and commercial ideas to the studio. The upstart New Orleans-based labels also signed younger New Orleans artists and employed session musicians with open ears. Subsequently, there was a change in instrumental dominance on New Orleans R&B recordings. Pianos and saxophones-once the standard solo instruments-were often returned to being rhythm instruments. There place was taken in many cases by guitars, trumpets and organs. In addition, they were backed by modern electric basses rather than plodding string basses.

It must also be cited that by the 1960s, New Orleans was no longer the isolated outpost it once was. Jet planes and modern highways ushered New Orleans music in and out-of-town much more conveniently and it also made other styles more accessible to the Crescent City. Recording artists from other cities performed in New Orleans more often, subsequently influencing local musicians. Radio also nurtured the metamorphose, as records from New York, Chicago, Philadelphia, Detroit, Memphis, Cincinnati, Houston and Los Angeles were programmed on New Orleans stations that listeners and musicians absorbed.

By the beginning of the 1970s, the New Orleans R&B sound had been swept into a corner as the black record industry—developed and nurtured by innovative independent labels—was now controlled by major labels. The majors vice-like grip, extended to New Orleans radio and made it increasingly difficult for local labels to get their records played even in the town where they were made. When records didn't get played on the radio, they obviously didn't sell. As a result, many local labels threw in the towel, meaning fewer New Orleans R&B artists were recorded. Those that did could only hope a major would lease their material, otherwise they'd have to be content with local sales. However, many preserved and fought the odds. In the 1980s and 1990s, a revival of the sound occurred and many artist benefited. Here are some of their stories.

CHAPTER THIRTY SIX
~ Deacon John: The Creole Chameleon ~

Deacon John Moore is reflecting on his career in the spacious kitchen of his renovated camel back in Uptown New Orleans, a house which doubles as his residence and his band's rehearsal space.

One of the two phones on his antique thrift store bought porcelain table rings, and he grabs it on the the second ring. "Yeah," says Moore with caution in his voice. (Pause) "Oh yeah, I remember those dances— you guys really partied." (Pause) "Sure, we can play that night, no problem." (Pause) "Tipitina's old big room? You mean Tipitina's Ruins. Yeah we'll be looking forward to playing there."

Moore and the client take about one minute to agree on terms. With a look of satisfaction on his face, Moore puts the phone down and scribbles some notes in his date book.

"You know I played at that guy's high school prom," said Moore with a trace of amazement in his voice. "Now I'm going to play at his daughter's wedding."

If New Orleans has such a thing as a musical chameleon, it is certainly Deacon John. A war horse and model showman, he's entertained three generations of New Orleanians playing classic rhythm and blues, rock and roll, British rock, psychedelic music, pop, soul, disco, and blues.

Born June 23, 1941, Moore's mother knew her son would someday have a great voice because he cried loudly as an infant. Just to be safe though, she took the advice of an aunt and cut his fingernails under a fig tree. According to a Creole folk tale, this insured he would become a great singer.

"I grew up at 2252 North Tonti Street," said Moore. "I was the fifth of 13 kids. Technically, our family lived in the Eighth Ward but we lived just a block and a half from Elysian Fields, the dividing line between the Eighth and Seventh Ward. I went to school in the Seventh Ward at Corpus Christi and later St. Augustine High School. All my friends lived in the Seventh Ward. Back then it was mixed neighborhood. It was kind of rural. Down the street from us was a dairy farm and my father raised chickens, goats and ducks that we'd eat or he would sell or trade."

"My grandfather played banjo in Harrison's Creole Serenaders. I also heard music coming out of the barrooms on jukeboxes and people would play 78s at house parties. I was really lucky because my parents would send me to chaperone my older sisters when they went to high school dances. I got to see Snooks Eaglin when he played with the Flamingos, Art Neville and the Hawkettes, and Lil Millet and the Creoles. That was in the mid-1950s."

With a voice that earned solos at Midnight Mass, Moore joined a group called the Rockettes in the seventh grade which patterned themselves after the Hawkettes. However, he quit when the group's other vocalist proved to be more popular with female admirers.

"At that point I wanted to play the guitar too," said Moore. "People would jump over ten singers to get to a guy that played guitar and sang. I was delivering groceries then and I saved up enough money to go down to Abe's Pawn Shop on Canal Street and buy a Supro electric guitar. My first amp was a small Alamo, but then I got an old Gibson amp with two 10 inch speakers that I bought for $35 from Albert Scott."

"I was self-taught. I went down to Werlien's and bought a bunch of instruction books which taught me chords. I also bought a lot of records and learned to play by ear. One of the first songs I learned was Bill Doggett's "Honky Tonk." I never really took lessons, but I'd go over to the homes of Roy Montrell, "Papoose" Nelson, Justin Adams, and Prince La La's to get them to show me this and that. Once I went by La La's house and he was there with his bother "Papoose" and their father. They were passing the guitar around arguing how a certain song should be played. I used to see La La at Edna's Place. He'd sit at the bar drinking black port and lemon juice. Later on, I played on La La's first record ['She Put The Hurt On Me']. Roy Montrell was supposed to play on it, but he was on the road with Fats Domino. That's sort of how I got a lot of studio work. Papoose, Roy, Edgar Blanchard and Justin Adams were always the first choice, but if they were on the road when a session came up, I got called."

Moore's favorite New Orleans guitarist though is a musician not often mentioned.

"George Davis really blew me away," confirmed Moore, referring to the guitarist who is best known for co-authoring and arranging Aaron Neville's 'Tell It Like It Is.' "He played several instruments and excelled at them all. He could pick up an alto saxophone and blow Hank Crawford out of the way. But I really liked the way he played guitar."

Moore decided to start his own four piece band, The Original Echoes, with himself and Terry DeRouen on guitar.

"During that time not too many bands had a bass player," explained Moore. "Terry tuned his guitar down a whole step and played bass on the guitar behind me."

The Original Echoes disbanded when DeRouen's family moved to

California and the saxophonist left for college. Around 1957, Moore formed the Ivories along with saxophonist Roger Lewis who now plays in the Dirty Dozen Brass Band. The group has survived scores of personnel changes, but amazingly, is still very active today.

"The group's name came from the keys on the piano," said Moore. "But it was kind of a ironic because all dudes in the band were black. That's when they started calling me Deacon John. That name really came from a line in Roy Brown's song 'Good Rockin' Tonight.' The drummer in the band at that time was Al Miller who used to play with Roy Brown. He stuck me with the name at rehearsal. I was there with my short hair and a tie on. The bass player said to Al, 'He looks like a deacon.' Al turned to me and said, 'Let's call you 'Deacon John' then'."

Although the Ivories played many small black clubs in New Orleans, they also became phenomenally popular on the Tulane and LSU fraternity circuit. Led by Moore, who was a natural showman in the tradition of Chuck Berry, the Ivories were known for their sharp appearance and versatility.

"This was in the days before 'Louie, Louie,'" laughed Moore. "We played R&B—Fats Domino, Bo Diddley, Chuck Berry the Coasters. The frat kids ate that stuff up."

"We got on the frat circuit through a guy called Solomon Spencer. He was the entertainment director at Lincoln Beach and the band director at Cohen High. He booked bands at Lincoln Beach and the colleges, and the fraternity houses. He got us into Valencia [a private Uptown youth club], which introduced me to the higher echelon of New Orleans society. Spencer had a lot of bands. Spencer drove a Studebaker we called 'the whirly bird.' He'd pick up one band at 5:00 and then drop them off at their gig. Then Spencer would get another band and drop them off. Some nights he'd have four or five bands working and he'd pick'em all up at the end of the night and bring them home. He really got a lot of careers in New Orleans off the ground."

In 1960, the Ivories became regulars at the Dew Drop and eventually became the house band.

"Playing there was a little more bruising than playing at the fraternities," said Moore. "At the Dew Drop you played 'Don't Cry No More' instead of 'Yakety Yak.' Frank Painia [the proprietor] really liked the band because we had a lot of variety. We did a comedy as part of our act, but we also played hard R&B.

"One night Frank called me in his office and said, 'Look you red nigger, you could be a bitch, but I got to get some ink on your ass. You sign a contract with me and I'll make a deal so you can cut some records.' I never did sign his contract but we were hired and Frank booked us outside of New Orleans a lot."

A hotbed for up-and-coming talent, the Dew Drop Inn attracted scores of talent scouts, label owners, and producers. Moore's playing fascinated one producer in particular.

"One night Allen Toussaint came in and said, 'I like the way you sound. Would you like to play on a recording session?' Naturally I said 'Yeah.' The next day I was in the studio. That first session might have been Lee Dorsey's 'Lover of Loves' and then I played on K-Doe's 'Where There's A Will There's a Way.' Later there was Benny Spellman, Esquerita, Irma Thomas, Eldridge Holmes, Lee Diamond, and Chris Kenner.

"A usual Allen Toussaint session back then was besides me on guitar, Chuck Badie on bass, Red Tyler on baritone, Nat Perilliat on tenor, Melvin Lastie on trumpet, John Boudreaux on drums. We got paid $50 a man for a four song session."

Moore was present on several of the early Toussaint productions although at times he's barely discernible.

"If you listened to those early Allen Toussaint productions you can hear they were built around the piano," said Moore. "The other instruments were just dressing. Allen was trying to create his own identity. He'd always be telling Cosimo Matassa, 'Turn up the piano and turn the other instruments down.' My job was to accent the rhythm or the drum beat. Allen would only feature the guitar on a line or two. Often the chords I played were on the middle four strings of the guitar so it wouldn't stand out.

"Allen was a perfectionist and sometimes those kind of people can be temperamental. I've seen him throw tantrums in the studio and cancel a session. He was very particular about the way you played his music. If you played an upbeat instead of a downbeat, he'd stop the whole session and get mad."

"He used to get pissed off at the guitar because he couldn't make the piano cry like a guitar. Later though he had to adapt to change and let the piano play the fills behind the guitar."

Toussaint had approached Moore about recording for Minit but opportunity never materialized. However, in 1962 Moore cut his first record, "I Can't Wait"/"When I'm With You" for Rip Records.

"That was Rip Roberts' label," said Moore. "He had earlier had a record on Reggie Hall called 'The Joke' that did pretty well. At the time he had a gambling facility at his house on Duels Street and his brother sold used clothes. He was also the only guy in the area that could book Ray Charles. [Charles was once "involved" with one of Roberts' daughters.] Al

Reed wrote "When I'm With You" and Earl King contributed the flip side. Wardell Quezergue did the strings and played piano on it."

Another track Moore recorded for Rip, the aptly titled "Preacher Man," was leased to Frisco Records but was never issued and the tapes have seemingly disappeared.

Moore's initial single got a few spins on local radio but not much happened. The Ivories stayed busy though playing proms, highs school dances and frat parties while Moore continued to play sessions produced by Toussaint, and occasionally Dave Bartholomew, Harold Battiste and Red Tyler.

However, by the beginning of 1964 there was tremendous change in the New Orleans music industry, most of it not good. The Minit, Imperial, AFO, Ric and Ace labels had moved, were sold or folded. To make matters worse, Allen Toussaint was drafted so there was quite suddenly very little recording going on in New Orleans. If that wasn't enough, the British music invasion was in full swing and it knocked the New Orleans sound out of the charts. It also kicked many of the musicians that played that style of music out of the clubs and dances. For many artists, the shift in styles proved to be the kiss of death. Moore, however adapted.

"When the hair bands came in I jumped right on the bandstand with them," said Moore. "I was in competition with other bands for the proms and fraternity dances. I could see the R&B bands were getting less and less work, and it was because of the British Invasion. Personally, I really liked the Beatles—I was the only black guy that went to see them at City Park. They had a fresh approach to R&B and they had a lot more chord changes than a standard 12 bar blues. I loved the harmonies and the chord structure in their songs."

"R&B wasn't dead, but if I wanted to work, I had to play what the hair bands played because my audience was mostly high school and college kids. At the time I had a fabulous band. Zigaboo [Modeliste] was on drums, James Rivers on tenor, George French on bass, Sammy Berfect on keyboards, Sam Alcorn on trumpet and a girl named Veronica sang."

In 1967, Moore was doing a session with the Aubry Twins when he met their manager, Stanley Chaisson, who doubled as promotion man for All South Distributors. Moore signed a contract with Chaisson which led to his second single, "Haven't I Been Good To You"/"$1.98," which was issued on Wand under the name Johnny Moore. However, the contract he signed wound up stalling his career.

"I signed a five year deal with options and I wound up tied up 10 years," said Moore. "He kind of sat on my contract and didn't cut many records because it had to be under his conditions. He wanted to only record original songs and he wanted me, him and Paul Varisco [the leader of another band Chaisson managed] to be the songwriting team. But he wanted to split the publishing so there would be an extra points to go to him so he could pay off disc jockeys and the promotion people. Later he wanted to merge my band with Paul's band which I thought was ridiculous. The deal I signed really hurt my career as a recording artist."

That same year, Moore's music turned in yet another direction.

"A guy in the Paper Steamboat band told me about Jimi Hendrix," said Moore. "He said he was tearing up the whole world. I bought that first album, *Are You Experienced?,* and I said to myself, 'This the kind of music I had been wanting to do.' I went out and bought a used Stratocaster for $100 because that was the guitar Jimi used. I saw him play in Baton Rouge and it was the first time I heard music so loud it made my skin shake. After that I made the change from the Beatles to harder rock."

Right around this time Moore contracted hepatitis and was forced to take several months off. The Ivories continued to play, but without Moore's direction they split up. After he recovered, Moore formed another band, which he called Deacon John and the Electric Soul Train.

"I got rid of the horns and just had a four piece," said Moore. "We went from tuxedos to bell bottoms and fringe. I bought the big amps and all the effects. I had a tape delay effect where I could put the guitar down or throw it into the audience and it would keep playing."

"When the Electric Soul Train first started working it was in black clubs. In the beginning we didn't have much work but eventually we were playing almost every night of the week. I think black people went for us because the music we played was blues based and they'd never seen a show with strobe lights and all the effects. We started playing at the Night Cap on Louisiana Avenue where the Meters started out, but we wound up drawing more people than them. When we played the Nitecap, there would be as many people on the street trying to get in as there were inside the club. The sidewalk and neutral grounds would be packed but it started turning into a bad scene. People were dealing drugs outside the club and that attracted the police. Eventually that scared a lot of people away. For awhile I had Art Neville on organ in the band and Cyril Neville on drums. Art left the Meters for awhile because he'd had a disagreement with the other guys in the group."

During his psychedelic period, Moore was the first rock musician to perform with the New Orleans Symphony. On the recording front, he covered Jimmy Cliff's "Many River's To Cross" which landed on Bell Records in 1970.

"That was Stanley's idea," said Moore. "He wanted a softer approach than my hard rock stage act. He thought if I cut hard rock I'd be labeled 'a dinosaur.' We cut 'Many River's to Cross' in Baton Rouge. Stanley added strings to it to make it more pop and added background vocals. It got played and crossed over in the Gulf Coast from black radio to white radio. I didn't change my stage act though because I had a fan base that wanted me to play hard rock."

By the mid 1970s, Moore was faced with an old, and a new challenge.

"Disco came in and I jumped on the disco bandwagon," chuckled Moore. "That was also around the time that movie *Animal House* came out. Everybody wanted a band that played the kind of music that was in *Animal House*. I started getting calls to play toga parties, as well as high school and college reunions because I was the real deal. People remembered me from the old days. I brought the horns back and we did the material we played in the 1950s and 1960s. That kind of work has continued to this day."

Never one to stagnate musically, Moore also got interested in playing hard urban blues, ala Bobby "Blue" Bland, Little Junior Parker, Elmore James, and B.B. King. In fact he began teaching a course on blues in the New Orleans Public Schools.

"I got into playing blues on the slide guitar in the mid-1980s," said Moore. "I walked into a music store one day and saw Lenny McDaniels play slide. I asked him, 'How do you do that?' I started fooling around with it and doing open string tuning and raising the action on my guitar. It's not as easy as you think. That slide has to be right on top the frets. You got to think a whole different way than playing regular guitar. It took a lot of practice."

Around this time, Moore put together the New Orleans Blues Revue, which at one time or another featured Earl King, Chuck Carbo, Mr. Google Eyes, J.D. Hill, Juanita Brooks, Sadie Blake, Walter Washington and J. Monque'D.

Despite a return to the blues on stage, in 1990 Moore made a pop CD, *Singer of Song*, which he produced along with George Davis and put out on his own label, Jogeo.

"I wanted to make a CD designed for radio so I went in the studio with that concept," explained Moore. "The problem was when it came out, I couldn't get any stations to play it."

A couple of years later, Moore decided to take a more active role in the Musicians Mutual Protective Union Local 174/496, an organization he had joined in 1958.

"I felt like it was time for me to give something back and help other musicians," said Moore. "I've been a musician all my life, but I've done a whole lot of things besides just playing the gigs. Hopefully some of the younger guys can learn from my experiences."

In 1999, Moore started another label, Red Bone, and released his live set from the 1994 New Orleans Jazz & Heritage Festival.

"WWOZ had done a live broadcast of the gig. They had the rights to broadcast the show and then they were going to preserve the recording for archival purposes. I knew it was good set so I approached WWOZ and the Festival so I could put it out. When I played that set, I wanted to capture the authentic 1950s blues sound. A lot of the stuff I played I listened to when I was coming up. I didn't want to be a copy cat, but I wanted to sound authentic. Technically it was done on two tracks. Whatever the sound was on the preset mix that was it. I'm distributing it myself, getting it to record stores, and trying to get it to all the blues magazines so they can review it. I'm hoping it will be my ticket to get on other festivals."

Although he's been a musical icon in New Orleans for four decades, amazingly Moore has never played in Europe and rarely gets invited to play out-of-town blues clubs or festivals. He feels he is often overlooked because of his skin color.

"You see there is a white blues category and a black blues category," explained Moore. "I don't fit into either one. If you look at the real deal blues performers that go to Europe and Japan, they all have one thing in common—they all have dark skin. None of those artists look like me. Most people say it's not true, but there's definitely a color thing linked to blues. Europeans like their coffee black. I've also gone to several movie and television commercial auditions where I was told, 'Sorry, this part is for a black man.' I play the role of the tragic mulatto—I'm not black enough for this job, not white enough for that job."

At this point in Moore's career, working overseas would just be icing on the cake. Few New Orleans musicians have enjoyed a career as long and as successful.

"The only regret in my entire career is that I haven't recorded more," said Moore. "I've played music for 42 years and all I've got to show for it is three 45s, only one of which sold, and two CDs. That's not much. There are people that have been playing half as long as I have and have had 15 albums. But that's because I'm not a writer. I've tried to write songs, but I came to the conclusion that I was a better performer than songwriter."

"But I've been able to support myself with music all my life. Even some artists with hit records can't say that. I never had any royalties from hit records to supplement my income but I own my own home and I bought the house next door. The way I look at things, I think I'm pretty successful."

CHAPTER THIRTY SEVEN
~ Aaron Neville: The Voice ~

Aaron Neville has made a Manhattan hotel suite his headquarters for nearly a week. His stop in New York is part of A&M Records' promotional push behind the CD *To Make Me Who I Am*. Neville has been huddling with record company executives, tapping television appearances, performing charity benefits, meeting with his brothers to discuss the Neville Brothers next album, and doing telephone interviews with numerous newspaper and magazine journalists. After two more calls and a session of lifting weights in the hotel's gym, he'll perform with his band at the Beacon Theater before moving on to a Washington date. Neville will then return to New Orleans and begin recording tracks for an upcoming Neville Brothers CD, *Valence Street*.

"It's been pretty hectic since the album came out [October 1997]," said Neville on a call back to New Orleans. "I've been playing dates with my own band between dates with my brothers. I'm doing a lot of material from my new album but I'm also doing a couple of Neville Brothers songs."

A&M is trying to market Neville's *To Make Me Who I Am* strategically beyond mainstream audiences to include the adult R&B market, listeners that previously have ignored Neville's contemporary recordings. A&M's effort seemed to be working which is good news for Neville.

"I've heard the album on all kinds of different stations in all kinds of different cities," he reported.

Although Neville is largely pleased by the acceptance of his solo work nationally and the recorded work he's done with his brothers, he is annoyed by the criticism and occasional negative reviews he and the Neville Brothers seem to occasionally receive in New Orleans.

"In *Billboard*, *USA Today*, and magazines around the country we get four and five star reviews," said Neville. "People in other cities write great things about our music. But it seems like New Orleans writers and critics are quick to put down my records and the Neville Brothers records. I just don't understand that."

When asked if people in New Orleans have different tastes in music than the rest of the country, or have different expectations from him and his brothers, Neville responded: "The people in New Orleans are no different than anywhere. It's the media that's different. You know they say the hardest place to make it is in your own home town. Believe me that's true."

Clearly no matter what anyone writes about Aaron Neville, he has definitely made it. His success is attributed not only to his voice—which at times seems to be on loan from a higher power, but also his perseverance, and his abilities to conquer his inner demons, many which he addressed in the title track of *To Make Me Who I Am*.

The third of four brothers, Aaron Neville was born January 24, 1941, and grew up in a close knit family on Valence Street and later in the Calliope projects. Neville's father, Arthur, worked in the merchant marine and drove a cab, while his mother, Amelia, took care of the children.

"My mother was the sweetest and most understanding woman I ever knew," said Neville. "She read us *Peter Rabbit*. When we were children we all got a spanking if we did something wrong. I've always felt I got my strength from my father— my compassion from my mother."

As a youth, Neville was a fan of radio serials, especially those with a Western theme. When he had some change in his pocket, he'd go to the Gallo or the Carver Theater to watch Roy Rodgers, Lone Ranger, Hop Along Cassidy and Gene Autry films. Inspired by what he saw at the movies, Neville organized games of Cowboys and Indians in the Calliope's courtyard. He called himself "Apache Red" and terrorized his playmates on a stick horse he made from his mother's mop.

Singing cowboys left an impression on Neville, but not as deep as the spiritual music and doo-wop he heard on the radio. As an adolescent, Neville was big fan of Sam Cooke and Soul Stirrers, the Spaniels, the Moonglows, the Flamingos, the Drifters, and the Orioles.

"Doo-wop has always been my medicine," confirmed Neville. "There was a lot of dumb stuff going on then, and even dumber stuff now, but that kind of music is like a temporary escape from the real world for me."

Two other direct influences on Neville were his uncle George Landry and an otherwise obscure New Orleans singer, Issacher "Izzacoo" Gordon.

"Izzacoo sang with Huey Smith," said Neville. "We grew up together. He never got a chance to really step out, but he had a beautiful voice, especially for doo-wop. We used to harmonize a lot."

Neville made his professional debut with the Avalons at Lincoln Beach in 1956. He would later win several talent shows at Lincoln Beach, New Orleans' black amusement park, and occasionally sit in with Snooks Eaglin's group, the Flamingos, at the Driftwood Lounge in the French Quarter. In 1958, Neville's brother Art joined the Navy and Aaron took over his band, the Hawkettes. With the recently married Aaron at the helm, the Hawkettes were hired by rock and roll bad boy Larry Williams.

Williams took the band on the road to help promote his hits "Short Fat Fanny" and "Bony Maronie."

Like his older brothers Charles and Art, Aaron was on the road to a career in music but ran into a roadblock. Neville was arrested for joy-riding in a stolen car with some buddies and wound up doing six months in Orleans Parish Prison. During his incarceration he wrote several songs including "Every Day." When Neville was released, he sported several jail house tattoos including daggers on his cheeks.

Once back on the street, Neville was taken to a Minit Records audition by Larry Williams that was held at radio station WMRY. Producer Allen Toussaint was drop dead impressed with Neville's original songs and his voice.

"Aaron had a voice that sent shivers down your back," said Toussaint. "He had the voice of an angel. I don't think there's a vocalist alive that can match him especially when it comes to singing ballads."

Neville's first Minit single paired "Every Day" with the low-down "Over You" written by Toussaint and Allen Orange. The record sold well in New Orleans and in several key markets. It eventually nudged into the *Billboard* R&B charts for two weeks, making it to number 21. Neville waxed several superb ballads while at Minit, including "Lets Live." "I Found Another Love," and "Wrong Number (I'm Sorry Goodbye)." However some of his best performances were heard on up-tempo songs like "Sweet Little Mama," "Get Out Of My Life," and "Waitin' At the Station."

"Compared to what recording is like today those sessions were easy," recalled Neville. "You'd go in the studio, learn the songs, and record them. You were done in a couple of hours. There were no such things as overdubs. Allen was a great producer and wrote a lot of songs just for me. I think we worked well together and put out some great records."

Unfortunately, except for a few decent paydays on local gigs, Neville's seven Minit singles didn't amount to very much financially.

"I never got any royalties or even a statement from WMiit," claimed Neville. "Back then when you finished a session you owed the company money for studio time. No matter how many records you sold, it was never enough to pay back what they said you owed them."

When Lew Chudd sold Imperial to Liberty in 1963, Minit was included in the deal. However, the Los Angeles-based label didn't pickup Neville's contract. From 1963 to 1965, Neville split time between New Orleans and Los Angeles working with Larry Williams who unsuccessfully tried to secure him a recording contract. During this period he increasingly became dependent on heroin.

"I was still riding pretty rough in those days," admitted Neville. "I remember driving Larry's Jaguar from New Orleans to Los Angeles where I might have set the world's land speed record."

Once back in New Orleans, Neville made some gigs with brother Art's latest group, The Neville Sounds, but to make ends meet he toiled on the city's docks. Late in 1965, Neville was approached by writer and arranger George Davis, session man Red Tyler, and art teacher Warren T. Parker, who were partners in a production company, Par-Lo Enterprises. A friend of Davis', Wilbert Smith, a.k.a. Lee Diamond, once a member of Little Richard's Upsetters, and Neville's Minit label mate, had a title for a song he thought had a hook—"Tell It Like It Is".

Davis agreed, but Diamond went to jail before he could supply any lyrics for a song. Eventually, Davis wrote several verses which fit the title. Neville then went to Cosimo's studio to record "Tell It Like It Is" and three other Diamond/Davis compositions. On the session, Davis was on baritone sax, Tyler on tenor sax, Willie Tee on piano, Deacon John Moore on guitar, Emory Thompson on trumpet and June Gardner on drums. Tami Lynn and Moore supplied background vocals.

Davis and Parker shopped the session to several New Orleans labels but had no takers. They then took it to New York, but met with similar results. Finally, Davis, Parker and Tyler decided to put "Tell It Like It Is" out themselves. They pressed 2,000 singles and signed a distribution deal with Cosimo Matassa's Dover Records. To nurture local air play, Par-Lo agreed to give WYLD's Larry McKinley, then New Orleans' most popular deejay, half of the publishing on "Tell It Like It Is." Obviously McKinley played the single often and other New Orleans deejays quickly followed suit. In just a week, Dover reportedly sold 40,000 "Tell It Like It Is" singles in the New Orleans market alone. Shortly after, it began breaking in other markets and jumped into the charts.

"Tell It Like It Is" would top the R&B charts for five weeks and climb to number two in the pop charts. Eventually the single exceeded two million in sales and Par-Lo rushed a *Tell It Like It Is* album onto the market. Liberty, who still owned Neville's Minit masters, repackaged most of them on the *like it 'tis* album to coattail some sales from the Par-Lo hit.

With a gold record in his resume, Neville should have been strutting down easy street. However, besides some well paying tour dates with Otis Redding and Stevie Wonder, Neville didn't see anything but frustration from his biggest hit. Par-Lo and Dover overextended themselves by giving their accounts credit terms that were far too liberal. When Neville's follow ups, "She Took You For A Ride" stalled at number 92, and "Those Three Words" missed the charts entirely, the one-stops and distributors that sold "Tell It Like It Is" didn't pay for the 45s and LPs they had bought. Suddenly, Par-Lo and Dover couldn't pay their pressing, shipping, promotion, or tax bills. In the end the Internal Revenue Service seized their assets. Not only did Neville find himself without a record label, he never collected any royalties from Par-Lo for "Tell It Like It Is."

"It was a bad deal made by people from New Orleans who didn't know the business," said Neville. "There's still companies out there pirating that material—especially in Europe—and they've been doing it for years. I even saw a Neville Brothers CD box set over there that didn't have Cyril or Charles on it at all. It was just old stuff Art and I recorded back in the days."

Back at square one, in 1968 Neville had, "Ape Man"/"Forever More"on Safari that were left over George Davis produced Par-Lo tracks. He also had a release on Instant, "For Every Boy There's A Girl"/"I've Done It Again," that was spoiled by an inappropriate flute overdub. Later in the year, Marshall Sehorn and Toussaint produced "Where Is My Baby" for Bell which was a minor local hit.

Neville had two more singles on Bell including a superb remake of Art's "All These Things." In 1972, Sehorn struck a new deal with Mercury who released "Mojo Hanna"/"Baby I'm A Want You." The following year he recorded the street classic, "Hercules," but by now Neville's career was in deep mud. He and Cyril joined the Soul Machine, a band that temporarily relocated to Nashville, but eventually fell apart. With gigs infrequent, Neville returned to New Orleans and again toiled on the docks to support his family.

Things began to look up for Neville in 1976 when he and his brothers recorded the highly acclaimed *Wild Tchoupitoulas* album for Island with his uncle George Landry—Big Chief Jolly—and the Meters. The following year, he had a sizable local hit on Polydor with Joe South's country ballad "The Greatest Love." Around this time, Art and Cyril left the Meters and together the brothers rolled the dice and formed the Neville Brothers band.

The Neville Brothers quickly became New Orleans top club attraction and the group began a two decade-long role as emissaries of New Orleans music. While attaining the reputation as one of the funkiest bands in America, the Neville Brothers shows and albums included Aaron's vocal cameos. The band would slow the pace down and let Aaron display one of the sweetest voices in contemporary music.

Neville's next solo release, *Orchid In the Storm*, was an EP that included elegant renditions of several doo-wop classics. A big fan of the New Orleans Saints, in 1985 (the year the team experienced their first winning season) Neville cut "Who Dat, (Gonna Beat Them Saints)" for Who Dat/Mardi Gras Records. When the Neville Brother's weren't touring, Neville continued to do oldies gigs in small New Orleans area clubs in order to pay the rent on half of a double shotgun house on Valence Street and keep gas in his 1978 Thunderbird.

While Neville's celebrity fans could barely squeeze into Tipitina's, it was Linda Ronstadt who proved to be his eventual benefactor. In 1989, Ronstadt invited Neville to join her on the A&M album, *Cry Like A Rainstorm*. The LP, which contained the duet, "Don't Know Much," won a Grammy. The following year Neville was signed by A&M and his debut for the label, *Warm Your Heart,* became a soft rock favorite. Neville's momentum continued with *The Grand Tour* and *Tattooed Heart*. By the mid-1990s, his quivering falsetto was regularly heard on mainstream FM radio and on several radio and television commercials. All of this was accomplished between recording and tour dates with the Neville Brothers. Finally physically and financially stable, Neville was able to afford a comfortable home in the exclusive Eastover subdivision and dabble in a new hobby, collecting late model high performance automobiles.

"I've really been blessed," concluded Neville. "My life has been a gift from God."

POSTSCRIPT

This is the way it was in December 1997. *To Make Me Who I Am* didn't live up to expectations and after five CDs on A&M, Neville's contract wasn't renewed by the label. Neville took matters into his own hands, built a small studio, and created his own label, aptly named Tell It Records. The first release, *Devotion*, was issued in September of 2000 and nominated for a Grammy.

CHAPTER THIRTY EIGHT
~Danny White: Kiss Tomorrow Goodbye ~

Although the late Danny White was never able to crack the national charts—as did several of his contemporaries—his singles were as good, if not better than many of the national New Orleans hits of the era. His best known releases, "Kiss Tomorrow Goodbye" and "Loan Me Your Handkerchief," are still New Orleans favorites and justifiably remembered.

Allen Toussaint put White's importance into perspective:

"Danny White was never really a big name artist, but he had a band that used to work at the Sho Bar on Bourbon Street that was really hot. Danny inspired me to write some songs, but unfortunately we [Minit and Instant Records] weren't recording him at the time, so I gave the tunes to K-Doe. I'm speaking about "Mother-In-Law" and "Certain Girl"–that was Danny White's style. There was something very influential about Danny White that was absorbed by a lot of artists that had records here."

Born Joseph Daniel White, July 6, 1931, at New Orleans' Charity Hospital, he was the youngest of seven children and grew up in the Hollygrove and Seventh Ward sections of the city.

"There was always lots of music around growing up," said White in 1985. "I sang in church and in plays at school. It was really my teachers who thought I had a good voice and encouraged me."

White's professional debut didn't occurred though until he was a 20-year-old marine stationed at Fort Pendelton, California.

"I used to go this club, the Offshore Lounge, to listen to music," he explained. "I saw people like Al Hibbler there. They had a house band but one night the vocalist didn't show. People started asking the band for requests but they said they couldn't do them without the singer. I got up and told the band I could do the requests. I ended up singing the rest of the night and the owner offered me a full-time job as vocalist. I told him I couldn't because I was a marine, but I agreed to sing weekends and he paid me $10 a night."

When White's enlistment concluded he returned to New Orleans.

"I went back to school on the GI Bill," he said. "I used to go out to clubs like Hayes' Chicken Shack, the Dew Drop and Shadowland to hear music. I got to know a lot of musicians, so me and a guy called Jack decided to start a small band that worked weekends. One of the first places we played was Dupree's Lounge on North Claiborne and St. Bernard. We played there one Saturday night and the place was packed. During the break, someone came up to me and said, 'Danny, there's a white guy outside in a Cadillac who wants to talk to you.' I went outside to see what he wanted. The guy told me he was going to reopen a club called the Golden Cadillac. It was a big club across the road from the Fifth Precinct on Poland Avenue near the Industrial Canal. It had been a country and western place [Elvis Presley performed there] but he wanted to book R&B. He offered to pay us much more money than we made at Dupree's, so I brought Jack out to talk to him, It worked out that our band actually reopened the Golden Cadillac. That was 1955.

"We played the Cadillac every Friday and Saturday and were really popular. So popular that they expanded the club's capacity from 700 to 1,000. After a few months, Jack wanted to go back to playing black clubs [the Golden Cadillac's clientele was strictly white] but I didn't want to and the band split up. I had to recruit some new musicians to keep playing there. I got a good six-piece band together but I didn't have a name for it. At the time, there was a new brand of cigarettes that I had bought. I looked at the package and they were Cavaliers. I thought, 'Hey that's a great name. I'll call the band Danny White and the Cavaliers.' We played the Cadillac for five years solid."

During his Cadillac tenure, White cut a single for Nashville record man, Shelby Singleton, who leased it to Dot. Huey Smith also brought White to the attention of Johnny Vincent at Ace Records. White cut some excellent up-tempo material for Ace, but Vincent didn't think it was suitable to release.

"A lot of club owners started coming by the Cadillac to see what was happening and ask me if I wanted to work for them," said White. "I'd always said 'No,' but after awhile I wanted to circulate. I told the owner of the Cadillac that I wanted to play at some other places and he said, 'Danny, I hate to lose you, but you can always come back when you're ready.'"

Danny White and the Cavaliers became a regular attraction at the Dream Room on Canal Street and the Safari on Chef Mentuer Highway. However, most people remember the band from their lengthy tenure on Bourbon Street.

"My saxophone player at the time was John Payne," said White. "He had his own gig on Bourbon Street at the Sho Bar. I started dropping in to see him and I said to myself, 'Hey I like this scene.' I talked to the club owner, Sam Anselmo, and gave him my card. He hired me to play a morning jam session on the weekends from 2 a.m. to 6 a.m. I didn't know if it would work, but people started following us from our gig at the Dream Room or the Safari to the Sho Bar. We'd get 300 people in there on a Sunday morning."

Anselmo's son, Jimmy, who later owned Jimmy's Music Club on Willow Street, recalls a typical evening with Danny White and the Cavaliers at the Sho Bar.

"Danny White and the Cavaliers were the hottest band in town in the early 1960s. You'd have to compare them to the Cold or the Neville Brothers when they were at their peak. Imagine Tipitina's or Jimmy's packed full of people with the sun coming up. That's what it was like when Danny played the Sho Bar. Danny had a strong following. We'd go see him at the Safari on Chef Menteur Highway, then jump in our cars and race to the Sho Bar for the early morning set. Every time a fight would break out, the band would cut whatever they were playing and break into 'When the Saints Go Marching In.' That was a signal for the bouncers to break up the fight."

In 1961, White and the Cavaliers were one of the highest paid and and most popular bands in New Orleans, despite not having a record out. That changed when Connie LaRocca, who had recently formed the Frisco label, approached him.

"Connie dropped by the Safari one night and talked to me about making a record," recalled White. "But to tell you the truth, we didn't have much time to think about recording. Once the college fraternities started booking us we only had one night off a week. Man we were hot then and we were really professional. We had sharp uniforms and we were very disciplined. We played places where they wouldn't hire other black bands. Anyway, Connie finally talked me into coming down to her office. Al Reed was down there—he was her writer and arranger. He played something on the piano and it sounded real good—it was 'Kiss Tomorrow Goodbye.' But he did it up-tempo. I said, 'If I was going to record it I'd slow it down.'

"Right away Connie said, 'Well why don't you cut it that way?'

"At first I wasn't interested, but I agreed because I didn't think anything would become of it. The next week we went down to Cosimo's Studio. Wardell Quezergue arranged both sides. Cosimo told Connie that 'Kiss Tomorrow Goodbye' sounded like a hit. She called Hal Atkins, who was her partner and a deejay at WYLD, to come down and listen to it. He got real excited and got Cosimo to press a demo so he could break it on his show the next day. People started calling him right away wanting to know where they could get the record, but he had to tell them they'd have to wait until it hit the shops. When I got a copy of the record, I took it to the Safari to gauge the people's reaction. Everybody liked it right away, but it was the flip-side they liked best, 'The Little Bitty Things.'"

Nevertheless, it was the haunting "Kiss Tomorrow Goodbye" that became the public's favorite and it eventually was the number one single on every New Orleans radio station. As a small New Orleans label, Frisco was hard pressed to distribute the single outside of the Gulf South, but they were approached by Arleen Records who distributed it nationally.

"I guess 'Kiss Tomorrow Goodbye' could have done better," speculated White. "It got good reviews in *Cashbox* and *Billboard* [although neither magazine charted the record]. It might have done better if Connie would have leased it earlier but she wasn't interested. I didn't make any big money off the record, but I liked everyone involved with the label."

White followed "Kiss Tomorrow Goodbye" with the popish "Never Tell Your Friend" and the dance novelty "The Twitch." Both singles showed that White and Frisco were reaching for an audience beyond New Orleans. Although it didn't get any attention, a better track might have been the passionate minor-keyed blues ballad "Why Must I Be Blue"—the B-side of "The Twitch."

His first release in 1964 was the emotive Earl King composition, "Loan Me Your Handkerchief," which rose to the top of all the New Orleans radio charts and attracted attention from several national labels. Decca eventually leased it and it sold around 100,000 singles.

"That record did real well in areas like Philadelphia and Washington," said White. "Universal started booking me and I went on the road with some package shows with Marvin Gaye, Otis Redding, and Jimmy Reed. I played the Apollo and a lot of big theaters."

After "Loan Me Your Handkerchief," White's Frisco sessions were transferred to Memphis.

"Hal Atkins started working for WDIA in Memphis," explained White. "He got to know Jim Stewart and Booker T at Stax. He arranged for me to fly up to Memphis to cut with Isaac Hayes and Dave Porter."

White's last Frisco single, "My Living Doll," was a fine ballad with shadings of the early Stax sound. Frisco did continue to record White in Memphis, but his singles began appearing on ABC-Paramount. The Earl King compositions "Mr. Moonbeam" and "Hold What You Got" were great performances, but the British music invasion ensured that they got little airplay.

"Connie got out of the record business then and I was between labels," said White. "Stax used to lease material to other labels—not just put their own stuff out. They got me a deal with Atlas out of New York. That's when 'Keep My Woman at Home' and 'I'm Dedicating My Life' came out."

White's later recordings were leased to Decca, including "Cracked Up Over You"/"Taking Inventory," a rousing two-sider with Booker T & the M.G.s, and the Memphis Horns supporting. The single got some airplay in New Orleans but little elsewhere. By the mid-1960s, White and the Cavaliers had to contend with a bizarre new prejudice integration created and the style of music imported from England. Well paying fraternity gigs and white club dates suddenly disappeared when club owners and booking agencies became convinced that R&B bands would attract black patrons that they felt would scare off their white clientele. In addition, many listeners now preferred the bands inspired by the Beatles and the Rolling Stones over R&B bands. With gigs becoming few and far between, in 1966 the Cavaliers disbanded and White searched outside the field of entertaining for employment. In 1969, he began managing New Orleans hottest groups, the Meters. White, who had earlier worked with members of the group, was the ideal individual to show the youthful Meters the discipline they needed to survive on the road.

The following year, White cut one last single, "Natural Soul Brother"/ "One Way Love Affair," which was produced by Allen Toussaint and leased by Marshall Sehorn to SSS-International. However, the single failed to sell even in New Orleans. Three years later, he had abandoned the music business again and moved to Washington, D.C., where he became a furniture salesman.

Over the next two decades, White returned to New Orleans periodically to visit family, enjoy Mardi Gras and appear on oldies shows. He hoped that one day his Frisco singles would be reissued, and he nurtured the idea of one day returning to New Orleans to perform and open a booking agency. Unfortunately these goals would never be realized. Danny White died January 5, 1996 at his home in Capitol Heights, Maryland, after suffering a stroke. Two years later, many of his best recordings were reissued on *The Frisco Records Story*.

CHAPTER THIRTY NINE
~Warren Lee: Climb the Ladder ~

In 1982, Charly Records released one of the all-time best collections of New Orleans soul and R&B material aptly titled *Sehorn's Soul Farm*. The anthology included tracks by Aaron Neville, Benny Spellman, Earl King, and Ernie K-Doe among others, but it was the otherwise obscure Warren Lee who stole their thunder with the storming "Star Revue," and the irresistible "Climb the Ladder."

Warren Lee, whose full name is Warren Lee Taylor, garnered a name check in John Broven's *Walkin' To New Orleans*, but most of his contemporaries barely remembered him. Over the years I'd collected several of his singles, which only added luster to his legend, but even after spending hours of detective work—combing newspaper obits, city directories, discographies, library files and Social Security records—I couldn't track him down.

Finally, with the assistance of Marshall Sehorn and BMI, in the fall of 2000 I tracked down a West Bank address on Taylor. Upon reaching him via telephone, admitting my admiration for his recordings, and desire to interview him, Taylor declared that not only would he be happy to discuss his career, but he wanted to come to my house the next day to talk about it! Sure enough, the next afternoon a compact gregarious gentleman in his early 60s arrived to tell his story.

Warren Lee Taylor was born May 11, 1938, at Vacherie, Louisiana, and grew up on the Laura Plantation. At the age of nine, Taylor moved to New Orleans with his family and they lived in the Uptown section of the city.

"I loved the strings," recalled Taylor. "When I was 12, I begged my daddy to buy me a guitar. As a little boy I used to watch Guitar Slim. I understudied this man. Everywhere he went I followed. He was the first man I ever saw play the guitar with his teeth. I practiced doing that until I chipped most of mine. I wanted to be just like him. Guitar Slim stayed at the Dew Drop and I ran around in there every day with tennis shoes on chasing after him."

Other guitarists Taylor befriended at the Dew Drop included Walter "Papoose" Nelson, Roy Montrell, Irving Bannister, Smiley Lewis and Earl King.

"Earl and I were partners in mischief," laughed Taylor. "One night we poked a hole in the sheet rock with a pencil outside of Patsy's [Patsy Valdalia, the transvestite emcee at the Dew Drop] dressing room so we could peak in and see what was going on in there. Oh man it was a crime. Did we see some stuff."

"I remember when Earl came out with 'Mother's Love' and it sounded just like Guitar Slim. People started saying Earl was going to take Slim's place. Earl played the Dew Drop one night [shortly after it came out] and the place was packed. Meantime, Slim was in Flint-Goodrich Hospital down the street [he'd been involved in a car wreck] and he shows up that night in a hospital gown. Slim comes up to the bandstand and says 'Earl you can't do that song. It's too close to my style.' Earl thought Slim was gonna beat the hell out of him. But Earl has paid his dues and came up with his own style. Earl has wrote some beautiful songs and he's a great entertainer. I really admire him."

A fabulous showman, ("If you missed my show you only lived half a lifetime.")Taylor and his combo played regularly at the Dew Drop, Jessie's in Marrero, the Sugar Bowl in Thibodaux, and he was booked into other surrounding towns by Percy Stovall along with Chris Kenner, Joe Tex, and Ernie K-Doe.

"One night in 1959 we had a job at James' Bar in Marrero with K-Doe," said Taylor. "I got there and the owner started wondering where K-Doe was. We called K-Doe's house and got Shirley [K-Doe's first wife]. She yells, 'K-Doe, it's James and he wants to know why you're not there.' K-Doe didn't have bus fare! K-Doe lived on Second Street. The New Orleans bus was seven cents then. Catch the Jackson Avenue Ferry which was free. Then get on the Gretna bus, which wasn't but a dime, and you'd be at the joint. K-Doe didn't even have 20 cents to make the gig."

Taylor caught his first break in 1961 when Eddie Bo—who was recording and scouting talent for Joe Ruffino's Ric and Ron labels— approached him at the Dew Drop.

"Eddie said, 'Lee you're good enough to go on a record.' I told him, 'Eddie I've been looking to make a record.' He asked me if I had any original material. I said,'Sure.' We went to Cosimo's on a Monday and the following Saturday, 'Unemployed' was out. It was that fast. 'Unemployed' was a comical song."

The flip side, "The Un-Huh," was the first of a series of catchy dance records Taylor would record. The Ron single did well around New Orleans and in 1962 Taylor was back at Cosimo's. In the interim, Ruffino had set up Soundex as a subsidiary label and transferred Taylor's recordings to it.

"That's when Eddie Bo, Mac Rebennack and myself came up with the answer to 'Anna,'" said Taylor. "His [Arthur Alexander] record was

'Anna (Go With Him)', mine was 'Anna (Stay With Me).' It did pretty good around here and I started working better jobs and making more money. After that my contract was up, I went to Wardell Quezergue's new label NOLA. They were promising big things. I did 'A Letter To Santa' and 'Anna (We're Gonna Get Married).' They did okay around here, but NOLA didn't have national distribution so not much happened."

Taylor also accounted for the sensational "Every Hour, Every Day," and "The Key To Your Door," one of the toughest blues sides to come out of New Orleans in the 1960s. After NOLA, Taylor cut "Geraldine"/"London Bridge" for New Orleans disc jockey/promoters Herb Holiday and David Nebel who leased both sides to Floyd Soileau at Jin Records.

In 1965, Taylor was approached by Allen Toussaint, who along with his new partner, Marshall Sehorn, were beginning to release New Orleans singles fast and furiously.

"I'd been knowing Allen from the Dew Drop," said Taylor. "Some nights he'd get up and jam with my band and he'd say, 'Lee, you're funky.' One night after a show we sat down and he asked me what was happening? I wasn't recording at the time and I told him I wanted to get something out. He said, 'You ever thought of trying me?' I knew he had records out on Lee Dorsey, but I didn't know he was searching for other artists. Allen said, 'If you come up with something good, bring it to me and I'll go with it.' Three months later, I was fooling around with my tape recorder and I came up with 'Star Revue.' I took it to Allen and we rehearsed at his house on Earhart Boulevard. He said, 'Lee that's what I'm looking for.' Allen came up with a hip piano arrangement and I put all the star's names in the song. James Brown, Solomon Burke, Wilson Pickett, Otis Redding, Irma Thomas and me—I was the Mighty King Lee [laughs]."

"When that record came out [on DeeSu] as soon as the needle hit it— BAM—that sucker smoked. I never understood—still can't—why that record didn't hit. The black stations here played it but didn't break out of New Orleans. But every time I played "Star Revue" on the bandstand, the house would go wild. Even Allen said, 'Lee I don't understand it. That record's got everything. A great arrangement, great lyrics and you sang great.'"

Taylor followed with another solid dance groove "Climb the Ladder" ("Make like a fireman when a house is burning down."), but outside of a few plays on WBOK, WNNR and WYLD, it strangely didn't even grab New Orleans' attention.

"It's not always what's on a record that makes it a hit," reflected

Taylor. "It's what you got behind a record. You had to have money to get records played then. I didn't have the connections and wasn't the kind of guy to sniff a deejay's behind to get mine played."

Taylor kept plugging though and accounted for other great DeeSu sides like "Lady," "Mama Said We Can't Get Married" and "Underdog Backstreet."

"'Underdog Backstreet' did great," said Taylor. "Shelly Pope [at WNNR] played it four times every hour. I got so embarrassed I asked him not to play it so much."

By the late 1960s, New Orleans labels were becoming hard pressed to keep up with the demands local radio stations were placing on them. As a result many labels—including Deesu—began leasing material to national labels with larger promotional budgets. As a result, Taylor wound up on the New York-based Wand label with another great dance record that was produced by Toussaint and featured the Meters as background musicians.

"'Funky Belly' came out but the radio stations wouldn't play it," said Taylor. "They said it was too vulgar. Larry McKinley at WYLD told me 'You're talking about something under people's clothes. We can't play that.' But two months later, Johnny "Guitar" Watson came out with 'Ain't It A Bitch' and it was a smash. Larry sat on that sucker."

In the early 1970s, Toussaint and Sehorn opened SeaSaint Studio. In order to make it successful, they began concentrating on attracting business from national labels and for the most part discontinued releasing singles aimed at the local market. As a result, Taylor and several other New Orleans artists were cut loose. In 1974, Taylor cut "Direct From the Ghetto" and "So Suddenly" for Choctaw, a label connected with Cosimo Matassa. It was another solid release, but the advent of disco kept it off the airwaves. Although Taylor primarily supported his family with his earnings from repairing air conditioners, he kept his band—Past, Present and Future—busy until 1977 when he was felled by a stroke.

"I came home from a job in Vacherie, went to bed, woke up the next morning and nearly dropped dead," said Taylor. "I didn't remember anything from April 20 to August 26 because I was in a coma. Stayed in a wheelchair over a year. An old man came to see me—'Gospel Pa.' He said, 'Lee why can't you move your hand?' I told him, 'I had a stroke.' Then he asked me, 'Did you ask Jesus to move it?' I had to say, 'No.' Then he said, 'Think it and say it.' I did and it worked. Eventually I got out of the wheelchair and taught myself to walk again. I tried playing after awhile but they wouldn't hire me at the World's Fair [1984] because I had a limp. I put music down after that but I've got no regrets. My wife and I have been married 41 years and we raised six great kids. I think that's more important than having a hit record."

234

CHAPTER FORTY
~ Martha Carter: You Can If You Think You Can ~

One of New Orleans' great rhythm and blues unknowns is Martha Carter who cut four great singles, and whose local popularity rivaled that of Irma Thomas and Barbara George in the early 1960s.

Born Martha Nelson, June 9, 1941, she grew up in the Ninth Ward. A member of the Greater Mount Carmel Baptist Church, her voice originally sang praise to the Lord. Carter's break into secular music occurred at the age of 16 when she asked Oliver Morgan to let her sing with his band one evening at Mary's Bar on Tchoupitoulas Street. Morgan was impressed by the youngster's voice and bold stage presence, so he invited her to become part of his revue.

By 1960, Carter was appearing around New Orleans with Porgy Jones' group, singing jazz, standards, as well as rhythm and blues. Spotted by Ric and Ron A&R man Eddie Bo, he brought Carter to his boss Joe Ruffino to audition. Her powerful voice impressed both men and she was signed. Carter's first trip to the studio was in August 1960, when she was featured on Bo's tough second line opus, "Ain't It The Truth Now." The following month, Carter cut her own single "I'm Through Crying"/"Nobody Knows," both written and cleverly arranged by Bo. The pleading ballad "I'm Through Crying," released on Ron, got a lot of airplay locally and sold quite well. With a hot record out, Carter began appearing with Bo and his band on several shows around New Orleans. It was Carter's fortune (or misfortune) to join Ric and Ron when Joe Jones' Ric single, "You Talk Too Much," was beginning to make some noise nationally. Unfortunately for Ruffino, he was strong armed into signing away the ownership of the record and publishing by Roulette Records. Embittered by the situation, Ruffino attempted to extract revenge on Roulette by having Carter record an answer to Jones' hit.

Although Carter was less than enthusiastic about cutting Bo's composition "I Don't Talk Too Much," the song's one-upmanship is irresistible. Ruffino issued the record on Ric, using Carter's maiden name. Despite a heavy ad campaign in the trades, "I Don't Talk Too Much," stole little of the thunder from Jones' record, although it did well in New Orleans.

Carter's third release, the attractive "One Man's Woman"/"You Can If You Think You Can," was produced by Harold Battiste and employed the AFO Combo. "You Can If You Think You Can," was especially memorable because the shave-and-a-haircut arrangement was a prototype for Barbara George's "I Know," which Battiste produced a few months later for AFO Records.

Carter's last release, "Then I'll Believe"/"You Shall Not Be Moved," was issued early in 1962. Bo again supplied the lyrics and arrangements, but the material was a departure for him. Unlike previous songs, he borrowed heavily from traditional spirituals and was less than original. It was Carter's least popular single. Later in the year, Ruffino died leaving Carter without a label. Shortly thereafter, her career as an entertainer ended when her doctor found polyps on her vocal chords and advised surgery. The operation was unsuccessful. Not only was Carter's voice altered, but singing began causing her a great deal of pain. Today Carter still lives in New Orleans and works as a seamstress.

CHAPTER FORTY ONE
~ Robert Parker: Barefootin' ~

Although he's best known for the unforgettable New Orleans hit, "Barefootin'," Robert Parker is also a very important figure in the development of the city's rhythm and blues tradition. Born October 14, 1930, Parker has made a name for himself as a session musician and a solo recording artist. He has also played in several of the great New Orleans R&B bands and backed scores of artists.

"I grew up on Melpomene [now Martin Luther King Jr. Boulevard] Street between LaSalle and South Liberty," recalled Parker. "My grandmother played the piano, but it was Louis Jordan who really inspired me. I used to go see all his movies and I liked his music. I decided I wanted to play saxophone. I played in the band at Lafont and Booker T. Washington High School. Everybody I hung around with in my neighborhood played music—June Gardner, Huey Smith, Lee Diamond, Sugar Boy Crawford, Big Boy Myles, Danny White, and Irving Banister. Guys like Fats Domino, Dave Bartholomew, and Professor Longhair would come to our neighborhood looking for musicians."

It was the legendary pianist Longhair who gave Parker his first break while he was still a teenager.

"Fess was playing downtown at the Caldonia Inn," said Parker. "I'd go down there on Sunday evenings when they had jam sessions. Fess asked me if I wanted a job because his band needed a saxophone player. He had a Tuesday night gig in Gretna at the Pepper Pot. I played with him there about two years. Al Miller was on trumpet and Louis Joseph on drums. When he got a contract to record [1949], we did the first version of 'Mardi Gras In New Orleans' [for Star Talent]. That was a song I'd been playing with him well before it was recorded. Later we did 'Baldhead' and 'Hadacol Bounce.' That was on Mercury and then we did some things for Atlantic [where Longhair recut 'Mardi Gras In New Orleans'.] Fess taught me the ropes."

After his stint with Longhair, Parker moved to the Tiajuana Club where he led the house band which also included David "Fatman" Mathews on piano, and Billy Tate on guitar.

"I was there five years," said Parker. My job was to warm up the house and back the featured artists. I was a showman—I walked the bar, took my horn out in the audience and played under the tables on my back.

The Tiajuana was a small place, but a lot of big talent came through there like Little Richard and Gatemouth Brown. We played behind Guitar Slim the first time he worked there and he worked there a lot. Bobby Marchan was emceeing then and was real young at the time. He was dragging [impersonating females] then and he booked a lot of drag shows in there too. A lot of talent scouts came by the Tiajuana. Johnny Vincent [Specialty Records and Ace] came in there. That's where he found Guitar Slim. Dave [Bartholomew] came by there and so did the guy from Aladdin [Eddie Mesner]."

By the mid 1950s, Parker had been hired by booking agent Percy Stovall. He put a new band together, Robert Parker and the Royals, that included George Fortier on sax, Bobby LaCour on guitar, Joe Butler on drums, Raymond Jones on piano, and Walter Bourgeois on bass.

"We had a strong front line," confirmed Parker. "Stovall hired us to back people like Roy Brown, Big Joe Turner, Wynonie Harris, Solomon Burke, Charles Brown, and Amos Milburn. We played every city and country town between Texas and Florida. We made $25 a night on the road and $10 a night in New Orleans."

Parker was also starting to get calls for studio work from labels like Ace, Chess and Specialty. He cut four instrumentals for Specialty in 1956 but none were released at the time. Parker later played on Huey Smith's hit, "Don't You Know Yockamo," and he joined the Clowns on a lengthy tour.

"Once Cosimo put me on his list, I did a lot of sessions," said Parker.

Parker's first solo release was the rousing R&B instrumental "All Night Long," which appeared on Ron in 1959.

"That came through Eddie Bo," said Parker. "He was doing A&R for Ric and Ron. I'd been knowing Bo from doing gigs with him. He had the house band and he started using me on the sessions he produced. I played on Al Johnson's 'Carnival Time,' Irma Thomas' 'Don't Mess With My Man,' and on records by Martha Carter, Johnny Adams, and Chris Kenner. We also did the first tune that I sang on, 'Across the Tracks.' Playing with Bo made me realize I had my own style. Before I got with him, I played what I was told to play in the studio. Bo told me, 'Do your own thing man. Play what you feel.' For the first time I finally did."

After Ric and Ron folded in 1962, Parker cut a single for Imperial, "Mashed Potatoes All Night Long"/"Twistin In Outer Space," and did a session for the Booker label. Parker continued to work for Stovall on weekends, but gigs were becoming increasingly scarce for R&B musicians in the mid-1960s. To make ends meet, Parker worked at Charity Hospital as an orderly. However, Parker's fortunes would soon change for the better.

"Stovall booked a job at Tuskegee University in Alabama," said Parker. "The kids there had a saying, 'Hell Yeah,' for when they really liked something. That stuck in my mind. So when we came back to New Orleans, I came up with a song with, 'Hell Yeah' in the lyrics. Next time we played there, I did the song and the girls took off their shoes piled them in front of the bandstand before they danced. That stayed with me. After that I went on the road with Chris Kenner. We played a show in Miami with a comedian who had two daughters that were shake dancers. When he came on stage he said, 'Everybody get on your feet, you make me nervous when you're in your seat.' Well that rang a bell. When I started writing 'Barefootin',' that was the opening line and then I worked in the other ideas. I finished the song and I took it to Wardell Quezergue. He was the A&R man for NOLA Records. NOLA was Clinton Scott, Ulis Gaines, Wurley Burley and Wardell. I cut a demo that Wardell liked but Gaines and Scott didn't. They offered the song to other artists, but I wound up cutting it. Wardell's musicians played on it—George Davis played guitar and James Rivers played sax."

"NOLA sat on the tune for nearly a year. Finally Hank Sample, he was a singing disc jockey who had a couple of records out, heard it. He had a record shop on Claiborne Avenue. He told Gaines, 'Man you better release this it's going to go big.' So NOLA pressed some records and gave him two boxes and they sold right away. Then Gaines took the record to the radio stations in town and it started to bust open. NOLA made a deal with Cosimo who distributed the record through Dover. All of a sudden my life changed from worse to better. The Queen's Booking Agency picked me up and my first out-of-town job was seven days at the Apollo in New York. On the first show I did 'Barefootin',' but it didn't go over. Before the second show, the emcee came to my dressing room and said, 'Robert you got to sell yourself. You got a hit record out there called 'Barefootin'.' Go on stage without your shoes on.' I did and the audience gave me a big ovation. After that I was on the road with the Marvelettes, the Temptations, the Four Tops, and Joe Tex."

"Barefootin'" was especially appealing because it had the contemporary soul flavor but still retained the syncopated New Orleans beat. The single reached number two in *Billboard's* R&B charts and number seven in the pop charts during the spring of 1966. It also did especially well in England and Canada. Still Parker felt the record didn't reach it's full potential.

"I don't think NOLA promoted the record as well as they could have," he claimed. "Some of the NOLA people got greedy. I'm sure 'Barefootin'' sold over a million but I never got a gold record."

Parker stayed on the road doing one-nighters behind "Barefootin'" for more than a year. On the record front, a hastily assembled Barefootin' album was released and his next single, "Tip-Toe" (a clever answer to "Barefootin'"), reached the national charts briefly in 1967. Excellent NOLA singles like, "Yak Yak Yak," "Foxy Mama" and "Everybody's Hip-Hugging," only did well in New Orleans. Parker stayed with NOLA until they and Dover folded in 1968. As events transpired, NOLA played a major part in Dover's demise, owing Matassa $70,000 in studio costs when the IRS shut his doors. Two years later, Marshall Sehorn and Allen Toussaint signed Parker and leased a couple of strong singles to the Nashville-based Silver Fox label. However, "Your Shakin' Things Up" and "The Hiccup" did little. With "Barefootin'" yesterday's news, Parker was back home playing in Clarence Henry's band on Bourbon Street and occasionally doing oldies shows in Jefferson Parish.

In 1974, Parker was reunited with Wardell Quezergue at a session at SeaSaint Studios. Sehorn leased a couple of singles to Island Records including, "Give Me the Country Side of Life," a local hit that just missed breaking nationally. He also appeared on Island's landmark LP, *New Orleans Jazz & Heritage Festival 1976*.

Parker performed sporadically around New Orleans in the late 1970s and 1980s, his marquee gig being the Jazz & Heritage Festival. He caught a break when "Barefootin'" was used on a Spic 'n' Span television commercial in 1983, which produced some unexpected royalties and attention. In 1987, "Barefootin'" was re-released in England and was a moderate hit overseas again.

In 1994, Parker and his wife of 40 years moved to Sunshine, Louisiana, where he began driving a school bus. However, music remained the biggest part of his life.

"I still practice the saxophone every day and I try to write new material," said Parker. "I still feel like I'm creative. I've recently been doing some recording again with Marshall Sehorn. I know I'm old school rhythm and blues, and I don't do any new sounding stuff, but I don't think that sound has gone away."

In 1999, fortune smiled on Parker again when, Harrah's, the land based New Orleans casino, used "Where the Action Is"—the flip side of "Barefootin'"—in their radio and television commercials, albeit a version recorded by Luther Kent.

"I was surprised they wanted the song," said Parker. "But it looks like good things might happen because of it. Harrah's paid me up front for using the song and they want me to do promotion for them and to perform there. I'd really like to get start playing more and recording again. I'd really like to keep the New Orleans R&B sound going and I still think I've got something to offer."

CHAPTER FORTY TWO
~ Prince La La: She Put the Hurt On Me ~

Prince La La hasn't reached the mythical proportions of Stagger Lee, but he has become a musical legend via Oliver Morgan's signature tune "Who Shot The LaLa." Every day of his life Morgan gets asked, "Was there really a person named La La?" The answer is definitely yes.

Prince La La's career was brief, but he left an important footnote in the history of New Orleans music. Had he not died under tragic and mysterious circumstances in 1963, Prince La La might have extended a promising career, and perhaps been the rock icon Mac Rebennack—Dr. John—became.

Prince La La's given name was Lawrence Nelson. Born in 1936, and the youngest of four children, he came from a desperately poor, but talented Ninth Ward family. La La's father was Walter Nelson, a. k. a. "Captain Midnight" and "Da Da," a guitarist who played with Smiley Lewis and Noon Johnson. His older brother, Walter "Papoose" Nelson Jr., played with Professor Longhair before becoming Fats Domino's longtime guitarist. Papoose tutored Mac Rebennack and was a popular studio guitarist in the late 1950s.

"La La," a common New Orleans alias for Lawrence, was hung on Nelson as a child. Like his older brother, La La began playing the guitar at an early age.

"Papoose played more like his father," recalled Oliver Morgan, who befriended the Nelson family when he was 13. "He played a lot of heavy chords. I wouldn't say that La La was as good of a player as Papoose, because Papoose was a legend around here. But La La played a funk style of guitar long before funk got popular."

Several New Orleans guitarists, including Rebennack, Deacon John and Walter Washington have confirmed this, and that La La was an influence on their playing.

"I used to go by La La's house and play Charles Brown's 'Driftin Blues' on the piano," added Morgan. "La La, Papoose, and their dad would all play guitar behind me at the same time. I never knew La La to do anything but play music. He played a lot at a place called Picou's that was on St. Philip Street next to the Iberville Projects. Miss Edna (Picou) owned the joint. She was the woman La La's father stayed with. When I played in there with Jessie Hill and La La, the place would always be packed."

Hill, who was married to La La's sister Dorothy, invited his brother-in-law to accompany Barbara George on an audition he arranged with the recently formed AFO label in 1961.

"La La was in Jessie Hill's loop," recalled AFO Records founder, Harold Battiste. "Jessie brought him with Barbara George to help her audition. La La had a song, 'You Put the Hurt On Me,' that Barbara was going to record, but she couldn't get the words right. La La sang it and played during the rehearsal. Finally, one of the musicians, maybe Melvin Lastie, said, 'Hell, he sounds so good let's record him.' The first session was split between La La and Barbara. [George recorded the hit "I Know."]

La La was a shy, reserved guy, but when he sang, he came across as extroverted. We were all fascinated by his voice. I compared it to Ray Charles. He was easy to work with, certainly a lot easier than Barbara was. He was a smart guy, but he grew up in a neighborhood where if you displayed any type of intelligence, it wasn't exactly cool. He wasn't the kind of person you could sit down and talk politics with, but he wasn't the kind of guy that had to have his behavior monitored."

"You Put the Hurt On Me"— a popular street expression—became "She Put the Hurt On Me," and was the initial release on AFO Records in the summer of 1961. It was a bouncy, funky song that embodied the early 1960s New Orleans sound. Battiste and his fellow AFO executives came up with the Prince La La nom-de-disque and they subsequently created the Prince La La stage persona.

"We'd recorded an African thing, 'Need You', that I played soprano sax on," continued Battiste. "It was never released on AFO [The song was included on *More Gumbo Stew*, an AFO anthology reissued in 1994.], but we picked up on that sound. La La started wearing Africian-styled clothes on stage to create a different kind of image."

Considering this was an era when male performers often wore tuxedos on stage, and the symbols of black pride weren't displayed prominently, in 1961 it was a radical idea for an artist to dress like an African Prince.

"Need You" was written by Jessie Hill, but credited to his wife Dorothy, because Hill was then under contract as writer to Minit Music, the publishing arm of his label, Minit Records. "Need You" would later become the inspiration for the original Dr. John sound that was heard on the *Gris Gris* album which Battiste produced in 1967.

"The arrangement was an African/New Orleans/Congo Square type of spiritual thing that you can only find here," said Battiste. "It was something we at AFO felt. Mac eventually made that sound commercial, but we never cut anything with commercial as a forethought—only as an after-thought."

"She Put the Hurt On Me" got AFO out to a fast start. Although Battiste considered it a regional record, "She Put the Hurt On Me" entered the *Billboard* R&B charts in October of 1961 and reached number 28 during its month long stay. La La's record and George's "I Know" attracted the interest of Juggy Murray, the owner or the New York-based Sue label. He signed AFO to a national distribution contract and picked up both singles. The deal helped La La's record, but George's "I Know" stole the thunder, rising to number three in the national pop charts early in 1962.

"La La did some local shows and I went to Detroit with him," said Battiste. "I didn't play in his band, but I took him to some radio stations and looked out for him. He was a regular guy that didn't adapt to the star persona. I think all of that mystified him."

On the strength of his hit, La La toured briefly with Fats Domino in North Louisiana. In December of 1961, La La and several other AFO musicians backed Smiley Lewis on his lone Okeh session. That same month, La La and Morgan—who recorded for AFO under the alias Nookie Boy— performed on a huge New Orleans show at the I.L.A. Hall headlined by George.

"They called us the AFO family," said Morgan. "To be honest with you, La La and Barbara weren't showmen, they left that to me. They just did their songs and got off stage."

La La's second and last single, "Getting Married Soon," is a great record that showcase superb vocals and a punchy arrangement. The song include some interesting lyrics, including one where La La invites his father, Miss Edna and Papoose to his wedding. The single sold around New Orleans, but did little elsewhere.

The AFO/Sue deal fell apart after just six singles, after Murray objected to AFO musicians playing on Lee Dorsey's "Ya Ya" without his permission. Murray assumed George's contract, but everyone else at AFO, including La La, had to scramble. AFO survived briefly with only local distribution, but eventually Battiste and most of the musicians/executives moved to Los Angeles late in 1962.

La La remained in New Orleans however and continued to play at Picou's and a few other small clubs, but sadly not for long.

According to *The Louisiana Weekly*, at 8:00 p.m. on the evening of October 27, 1963, La La (who at the time was separated from his wife and living in Treme) went to a sister's (not Hill's wife) rooming house on Pauger Street to watch television. La La's sister and brother-in-law left for the evening and returned around 2:00 a.m. and found him unconscious.

Although they tried to revive La La, he died before they could get him to the hospital.

For weeks La La's death was unclassified pending the toxicology reports. Although Morgan contends La La had a taste for liquor but never drugs, rumors of a narcotics overdose circulated. These rumors were fueled in part by the fact that Papoose had died of a heroin overdose the previous year in Harlem's Theresa Hotel while touring with Fats Domino. Evidence pointed to a heroin overdose, but apparently one that wasn't self-inflicted. Word on the street was that La La was given a "hot shot" by a dealer who had a new score of heroin and wanted to know the strength of his purchase. Obviously it was far too strong for La La, who was just 27 when he died, leaving a wife and two sons. A well-attended jazz funeral was held at the Bladdin Funeral Home in Treme.

Oliver Morgan claims he composed "Who Shot the LaLa" on the way home from a gig not long after La La's death even though the credits on the single don't list him as the writer. Morgan said he was unaware of copyrights at the time and allowed Eddie Bo to take co-writers credit. While the lyrics to Morgan's classic aren't historically accurate, La La was apparently shot, although not with a .44. A classic New Orleans performance, "Who Shot the LaLa," recorded in 1964 for the GNP Crescendo label, provided a springboard for Morgan's career and allowed him to pay tribute to a good friend, and a deserving artist who might otherwise have been forgotten.

CHAPTER FORTY THREE
~ Wallace Johnson: I'm Grown ~

Of the dwindling number of 1960s New Orleans recording artists still active, the talented Wallace Johnson remains one of the most underrated and unappreciated of all. Johnson's anonymity can easily be explained, as he didn't perform in New Orleans until the late 1990s. Nevertheless, his clutch of fine singles on AFO, Sansu, and RCA, rank as some of the era's best examples of Crescent City rhythm and blues.

Johnson was born October 8, 1937, at Napoleonville, Louisiana, a small town 65 miles west of New Orleans on Bayou Lafouche.

"I was born on the Martin Plantation," recalled Johnson. "My father did every conceivable type of work expected on a sugar cane plantation. My mother sang in the church choir and was a seamstress. I wanted to be in the choir too, so when I was three, she made me a choir gown and a cap so I could sing with her. When I was 13, I saw Roy Brown in a little town called Bertranville. There was a real popular priest there, Father Maloney, who gave dances. I stood in front of the bandstand the whole night focused on nothing but Roy Brown. This was back when he had records like 'Cadillac Baby,' 'Brown Angel' and 'Good Rockin' Tonight.' Roy was a big star. He was the first black entertainer I ever saw who advertised something. There used to be posters up everywhere for Jax Beer with Roy's picture on them.

"I went in the service in December 1954. After basic training I was stationed in Fort Lewis, Washington. One day in the service club, a guy asked me if I sang. He mistook me for someone else so I said, 'No I don't.' But then he said, 'Well anybody can sing, let's get a group together.' I knew some guys in my barracks that sang so we started harmonizing. Next thing you know, we had a five-member group. This was during doo-wop times. We performed at all the talent shows and usually we won. In 1956, I got transferred to Alaska. The only group I could find to sing with there was a gospel group and we performed spirituals in church."

Johnson had gotten married while in the service and after his discharge in December 1957, he and his growing family moved to New Orleans where they had several relatives. Interested in pursuing a career in music, Johnson began attending Houston's School of Music on North Claiborne Avenue. After auditioning and being turned down by Imperial's Dave Bartholomew, he approached Harold Battiste who ran Specialty

Records' New Orleans branch office on the second floor over Houston's. Battiste was interested in recording Johnson, but couldn't because Specialty was in the process of closing their New Orleans operation. However, he told Johnson about a new enterprise he was planning.

"Harold was going to start his own label—AFO [All For One]," said Johnson. "He said it was time for the New Orleans musicians that make music, start making money from it, not the out-of-town companies that came here to record it. I agreed with him and that's how I wound up on AFO."

In 1962, Johnson debuted on AFO with, "Clap Your Hands"/"Peace of Mind." Unfortunately, it came out immediately after AFO acrimoniously split with Sue, a New York-based label with a national distribution network that AFO was affiliated with. With only a New Orleans distributor (All South) pushing Johnson's release, it remained a local single. He also recorded the brilliant "Private Eye" for AFO which amazingly didn't see the light of day until Ace issued it on *Gumbo Stew*, a CD released in England in 1993.

"That session was done in a studio built behind Ric Records on Baronne Street," recalled Johnson. "I met Allen Toussaint there that night. He couldn't do the session because he had a contract with Minit, but the rest of the AFO Combo played on it. We started recording at midnight and didn't get out of there until day break. 'Peace of Mind' was the first song I ever wrote. 'Private Eye,' that was a funny tune ['I'm gonna hire a private eye to help the two I've got.'] but it was a true story about somebody I knew. I cut the session and went back to Napoleonville. I moved back after I broke my ankle in an accident. Later, I found out the label folded and all the AFO cats went out to the West Coast. Then I started seeing Harold ever Wednesday night on *The Sonny & Cher Show*."

Johnson was then performing clubs along Bayou Lafourche most weekends, his marquee gig being Thibodaux's Sugar Bowl, where he often opened for touring acts like Bobby Bland, and Ike & Tina Turner. In 1965, Johnson was back in New Orleans and ran into Toussiant again.

"Allen had just gotten out of the service and became partners with Marshall Sehorn," said Johnson. "This was right after Allen produced Lee Dorsey's 'Ride Your Pony.' I wound up doing several singles with Allen that came out on on Sansu and RCA."

Johnson's Sansu debut, "Something To Remember You By"/"If You Leave Me," was splendid. "Something" sounded like a second line answer to Martha Reeve's "Dancing In The Street" and begged to be a hit. However, as catchy as it was, and even though it was distributed nationally by Bell, it didn't get further than New Orleans. The follow up, "I'm

Grown"/"Baby Go Ahead," was also a funky single, driven by Toussaint's in-the-pocket piano and George Davis' distinctive guitar. However, it also remained a neighborhood record.

"None of those records were cut live," recalled Johnson. "Allen would have the musicians record a backing track and then I'd come in and do the vocals. I though "Something To Remember You By" was pretty good. "I'm Grown" was an arrogant tune that told a different story. The last single I did with Allen, 'I Miss You Girl' and 'On My Way Back Home,' came out on RCA in 1973. That was cut in Atlanta. I flew there with Aaron Neville. He cut "Hercules" [which appeared on Mercury] at the same session. We recorded in Atlanta because they were building the new studio [SeaSaint] on Clematis Street and it wasn't ready yet."

The RCA single stalled and Johnson returned to Napoleonville, gigging occasionally on weekends. Eventually he abandoned the idea of becoming a recording star and concentrated on supporting his family—driving trucks and working in a lumber yard. After his wife died and his children were grown, Johnson returned to the New Orleans area and began working for a company that laid sewer lines. In the mid-1990s, several events happened which revived Johnson's music career.

"I met some of the guys that played with Rockin' Dopsie Jr. including [bassist] Alonzo Johnson," said Johnson. "I also talked to 'Junk Yard Dog' [Wilbert Arnold], Walter Washington's drummer. I wanted to do a four song demo to try and get somebody interest in doing a full CD on me. They said both said, 'Just call when you're ready.'"

"My girlfriend at the time was a teacher and she had an exchange student from Germany who wanted to buy some New Orleans music to take home. He came over to her house with a CD he bought in the French Quarter called *Gumbo Stew* and asked me if I thought it was any good. I saw Barbara George, Prince La La, Dr. John and Willie Tee were on it and then I saw my name. "Private Eye" was on there—I couldn't believe it. We played the CD and I told him, 'Yeah this is great!' Discovering that really fired me up.

"At the time, I used to go by Allen's [Toussaint] house to shoot pool with him and Marcel Richardson. I asked Allen what he thought of me cutting a demo? He said, 'Yeah, go ahead. Get the musicians together and you can use the studio [SeaSaint] any time.' I had, 'Write My Baby A Letter' and 'Something's Wrong,' and Allen gave me a song, 'I'm Your Man.' I got the musicians together and we did four tunes. I paid them $100 each. Allen heard the demo and a couple of weeks later he came by my house. He said he had some friends in New York that were interested in starting a label and would I be interested in being involved? Of course I was, that's why I cut the demo. I wound up doing a CD for NYNO, *Whoever's Thrilling You,* which Allen produced that came out in 1996.

The CD set off a brief fire storm of activity which included a cameo at the Jazz Fest, several in-stores, club appearances (the first time he ever appeared on a New Orleans stage) and a two week NYNO promotional tour. However, the excitement eventually died down and Johnson returned to driving a truck, and scuffling for local gigs. Four years after the release of *Whoever's Thrilling You,* Johnson realized that to jump start his career, he needed a new release.

"I consider myself a blues singer but I've found out from trying to gig in clubs, New Orleans isn't really a blues town," reflected Johnson. "If I do get to record again, I'd like to do more mid-tempo and up-tempo material. I've talked to a few labels, but they all have a different way of saying they're not interested. I thought about doing a CD myself, but I don't know if that's the way to go. I want to get a new CD out—not to be a star—but I'd like to be able to put a good band together, jump in a van on weekends, and gig in Houston, Jackson, or anywhere there's an audience for the blues. My one dream though is to someday perform overseas. One day I'd love to be able to say I did that."

CHAPTER FORTY FOUR
~ Willie West: Did You Have Fun? ~

A contemporary of Ernie K-Doe, Johnny Adams, Aaron Neville, and Danny White, Willie West's career has been largely overlooked because his resume lacks the one identifiable hit that can shape a recording artist's career. Nevertheless, West's string of excellent singles confirm that he is a top ranked New Orleans artist with an attractive and adaptable voice.

Miller William West was born December 8, 1941, at Raceland, Louisiana, a town southwest of New Orleans in sugar cane country. As a teenager West listened to Bobby Bland, B.B. King, and Eddie Bo records he heard on the radio. Occasionally, West would visit nearby Thibodaux where two of his early influences lived—Guitar Slim and James "Thunderbird" Davis.

"Slim had a room at the Sugar Bowl," recalled West. "He'd sit outside of it during the day with a jug of port wine plucking on his guitar. I was too young to go in the Sugar Bowl, but one night I looked in the window of the club and Slim was playing the guitar and hanging from the rafters. Thunderbird was Slim's buddy and they performed together. I learned a lot from Thunderbird. He could sing spirituals that would make you want to cry and he was a great showman. He could do acrobatic things with the mike stand that were outrageous. After Slim died, Thunderbird made lots of gigs with my band before he moved to Houston and started making records."

West had a cousin that played guitar and together they founded the Sharks, a four-piece band with West on vocals. The Sharks played Raceland clubs like Tee Maws, a white club, and the Two Tone, the town's only black club. They also appeared at clubs in nearby Bayou Lafourche towns like Donaldsonville, Napoleonville, Morgan City and Houma. The Sharks were performing in Houma when they were spotted by Dorothy Lee, the owner of the Rustone label. Lee saw potential in West and the Sharks and sent them to New Orleans to record at Cosimo's Studio. West's initial single, "You Stole My Heart" didn't do much, but his second release, "Did You Have Fun" made a lot of noise.

"When 'Did You Have Fun' came out, Dorothy gave a copy to Diggie Doo and Rootie Tootie, disc jockeys at WXOK in Baton Rouge," said West. "She told them if they played it she'd buy them both a fifth of scotch. They both played it and the record started to sell."

Lee didn't really need to provide the liquor, as the ballad was the perfect fit for South Louisiana. "Did You Have Fun" started to break in New Orleans, Baton Rouge and along the Gulf Coast. Chess Records leased the master which gave it a significant push, but it just missed the charts.

"Percy Stovall was calling me for dates but I couldn't make them because Rootie Tootie and Diggy Doo had me tied up," said West. "They booked me everywhere between Baton Rouge and Texas. I never got royalties from 'Did You Have Fun.' All I got was $70 to buy an outfit for a show once. But I got a lot of work from the record."

With "Did You Have Fun" as a calling card, West was invited to open local shows for Eddie Floyd, Jimmy Reed, Freddy King, and Solomon Burke. Rustone issued one other single, "Willie Knows How," that paired West with a Houma frat band, Emmett and the Jades.

"I was the first black singer to record with a white band in that area," said West. "Considering the era, that was a pretty big deal."

In 1962, Rustone folded and West was recruited by Porgy Jones who was a producer and talent scout for the Frisco label. West's first Frisco single, "Lost Love," was memorable because as he sang most of it in high falsetto. However, his best single on Frisco was his third and last one, "I'm Back Again"/"Am I the Fool," which was produced by Wardell Quezergue.

"Those records got a little bit of airplay but they never really got off the ground," said West. "At Frisco I didn't feel like I always got the best material to record."

By 1963, West had moved to New Orleans and was working with several bands, including Deacon John and the Ivories, Edgar Blanchard and the Gondoliers, and Oliver and the Rockettes.

"I worked with several groups in the 1960s," said West. "I played fraternities, clubs, bars, dance halls, and traveled quite a bit too. Back then you really had to put on a show to get over. I didn't just sing—I danced too. I did all those James Brown and Jackie Wilson splits. They called me Lil' Willie West because I only weighed 125 pounds. I was so small I used to buy my pants off the boys rack at the department store."

In 1966 West signed with Deesu, one of several labels owned by Marshall Sehorn and Allen Toussaint. Toussaint had West overdub new vocals on, "Hello Mama" and "The Greatest Love," tracks that had earlier been recorded on Amy by Lee Dorsey. The performances were good, but West likely would have benefited by recording fresh material. He then remade "Did You Have Fun" but before it could make any noise, Deesu and it's distributor Dover went out of business.

"That was frustrating," said West. "I had records out but they weren't being played on the radio and you couldn't find them in the stores."

In the late 1960s, West joined Deacon John's new band, The Electric Soul Train, then one of New Orleans's top live attractions. He later joined the Meters who periodically used him to sing on their live dates. In 1972, the Meters   backed him on a Warner Brother's single, "Chasing Rainbows," a song later covered by Johnny Adams.

In 1973, West was forced out of the Meters when Cyril Neville joined the group as vocalist. Later that year, Toussaint used West on the sound-track for the film *Black Sampson* which starred Bill Cosby. By the mid-1970s, West began performing at several clubs in the French Quarter, employment he tolerated off-and-on for two decades. In 1977, Cyril and Art Neville had left the Meters and West was invited to rejoin the group. He cut an album with the remaining members of the group but it was never released. By the early 1980s, the Meters were pretty much defunct and West returned to the Bourbon Street grind and occasionally appearing at upscale New Orleans black venues like Prout's Alhambra and Mason's Las Vegas Strip.

By the mid-1990s, West had enough of Bourbon Street, but continued to work weekends in small neighborhood clubs and hope for the best. In 1999, he recorded *From West With Love* with keyboardist Bobby Love producing. A strong set of Southern R&B, hopefully West will benefit from it's release.

CHAPTER FORTY FIVE
~ Rockie Charles: The President of Soul ~

Guitarist and vocalist Rockie Charles recorded a handful of well-crafted 45s during the 1960s and 1970s, but until 1997, when his first CD, *I Was Born For You*, was released, only the most fervent blues and soul record collectors were familiar with his down home style.

A powerfully built man with a quick smile, "Rockie" Charles Merrick was born November 14, 1942, at Boothville, Louisiana, a tiny fishing community located near the mouth of the Mississippi River in Plaquemines Parish. Charles' parents separated when he was quite young and he was raised by his father, Earlington, who trawled the Mississippi for fish, shrimp and oysters. Earlington also played guitar with the Boothville Hot Five, a group that performed at juke joints in the area.

"He had a regular [acoustic] guitar," recalled Charles. "He played blues, hymns and country. Songs like 'Careless Love,' 'Just A Closer Walk With Thee' and 'What A Friend We Have In Jesus.' He taught me how to hold the guitar and how to pick out a few chords. I've been playing the guitar as far back as I can remember. Back then kids could go in the bar-room with their parents. My dad used to take me to a bar around the corner and I remember hearing Louis Jordan's 'Caldonia.' I liked his kind of stuff—Ray Charles and Nat Cole too."

At the age of 13, Charles moved to New Orleans' Ninth Ward where he stayed with an aunt and attended Caffin High School. He also enrolled at Houston's School of Music on North Claiborne Avenue, where he studied theory and learned how to read and write music.

"I used to enter the talent shows at Lincoln Beach in the summer," said Charles. "Ernie K-Doe or Aaron Neville would usually win every week, but once in 1958, I won second place and my picture appeared in *The Louisiana Weekly*. That inspired me to go some place with music."

While at Caffin, Charles joined the Eagles, a group that played R&B in several small Ninth Ward clubs. Charles dropped out of school in the 10th grade and moved to Venice, Louisiana, where he worked as a deck-hand. While in Venice, Charles got to see one of the most influential blues guitarist and singer of the era, Guitar Slim.

"Slim played at Club Good Rockin' in Sunrise which was just down the highway from Venice. 'The Things I Used To Do' was popular then and the place was packed. He came out with a red suit, then a blue suit, then a yellow suit. Slim was playing a big Gibson hallow-body with a pickup and he was hell on that guitar. The whole place went wild like I'd never seen before."

On his 18th birthday, Charles got his pilot license and began captaining tug boats on the Mississippi River. However, after moving back to New Orleans, he began playing music again, forming a five-piece group called the Gadges (sic) Soulful Band. Their first job was at John's on the corner of Clio and LaSalle. Eventually the Gadges began playing other clubs and dances in nearby small towns. By the early 1960s, the Gadges had become popular with Tulane students, often working three nights a week on Broadway Street's fraternity row.

"By working all those different type of gigs you had to be really versatile," said Charles. "You'd get all kinds of requests. We had to play stuff by Chuck Berry, Jerry Lee Lewis, Fats Domino, Hank Williams, and Ray Charles. You had to be ready to play jazz, rock and roll, blues, soul and country. I think that affected me when I started writing my own songs."

From working local clubs and hanging out at the One Stop Record Shop, Charles got to know the eclectic Earl King, who in the early 1960s was producing sessions for several local labels. King employed Charles as a supporting musician in the studio many times. Unfortunately the tapes from these sessions were stolen out of King's room at the Dew Drop and are now lost forever. Another character Charles met at the One Stop was Senator Jones, an aspiring producer and label owner.

"I tried to record for Allen Toussaint [Minit and Instant] and Dave Bartholomew [Imperial] but they turned me down," said Charles. "Senator used to come by my gigs and he talked me into making a record for him. That would have been the mid-1960s. He started a label called Black Patch. We did "Mr. Rickashay" and "Sinking Like a Ship." The record didn't turn out the way I thought it would and didn't sell."

Around this time, Charles and the Gadges were hired by Al While, a promoter and bandleader who booked local acts like Ernie K-Doe, Benny Spellman, and Irma Thomas. A lot of White's bookings took the Gadges to Nashville, where they were spotted by another booking agent "Good Jelly" Jones.

"In the late 1960s the band and I moved to Nashville because Good Jelly started booking us," said Charles. "We went on the road with O.V. Wright, Percy Sledge, Roscoe Shelton, Little Johnny Taylor, Otis Redding and really more artists than I can remember. You see any record I hear I can play, but I have my own style of playing for myself."

Charles also recorded a session with Joe Simon in Nashville produced by WLAC deejay John Richbourgh. However, recording sessions were rare because Good Jelly kept the Gadges busy for two years, often send-ing them on the road for six weeks at a time. Things went well until 1969 when Charles and the band got stiffed after playing three weeks worth of dates in Texas. After paying off the other musicians out of his own pock-et, Charles decided it was time to return to New Orleans.

Back at square one, Charles realized that he needed a new record out to help him find work. Charles had difficulty finding a company willing to record him so he formed his own label, Soulgate. Charles cut three good singles on Soulgate, "Living the Good Life," "Show My People Around the Curve," and his biggest record, "The President of Soul."

"I cut the 'President of Soul' at Malaco in Jackson, Mississippi, just before King Floyd and Jean Knight went up there," pointed out Charles, referring to Floyd's 'Groove Me' and Knight's 'Mr. Big Stuff'. "I had written the song and we were doing it at a dance in Yazoo City, Mississippi. A guy came up to me and said 'The President of Soul' was a good song and I should record it. He told me about a new studio in Jackson. When I got back to New Orleans, I called Malaco and talked to Tommy Couch. We worked out the song here and went up there to cut. It got real popular in New Orleans and did about 7,000 singles. I got a lot of work off 'The President of Soul.' In fact a lot of people started calling me The President of Soul on gigs."

Charles last Soulgate effort, "Show My People Around the Curve", was very much a 1970s social statement where Charles addressed many of the problems black America was then dealing with including crime, poverty, and broken homes.

"There was a lot of trouble going on back then," explained Charles. "There was crime, the war in Vietnam, the civil rights problems. From growing up where, and when I did, and working on the road, I had to go through a lot of back doors to eat. I made marches with Dr. King—I was aware of the problems at the time."

Unfortunately, Charles' message largely went unheard.

"Disco had come out and it took a lot of work away," he said. "I'd moved to the West Bank and withdrew from gigging. I began working the river again on tug boats. I kept playing, but being gone 14 days at a time, it was kind of hard keeping a gig."

Charles can testify that there's rarely a dull moment on the Mississippi River or Gulf of Mexico when you're a tugboat captain.

"I've had several close calls," confirmed Charles. "I've spent two days without seeing no daylight, just running in the fog with my head in the radar. A tugboat is like a taxi cab. You get paid by the hour and you get sent everywhere. It's a 24 hour a day job. Once I got called upriver to

Norco and I picked up two gasoline barges. The tanker man from the barges came on board and told us to take the barges to Twelve Mile Point. On the Mississippi, there's a Lower Twelve Mile and an Upper Twelve Mile. I assumed he was talking about the Lower Twelve. But when we got to the Upper Twelve he said, 'This is where we want to go captain.' I said, 'Jeez why didn't you tell me that before.' I had to stop two 200 foot barges in high water and turn 'em around. The river was clear for a couple of miles, but the barges got crossways and I couldn't turn them around in the current. When we got a mile or two down the river, they had ships anchored in the river and we were drifting down on them. At the last second I got the barges to turn around with just 20 feet to spare. My mate, the deckhand, and the tanker man were screaming and ready to jump overboard. When we got back, the whole crew quit. My pilot's license expired in 1986 and I quit the tugs. I built an oyster boat and caught oysters for eight years."

Charles had continued to write and play music in his spare time, but performing stayed on the back burner until 1994 when he placed a classified ad in *Offbeat* magazine's Louisiana Music Directory, advertising that the "President of Soul" was accepting engagements. The ad caught the eye of Orleans Records producer Carlo Ditta, who noted that Charles' telephone exchange was the same one his parents had when he grew up in Gretna. Ditta called Charles and after a lengthy conversation was intrigued. Ditta went by Charles' house to listen to some original songs, and quickly recognized that Charles was an R&B diamond in the rough. Together they began working on the *Born For You* CD.

"We took a couple of years recording to get the CD out," said Charles. "I got a lot of stuff in my repertoire and it took a long time to try different tunes to decide what we were going to record. Believe me, I've written so much material that I could go in a studio again tomorrow and record another entire CD. A lot of the tunes, like 'Born For You,' were written before I made my first single. I was going to record it when I cut 'Mr Rickashay' but I didn't get around to it. I laugh when people say "Born For You" sounds like an Al Green song—I wrote it six years before Al Green came along.

"I wouldn't put my music strictly in a blues category. My style works off the blues, but it's not confining, and I don't mean that in a negative way. I've had to play a lot of different types of music because of the situation I was in. I've incorporated those styles into what I write. I still feel what I write, but I want to be different than the next guy. That means taking the blues a step further."

Born For You got a lot of local attention and Charles made a successful last minute appearance at the 1997 New Orleans Jazz & Heritage Festival. Charles, who at the time was building a 40 foot boat in his backyard out of scrap lumber, started making gigs at several Uptown music clubs, but uneven and unrehearsed bands often undermined his performances. When the fuss died down, he went back to completing the boat.

In 1999, Charles finished a new CD with all new original material. However he hasn't been able to find a label willing to release it. Charles hopes though that when it does come out, his ship will have finally come in.

CHAPTER FORTY SIX
~ Lee Bates: Bad Understanding ~

A prolific New Orleans recording artist during the 1960s and 1970s, today Lee Bates remains unfamiliar to a many rhythm and blues aficionados, even in his home town. Possessor of a raw rural voice that invites comparison to Otis Redding, Bates is a naturally talented deep soul vocalist.

Born Obie Leroy Bates in 1941, at Magnolia, Mississippi, as a youth he moved with his family to the Central City neighborhood in New Orleans close to Dryades Street.

"I had to fight every day," recalled Bates. "The other kids called me 'Country' because I talked real Mississippi country talk. But I was a strong kid. I ate cornbread and collard greens three times a day, and I never backed down from a fight."

A strapping adolescent, Bates dropped out of high school in his midteens and unloaded ships to help support his family. His life's calling seemed being a longshoreman until fate drove up to his house in a brand new 1958 a Chevy station wagon.

"Chris Kenner was going with my sister around the time 'Sick and Tired' was selling," said Bates. "He came by where we lived on his way out of town. I jumped in his car just to be smart and he threw me out. The next time I saw him was a couple years later when 'I Like It Like That' was hot. I asked Chris if he remembered me and he did. Chris was looking for a valet and a chauffeur at the time. He asked me if I was interested in the job. I said, "Yes." Chris was a great entertainer if you could keep him from drinking—but if you couldn't he was a mess. Besides driving and trying to keep Chris sober, I brushed down his suits, took his clothes to the laundry and kept his shoes polished. A lot of people called me Chris' flunky, but I knew if he didn't make any money neither did I."

One evening Kenner and Bates were on the road in North Louisiana with Robert Parker's band. Looking for some diversion, Bates told Parker that Kenner wanted him to do a number to open the show, even though he hadn't.

"I did 'Tossin' and Turnin' and tore up the house," claimed Bates. "People asked me to do another number, but I didn't know any other songs so I couldn't. After that Chris started letting me open the show for him."

A phenomenal songwriter, Kenner was known for squandering large sums of money and the occasional brushes with the law. (Kenner did time in Angola on a questionable statutory rape conviction.) Bates recalls Kenner might stay in a posh hotel one day, the next, out on Rampart Street bumming spare change for a plate of red beans. After a couple of years worth of opening shows for Kenner, in 1964 Bates recording career took it's initial step.

"I was walking on Dryades Street singing to myself when somebody stopped me," said Bates. "He said his name was Doc [Victor Augustine, a local songwriter who also ran a candy and curio shop.] He had a room with a piano in it. He said he had a song he wrote called 'She's Got Bad Understanding' and wanted me to sing it. I didn't want to at first because I thought he was an old sissy. Anyway, I sang it and he recorded me on a little tape recorder. He told me to take the tape to Cosimo Matassa and let him hear it. Cosimo liked the song and I went in the studio and recut the song."

Billed as Leroy Bates, "Bad, Bad Understanding"/"I'm Forever Crying" appeared on Matassa's White Cliffs label. The single didn't set the town on fire, but Bates picked up a few local dates and gigs as far away as Grand Isle, Louisiana. Bates' group at the time included two future members of the Meters, George Porter and Zigaboo Modeleste.

When White Cliffs folded in 1968, Kenner brought Bates to his label, Instant. Bates' Instant debut reworked "Bad Understanding," and was backed with a dance tune, "Simon Says." The single did well enough to keep Instant interested in recording Bates and he wound up having several local hits on the label including "Why Don't You Write," "Key To My Heart," and "I Do Things Come Naturally."

"I made money on Instant," insisted Bates. "I stayed with them until they went out of business [1977]. Then I signed with Allen Toussaint and Marshall Sehorn at SeaSaint [Sansu Records] I was with them for eight years. We had some hits around here with 'Shake Baby Shake,' 'Help Me Make It Through the Night' and 'Wishing, Waiting, Hoping.' Issac Bolden produced a lot of those records."

During the 1980s, Bates was a fixture in the French Quarter playing at clubs that catered to tourists.

"I worked every club on Bourbon Street except the 544 Club," confirmed Bates. "Around 1983, I went to see Louis Karno at the Famous Door. I wasn't doing too good at the time and neither was his club. I convinced him to give me and my band a try. He did, but he told us business was slow and probably nobody would show up. Just 15 minutes into the first set the place was packed. I built that club back up. Later Louis moved me over to the Crazy Corner to get something going over there. Back then, you could make $700 to $800 a week working in the Quarter which was good money."

Declining pay eventually prompted Bates to abandon the French Quarter and look for work elsewhere. He admitted it's not easy though, and that jobs for soul and rhythm and blues artists without hits are few and far between in New Orleans. Bates put out his own CD in 1998, *Stop Leanin' On the Wall*—produced by Carl Marshall at Giftt Studio—to help shop for better gigs.

"It doesn't have a New Orleans type sound," said Bates, referring to the CD. "I didn't want that. I wanted a brand new sound, one that would get my records played outside of New Orleans for a change."

CHAPTER FORTY SEVEN
~ Jean Knight: Mr. Big Stuff ~

Jean Knight delivered one of New Orleans biggest hits ever in 1971 with "Mr. Big Stuff," a saucy syncopated deep soul single that incredibly was almost never released. A decade latter she had two other major international hits, "You Got the Papers (I Got the Man)" and "My Toot Toot." Combined, these three hits have provided Knight with a quiet comfortable lifestyle. Today she lives in a spacious home in a gated community in Eastern New Orleans adjacent to a lake and a golf course, not far from Aaron Neville's abode. Knight decides when, and if she wants to perform.

"I'm not a hungry musician anymore," Knight said with a laugh in 1997.

When she has time between gigs, Knight works at her second profession, nursing, which she enjoys just as much as performing.

"I must admit I've been blessed,"continued Knight. "Everything I've dreamed I've attained. I'm able to entertain and help people."

Jean Knight's given name is Jean Caliste and she was born January 26, 1943, the seventh of eight children. Raised by Creole parents who performed in vaudeville, Knight grew up in the Seventh Ward before her parents moved to the Ninth Ward. She sang in grade school, but didn't take music seriously until high school.

"I listened to Sarah Vaughan, Billie Holiday, and Etta Jones," she recalled. "I was into jazz until I heard Etta James sing "All I Could Do Was Cry." I had to learn that song and it changed what I listened to forever."

Knight first began to sing in public at her cousin's bar, Laura's Place on St. Bernard Avenue.

"I called myself 'Little Etta,'" said Knight. "A lot of bands played there and they'd let me sit in. People teased me about singing in there, but I told them that one day I'd have my own records out."

In 1965, Knight's first husband encouraged her to cut a demo and introduced her to vocalist Alex Spearman, who arranged an audition with producer Henry Hines. Knight went to Cosimo's and recorded several tunes, including a cover of Jackie Wilson's "Stop Doggin' Me Around." Texas producer Huey Meaux, in town to supervise a Barbara Lynn session, heard the demo and felt Knight had the potential to sell records. He signed her to his Tribe label. Knight came up with her nom-de-disque for

her debut single ("Lonesome Tonight"/"Love"), feeling that Caliste would
be too hard for the public to pronounce, deciding Knight was catchier.

"I did three singles for Huey," said Knight. "We covered [Ernie] K-
Doe's 'Taint It the Truth,' but nothing big happened. I did some regional
touring, but mostly it was local stuff. I'd play the Dew Drop and clubs like
that."

By the end of the 1960s, singing was just a pleasurable hobby and
provided part time income for Knight, as she spent 40 hours a week baking bread at Loyola University's cafeteria. That would soon change.

"One day I was downtown paying a utility bill when a guy came up
to me I never met before," recalled Knight. "He said his name was Ralph
Williams and he had written some songs for me that Wardell Quezergue
wanted to record. I'd never met Wardell before, but when I did, he said he
wanted to do some recording with me. After that, Ralph brought a tape of
some songs for me to listen to. Right away I picked out 'Mr. Big Stuff, '
but the demo was done as a ballad. I told Ralph and Joe Broussard [one of
the co-writers] that I liked the song, but I wanted to put some sass into it.
Joe said, 'Jean sing it the way you feel it.' I knew right away that the song
was going to do something because when I'd rehearse it at home, all the
kids in the neighborhood would be outside the window dancing."

"Wardell set up the session at Malaco in Jackson [Mississippi] and
one Sunday in May [1970] we drove up there. Bonnie & Sheila, the
Barons, Joe Wilson, and King Floyd recorded that same day. We had just
four tracks to work with, but we nailed 'Mr. Big. Stuff' on the second
take."

Knight and the other artists were backed on the session by the
Chimneyville Express: Guitarist Jerry Puckett, drummer James Stroud,
and Vernie Robbins on bass. Quezergue handled the keyboards and he
used some local horn players to fill out the sound.

Even though Knight was sure the song was a hit, she went back to
baking bread and eventually forgot about "Mr. Big Stuff." Malaco tried
feverishly to lease all the Quezergue produced sessions, but initially no
label was interested. As a last resort, Malaco started their own label,
Chimneyville, and released Floyd's "Groove Me." The single started to
break in New Orleans and subsequently spread like wildfire across the
nation. Floyd's success renewed interest in the rest of the Quezergue produced tracks. It was then that Stax—one of the companies that initially
rejected "Mr. Big Stuff"— picked up Knight's session. Issued nearly a
year after it was recorded, the jerk-rhythm of "Mr. Big Stuff" proved irresistible to record buyers all around the world.

"Right away it broke in New York and Washington," said Knight.

"Shelly Pope at WBOK played it, but like a lot of my records, New Orleans was slow getting behind it. Wardell called me when it started to break and told me I'd better get on the road because his phone wouldn't stop ringing. I was still working at Loyola and didn't want to leave them without a baker so I waited until school was out in June. My first job was a week at the Apollo in New York. I was real lucky. Maceo [Parker] and his band had just quit James Brown and they backed me. I got over like a fat rat. I started out the fifth attraction, but in two days I was the co-headliner."

New York's Universal Attractions began booking Knight all over the country. She recalls at one point working 21 consecutive one-nighters with a different band at each stop. That included flying to each city and rehearsing with each group.

"Wardell wrote my arrangements so there never was a problem with pickup bands," said Knight, who was averaging $5,000 a night at the time. "I was so busy I didn't even have time to spend the money I was making. I didn't even buy a new car for a long time because I was never home long enough to drive one. I had to fly to Jackson between dates in order to finish the *Mr. Big Stuff* album."

Although life didn't really settle down for a couple of years, Knight did pause long enough to attend the Grammy awards in New York where "Mr. Big Stuff" was a runner-up to Aretha Franklin's "Bridge Over Troubled Water" for song of the year. Knight was later named the most promising new female artist of 1971 by the NAACP.

"Mr. Big Stuff" surpassed three million in sales garnering Knight a gold and platinum record. The follow ups, "You Think You're Hot Stuff" and "Do Me," did respectably, but Knight got the feeling that her tenure at Stax would be brief.

"After I got the gold record and met all the people at Stax, Jim Stewart [Stax's owner] came up to me and said the label couldn't do any more for me. I thought that was strange, especially since I just got a gold record. They did give me some great songs to listen to including 'Cold, Bold and Real,' which I thought was a sure hit.

"When I got back to New Orleans, I called Wardell and told him that Stax had gave me some good material and I wanted to go to the studio right away. I went by his office and played him the demos. Wardell said he didn't like them and that his people [the writers that worked for Quezergue's Big Q productions] could come up with material just as good. He threw the material I brought back from Memphis away. I didn't think it was right for a producer to shoot down material, especially when an artist was really gung-ho to record it. But I had a contract with Wardell and there was nothing I could do."

Because of the breakdown in communication, Stax and Quezergue were out of the picture by 1973. Knight cut a couple of singles for Buddy Killen's Nashville-based Dial label, but none clicked. She had an offer from Epic, but had to turn it down because she had signed a deal with Los Angeles-based Chelsea Records. Chelsea recorded her, but never released the session.

In the late 1970s, Knight did some recording for Traci Borges in Metairie (the excellent local hit "Humpin' To Please" came out on OLA), and she worked numerous oldies shows at VPs Club on Jefferson Highway as well as Bobby's in Chalmette with Tommy Ridgley and the Untouchables.

However, by 1981 Knight was back on top. She'd met local producer Isaac Bolden who was interested in recording Knight on his Soulin' label. Together they came up with the idea to write an answer to Betty Wright's hit, "I've Got Papers On the Man." Knight's sassy answer, "You Got the Papers (I Got the Man)," was picked up by Atlantic's Cotillion label.

"The phone started ringing again and the next thing I knew I was working in New York, Miami and Chicago," said Knight. "The record stopped 100,000 short of a million. We did a couple of other singles for Cotillion and an album [shared with an artist called Premium]."

Quite often, life on a major label is brief and 12 months later she was back cutting "neighborhood records" on Soulin'. However, the lull allowed Knight to enroll in nursing school, something she had wanted to do since childhood.

In 1985, Bolden heard a popular zydeco single he thought Knight might want to cover.

"It was the day after Mardi Gras," recalled Knight. "Isaac came by and played Rockin' Sidney's 'My Toot Toot.' I said, 'Yeah I can do that.' I wanted to add another verse to the song, but Sidney didn't want me to. It was my idea to add that little break in the middle though and we cut it. Right away Atlantic was interested in it."

At one point during the spring of 1985, three versions of "My Toot Toot" were on the Billboard charts. Rockin' Sidney's original was in the country charts, Denise LaSalle's treatment was in the R&B charts, and Knight's version reached the pop charts. In the end, Knight earned a spot on *Solid Gold* and sold 850,000 singles. Atlantic rushed out an album, but the material was primarily padding around "My Toot Toot."

"A lot of work started coming my way again," said Knight. "But I was in the middle of nursing school and didn't know what to do. Finally my son said, 'Mom you can always go back to school. This opportunity might not come along again.' I wound up doing a lot of touring, but I did go back and get my degree after 'My Toot Toot' settled down."

With three huge records in her resume and a nursing degree to fall back on, Knight is able to take life a lot easier. Today she rarely works clubs but occasionally does appear at local music festivals. About half-a-dozen times a year, she flies to New York, Chicago or Los Angeles, where she does "Disco Diva" concerts with Gloria Gaynor and Donna Summers. In 1996, she worked her first "track gig" at Madison Square Gardens.

"I love those kind of shows but you'd never get away with doing one in New Orleans," laughed Knight. "There's no band, just a prerecorded track. The promoters time the track to fit the show exactly. It's easy to rehearse those types of gigs because all you have to do is listen to the tape and sing along with it."

In the late 1990s, Knight waxed two CDs, both produced by Bolden. Ichiban released *Shaka Da Booti*, which consisted of some tracks a decade old, and the Australian Aim label issued *The Very Best of Me*, where Knight covered R&B classics.

While Knight obviously would like another hit, she isn't losing any sleep over it. She's been to the top, and near the top of the charts three times. That's more than most recording artists can ever hope for.

CHAPTER FORTY EIGHT
~ Charles Brimmer: Where Have You Been? ~

With almost none of his material available on CD, Charles Brimmer is just a name on several hard to find 45s and LPs. However, during the 1970s, Brimmer was one of New Orleans' top selling recording artists and a solid exponent of deep Southern soul.

Brimmer was born October 10, 1948 and grew up in New Orleans Ninth Ward. Gospel music was his initial calling although he was eventually drawn to secular music.

"I started going to the R&B shows at the Auditorium," recalled Brimmer. "I saw the sharp way the artists dressed and the way they handled themselves. I said to myself, 'That's what I want to do.'"

As a sophomore at St. Augustine High, Brimmer began singing with the group called the Ravens, replacing Carl Weathers, who later would be cast as Apollo Creed in the *Rocky* series of films. Shortly thereafter, Brimmer cut his first single for Camile Incadon's ABS (Always Better Sounds) label.

"Wardell Querzergue was Camile's arranger," said Brimmer. "He took me to his production company [Big Q productions]. He asked me to pick some songs to record. I chose 'Barefootin'' which was written by Robert Parker. I rehearsed it, but a week later Wardell said Robert wanted to record it so I couldn't."

Brimmer wound up cutting "Now She's Gone, Gone" which sold around 3,000 singles around New Orleans. His second ABS single, "The Glide," did about the same. After graduating high school, Brimmer joined David Battiste and the Gladiators.

"We did all the latest soul and R&B stuff," said Brimmer. "Whatever was on the, radio. I became popular because I could sing anything that was out. But I projected myself—I got inside the material."

While Brimmer's reputation as a first class entertainer grew, he continued to pursue an education, eventually graduating with an accounting degree from Southern University of New Orleans.

"Music paid my way through college," said Brimmer. "During the breaks, I'd be in the corner studying while the rest of the band partied."

Brimmer's next two singles, "Black Is Beautiful," and the splendid "The Feeling Is In My Heart," appeared on Dave Bartholomew's Broadmoor label in the early 1970s.

"'The Feeling In My Heart' gained a lot of notoriety," recalled Brimmer. "I got a lot more airplay and my career picked up a little more momentum. I started opening shows for national acts. At that point, I got in a dispute with Broadmoor and ABS [they had a joint production deal on Brimmer]. My contract called for the release of an album once I sold a certain amount of singles. The sales were reached, but Broadmoor and ABS refused to do an album. I got mad. I still performed, but as far as being a recording artist, I kept myself dormant. In fact, I had a chance to cut 'Groove Me.' King Floyd offered me the song after a show at the ILA Hall but turned it down because I didn't want to cut anything."

In the early 1970s, Brimmer was performing with Oliver and the Rocketts, then a popular soul revue on the New Orleans club circuit. During this period he met producer Senator Jones, who ran several small labels including JBs and Hep' Me.

"Senator used to come around and watch me sing," said Brimmer. "He wanted me to cover O.V. Wright's 'Afflicted.' We cut it, but everyone went wild over the flip side—'Your So Called Friends.' It was a preaching type monologue that I wrote. It was deep soul—it was an inner expression of feelings. Not many artists can express that kind of feeling today."

Brimmer's JBs single did well enough in the South to attract the interest of the Memphis-based Hi label, which was distributed nationally by London Records. Hi was interested in leasing the single and cutting an entire album. However, Brimmer's ABS/Broadmoor contract still hadn't expired and the labels insisted on producing the album. Because Hi wanted control of the recordings, they eventually passed on Brimmer. Naturally he was disappointed.

"That was the year before Hi signed Al Green," lamented Brimmer. "I was disgusted and got releases from every record company I'd been involved with."

However, in 1974, Senator Jones was back in the picture. At the time, Al Green had just released the album *Al Green Explores Your Mind*. The LP contained the track "God Blessed Our Love," that black radio stations wore out. Record shops and juke box operators were begging for the song on a single, but Hi wouldn't release it because they thought it would hamstring album sales. However, Jones realized there was a demand for a "God Blessed Our Love" single, even if it wasn't recorded by Al Green. He asked Brimmer to cover it.

"We went to a studio in Baton Rouge [Deep South]," said Brimmer. "My music director, Raymond Jones, said, 'Lets do 'God Blessed Our Love.'" We already did the song on the bandstand so we rehearsed it the way we played it live. After we rehearsed it, I said, 'Okay I'm ready.' But

Senator had the engineer record the rehearsal and said he wanted to go with that. What he got on tape was a live relaxed performance of 'God Blessed Our Love.'"

Always the hustler, Jones rushed a dub of the song to Slidell's WXEL, who promptly aired it. Within 48 hours, Brimmer's treatment of "God Blessed Our Love" had caused a major commotion in New Orleans.

"All South Distributors had orders for 10,000 singles but Senator didn't have have any money to press records," said Brimmer. "All South contacted Chelsea Records in Los Angeles and told them what the situation was. They came here and leased the master. We wound up doing 60,000 singles in New Orleans. It was the biggest single in the city since the Jackson Five's 'ABC.' We did 300,000 nationally, but we could have done more if disco hadn't affected it. We did an album, *Expressions of Soul*, which did around 10,000."

Brimmer spent nine months on the road on the strength on "God Blessed Our Love," largely touring Southern clubs and appearing on package shows in auditoriums. Chelsea released a couple of decent selling follow-up singles, and a sensational second album, *Charles Brimmer:Soulman*. However, the relationship between artist, producer and label began to deteriorate.

"I was disappointed with the production on my records," pointed out Brimmer. "I was on the threshold of being really successful. I wanted to compete with the big artists—I wasn't satisfied with just being a local artist. But that's the way the record company looked at me. There was some material I recorded that called for strings, but they [Jones and Chelsea] cut corners and didn't use any. I also found out that my royalties were being spent on studio time for other artists. Finally I got disgusted and moved to Los Angeles in 1976. I went there because that's where the entertainment business is. I wanted to see if I was as good as I thought."

Brimmer had mixed luck in California. Gigs were hard to find and it was difficult and to find a label interested in recording his brand of deep soul, although Motown at one time expressed interest. By day he worked as an accountant, at night he made pocket money appearing in talent shows.

"I was a small fish in a big pond," admitted Brimmer.

In 1983, Brimmer came home to record a cover of Marvin Gaye's "Distant Lover," issued on his brother's King Kokomo label. It was a decent rendition but not much happened. Brimmer returned briefly to California, but came back to New Orleans to be closer to his family. (Brimmer is married to one of Fats Domino's daughters.) Since then, he has concentrated on raising a family and his business career. Currently he's a financial controller for a health care company, and owns an industrial cleaning business. The last time he sang in public was in 1991, when he stopped by Tipitina's for a Jessie Hill benefit.

"I went there because a lot of artists that I hadn't seen in a long time were scheduled," said Brimmer. "Half of them didn't show up, so Jessie asked me if I could sing a couple of tunes. I hadn't been on stage in New Orleans in nearly 15 years but the crowd went crazy after I started to sing. People kept coming up to me after the show and asking, 'Charles Brimmer, where have you been?'"

CHAPTER FORTY NINE
~ Tony Owens: Confessin' A Feelin' ~

Seventies hit maker Tony Owens no longer sings for a living but he certainly hasn't abandoned the field of entertainment. Owens, who reached the national rhythm and blues charts in 1971 with the polished ballad "Confessin' A Feelin'," currently shuttles tourists through the Vieux Carre in a mule drawn carriage, dispensing New Orleans history on his tours and peppering his litany with one liners for good measure. If the tip is large enough, Owens has been known on more than one occasion to entertain his passengers with an a Capella treatment of one of his hits.

"It's really a job I enjoy and it's been an education," said Owens. "I've met a lot of interesting people from all over the world—people I otherwise would have never had the opportunity to encounter."

Present employment aside, along with King Floyd, the Meters, Jean Knight, Charles Brimmer, and Chocolate Milk, Owens' was one of New Orleans most successful recording artists of the 1970s. Although he curiously never had an album, and none of his work is currently available on CD, Owens had several major label releases and has toured the country on more than one occasion. Primarily a balladeer, with roots in the fields of gospel and close vocal group harmony, Owens' voice had a polished yet haunting quality.

Owens was born in New Orleans in 1948 and grew up in the Zion City section of the city. His mother was a member of the neighborhood Baptist church choir and his father, Osborne Owens, was a barroom blues piano player. Quite naturally music was a major part of growing up.

"When I got involved in church I began singing at Sunday school and in the choir," revealed Owens. "When we were kids we'd sit at the canal bank at [South] Dupree and Melpomenee [now Martin Luther King Boulevard] and harmonize. Sometimes I'd go over to the Calliope Projects because there was always a bunch of guys there that could sing. I remember they had a guy living there called Buckwheat—Little Buck [Edwin Ross]. He did a record on Duke ["Let It Be Now"/"I'll Follow You"] and he sang on [Huey Smith's] 'Coo Coo Over You.' There was another guy called Charles Diggs, we called him 'Diggy.' He shook his head like he had a nervous condition, but when he sang he had a strong vibrato in his voice. Izzacoo Gordon [who recorded "Blow Wind Blow" as 'Junior' Gordon] was another bad dude. In fact, Aaron Neville got a lot of his style from him.

"We had an attitude about music in my neighborhood then that we called 'ratty.' That meant hip, fancy, improvisational, but really, really funky. If you wanted to sing like the guys in the neighborhood, you had to sing 'ratty.' I think that was what the New Orleans sound was about back then."

By the time he was in junior high school, Owens was entering talent shows and often winning first or second prize.

"After I got out of junior high, my confidence level as a singer was at an all time high," said Owens. "I'd sung with a vocal group called the Emeralds and I sang a solo at my graduation ceremony. I wanted to go to Cohen High School because they had the city's biggest talent show [the WALOCO, as in Walter Louis Cohen] and a lot of entertainment type people went there. It was there that I met Isaac Bolden. He was a piano player and we did many things together. Through Isaac I met Earl King. Later Earl and I used to go sit in the Gladstone Hotel on Dryades Street and listen to big band records on the jukebox by Joe Williams. We'd break them down to figure out how they put those recordings together from the bottom to the top. From Earl I became inspired to write my own songs."

"Isaac's father's business partner [Sam Whitfield] made an investment with Isaac and together they started the Soul Sound label. That's how the first record came about, 'I Got Soul.' We did it at Cosimo's in 1966. It was simple concoction and it sounded pretty good. But to be perfectly honest it didn't really do anything. The next record was 'Wishing, Waiting, Hoping' in 1968. [In the interim Whitfield was out of the mix and Bolden changed the name of the label to Soulin'.] That got a lot of airplay and a lot of people liked it. [It was also covered by Lee Bates on Instant Records.] I didn't do any public appearances at the time though. I was still in the woodwork—I was working and had already started a little family."

Owens third single, "I Need, I Need Your Love," sold modestly well locally and was played on WYLD, WTIX and WBOK. By 1970, Bolden had a new partner, Virgil Engeran, and together they began working on some new material for another another Owens single. However, in the midst of rehearsals, Owens moved to New York to be with his father. During his stay in the Big Apple, Owens was constantly badgered via the telephone by his girlfriend who wanted him to return to New Orleans in order to complete the session.

"I came back in the summer [of 1970] and we cut 'Confessin' A Feelin'," recalled Owens. "It came out on Soulin' in September. In around six weeks it began to take off. Every station in the city went on the record. Henry Allen at Cotillion Records [an Atlantic subsidiary] picked it up. I think Larry McKinley at WYLD had something to do with shopping the record to Cotillion. Once it got on a national label it made the charts. ["Confessin' A Feelin'" entered the *Billboard* R&B chart in January of 1971 and rose to number 39 during a four week stay.] I went on a promotional tour for Atlantic around the entire country and played every major club in the city—Club 77, the ILA and the Prime House. At that time, I was one of the hottest artist in New Orleans."

After the success of "Confessin' A Feelin'," Cotillion was interested in more material from Owens. Bolden submitted several tracks on Owens for their consideration but they were rejected. One of the tracks, "I Can Hear Music," was released on Soulin', but outside of a few spins on the local soul stations, it didn't do much. With "Confessin' A Feelin'" cooling off, Owens began working on Bourbon at the La Strada.

"I had a great band then," confirmed Owens. "I had Antoine Domino Jr. and Lloyd Gaines with me. At the time James Black wanted to play drums with me, but I didn't have room in the band for him. We used to pack them in every night. At the time [1973] Isaac got involved with the Allen Toussaint, Marshall Sehorn organization [SeaSaint]. We did 'One Man's Woman, Another Man's Wife.' [on Listening Post] It was a blues record, but it had that special ingredient that made people want to listen to it and buy it."

"One Man's Woman" sold a couple of thousand and looked like it was going to take off. However, just as local sales were building, WYLD hired Bob Hudson, as program director who pulled all New Orleans releases from the station's play list. That killed the Listening Post single. The next effort was the Bolden produced "I Don't Want Nobody But My Baby"/"All That Matters." released on Buddha Records.

"Shelly Pope [the infamous deejay who referred to himself as "Sputnik Shelly" and "The Black Pope"] had moved from New Orleans to Birmingham," said Owens. "He started playing the record and it bust wide open. It was number one in Birmingham, Baton Rouge and a lot of other cities. Every record store and distributor in the South was trying to get the record, but Buddha went out of business right after it came out and nobody could buy it."

Owens then cut another Bolden ballad, "The Letter That Broke My Heart," which Sehorn leased to Island Records. Unfortunately disco was beginning to dominate the air waves and the single stalled. Although Owens almost exclusively recorded Bolden's songs, with Earl King's encouragement, he continued to write original material and formed his own publishing company, Ellie's Music.

"I got my writing and publishing feet wet with Charles Brimmer," said Owens. "He cut one of my songs ['Your Man's Gonna Be In Trouble'] on Chelsea. I was ready to elevate to the next level. Besides, in the decisions about my records, it was always what was best for the dee-jays, or the record company. Nobody thought about what was best for Tony Owens. Me and Isaac are still good friends, but I needed to develop on my own."

In 1990, Owens recut "Confessin' A Feelin'" on his own Melody World label with Willie Tee supporting. He also produced a Sharon Henderson's single "Morning After." In the mid-1990s, Owens opened a small bar in Treme called Tony's, on the corner of Villere and St. Philip Street.

"It had a small bandstand and we had a few brass bands in there," said Owens. "It was open a couple of years, but to run a neighborhood bar you've got to be married to the place. People come to the bar to see you. Your personality sells a bar, so you have to be there at all times. It got to be too much. I closed it [in 1997] and started driving the carriage."

Although Owens' hasn't gigged regularly (or irregularly) in over a decade, he proved at a 2000 Otis Jenkins funeral benefit, held at Ernie K-Doe's Mother-In-Law Lounge, that his voice is still still strong and that he still possesses a lot of stage presence.

"I miss performing and I especially miss having a record out," admitted Owens. "People, especially the musicians in the French Quarter, see me on the carriage and they say, 'Damn Tony Owens, when are you gonna go back in the studio?' I've got some material ready to record, in fact I think I've developed into an exceptional songwriter. My songs are a little bit different but they tell a story. They might not necessarily all be commercial, but they're real. One day I will get back in the studio and record them though."

CHAPTER FIFTY
~ C. P. Love: You Call the Shots ~

Vocalist C.P. Love has the rare distinction of being better known for a song he didn't record rather than one he did. Love had been offered "Groove Me" by King Floyd but passed on recording the song, feeling Floyd deserved to record it and would do a better job. However despite missing out on a certified hit, Love managed to notch a couple of regional successes and assemble a compact, but enjoyable resume of soul and R&B recordings.

Love was born Carleton Pierre Love at New Orleans in 1945, and was raised on the West Bank, at various times in Vacherie, Algiers and Marrero. At the age of 12, he began playing guitar with some pals in Marrero that had formed a four-piece band. Love eventually switched to bass when the group found a guitarist who was better than he was. Later he joined Little Benny and the Creoles, a group which occasionally featured guitarist Walter Washington. Originally Love didn't sing, but when the vocalist couldn't learn the material the other members of the group wanted to play, Love began fronting the band on bass and vocals. Eventually he dropped the bass and concentrated solely on singing.

"I liked Sam Cooke, Buster Brown, Elmore James, Danny White, and Smiley Lewis," said Love. "Those were the artists you heard on the radio then. I started going by the Dew Drop where I hung with Deacon John, Esquerita, Curley Moore, and Earl King."

One of the first marquee jobs Love got was at Jessie's El Grande Lounge in Marrerro sharing the bill with Professor Longhair.

"I came in and sang some Bobby Mitchell tunes and Fess backed me," said Love. "The band consisted of just Fess and a drummer. I think his name was Lionel and he was from Algiers. All he had was a snare, bass drum, and one cymbal. But when he played he sounded like two drummers. We were in the middle of the set when a guy came in the club with a shovel and hit two guys over the head with it. They were fighting over a woman and all hell broke loose. Me and Fess grabbed his [electric] piano and carried it outside. He was driving an old limousine with the seats pulled out of the back. We just slide the piano inside and sat in the front seat. Jessie [the owner] came outside after the fight was over and asked us to start playing again. Fess said, 'No we're going home.' He was a quite guy who didn't go for any humbug."

In the mid-1960s, Love joined Eddie Gilmore and the Invaders, a band that played at the GTO and the Devil's Den on North Galvez Street. The Invaders also became popular on the fraternity circuit which led to one especially memorable gig.

"There was a young Italian-looking guy booking us at frat dances that paid real well," said Love. "He called us and said he booked us a job at the F&M Patio backing the Coasters and Aretha Franklin. Aretha was really popular then and we couldn't believe she'd play at a little joint on Tchoupitoulas Street. When we got in the dressing room, we looked at who was supposed to be Aretha and the Coasters and knew right away they were impostors. We did the gig and the girl impersonating Aretha ran off the stage at the end of the set and took off in a car. Of course everybody in the audience knew it was a fraud and the promoter wound up getting busted."

One evening, Elijah Walker, a longshoreman turned music business entrepreneur, caught the Invaders at a club and liked what he heard.

"Mr. Walker booked dances and shows," said Love. "He'd bring in whoever had a hot record and hire a New Orleans band to back them. One of the bands Mr. Walker hired canceled a date and he asked us to take their place. After we did the show he asked if I was interested in making a record with him. Naturally I said, 'Yes.' Mr. Walker had learned the music business the hard way and he didn't take any shit. If Mr. Walker didn't get what he was paying for, or somebody was trying to get over on him, he would get pissed off. Mr. Walker didn't get kicked in the ass—he was the one doing the ass kicking. Mr. Walker was very generous to me and helped my career."

In 1968, Walker and Earl King became partners in the King Walk label and they recorded Love doing "Plenty Of Room For More"/"You Call the Shots" at a Conti Street studio located behind an auto body shop owned by Lionel Worthy. A solid Earl King arrangement and composition, "You Call the Shots" reminded listeners of Wilson Pickett and sold well locally. Love's ability to sound like artists with hit records got him a job doing what he referred to as "sound a like records." At the time it was common to find albums and 45s in department stores containing covers of current hits at a fraction of price of releases by the original artists. Walker had a connection with MGM Records—who had a budget/cover label—and Love recorded in a Baton Rouge studio mimicking James Brown, Wilson Pickett, and Otis Redding.

In the meantime, Walker and King amicably folded King Walk. Walker, who was assembling a stable of New Orleans talent, then formed a new partnership with Wardell Quezergue. Together they formed Pelican

Records, a production company and label. Then along came King Floyd and "Groove Me."

"I told Mr. Walker about King," said Love. "I knew him from my cousin who was going with his sister. King had just come back from California. He heard I had made a record and that was when he offered me 'Groove Me.' I heard the song and immediately realized he had something. King just wanted the song recorded, be it by him, me, or somebody else. But I thought King had a really unique voice and that he should be the one to record it. I was working with a gospel group at the time and we made a tape with King doing "Groove Me" at a school in Shrewsbury. I brought the tape to Mr. Walker and that was the first time I meet Wardell. Wardell heard 'Groove Me' and told Mr. Walker, 'I believe we have something.' Mr. Walker said he'd take a chance on King, but if he lost money, I was going to have to pay him back."

In May of 1970, Love was scheduled to record a Joe Broussard song called "I Found All These Things" at the Malaco studio in Jackson, Mississippi. However Love suggested that Floyd should replace him on the session.

"Walker said, 'Man why do you want to look out for him all the time,'" said Love. "I just thought it was a good song and King should record it. I never regretted not recording 'Groove Me'—I felt glad for King. I never gave not recording the song a second thought."

Later Love did record "I Found All These Things," and like "Groove Me," it was picked up by Atlantic. The single did well in New Orleans and in some areas of the South. However, Love couldn't make a tour opening for James Carr that would have taken him from Gulfport to the Apollo in New York. Love felt that if he'd have made the tour, the single might have broken into other markets.

With "Groove Me" in the charts, Floyd returned Love's favor by hiring him to open his shows along with the Invaders. After nine months with Floyd, Love then toured with Candi Staton and Bobby Womack. By 1972, he was back in New Orleans. On the recording front, Love did sessions as a background singer and he cut a single for Janis Records in Philadelphia. He also recorded "Wonderful World, Beautiful People," but he doesn't recall the label it appeared on. By 1977, Love was working six nights a week in the French Quarter.

"I did Bourbon Street for 10 years at several clubs," said Love. "That was the best lesson I ever got as a singer. At first it was a job I looked forward to, but near the end it was job I looked forward to getting away from. I started at the Sho Bar and later I worked at the La Strada. At the La Strada, we'd come on at 7:00 and play until 9:00 p.m. Then 'Frogman'

Henry came on and played until 1:15 a.m. Then we'd come back and play until 5:30 or 6:00 a.m. I did that for two-and-a-half years doing soul covers and New Orleans tunes. My job was to make the cash register ring and I was good at that. But after Bourbon Street went non-union, you had to work your ass off to make any money. You see there are more musicians than jobs. The club owners started hiring bands for a lot less money and getting rid of the bands they already had. If you wanted to work on Bourbon Street, you had to take a big cut in pay. I wouldn't accept that."

A change of scenery was in order and in 1986, Love moved to the Bay Area. He made several good connections there and worked the club and festival circuit between San Diego and Seatle. While in California, Love cut a four-track EP for Award and an album for Orleans.

"Carlo Ditto asked me if I wanted to make a record with him and I agreed," said Love, referring to Orleans' producer and owner who briefly lived in California. "I wrote three of the song on it [*C.P. Love*]. Carlo mentioned that we weren't going to have very much time to do the recording. George Porter and Leo Nocentelli were going to play on the session and they were only going to be in San Francisco for one day. We did the session at Fantasy Records. I wanted to do my voice over, but we didn't have time and the next thing I knew it was out."

After 13 years in California, in 1999, Love returned to the New Orleans area to assist his ailing mother. He made a couple of appearances at the House of Blues and at Tipitina's, but he admitted readjusting to the Crescent City isn't easy.

"As far doing gigs, it feels like the same old same old. The clubs don't want to pay any decent money and I'm not going to embarrass myself by working on Bourbon Street for $8 a set. But if the money is there, and I can rehearse a good band, I'd be interested in that. What I'm really interested in is going in the studio and cutting a gospel album. I was working on a gospel project before I left California and I'd like to complete that."

CHAPTER FIFTY ONE
~ Snooks Eaglin: Wild Man On the Guitar ~

In a town dominated by awesome pianists, funky drummers and swinging horn players, Snooks Eaglin is New Orleans' ruling guitarist. An amazing musician, Eaglin is equally at home playing country blues, standards, funk, classic New Orleans R&B, soul, gospel, country, Dixieland and even flamenco. Although he is blind, Eaglin is blessed with the ability to mimic nearly any song after a cursory listen. While he estimates his repertoire is more than 2,000 songs, it is possibly double that.

Besides his amazing versatility, Eaglin gets a most unique sound out of his instrument. The way he plays the guitar is the secret to his style. First of all, his fretting hand works like a vice on the guitar neck. He often uses his left thumb to complete chords or to play bass runs that compliment his rhythm and lead playing. Secondly, Eaglin's plays without a pick, flailing at the guitar strings with his thumb and all of his picking fingers. When he's really playing hard, it appears as if his right fingers are actually bending backwards at a 90-degree angle. Although he plays with heavy gauge strings—which adds to the sustain of his sound—he probably breaks more strings than probably any other guitarist.

"Snooks is a unique musician," said Earl King. "He can play a job with just a drummer and make it sound like a four-piece group. He can cover the bass strings with his thumb and pick out the rhythm and lead at the same time with his fingers. I've seen Snooks play for years, but I still shake my head every time he picks up the guitar."

For someone with such a seemingly complicated style, Eaglin rarely touches a guitar unless he's on a gig. Instead he prefers to "watch" soap operas with his wife Dee, or listen to WWOZ at his home in St. Rose, Louisiana. While friends and benefactors have given him expensive new and vintage guitars, Eaglin is just as comfortable playing the cheap Japanese pawn shop guitar he keeps in his closet. However, no matter what instrument he plays, he'd still get a sound that is impossible to duplicate. Occasionally, Eaglin forgets to carry an extra set of stings and has completed jobs with just four or five strings on his instrument but his sound is nearly unaffected.

Born Fird Eaglin Jr. in New Orleans on January 21, 1936, he was rendered blind at the age of 19 months, after an emergency operation to remove a brain tumor.

Being blind though didn't keep Eaglin out of mischief as a child.

"That's how I got the name Snooks," said Eaglin. "There used to be a radio program with a character named Baby Snooks in it. Baby Snooks was always getting into trouble. They started calling me Snooks because I was always getting into something too."

Eaglin was five when his father brought home his first guitar, an inexpensive Harmony acoustic. Being blind meant spending a lot more time around the house, but Eaglin used the extra hours to learn how to play the guitar and listening to the radio. His father, who played harmonica, purchased an used disc cutting machine and together they made acetates that they played on their 78 player. Snook's progress on the guitar was rapid. At the age of 11, he won a talent contest sponsored by radio station WNOE, playing "Twelfth Street Rag." Around this time, he joined his first band with Joe Smith on drums, and Bill Sinigal on saxophone. At the age of 15, Eaglin got his first electric guitar, a Twintone, and a small amplifier. He briefly attended the Louisiana School For the Blind in Scotlandville, Louisiana, but dropped out in order to play music professionally.

Back in New Orleans, Eaglin began hanging out at Victor Augustine's curio shop on Dryades Street. Augustine, a part time songwriter, also had a rehearsal room and briefly his own label—Wonder. Augustine arranged for Eaglin to record some material at his shop and a gospel 78 was released—"Jesus Will Fix It" crediting "Blind Fird"—which sold around the neighborhood. Around this time, Sugar Boy Crawford hired Eaglin to replace Irving Banister who'd been drafted. This led to a historic recording session in November 1953, where Eaglin provided the slashing guitar on Crawford's Carnival classic "Jockamo." During the "Jockamo" session, Eaglin cut an Augustine composition, "If I Love You Darling," which wouldn't be issued until two decades later. However, the song was heard by bandleader Dave Bartholomew, who recorded it as "Would You" and it sold quite well around New Orleans in 1955.

Banister got his old job back with Crawford when he got out of the army so Eaglin joined the Flamingos, a seven-piece group with Allen Toussaint on piano. The Flamingos, patterned themselves after Art Neville's Hawkettes, playing high school dances as well as social aid and pleasure club functions.

"Snooks was phenomenal even then," said Toussaint. "He was just all over the guitar. People in the audience would call out popular songs of the day and Snooks would play them all note-for-note. The rest of us would just stumble along behind trying to keep up."

By the mid-1950s, Eaglin was already considered one of New

Orleans' top guitarists. Although he contends he is completely self-taught and never took a music lesson in his life, the renown blues guitarist Robert Jr. Lockwood disagrees.

"His playing is too far advanced to have never been taught music," said Lockwood, who spent a number of weeks alternating sets with Eaglin at the 1984 World's Fair in New Orleans. "It would take most guitarists years of music school to learn what Snooks knows about music and chord progressions."

In March 1958, Dr. Harry Oster and Richard Allen, taped 57 songs by Eaglin that appeared on albums released on Folkways, Folk-Lyric and Storyville. Oster and Allen heard about Eaglin from his neighbors. When they went to his house, the folklorists found Eaglin playing on the porch. Just 21 when these tracks were recorded, Eaglin display not only his guitar mastery, but also his amazing versatility. There are traditional blues like "See See Rider" and "Rock Me Mama," but there's also a mix of pop, gospel, rhythm and blues, rock and roll and Dixieland. The liner notes on these albums wrongly cast Eaglin as a wandering street singer, a troubadour who played for spare change in the the French Quarter. However, the information provided by Oster and Allen was a total fabrication .

"I never played on the street once in my life," said Eaglin. "I didn't have to because I was making plenty of money playing in nightclubs. I used to play the guitar on my mother's porch and some people stopped by to listen. Somebody told Dr. Oster about me and he came over to the house to introduce himself."

Eaglin unsuccessfully tried to get Oster to record the Flamingos, who eventually disbanded when Shirley and Lee raided the band and hired Toussaint. Eaglin in turn began billing himself as Li'l Ray Charles and became a popular club attraction. He covered most of Ray Charles repertoire and often appeared at the Dew Drop and Rip's Playhouse.

"He not only sounded like Ray Charles but he looked like him too," said Earl King. "He always had a house full of people. Snooks played wide-open too. You could always hear him a block away."

In 1960, Eaglin was signed by Imperial's Dave Bartholomew, who in the previous decade had discovered most of the promising R&B talent in New Orleans. Bartholomew recorded Eaglin with a small rhythm section, as well as with a full horn section, using noted sidemen like James Booker, Bob French, Frank Fields and Clarence Ford. While Eaglin cut some fine blues and R&B for Imperial—using the name "Ford" Eaglin—Bartholomew was rather unimaginative about the way he handled Eaglin's sessions. Most of the material Eaglin cut for Imperial was either Bartholomew compositions recorded by other Imperial artists—"That

Certain Door," "I'm Slippin' In," "Nobody Knows"—or standards like "Guess Who" and "C.C. Rider."

"Dave and I never could see eye-to-eye," said Snooks. "He had his way of doing things and I had mine. Dave was the producer though so he won most of the arguments. I just thought those records could have come out a lot better and been hits."

Although none of Eaglin's nine Imperial singles sold well beyond New Orleans, they did well enough to maintain the Imperial's interest until the label was sold in 1963. He would cut only one other single during the 1960s, the humorous "Cheetah" and "Sweetness," which appeared on the tiny Fun label. Like many other New Orleans blues and R&B artists, Eaglin found work harder to come by once the Beatles' style emerged. By the late 1960s, he and his family had moved to Donaldsonville, Louisiana, where he performed at the Town and Country Club, as well as numerous other small clubs along Bayou Lafourche.

"That was really a lot of fun out there," said Eaglin. "I had my son with me on drums, and sometimes we added two or three other pieces. Paincourtville, Thibodaux, Belle Rose—man, those country people went crazy over the blues."

By 1970, Eaglin had moved to St. Rose, a rural community in Jefferson Parish not far from New Orleans. He began regaining local popularity, playing the Playboy Club and at the New Orleans Jazz & Heritage Festival. Eaglin was also paired at the Festival with Professor Longhair, an association that furthered both artist's careers.

"It was Quint Davis' idea to put me and Fess together," said Eaglin, referring to the director of New Orleans Jazz & Heritage Festival and Longhair's one time manager. "Quint booked us some pretty good jobs in Washington and London. Me and Fess even did some recording together in Woodstock."

Eaglin and Longhair's studio collaboration from 1971 wouldn't be released though until 1987, when Rounder issued the *New Orleans House Party* CD, which eventually won a Grammy. Eaglin cut his own session in 1971, when writer/producer Sam Charters recorded an album that was part of Sonet Record's "Legacy of the Blues" series. He also supplied some outrageous guitar sounds that found their way onto the two great Wild Magnolias albums that were recorded in 1974. There was one more album for Sonet, *Today*, but after that it was nearly a decade before he got back into the studio.

"The money just wasn't right," said Eaglin, referring to his recording lapse. "I had about half-a-dozen offers, but I'm not going to work for nothing. I don't like royalties—I want my money first."

Snooks continued to work occasionally at clubs like Tipitina's, and of course at the Jazz Festival, often playing with the Meters old rhythm section, George Porter on bass and Zigaboo Modelesti on drums.

In 1986, producer Hammond Scott finally coerced Eaglin into the studio to cut *Baby You Can Get Your Gun*, the first of five Blacktop CDs.

"It wasn't an easy project," recalled Scott, referring to the initial CD. "Recording-wise, we got everything done in one session but it took a lot of preparation. First I had to get Snooks to trust me and then we had find material that was suitable. Snooks isn't big on writing new tunes, so I went through my record collection find things that he might be comfortable with. I came up with Percy Mayfield's 'Baby Please' and Earl King's 'Baby You Can Get Your Gun.' Snooks cut 'Certain Door' for Imperial (a Smiley Lewis cover) but it was such a good song we recorded it again. He came in with 'Lavinia,' an old Tommy Ridgley song and 'Pretty Girls Everywhere,' a Eugene Church tune. Snooks got the verses tangled up, but he had such a good grove going that we decided to keep it the way it was. 'Drop the Bomb' and 'Sweetness' are tunes Snooks had done for years so they were naturals."

The Black Top CDs exposed Eaglin's music to a wider audience. By the mid-1990s, he'd been to Europe on several occasions and was one of the top R&B draws in New Orleans. Regularly using George Porter and his band, Eaglin packs hundreds of people into the Mid-City Rock and Bowl, where he plays several times a month. His sets are especially entertaining and unpredictable, as any witness can attest. Besides brilliantly fielding requests, he likes to play obscure R&B classics, tunes from his CDs and even a catchy radio jingle he heard on the way to the gig. He doesn't let his blindness handicap him on stage either, as he swings the guitar around like a machine gun as his hands fly across his instrument. He's also is fond of playing solos behind his head which always delights his audience.

Eaglin though will not play music between sundown Friday and sundown Saturday, because he and his wife are Seventh Day Adventists. This means that some job offers have to be turned down (he almost didn't play the 1994 Jazz Fest but was rescheduled at the last minute) and his tours have to accommodate his quirky schedule. Nevertheless, more so than any other New Orleans artist, Eaglin is capable of taking his listeners through a veritable maze of musical ideas and styles. His dominance is unwavering and his playing reflects past present and future.

CHAPTER FIFTY TWO
~ Little Freddie King: New Orleans Country Bluesman ~

Perhaps because it is considered the birthplace of jazz, New Orleans isn't often mentioned as a hotbed for blues. In truth though, the blues has always been popular in New Orleans, and it's the home of one of the last great country blues players, Little Freddie King.

Little Freddie lives the blues. He stays in a run-down apartment in a deteriorating neighborhood, rides a rickety bicycle several miles to and from a downtown garage where he rebuilds alternators and lives with a demanding wife. He is tormented by ulcers and headaches, but playing his cheap pawn shop guitars always makes him feel a little better at the end of the day.

Little Freddie has absorbed portions of various styles, making his playing quite unique. His primitive guitar style and singing reflects his Mississippi background, but it is also reveals the influence of the rhythm and blues of his adopted home town. In addition, he has also listened to lots of blues records that have shaped his playing. An unassuming man with a quick smile, he nevertheless plays with conviction and authority. Yet in an era when authentic country blues artists have become celebrities, Little Freddie King has largely been overlooked outside the network of rough taverns and clubs he has played in over the last four decades.

Little Freddie King's given name is Frederick Martin and was born at McComb, Mississippi, July 19, 1940. His father, Jesse James Martin, was a sharecropper and guitarist who often played picnics, juke joints and house parties around South Mississippi.

"My daddy showed me my first two songs when I was six," said Martin. "'Cat Squall Blues' and 'Baby Please Don't Go.' My daddy wouldn't let me play his guitar because I always broke the strings. I had to make my first guitar with a piece of wire and a cigar box. When I was 11 or 12, I got my first regular guitar."

As a youth, Martin spent his evenings listening to WLAC, where he heard the latest Muddy Waters, Elmore James, B.B. King, and John Lee Hooker records. Often he'd try to sing and play along with them on his guitar. As he got older, he began performing in some of the joints that lined McComb's Summit Street.

At the age of 17, Martin moved to New Orleans where he lived with a sister. He first worked in a grocery store but latter landed a better paying job unloading freight on the river front. There he met future blues legends Slim Harpo and Buddy Guy, who were also stevedoring. As Martin explained, adapting to city life wasn't very easy for a country boy from Mississippi.

"I got lost all the time," he said. "All the houses looked the same. I had to get the police to take me home so they wouldn't arrest me. Finally, one of the policemen told me to look at the street signs and the numbers on the houses. It got easy to get around after that."

One thing Martin didn't have trouble with was finding gigs and appreciative audiences for the type of blues he played.

"The first place I played was Martin's on Rampart Street," said Martin. "I kept a jammed house. Mostly I played for people that moved here from the country that liked Jimmy Reed, Muddy [Waters], and Elmore [James]. I could play all that stuff. First I had just a drummer but later I hired a bass player. We made $7 a man and we worked for six to eight hours a night."

It was in 1961 that Martin assumed the "Little Freddie King" moniker as he used his given name on gigs up to that point.

"Freddie King was really hot with 'Hideaway' and 'San-Ho-Zay,'" said Martin. "People kept telling me I sounded just like him, so they started calling me 'Little Freddie King.'"

Chicago's Freddie King spent several months in the New Orleans area in 1961, using it as a base when he toured the South. Martin got a chance to open some local dates for King, who invited Martin to accompany him on a swing through Texas. Martin declined though because he would have had to quit his day job

Generally, the 1960s were busy years for Martin, as he played with the likes of Polka Dot Slim, Guitar Grady, Guitar Ray, Snooks Eaglin, Billy Tate, Harmonica Williams, Boogie Bill Webb, Charles Jacobs, and Little Eddie Lang around the area.

"I pretty much stayed lit up all the time back then," admitted Martin. "I played a lot around Slidell with Harmonica Williams, and then after the job we'd go to Logtown or Bayou Liberty to play. Then we'd come back to New Orleans around one or two in the morning and play at some place that stayed open all night. I'd go from my gig to my job. After work I'd catch three or four hours of sleep and then get a pint of corn liquor. That would wake me up and I'd do it all over again."

Two New Orleans spots Martin often played were Curley's Place and the Bucket of Blood.

"The Bucket of Blood was really called Roussel's," pointed out Martin. "It was on the corner of Perdido and South Derbigny. It rocked day and night. I played there a lot. It seemed like every night somebody got shot, stabbed, or cut in there. Curley's Place was really a house just off North Broad Street owned by a bootlegger. A lot of musicians hung around there and drank his corn liquor and jammed. Little Johnny Taylor used to go there when he was in town and buy corn liquor. At Curley's you could buy $100 shoes for $10, a $600 suit for $20, and get your car fixed."

Martin recorded for the Booker label around 1965, but the session was never issued. His first appearance on vinyl was in 1971, when he recorded an album with Harmonica Williams, an artist from Yazoo City, Mississippi, for the Ahura Mazda label .

"I had met Steve [Johnson, one of the owners of Ahura Mazda]," said Martin. "He was coming to my gigs and I started teaching him to play guitar. He told me that since I was helping him, he'd help me. He was partners with Parker Dinkins at the company and we made an album."

"That really was a pretty horrible record," recalled Dinkins, referring to the *Harmonica Williams With Little Freddie King* LP. "I think all the musicians were drunk and they had absolutely no direction. Finally Newton Greer [who ran Ruthie's Record Shop on Freret Street] took control and he got the album finished."

The album proved to be a dud, but "Born Dead," a single pulled from the album, which Greer sang on, actually sold reasonably well around New Orleans and got airplay on WBOK.

A few gigs materialized after the album was released, but overall Martin's life didn't change much. However, he did start playing at the New Orleans Jazz & Heritage Festival, usually appearing with harmonica player Brother Percy Randolph. In 1976, he toured Europe for a couple of weeks with Bo Diddley, John Lee Hooker, and Texas Alexander. Five years later, he embarked on a six month government-funded tour of the Western states, where he hosted workshops on the blues at colleges and high schools.

"I played some of my songs and told people about what the blues is really about," said Martin. "I explained about hard times and how the blues helps people get through them."

After the trip, Martin returned to repairing alternators and working occasionally at tiny clubs around New Orleans. In 1994, Martin's then manager, Gary Rouzan, lobbied Orleans Records' Carlo Ditta at Orleans Records to cut a CD on Martin. After several months of rehearsals, Martin completed *Swamp Boogie*, a rough but attractive CD that drew attention locally and from abroad. On the strength of the CD, Martin played a few French Quarter clubs, festival dates, and a short tour of France was arranged in the fall of 1996. However, Martin eventually returned to repairing alternators.

In the summer of 1999, Ditta taped Martin and a small band playing live at the Dream Palace club and released the *Sing, Sang, Sung*, a raucous set of originals and recycled down home blues.

"I guess I don't really sound like anybody else," said Martin after listening to a playback of the CD. "But I don't think you should try to sound like somebody that you've heard. You've got to put yourself into your music or you're not going to go anywhere."

CHAPTER FIFTY THREE
~ Ironing Board Sam: The Eighth Wonder of the World ~

Though an active, talented and eccentric blues singer/keyboardist for over four decades, Ironing Board Sam Moore's resume is quite slim. He's recorded only a handful of singles, one vinyl album and a lone CD. For this reason, the blues press has pretty much overlooked him. Chalk this up partly to Moore's inability to be in the right place at the right time, as well as a mild distrust for record companies, producers and his amazing non-musical interests.

Besides playing music, Moore is an active inventor. He sews and designs his elaborate stage costumes, and his inventions run from baby bottle holders to a button keyboard without keys. He claims he can convert an automobile's gas engine to a diesel engine (and vice versa) and produce free electricity for a large building with a small machine that has only five moving parts. The tiny New Orleans East apartment he shares with his wife contains cardboard display boards stacked with packages of personal air pollution control systems—mothball-sized filters that fit in one's nostrils— next to piles of cloth and a haystack of different colored wires. The only sign that a musician lives here is the presence of a broken keyboard that looks like even a Goodwill thrift store would refuse it as a donation.

"I'd go further with these inventions but they cost a lot of money to develop and kind of drag me down financially," said Moore. "Now if somebody were to give me a million dollars and told me to work on them, that would be different. Besides I've always felt I should be concentrating on playing music."

Ironing Board Sam was born Sammie Moore in 1939 at Rockhill, South Carolina. He spent a year-and-a half in college but dropped out when he got married. Moore learned to play on his father's pump organ and worked with several groups as a teenager. His initial professional job was backing Robert "Nature Boy" Montgomery, a blues singer and harmonica player who worked out of Miami. After relocating to South Florida, Moore's confidence grew to the point where he formed his own group and worked small clubs in the area. In 1959, he moved to Memphis, where he picked up his unique stage name. Moore couldn't afford the legs that normally supported an electric keyboard, so he improvised, using a collapsible ironing board stand covered with a drape. Club patrons began looking under the drape and   teased Moore about the ironing board. Although he was annoyed initially, Moore was tagged Ironing Board Sam and the name stuck. One of the clubs he played regularly even gave away a free ironing board on the nights he appeared. Moore toured the Mid-South and at one time hired Jimi Hendrix, fresh out of the Army, to play with his combo in Nashville. In the early 1960s, Moore auditioned for Stax and Hi, but was told to try elsewhere. Hi producer, Willie Mitchell, suggested Moore try Chess Records in Chicago.

"I did a session at Chess," said Moore. "But when I went back to find out if they were interested, I was told that the producer I'd worked with had been fired. At that point I was totally discouraged with the record business. I knew I had what the people wanted to hear, but the record companies wouldn't let me prove it."

Moore played around Chicago for a year before guitarist Earl Hooker got him a lucrative gig in Waterloo, Iowa. After a year-and-a-half in Waterloo, in 1968 Moore moved to Los Angeles where there were more chances to record and better paying gigs. However, by 1973 he was back in Memphis playing small clubs. During his journeys he managed to cut some very good singles on Atlantic, Styletone, Holiday Inn and his own Board label.

The following year, Moore moved to New Orleans and found a regular weekend gig at the Streetcar Lounge. The Streetcar was part of Mason's Las Vegas Strip, an entertainment zone that took up nearly an entire city block on South Claiborne Avenue. The Strip included clubs, restaurants and a motel. Billing himself as "The Eighth Wonder of the World," Moore teamed up with drummer Kerry Brown. Anyone who saw the duo didn't soon forget them.

At the time, Moore was playing a bizarre keyboard instrument he had recently invented. The instrument appeared to be two keyboards. The main one looked like a regular organ keyboard, but underneath it had been fitted with guitar strings. This keyboard was fed through a wah-wah pedal and then into an amplifier which could produce the sound of a guitar, organ, piano or a combination of all three. The bass keyboard had 60 stationary furniture tacks connected to electronic sensors. Moore ran a wire down his arm to his fingers which conducted electricity to the buttons. The "button board" produced an electric bass sound that was sent to a separate bass amplifier. The instrument made the duo sound like a four-or-five piece band. Blues standards were Moore and Brown's staple but their shows offered more than just music. Moore would lift the instrument off the ironing board, strap it over his shoulders, and walk through the club. He often did knee bends in front of the patrons' tables while he sang into a microphone fitted around his neck on a rack. Brown, a solid drummer, who later make a name for himself in the jazz field, ended the night by dousing his snare with lighter fluid and played it as it burst into flames.

"The button keyboard really had a different sound," said Moore. "I wanted to transistorize it so I took it to somebody who said he could do it when I went on the road. When I came back after a month, the guy had thrown the keyboard away. After that, I went back to the regular electric keyboard because I didn't have time to build another one."

At the time Moore cut a striking profile around New Orleans. Not only did his colorful home-made sleeveless velour outfits and huge gold medallions draw attention, he also drove a customized flocked purple 1969 Cadillac with leopard print upholstery and gold-plated bumpers. To accentuate the Caddy, Moore had a matching purple motorcycle and power boat. During his stint at the Streetcar, Moore did a single for Sansu, "Man In the Street," and recorded an album on his own. Unfortunately, because Moore was in a rush to get the LP out, he neglected to print covers or labels for it, instead selling them on gigs in plain paper sleeves. In 1980, the Streetcar gig ended abruptly after the owner of the club was arrested for selling stolen New Orleans Public School food in his restaurant. Moore then faced a new adversary.

"Disco," lamented Moore. "After it came in it was hard to find work. I drove 1,500 miles in one direction looking for a place that had live music but couldn't find one. Then I drove 1,500 miles in the opposite direction and still couldn't find one. I tried to learn to play disco, but couldn't get the feel or the sound. I found out you had to have a special keyboard to play it. That's when I decided to concentrate on trying to become more of an entertainer and draw attention to myself."

One of Moore's early steps in that direction occurred in March 1978 when he made plans to perform 500 feet above the French Quarter in a hot air balloon. Moore was going to run cables down to a PA system and a bank of amplifiers in Jackson Square as he played in the clouds. After tacking up hundreds of posters all over New Orleans advertising the event, the performance had to be canceled when the balloon couldn't be stabilized because of high winds. Moore's next act of self-promotion involved a 20,000-gallon tank filled with water. He devised a way to play underwater and brought the tank to the 1980 New Orleans Jazz & Heritage Festival. After a few frightening moments, Moore played a one-hour set submerged under water, amazing a huge audience.

"I went on the road with the tank," explained Moore. "But I found out it was too big to get in a lot of clubs. I worked some in Nashville and North Carolina with it before I moved back to Memphis. In Memphis, I played in Handy Park and helped get Beale Street revitalized."

By 1982, Moore was back in New Orleans, but still finding it hard to get work. This necessitated yet another intriguing form of self-promotion.

"People didn't want to hear live music anymore. They just wanted to play records or the jukebox. I was hurting, so I decided to become 'The Human Jukebox.' I built a giant cardboard jukebox that I fit inside with my keyboard and amplifier. I put slots into it where people could put money in when they wanted me to play a request."

Moore busked in the French Quarter for several months when fate stepped in. The producers of *Real People* saw Moore and shot a television feature on him that aired nationally. However, before the piece aired, the New Orleans Police Department arrested Moore on a noise violation and a judge fined him $12. Although it took him off the streets, the attention from *Real People* got him a few out-of-town dates and helped him get booked into some New Orleans clubs.

In the late 1980s, Moore incorporated "Little George"—a small battery-operated monkey that played drums—into his act. Moore devised a way to program Little George to play in synch with his drum machine and placed him on top of his keyboard. It appeared that "Little George" was actually playing the drums along with Moore and he even took solos. Audiences thought this was spectacular and Moore rarely left work without a stuffed tip jar. George though became the property of an enthralled tourist after he offered Moore several hundred dollars for the toy monkey. In 1991, Moore made his first tour of Europe. That same year he cut an album for Bob Vernon, then Fats Domino's manager, but Vernon and the tapes disappeared soon after. The following year, Kerry Brown arranged for Moore to audition for Orleans Records. Together they cut an excellent session in 90 minutes with Sam's leathery voice supported only by drums and a vintage Wurlitzer electric piano. On it Moore mixed originals with covers from his live gigs.

"That's always been my formula," said Moore. "I prefer doing my own material, but you've got to play some things that are familiar in order to attract an audience."

Just before the session was going to be issued, Orleans owner, Carlo Ditta, thought the recordings sounded too primitive for release. He had Moore redo most of the songs using a regular piano and surrounding Moore with questionable accompaniment. The second session lacked the raw energy the original contained, so *The Human Touch* only offered only a glimpse of Moore's style and his clever original material. To date, Ironing Board Sam's magic has yet to be completely captured on a CD. Until it is, he'll probably continue entertaining tourists by playing oldies on Bourbon Street for $10 a set.

CHAPTER FIFTY FOUR
~ Mathilda Jones: Wrong Too Long ~

Mathilda Jones' career has yet to reach the apex of New Orleans song divas like Irma Thomas, Jean Knight, or Marva Wright, but it's clearly not because of a lack of talent. An engaging and energetic performer out of the school of Deep Soul, until the mid-1990s, Jones wasn't been able to stay still long enough for success to catch up with her. The wife of a career naval officer, Jones finally returned home in the late 1990s after transfers took her and her family around the country.

"I kept performing every place we lived," said Jones. "But when you move around as much as we did for 15 years, it's hard to create any kind of momentum. Now that I'm back in New Orleans, I'm starting to build something up again."

One of 13 children, Jones, who was born in 1952, actually sang before she could talk.

"The way my Mama found out I could speak was from hearing me sing, 'Mama She Treats Your Daughter Mean,' when I was under the kitchen table one day."

Raised in a strict Baptist family, Sundays meant lengthy church services at Kenner's Greater Mount Cavalry Church followed by Sunday school. While Jones loved to sing spirituals, she also enjoyed other styles of music.

"From listening to the radio, I began enjoying, pop, blues, country and even opera," she recalled. "I had favorite artists in several categories. In gospel, I liked Mahalia Jackson and Shirley Ceasar. In pop, it was Brenda Lee. In blues, Little Willie John and Big Mama Thornton. In country, my favorite was Patsy Cline. I borrowed from these artists and developed my own style."

Before Jones reached her teens she was winning talent contests at school—singing "Jingle Bell Rock," and "The Shoop Shoop Song." Word of her talent got around the neighborhood, and while still in her teens, she began performing in small Kenner clubs. One night she was spotted by the late Cleon Floyd, King Floyd's uncle and manager.

"I was working at the Cozy Lounge which was across the street from Perkin's Lounge where King was playing," said Jones. "Cleon liked my singing and asked if he could manage me. I agreed, but my mother had to sign the contract because I wasn't 18 yet. I really got my first break with

King and traveled nearly all around the world."

King Floyd was riding high with "Groove Me" when Jones joined his revue as a supporting act. One evening in 1970, Jones was on a bill with Floyd and Clarence Carter at Alcorn State University. Jones opened the show with an interpretation of "Stand By Your Man," which immediately got the audience stirred up. At the time, Carter's wife, Candi Staton, had a version of the Tammy Wynette song in the charts. Carter was so taken by the Jones treatment of the song that he ran out of the dressing room in his shorts to stand backstage and listen.

"Clarence really went for my singing," said Jones. "He had a record company then called Future Stars and he wanted to sign me. Cleon and myself went to Montgomery, Alabama, where Clarence lived and signed a contract. Then we went to Macon, Georgia, and cut a whole album at Roger Redding's' [Otis' brother and Carter's manager] studio."

Future Stars released a fabulous single, "Wrong Too Long," a spectacular Dan Penn/Spooner Oldham composition backed by "Part of the Game."

"'Wrong Too Long' started to hit big," recalled Jones. "It was getting real strong around New Orleans and in the South but the record got pulled. They never released the album or any other singles."

According to Jones and Floyd, "Wrong Too Long" was initially submitted to Staton but she passed on it. Carter then offered the song to Jones. When "Wrong Too Long" started to break, Staton got upset and had words with her husband. In order to maintain harmony in their household (not that it kept the couple from eventually divorcing), Carter was forced to squash a potential hit and a great deep soul record.

Bent but not broken, Jones continued to tour with Floyd until 1975, when she got married and started a family. Jones continued to perform around New Orleans sporadically, but she no longer carried a band.

In the late 1970s, Jone's husband (who'd joined the navy) was transferred and the family made the first of more than half-a-dozen moves. After crisscrossing the United States, in 1994 the Jones were stationed in Gautier, Mississippi. Conveniently close to the Gulf Coast casinos, Jones stayed busy entertaining gamblers and good-timers at several clubs. Cleon Floyd continued to assist Jones career and he recorded her on *New Orleans' Unknown Talent*, a CD she shared with Robert Williams and the Living Dead Revue. He also released a couple of good soul singles on her including a remake of "Wrong Too Long."

Jones finally returned to Kenner in 1996, eager to get her career revved up again, but realized it would take a lot of work and a few breaks to become successful again. She began playing small clubs like Joe's

House of Blues and Mr. B's, but found that jobs for blues and soul artists were few and far between around town and didn't pay very well.

"New Orleans used to be the easiest place to make it in the music business but lately it seems like it's the hardest," lamented Jones. "But I look at it as a challenge. I've worked with several bands since being home. The musicians are good, but for instance, one band didn't want to rehearse. That restricts you when you get in front of a live audience. I like to please a lot of different people, so that means doing a lot of different material. I can't do that if a band won't rehearse and learn new material."

Jones also pointed out that many New Orleans clubs are conservative about bookings and often won't take a chance on an unfamiliar artist, especially one that doesn't perform mainstream material.

"I did a new CD, *Dues Paid In Full*, in 1999 for George Buck's Southland label," said Jones. "We decided to do a blues CD because I like blues and I think it's making a comeback. I grew up listening to the blues and I can really feel it. A lot of younger people think the blues is just about hard times. It's not. It can be about good times and having fun. I tried to express that when I sing. Hopefully the CD will open some doors for me."

CHAPTER FIFTY FIVE
~ George Landry: Big Chief Jolly ~

Although the late George Landry left a minuscule body of recorded work, he was a important figure in the development of New Orleans music. As leader of Wild Tchoupitoulas, Landry helped popularize and preserve the music of the Mardi Gras Indians. In addition, he was an influence and inspiration to the city's premier musical family—the Neville Brothers.

Born at Convent, Louisiana, April 14, 1917, Landry moved to New Orleans as a child and his roots became deeply embedded in the city's musical traditions. Along with his sister Amelia Landry (later to be Amelia Neville), they were a dance team during the 1930s and performed at several New Orleans clubs. During the 1940s and 1950s, Landry hung out in several clubs and listened to the city's new brand of music, rhythm and blues. Landry banged out the blues on any piano he could get his hands on, but he was aware of his musical limitations. Rather than struggle to make a living playing music, he joined the merchant marine, one of the few occupations open to blacks that offered security and decent pay during the Jim Crow era.

When Landry would return from overseas, he'd visit his sister in the Calliope housing project and entertain his nephews with stories about his travels, and entertain them on the piano.

"He was part of my life," said Aaron Neville. "I didn't just want to learn to play music like him, I wanted to walk, talk, and dress just like him."

Landry's Mardi Gras Indian career began in 1967 when he became Second Chief with the Black Eagle Tribe. In doing so, Landry helped continue the tradition of the Mardi Gras Indians.

In a city of wonders, perhaps nothing is more amazing than the tradition of the Mardi Gras Indians, black carnival societies that named themselves after fictitious Indian tribes. These tribes march through the streets of New Orleans on Carnival Day in exotic and expensive self made costumes that often take an entire year to assemble. These tribes have existed since shortly after the Civil War, when former slaves still congregated in Congo Square to sing and dance. There are several theories as to why black New Orleanians masked as Indians, but it is probable that for oppressed blacks, Native Americans were admired because they resisted enslavement. These tribes are now organized along neighborhood boundaries, but in the 19th Century, membership might well have been dictated by African tribal affiliation.

Music binds the Mardi Gras Indians and it can be heard on weekends in black neighborhoods, particularly during the weeks immediately proceeding Carnival. Mardi Gras Indian music still has many of the characteristics of West African music, including polyrhythms, call and response singing, as well as ad-libbed vocals. Their songs describe their costumes, Carnival day exploits, fighting, prison, getting high and street life.

In earlier days, tribe members carried hatchets, guns, clubs and knives in anticipation of a skirmish with a rival tribe. On more than one occasion, a Mardi Gras Indian was killed during these battles. Today, however, violence is a rarity and the only thing the tribes are competitive about is who has the prettiest chief.

After stints with the Black Eagles, the Wild Magnolias, and the White Eagles, in 1974 Landry formed the Wild Tchoupitoulas tribe and installed himself as "Big Chief Jolly." The original members of the tribe were Flagboy Louis Scott, Third Chief Tom Jackson, and Second Chief Norman Bell. As Big Chief, Landry was leader and caller of his tribe. In preparation for Mardi Gras day, he rehearsed and imbibed with his tribe at Uptown bars like Dots and the Patio on the Sundays that proceeded Mardi Gras.

Because Landry had no wife or children, his sister's children remained special to him. He kept in constant touch with them as they grew up and pursued careers in music, albeit separately. It was Art Neville, then playing with the Meters, who thought recording their uncle with his tribe, his nephews, and the Meters, might be an interesting project. His producers Allen Toussaint and Marshall Sehorn agreed. In the spring of 1976, the *Wild Tchoupitoulas* album was recorded and leased to Island Records. The LP contained several traditional Mardi Gras Indian street chants, and some new material penned by Cyril Neville and the Meters.

Landry's rousing second line chanting, backed by New Orleans' premier funk band, was sensational. *Wild Tchoupitoulas* contained some of the most spirited music ever recorded in New Orleans. Suddenly a local celebrity, you wouldn't have known it from the 60 year old's demeanor. Clad in a Neville Brothers or the Peach Tree Road Race Tshirts, Landry enjoyed hanging out at Tipitina's and was always appreciative and somewhat surprised when someone approached him and said they enjoyed the *Wild Tchoupitoulas* record. Inside Tipitina's, the humble Landry seemed far removed from the Big Chief who stalked the streets in a spectacular Mardi Gras Indian suit on Carnival day.

In 1979, when the New Orleans Police Department strike canceled most of the Mardi Gras parades, Landry, his nephews, and the Wild Tchoupitoulas were determined to continue their tradition and have a good time. So eager was Landry to show off his tribe's colors that on Mardi Gras day he overdid it and had to be propped on the hood of a car to make their final stops on their route. That same year, Landry began playing blues piano and singing at Tipitina's. His style was traditional and loosely similar to Champion Jack Dupree. Landry's last solo performances were at the Professor Longhair benefit held at Municipal Auditorium in February of 1980 and a Monday piano night at Tipitina's. On Mardi Gras Day of 1980, he passed the title of Big Chief on to Norman Bell. Not long after Landry was diagnosed with lung cancer and was confined to Touro Infirmary.

According to Aaron Neville, who maintained a bedside vigil, Landry suffered greatly during his final days, but like the characters in his songs, he never let the pain show through his heart of steel.

"He taught me to die and told me all of his secrets," said Neville. "When they told me he died, I went to see him and he seemed like he was resting with a smile on his face. I knew he had made his peace with God and he was in heaven."

Landry's funeral mass at the Blessed Sacrament Church on Constance Street was quite spectacular. His white headdress accompanied the casket to the church and his funeral service included music by the Olympia Brass Band and several Mardi Gras Indian tribes. During the mass, the eerie sounds of tambourines and chanting from outside the church seemed to by calling to Landry's spirit.

After the service the casket was carried outside while hundreds of second liners waited to send Landry off. Since the burial was 20 miles away at Greenwood Cemetery on Old Gentilly Road, an abbreviated second line parade was planned to wind through Landry's old neighborhood. Along the route Indians and second liners joined in "Indians Here They Come" and "Indian Red," songs from the *Wild Tchoupitoulas* LP. Despite the sweltering July heat, the dancing was energetic and and uninhibited. Eventually the funeral procession wound up at Aaron Neville's house on Valence Street where Bo Dollis, Chief of the rival Wild Magnolias, took up the calling of the final tribute to Landry, "Brother Jolly." From there, the hearse and limousines speed towards the cemetery and the parade broke up. All left happy—just as Landry would have wanted.

CHAPTER FIFTY SIX
~ The Neville Brothers: Uptown Rulers ~

For the past two decades, the Neville Brothers—Aaron, Art, Charles, and Cyril— have been New Orleans' premier musical family as well as the city's foremost cultural ambassadors. They have preserved and popularized a tradition of music passed on from such greats as Jelly Roll Morton, Louis Armstrong, Professor Longhair, Fats Domino, Lloyd Price, Huey "Piano" Smith, Allen Toussaint, the Meters, Ernie K-Doe, and Lee Dorsey. The Neville Brothers have been a model in perseverance, having hung together in various incarnations for over four decades. Together they've overcome bad business deals, jail time, drug addiction, punishing tours, as well as most of the other disappointments and setbacks the music industry tends to provide. However, their strong spiritual and family ties have permanently bonded them and together they've overcome most of their adversities. The fact that until the early 1990s, the four brothers all still lived within a two-block area of each other only strengthened that bond.

While you can't exactly call them superstars—well, maybe Aaron reluctantly falls into that category—the Neville Brothers have a legion of fans around the world that are drawn to their irresistible New Orleans rhythms that blend African, Native American, hip-hop, French, Mardi Gras Indian, Dixieland and parade music. They've toured all over the world and have remained the city's most popular band.

The Neville family grew up in the 13th Ward on shady Valence Street, then an integrated, blue-collar community teeming with street-corner music, brass bands, and Mardi Gras Indians, who chanted and paraded through the streets at Carnival. During World War II, Amelia and Arthur Neville, Sr. moved their family to the Calliope Projects, located in a Central City neighborhood that was no less musical.

"We were raised in pre-television times," said Charles. "So music of course was our entertainment."

The Nevilles' immediate musical inspiration was their uncle, George Landry, who played blues piano in local joints and entertained the Neville boys with tales of his travels in the Merchant Marine. Landry later doubled as Big Chief Jolly, founder one of New Orleans' most celebrated Mardi Gras Indian tribes, the Wild Tchoupitoulas.

Through Landry, the young Nevilles were exposed to new musical worlds. From him they inherited a love of local ritual, traditional songs and showmanship.

"Jolly's influence was immeasurable and not just musically," said Art. "He was a hero to all of us. His example encouraged all the Nevilles to greater things and to stretch out."

Art, born in 1937, is the oldest Neville child. He got his start playing piano with the Hawkettes, who in 1954 recorded the Carnival anthem "Mardi Gras Mambo." Three years later, he signed with Specialty Records and recorded the rock and roll classics "Cha Dookey Doo" and "Zing Zing." After a stint in the Navy, in 1962 he was contracted by Instant Records where he enjoyed a huge regional hit with a superb Allen Toussaint ballad, "All These Things."

In the mid 1960s, Art formed the Neville Sounds, a group which would eventually become the Meters. For a funky decade, the Meters were New Orleans' most valuable musical resource, both on their own and in collaboration with other artists. In the 1970s, the Meters redefined rhythm the same way Booker T. and the MGs had in the previous decade. Some fans and writers have gone as far as claiming the Meters were the inventors of funk. Besides making their own records, producer Allen Toussaint used the Meters as his rhythm section when he produced visiting artists such as Robert Palmer, Albert King, Etta James, the Pointer Sisters, Paul McCartney, and LaBelle.

Silky-voiced Aaron of course enjoys a phenomenally successful solo career outside of the Neville Brothers Band. A fan of doowop, gospel, and cowboy music, as a teenager Aaron sang with the Avalons and the Hawkettes. His first record, "Over You," produced by Toussaint for Minit Records, made the R&B charts in 1960. After several local records, the Minit label was sold and Aaron dropped off the scene. He returned though with a bang in 1967 with the hypnotic "Tell It Like It Is," which made it to number two in national pop charts. Aaron's comeback was cut short however when his label, Par Lo, went broke. For the next decade, he pretty much spun his wheels. Isolated Toussaint-produced singles appeared on Mercury, Bell and Polydor, but they remained neighborhood hits and Aaron supported his family by laboring on the docks.

Cyril, the youngest brother, was born in 1949. He was an occasional member of the Neville Sounds, and later, drummer with Deacon John's Electric Soul Train. (Art was also briefly a member of the Electric Soul Train) Cyril had a single on Josie in 1969, "Gossip"/ "Tell Me What's On Your Mind," which launched a brief solo career. He went on to join Aaron in the Soul Machine, a group that relocated briefly to Nashville. In 1975, Cyril was invited to join the Meters to add some visual, vocal, and percussive flash.

Saxophonist Charles paid his dues playing in the house band at the Dew Drop and at other New Orleans clubs. He also toured the South with Gene Franklin and the House Rockers, playing behind R&B icons like Big Mama Thornton, TV Mama and Johnny Ace. In the early 1960s, he moved to New York in order to play jazz, but wound up paying the bills backing Joey "Peppermint Twist" Dee and the Star Lighters. He would later move to Eugene, Oregon, where he played jazz.

In 1976, while with the Meters, Art convinced his producers, Marshall Sehorn and Allen Toussaint, to record his uncle's Mardi Gras Indian Tribe. With Aaron, Cyril, Charles and the Meters in tow, the subsequent album, the *Wild Tchoupitoulas*, provided a rare example of the fascinating and bizarre music of the Mardi Gras Indians.

"The music we did on the *Wild Tchoupitoulas* album was very traditional," explained Cyril. "Some of the songs had been sung by the tribes for years, and some Jolly wrote. We recorded them in order to preserve them."

As it turned out, the *Wild Tchoupitoulas* LP would serve as the genesis for Neville Brothers band. In 1977, Art and Cyril split with the Meters to join Aaron and Cyril. The Neville Brothers quickly built up a large loyal local following via energetic, funky sets at the newly opened Tipitina's and Jed's College Inn on Oak Street. The following year, they were signed by Capitol and released their first album, *The Neville Brothers*. Although it was a very good LP, it didn't sell and the band was dropped by the label.

In 1980, the Nevilles released a great self produced single, "Sweet Honey Dripper"/"Dance Your Blues Away," on their own Cookie label (named after their late sister), but they wouldn't do a full album until 1981 when they recorded *Fiyo On the Bayou*, the first of six albums for A&M.

Veteran producer, Joel Dorn, pitched the Neville Brothers to A&M after catching them at the Bottom Line in New York, but initially he didn't have much luck.

"The first time I saw them they completely blew me out of the water," admitted Dorn. "A&M was kind of hesitant though. They thought the Nevilles were too ethnic and too regional."

Concurrently, Bette Midler, who Dorn produced, was also a huge Nevilles fan and she also lobbied A&M on behalf of the group. The label eventually relented and Dorn got the green light to do an album.

On *Fiyo On the Bayou*, the Neville Brothers set out to capture an intense and undisciplined sound descending from New Orleans Mardi Gras Indian music and Crescent City funk. They also wanted to commercialize the sound enough so it could reach a broader audience. This was evident on the dance floor burners "Hey Pocky Way," "Sitting In Limbo," "Fire On The Bayou," and the medley "Brother John"/"Iko Iko."

"It [*Fiyo On the Bayou*] one of the few times that I've made a album and was 100 percent satisfied with when we finished," said Dorn. "I felt *Fiyo On the Bayou* was the culmination of my career."

Rolling Stone guitarist Keith Richards thought *Fiyo On the Bayou* was the best album of 1981. Most listeners never had a chance to form an opinion. Unfortunately, the title of the album caused confusion. In 1975, the Meters, with Art and Cyril, had released an album entitled *Fire On the Bayou* on Warner Brothers/Reprise. The Neville Brother's inclusions of new versions of the Meters' signatures "Hey Pocky Way" and "Fire On The Bayou," only further muddied the water.

"We wanted those songs heard by more people," pointed out Aaron.

Radio stations outside of New Orleans were puzzled by the Neville Brothers style, which didn't fit easily into any one format.

"I knew it wasn't going to get played on the radio," said Cyril. "So I didn't build up any false hopes. We just made the best record we could."

"We just couldn't get any airplay," confirmed Dorn. "It was the kind of record where I wished I could have gone door-to-door and said, 'Here listen to this record.'"

After stalling at number 166 in the charts, A&M didn't renew the Neville Brothers' contract. Back at square one, the group wouldn't have another release until 1985, when the New Orleans inde label Black Top released *Nevillization*, a live album assembled from three-year-old-tapes. The album got rave reviews and stirred up a lot of national interest in the band. That same year, Rhino released the first of three Neville Brothers retrospective collections, *Treacherous*, which assembled tracks by the Hawkettes, Art, Aaron, The Wild Tchoupitoulas, and of course the Neville Brothers.

In 1987, the Neville Brothers signed with EMI and recorded *Uptown*. While the title referred to the neighborhood in which the Brothers lived, the music it contained was AOR slanted and didn't sound anything like New Orleans.

"*Uptown* was a departure for us," admitted Charles. "It was our attempt to make music that sounds like what you hear on the radio."

The following year, A&M was back in the picture and the group began working on *Yellow Moon*. Produced by transplanted Canadian Daniel Lanois—best known for his work with U2, Bob Dylan and Peter Gabriel—the album was recorded in a temporary studio Lanois built in the Nevilles neighborhood. For the first time, the Neville Brothers cut an album that had very strong New Orleans undercurrents.

While collectively the group maintained that there was no calculated return to their roots, for the first time the Nevilles successfully transferred their onstage sound into the studio. Lanois didn't tamper with the syncopated rhythms and the arrangements were uncluttered. *Yellow Moon* would interweave African rhythms, street music, ballads, and for the first time, rap music.

"Sister Rosa," the album's first single and video, was inspired by Rosa Parks, the woman who played a pivotal role in the Civil Right Movement when she refused to move to the back of a Birmingham, Alabama, city bus in order to give up her seat to a white man. The song's contemporary sound came with a quasi-rap beat.

"That was Cyril's idea," said Charles. "He was talking to his kids, who listen to rap and hip-hop. Cyril realized that was the way to reach them. They remember rap songs. We were hoping the story of Rosa Parks would reach younger kids—kids who didn't know anything about her."

Yellow Moon also contained a couple of sparkling solos by Aaron— Bob Dylan's "With God On Our Side" and the spiritual, "Will the Circle Be Unbroken." The album sold in excess of 800,000 units and finally provided the group with it's international break-through.

The Neville Brothers' savvy follow-up, *Brothers Keeper*, was very much an extension of the music heard on *Yellow Moon*. Recorded in 1991, the album's highlights, "Brother's Blood" and "River of Life," proved that the confident Brothers could produce funky New Orleans music that also makes a social statement.

The following year, the Neville Brothers recorded *Family Groove* which was produced by Hawk Wolinski and David Leonard. The album contained an interesting departure for the group, a cover of Steve Miller's "Fly Like An Eagle," which sounded commercial but nevertheless fit the group's style. More typically representative song choices were "On the Other Side of Paradise," spotlighting Art and a warm afro-calypso groove, and "Let My People," Cyril's passionate plea for the end to political and social injustice.

In 1994, the group did an unusual live album. Assembled from recordings made at several venues, *Live* included material that previously hadn't been recorded in the studio and were lesser known bandstand favorites.

All My Relations from 1996, again underlined the spiritual and musical bond between the brothers. The album was subtitled *Mitakuye Oyasin Oyasin*, a Lakota (Sioux Indian) phrase for, "we are all one." The music it contained was a partial return to tradition. Art returned to his rhythm and blues roots on the attractive "Love Spoken Here," while Aaron's rendering of "Ain't No Sunshine" recalled the golden age of soul.

In 1999, the Neville Brothers moved to Sony Records and recorded *Valence Street,* which was nominated for a Grammy in the traditional R&B category. The CD continued the family legacy and enriched the tradition of New Orleans music, the greatest gift the city has given the world.

CHAPTER FIFTY SEVEN
~ Mem Shannon: Cab Driver Blues ~

Mem Shannon is not a typical blues musician, but then again he does-n't play typical blues music. Shannon's style is a unique blend of classic blues, New Orleans rhythm and blues, and funk. It also includes some jazz overtones, old school soul, and of course some of his own innovative ideas. Because his style is not easy to pigeon hole, for a long time he found it hard working even in New Orleans, a city that normally accepts musical innovation. Before the Hannibal label released his first CD, *A Cab Driver Blues* in 1995, record companies were also hesitant on taking a chance on him.

Born December 21, 1959, in the Irish Channel section of New Orleans, Shannon grew up with two sisters and a brother. He is too young to remember the classic period of New Orleans R&B, but he recalls that Lee Dorsey, Ernie K-Doe, and Irma Thomas were still big names during his childhood.

Shannon's first instrument was the clarinet, which he played in ele-mentary and junior high school bands. One of his first memorable moments as a musician was when his junior high stage band learned the theme from the film *Shaft*. Shannon was the unofficial bandleader in high school and it was his job to make sure everyone was in tune.

"We didn't have a record player at home when I was growing up," recalled Shannon. "But my dad built us a stereo with an eight-track tape player that came out of a car. We listened to a lot of contemporary R&B and funk—Barry White, Earth, Wind and Fire, Kool and the Gang, and the Bar Kays. But the first time I heard B.B. King on the *Tonight Show* I was mesmerized. I'd seen other guys play the guitar, but with B.B. it was like the first time I'd actually listened to the guitar. It was an emotional thing about B.B. When one of his records played on the radio my parents told us to be quiet and listen. In the 10th grade I begged my dad for a guitar and he bought me a Japanese electric guitar and a little amp."

"I got a book that showed me how to play chords but I tossed it aside for over a year. When I played I just played single notes. Finally I looked at the book again and realized you had to play chords and tune the guitar. I never really had anybody show me anything until I met Dave Dixon, Vincent Toussaint, and Jimmy Mollier. Dave and Jimmy played with Fats Domino, but they drove cabs when Fats wasn't working."

By his senior year of high school. Shannon was doubling on clarinet
and guitar in concerts, an experience that prepared him for later bands. His
first post-high school band, the Ebony Brothers Hot Band, was a cover
group that played dances and at small bars. His second band, Free
Enterprise, also specialized in covers.

"We'd do blues in rehearsal," said Shannon. "When we did, the parents would come out and listen to us. When we started playing something
else, they would go back to what they'd been doing. I took note of that."

Shannon also played guitar in the Dedicators, a gospel group that
played around New Orleans, but as he put it, "Money was no where in
sight back then."

After his father died unexpectedly in 1981, Shannon took it upon
himself to support his family and he put music aside. A member of his
mother's church drove a cab and offered to help get Shannon into the taxi
business.

"I didn't know what I was getting into," laughed Shannon. "I made
nine dollars the first night. Then it started to pick up and I created my own
routine. I worked the airport during the day and the French Quarter at
night. Driving a cab you see more than you could ever expect to see.
People ask me what are some of the weirdest things I've seen driving a
cab? I can't even answer that. Once weird stuff starts happening to you on
a regular basis, after awhile nothing stands out."

In 1990, Peter Carter, the bassist in Free Enterprise, began encouraging Shannon to pick up the guitar again.

"I started getting ideas for songs from watching people out in the
street and talking to people in my cab," said Shannon. "I was also
noodling with the guitar and came up with a few riffs for songs. One of
the first songs I wrote was 'You Ain't Nothing Nice.' That came from
street slang. Peter kept in touch with me even when I wasn't playing.
Every once in a while he'd come by the house and we'd make some noise.
I had put these songs together so one day we decided to do something with
them and put a band together—the Membership. Finally we started fishing around for gigs."

Before he started playing in public again, Shannon had to overcome
one other musical challenge.

"I'd never sang before," he admitted. "At first I really wanted to hire
a singer. To me standing out in front of an audience was a frightening
thing. I don't think I'm really a great singer, but if I concentrate on pitch
and staying in key, I'm not too bad."

Eventually Shannon booked a regular Tuesday night gig at Cafe
Brazil and the band occasionally opened for Cyril Neville and the Uptown

All Stars. They also played on Bourbon Street at Rhythms and the Absinthe House, working from 7 p.m. to 2 a.m.

"We were doing originals and some Albert Collins tunes," said Shannon. "I was booking the band, but I found out that you can't book yourself. You just don't get any respect as an artist from the club owners and the money is never right. It took me years before I could even get in the door at Tipitina's or the other Uptown clubs. Now I let someone else do the bookings."

Shannon caught a break came in 1991 when he spotted an ad in the *Times-Picayune* newspaper announcing a talent contest co-sponsored by the Audubon Zoo and a local television station. Mem Shannon and the Membership won the contest which landed them a them a spot at the New Orleans Jazz & Heritage Festival, $1,000, and a television commercial.

"We had to chase roosters off the stage," laughed Shannon, referring to his first Jazz Fest appearance. "Hardly anybody came to see us."

Later in the year, the band won a preliminary talent contest co-sponsored by KLON-FM and the Long Beach Blues Festival. The group traveled to California but lost out in the finals and didn't play the festival. Undaunted, Shannon then made a demo tape of his own material to shop to labels and procure gigs.

"The tape didn't really sound very good," he said. "We paid a lot of money and the studio we used gave us a tape that wasn't mixed properly. But I started sending the tape out to record companies but without luck. Finally, JSP in England was interested, but they would only put up $1,000 for the session. I would have recorded it for free, but I had to pay the guys in the band for their work."

"I talked to Larry Garner who recorded for JSP with a small budget. He liked his arrangement with JSP because he made money off gigs overseas. Larry can go over to Europe and play with pickup bands. I can't play with a pickup band because my music is too complex. Anyway, I went back and forth with JSP for a couple of years. They weren't really out of the picture until *A Cab Driver's Blues* was recorded."

Shannon still had to jump a few more hurdles in order to get a CD on the market. His tenor player, Tim Green, gave one of the band's demo tapes to Mark Bingham, an eclectic local musician and producer, in hopes he could remix the session. Bingham, who maintained a small studio, listened to the tape and offered to start a new project over from scratch.

"Mark and I hit it off right away," said Shannon. "He said he'd like to record me but he didn't have any money. All he had was time and a studio. I told him I didn't have any money either. All I had was a handful of songs and some friends that would help me. The guys in the band did the session for free, but I told them that if I ever made any money they'd get paid. There was no record deal at the time."

Shannon's entire session with Bingham consisted of original material.

"I'm not always thinking blues when I write a song," he explained. "My music can go anywhere once I get an idea for a song. I'm bored easily so I try to keep the music different. The first person I have to satisfy is myself. Then I hope everyone can like what I've done. If I don't play something funky, I feel like I should have stayed home."

When Shannon finished the session he wanted to add something a little bit off the wall.

"We had a concept for *A Cab Driver's Blues,* but I felt like something was missing," he explained. "People have a tendency to label things and say, 'Oh, I know what that is,' especially when it comes to blues. Well I'd been recording conversations in the cab for a long time. I wanted to include that on the CD. Mark was going to give me a DAT recorder to do some taping but we couldn't figure out how to get a power source to it in the cab. So I just used the tape recorder I bought at Walgreen's that we used during rehearsals."

Once Shannon and Bingham had a finished product they had to search for a label. Initially Herb Albert's Alamo label was interested but a deal couldn't be struck. In 1994, Hannibal's Joe Boyd stopped by Bingham's studio and listened to the session. He was impressed and the following year *A Cab Driver's Blues* became the label's first blues release.

The CD got an overwhelming positive response nationally and allowed Shannon to take the meter out of his taxi. Although he'd driven cabs around New Orleans for more than 500,000 miles, he'd rarely been out of Louisiana until he was booked by clubs in Austin, Boston and New York.

"At first it was kind of scary giving up the cab," said Shannon. "But my calender filled up pretty quickly. It was an opportunity I might never have gotten again and I had to take advantage of it. Making a living playing music is something I've wanted to do all my life. I was kind of taken aback by all the attention. I was on CBS, PBS and in the New York Times. People told me it was the first time a new artist from New Orleans got that much attention."

"I think a lot of my songs are a change from a lot of the other blues material that's out there. For a while blues was stagnant, everything was a jump-shuffle. I got burned out on that on Bourbon Street. I want to take my music in a new direction. I don't necessarily feel like I'm leading a change in blues, but I want to be part of the change when it happens."

CHAPTER FIFTY EIGHT
~ Al Jackson: The Future? ~

The first impression of Al Jackson is that you simply can't believe what you are seeing and hearing. Young, sharp, energetic—Jackson, born in 1973, already sings and plays rhythm and blues with the authority of a master. Technique, sincerity, spirit—with your eyes closed, you might imagine you're listening to Smiley Lewis, Joe Turner, Tommy Ridgley, or especially Fats Domino—when he plays.

Jackson grew up on Jefferson Parish's West Bank and was raised by a close knit extended family. His grandmother owned the Vet's Club in Bridge City, a club that booked Domino, Lloyd Price, Ridgley, and other local R&B artists. When the records were changed on the club's jukebox, Jackson's grandfather kept the replaced ones, amassing a substantial collection of 78s and 45s.

"That's what I grew up listening to," said Jackson. "Before I was even in kindergarten, he gave me a stack of records that I listened to all the time. Fats Domino was my favorite but I especially liked 'The Wiffenpoof Song' by Art Neville, and Tommy Ridgley's 'When I Meet My Girl.' I listened to a lot of popular stuff on the radio when I was growing up. I liked some of it, but it didn't affect me the way New Orleans R&B did."

Jackson has never taken formal music lessons, but he was quick at picking up music.

"When I was going to Higgins High School, they raised the minimum grade requirement for students that played in the band," said Jackson. "That just about wiped out the band. One year I played five different instruments. One week trombone, the next drums—whatever the band director needed, I supplied. I played in a few bands at school, but always in support. I never imagined myself as a leader."

In his mid-teens, Jackson bought a small Casio keyboard and began duplicating the piano patterns he heard on the records in his grandfather's collection. Eventually Jackson learned over 200 songs, the majority coming from the Fats Domino song book.

"People tell me that stuff is hard to play, but I feel comfortable playing it," said Jackson. "I can't always duplicate what's being played on those early records, but I try to duplicate the feeling. That's more important. Playing keyboards was always a hobby to me. I never intended being a professional. Only my family had heard me play."

Nevertheless, Jackson's rise to the professional ranks was rapid and unexpected.

"My Mom worked for Judge Winnsburg," said Jackson. "They were having a Christmas party in 1992, and she wanted me to play piano. I didn't want to, but she insisted. I played four Fats Domino numbers and I was ready to get out of there. When I reached the door, a guy stopped me and said, 'Man you're really great. Where do you play?' His name was Joe Cardenia. I told him the only place I played was at home."

"Then he asked, 'If I can get you bookings would you play them?'"

"I laughed and said, 'Sure, that would be like getting paid for having fun.' He called me a day or two later and said he could get me $200 for playing a private party the next night. I played it and the people loved what I was doing. The next thing I knew, Joe had a bunch of work booked for me."

"At first I thought I'd just play music for a month or two and go back to work at Burger King. But I played steady for three months and had gigs booked for six months in advance."

Perhaps because of the way Jackson's career began, he doesn't play many clubs around New Orleans.

"At home, I do a lot of private work—festivals, fairs and a lot of casino gigs," said Jackson. "I haven't really pursued a lot of club work because it doesn't fit in my schedule."

In 1996, Jackson finally got to go one-on-one with his idol and mentor, Fats Domino.

"Oliver Morgan had been telling me for months that he was going to take me by Fats Domino's house," recalled Jackson. "One Sunday he told me to meet him at his house. He didn't tell me where he was going, but in the back of my mind I had a pretty good idea. We parked in front of Fats' house and Oliver knocked on the door."

"Somebody opened the door and led us towards the back of the house. Fats was in the backyard looking at an addition that was being built. He looked over at us and said, 'La La, how ya' doing?' They talked awhile and then Fats went in the kitchen and started stirring a pot of red beans. Oliver told Fats, 'This is the guy I've been telling you about.' Fats said, 'I heard your commercial.' [At the time Jackson was featured on a local Frankie & Johnny's furniture store television commercial.]

"Then he said, 'Let me hear what you got,' and he led us over to the piano. I sat behind the piano but my mind went blank. I couldn't think of anything to play. Finally, Oliver said, 'Play 'Blueberry Hill.''"

"I started playing and Fats was watching. Then he started playing, but his playing was so much easier and with different fingers. When I started playing 'The Fat Man,' he came back to the piano and we played it as a duet. It really opened my eyes. He plays 'The Fat Man' with double octaves. What I was playing with my whole hand, he plays with three fingers. That allows him to hit the higher octave with his thumb. When we finished, I was sweating bullets. Fats was cool as a cucumber. We talked about his early career and he gave me some advice. When we left, he patted me on the back and said, 'Man, you're all right.' I'll never have a bigger thrill in my life than when he said that."

In February of 1997, Jackson recorded *Poor Man's Blues* for the local Kolab label. Shortly after its release, radio stations playing *Poor Man's Blues* got calls from listeners who assumed they were hearing a new Fats Domino CD. While it wouldn't be fair to compare Jackson to Domino, Jackson has proved he can hold his own behind the keyboard. He has a bright future and if he stays on course, Jackson will help keep New Orleans R&B alive for several more decades.

Epilogue

Unfortunately, too many of the artists profiled here, and in *I Hear You Knockin'*, have died since I began researching this book. I don't want to eulogize New Orleans rhythm and blues, but every time we lose another artist or musician, another nail is driven into the genre's coffin. Sadly, most younger New Orleans musicians simply aren't interested in playing rhythm and blues. I interviewed scores of musicians in compiling *The Soul of New Orleans*, but just two were younger than myself, and I'm in my mid-40s.

Economics are partly to blame for this predicament. Frankly, musicians in New Orleans can make much more money playing and recording hip-hop, funk, Dixieland, contemporary jazz, swing, classical music, rock, cajun and zydeco. Few New Orleans clubs—even the so called "House of Blues"—book R&B bands and the chances of recording classic R&B are all but non-existent. This isn't a recent phenomena however, as the trend began in the early 1960s when British rock music, Stax and Motown swept New Orleans music out of the charts. As many of the artists here have revealed, they couldn't have survived economically by playing only R&B. They either had to perform other styles of music, leave town, or shuck and jive on Bourbon Street for tourists, in order to support themselves and raise families. Several in fact abandoned music for lengthy periods of time, or in some cases, relegated playing R&B to a pleasurable past time.

Image is also a problem, as R&B has become the city's red headed musical step child. The avalanche of publications focusing on jazz, the Louis Armstrong Centennial Celebration, and Ken Burns' PBS documentary, *Jazz*, have lavished copious and deserved attention on New Orleans' jazz and Dixieland tradition. However, because of their scope, they've totally ignored New Orleans R&B. Although New Orleans R&B artists have sold millions of records and CDs—far exceeding other styles of indigenous New Orleans music—many contemporary musicians don't view New Orleans R&B as hip or cool. They often refer to it as "oldies," and chide the style because of it's simple arrangements, and uncomplicated three and four chord structure.

Like prejudice, in many cases this is a learned behavior. NOCCA— the New Orleans Center for the Creative Arts—the University of New

Orleans and Tulane University offer Jazz Studies programs, and have placed noted New Orleans jazz scholars and musicians on their faculties. These instructors sometimes give the city's R&B tradition passing acknowledgment, but too often under emphasize it's importance next to jazz. Good students listen to their teachers. As a result, educated musicians aren't taught to play, listen, or study R&B, nor do many musicians that pay their dues in clubs. At this point, I'm sorry to say, the chances of seeing a band playing the style properly are becoming infrequent, even in the city that produced it. Unlike Dixieland, the city rarely attracts out-of-town musicians willing to study R&B. So called "traditional New Orleans jazz bands" exist almost all over the world. Traditional New Orleans R&B bands don't.

In an effort to broaden their appeal, many New Orleans R&B artists have compromised their styles in order to keep working by recording other styles of more popular music. In many cases, they've been successful, and who can blame them for reaching for prosperity? While a plethora of New Orleans R&B CD reissues are available, there is virtually no contemporary New Orleans R&B being conceived or recorded.

The demise of New Orleans R&B must also be partially shouldered by the New Orleans Jazz & Heritage Festival. The city's premier music venue, in the 1970s and early 1980s, the Festival championed the genre and helped spark a brief R&B revival. However, in recent years, the people that hire entertainment for the Festival have forgotten that people largely come to their event, both from nearby neighborhoods and abroad, to hear indigenous New Orleans music. The festival makes no attempt to rediscover important R&B artists. They rotate artists that try to continue the tradition —having them play alternate years—and local artists aren't paid nearly as well as national acts. Certainly there are fewer slots than artists that want them, but the Festival seems content hiring entertainment based on who has the most attractive press kit or whoever's record company/booking agency exerts the most pressure on them. Major and minor New Orleans R&B artists are too often overlooked in favor of hohum and worn out national acts.

Nevertheless, to an extent many New Orleans R&B artists ruined it for themselves. Once the Festival was a marquee gig, a chance to perform before a huge audience, a high percentage of whom had never seen them before. Performers and bands were rehearsed and put forth their best at the Fair Grounds. Unfortunately, for some, the Festival simply became another pay day. Too many artists showed up unprepared with unrehearsed bands, and stumbled through shoddy sets. This tendency in some cases also extended to club dates. Unfortunately, some artists alienated past, present and future fans, and did a disservice to the musical tradition they helped create.

Although its era seems to have passed, I plan to continue studying and researching New Orleans rhythm and blues, adding as best I can to it's lore, and information base. I can't really see myself leaving the world of R&B, as there are still many stories to relate. One day, I hope to again compile a collection of profiles and essays for a publication such as this one. Hopefully, by then I'll be able to tell the story of younger musicians who have discovered the genre and reveal that another New Orleans Rhythm and Blues revival on the horizon. Unfortunately, at this point I can't see that happening.

New Orleans
August 31, 2001

Martha Carter - 1962

Aaron Neville - 1966

Danny White - 1962

Warren Lee - 1960

Deacon John - 2001

Prince La La - 1961

Wallace Johnson - 1996

Robert Parker and the Royals - circa 1962
[Parker second from left.]

Charles Brimmer - 1975

Rockie Charles - 1967

Willie West - 1961

Tony Owens - 2000

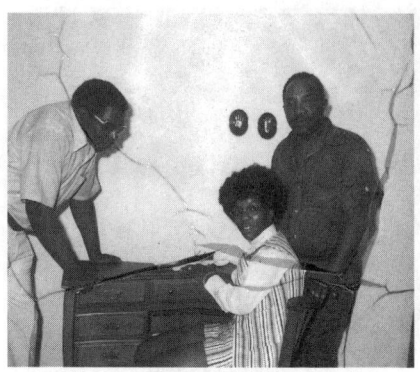

Clarence Carter, Mathilda Jones,
Cleon Floyd - 1972

Jenn Knight - 1971

Ironing Board Sam - 1975

Snook Eaglin - late 1980s

GEORGE "BIG CHIEF JOLLY" LANDRY

Born: April 4, 1917   Convent, Louisiana
Deceased: August 9, 1980   New Orleans, Louisiana

A beautiful human being; a respected musician;
an extraordinary Big Chief.
We loved him deeply.

WAKE
Tuesday, August 12, 1980   8:30 p.m.
Estelle J. Wilson Mortuary
2715 Danneel Street

FUNERAL:
Wednesday, August 13, 1980   10:00 a.m.
Blessed Sacrament Catholic Church
5018 Constance Street

There will be an Indian Jazz funeral. Participating will be the Olympia
Brass Band and the Mardi Gras Indian nation.

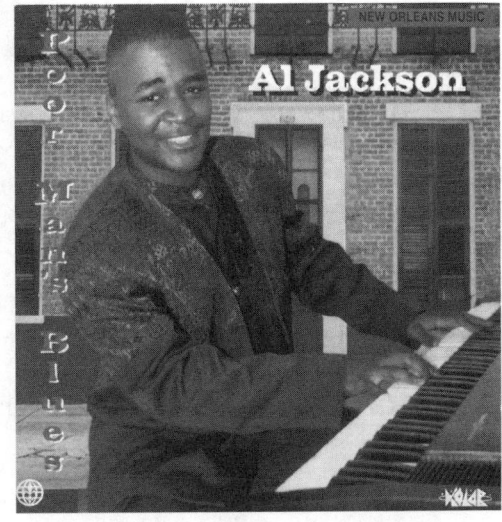

Mem Shannon - 1995

Neville Brothers - 1982: Charles (top left),
Cyril (2nd from top right), Aaron (top right),
Art (middle) with Jimmy Buffet (bottom center)

References/Bibliography

The following interviews, books, magazines, articles, programs and magazines were consulted for *The Soul of New Orleans:*

ORAL HISTORIES

Interviews with musicians, promoters and record industry people were the primary source for this book. The major interviews are listed below:

Lee Allen, New Orleans, October 1983.

Peter "Chuck" Badie, New Orleans, November 1999.

Joe Banashak, Algiers, LA, October 1982.

Irving Banister, New Orleans, February 1998.

Dave Bartholomew, New Orleans, April 1982; April 1985.

Lee Bates, New Orleans, October 1983; March 1998.

Harold Battiste, New Orleans, December 1992; September 1993; February 1999.

Eddie "Bo" Bocage, New Orleans, May 1982.

Isaac Bolden, New Orleans, May 2000.

Charles Brimmer, New Orleans, October 1996.

Chuck Carbo, New Orleans, October 1988; May 1989; October 1993; February 1999; April 1999; September 1999.

Martha Carter, New Orleans, June 1985; July 1986.

Jack Dupree, New Orleans, April 1990.

Billy Diamond, Los Angeles, May 1999; July 1999.

Antoine "Fats" Domino, New Orleans, May 1986; June 1991; July 1991; August 1991.

Fird "Snooks" Eaglin, St. Rose, LA, October 1987; New Orleans, April 1989; May 1993.

Robert "Skip" Easterling, Picayune, MS, July 1999; October 1999.

Bobby "Charles" Guidry, New Orleans, October 1986.

Herb Hardesty, New Orleans, September 1991.

Clarence "Frogman" Henry, Algiers, LA, March 1983; March 1986; March 1997; August 1999.

Johnny "Vincent" Imbragulio, Jackson, MS, August 1973; September 1980; November 1981.

Al Jackson, Gretna, October 1996; New Orleans, April 1998.

Kenneth Jackson, New Orleans, February 1985.

Senator Jones, March 1981; January 1985; October 1993.

Al Johnson, New Orleans, February 1985; February 1998; February 1999;
     October 1999.

Earl King, New Orleans, January 2000.

Jean Knight, New Orleans, March 1996; March 1997.

Lloyd Lambert, New Orleans, August 1984; April 1987.

Connie LaRocca, New Orleans, February, 1999; March 1999.

Roland LeBlanc, New Orleans, July 1999; August 1999.

Tommy LiPuma, New York, October 1993.

Fred "Little Freddie King" Martin, New Orleans, March 1995; March 1998.

Cosimo Matassa, New Orleans, June 1998; December 1999.

"Rockie" Charles Merrick, Marrero, LA, January 1996; January 1997; April 1999.

McKinley "L'il" Millet, New Orleans, May 1989.

Frank Mitchell, New Orleans, October 1998; February 1999; March 2000.

"Deacon" John Moore, New Orleans, July 1999; October 1999; September 2000.

"Ironing Board" Same Moore, New Orleans, October 1995; April 2000.

Oliver Morgan, New Orleans, October 1996.

Bobby Marchan, Metairie, LA, July 1997; October 1998; February 1999.

Aaron Neville, New Orleans, August 1980, New York, December 1997.

Charles Neville, New Orleans, November 1988; October 1989.

Cyril Neville, New Orleans, November 1988; October 1989.

Tony Owens, New Orleans, May 2000; June 2000.

Mac "Dr. John" Rebennack, New Orleans, 1980; London, England, June 1984;
     Metairie, LA, 1989; New Orleans 1993; New York, April 1998;
     New Orleans, February 2000.

Robert Parker, Roseland, Louisiana, October 1999.

Tommy Ridgley, River Ridge, December 1985, September 1987, March 1990,
     June 1992, June 1994; August 1997; April 1998; May 1999.

Clarence Samuels, New Orleans, June 1998; July 1998; February 2000.

Mem Shannon, New Orleans, March 1996; September 1997.

Bill Sinigal, New Orleans, February 2000; April 2000.

Huey Smith, Baton Rouge, August 1999.

Alonzo Stewart, New Orleans, September 1985.

Percy Stovall, New Orleans, March 1983.

Naiomi Swan, New Orleans, February 1985.

Warren Lee Taylor, New Orleans, September 2000; October 2000.

Alvin Tyler, New Orleans, February 1978; March 1988; January 1998.

Willie West, New Orleans, January 1998; July 1999.

Danny White, New Orleans, February 1985; February 1990.

BOOKS

Allan, Johnnie and Bernice Larson Webb. *Born To Be A Loser:The Jimmy Donley Story.* Jadfel, 1992.

Buerkle, Jack and Danny Barker. *Bourbon Street Black.* Oxford University, 1973.

Berry, Jason/Tad Jones/Jason Foose. *Up From the Cradle of Jazz.* University of Georgia, 1985.

Broven, John. *Walkin' To New Orleans/Rhythm & Blues In New Orleans.* Flyright/Pelican, 1974.

Charles, Ray. *Brother Ray.* Dial 1978.

Fancourt, Leslie. *Chess R&B Discography.* Self-published,1984.

George, Nelson. *The Death of Rhythm & Blues.* Pantheon, 1988.

Hannusch, Jeff. *I Hear You Knockin': The Story of New Orleans Rhythm and Blues.* Swallow, 1985.

Jancik, Wayne. *One Hit Wonders.* Billboard, 1990.

Lydon, Micheal. *Ray Charles: Man and Music.* Riverhead Books, 1998.

Al Pavlov. *The R&B Book: A Disc-History of Rhythm and Blues.* Music House Publishing, 1983.

Rebennack, Mac and Jack Rummel. *Under A Hoodoo Moon.* St. Martin's Press, 1994.

Topping, Ray. *New Orleans Rhythm & Blues Record Label Listings.* Flyright Records, 1978.

Whitburn, Joel. *Top Pop Records 1955-1970.* Gale,1972., *Top Rhythm & Blues Records 1949-1971,* Record Research, 1973.

White, Adam and Fred Bronson. *Number One Rhythm & Blues Hits.* Billboard Books, 1993.

Zur Hiede, Karl Gert. *Deep South Piano:The Story of Little Brother Montgomery.* Studio Vista, 1970.

ARTICLES

Baker, Cary. "Ronnie Barron," *Goldmine,* 1982.

Baptisa, Todd. "The Spiders," *United In Group Harmony Induction Ceremony Program,* 1999.

Broven, John. "Bobby's Happy House of Hits," *Juke Blues,* 1989, "I Knew Leonard At the Macombo, I Really Got Tired of the Road, One-Nighters, Buying New Cadillacs Every Year," *Blues Unlimited,* 1975, "Paul Gayten," Obituary, *Juke Blues,* 1991.

Coleman, Rick. "Chuck Carbo and the Spiders," *Wavelength,* 1982. "Eddie Bo," *Wavelength,* 1986, "Snooks Eaglin," *Wavelength,* 1987.

Fry, Macon. "Aaron Neville," *Wavelength,* 1985.

Gayten, Paul "Paul Gayten Speaks," *Artists Musical Direction Service,* 1949.

Hess, Norbert. "Champion Jack Dupree," Obituary, *Juke Blues,* 1982.

Joyce, Mike. "Intermission with Fats," *Living Blues,* 1977.

Marsh, Dave. "Dr. John," *Ann Arbor Jazz and Blues Festival Program,* 1972.

Matthews, Bunny. "Robert Parker," *Wavelength,* 1983.

Newlin, Jon. "Fats Is Skinnier, Still Loves N.O.," *Figaro,* 1972.

Santeli, Robert. "Dr. John: Gris-Gris Gumbo Ya Ya," *Goldmine,* 1987.

Skelly, Richard. "Right Place, Right Time: Dr. John Retraces His Roots," Unknown Publication, 1996.

Smith, Chris. "Come On And Shake It Like Jack Dupree," *Blues & Rhythm, The Gospel Truth,* 1990.

Sinclair, John. "Roland Stone: Remember Me?," *Offbeat,* 1993.

Spera, Keith. "On the Road Again," *Offbeat,* 1995.

Unknown writer, "Introducing Those Fabulous, Zany Torrid and Entertaining Gondoliers, brochure, circa 1959, "Lawrence Nelson," Obituary, *The Louisiana Weekly,* 1963, "Edgar Blanchard," Obituary, States-Item, 1972.

In addition, several liner notes from CDs and LPs as well as label information was consulted in researching *The Soul Of New Orleans.*

CD DISCOGRAPHY

There has never been more New Orleans rhythm blues available to listeners than at any other point in history. Unfortunately, because of the on-going trends and upheavals in the music industry, quite often titles appear and disappear with disturbing frequency. The abbreviated list of legitimate releases that follows is a suggested list of important, enjoyable and available recordings by artists covered in this book at the beginning of the new millennium.

RONNIE BARRON
My New Orleans Soul, Aim 1038.
Contains some of his great latter recordings.

EDDIE BO
Check Mr. Popeye, Rounder 2078.
Most of Bo's great early 1960s Ric sides are on this CD.

CHUCK CARBO,
Drawer's Trouble, Rounder 2123.
Excellent comeback CD from a superior singer.

RAY CHARLES
The Birth of Soul: The Complete Atlantic Recordings, 1952 - 1959,
Atlantic 82310-2.
   The title tells it all. Contains Charles' landmark New Orleans recordings.

ROCKIE CHARLES
Born For You, Orleans 1911.
   Superior soul blues effort. Will suffice until his early 45s get reissued.

DEACON JOHN,
Live, Red Bone 1994.
   Energetic and enjoyable recording from the under-recorded New Orleans legend.

FATS DOMINO
Out Of New Orleans, Bear Family 15540.
The Paramount Years:The Most Wanted Albums, Disky 87152.
   The eight-CD Bear Family set contains each and every track Domino record-
ed for Imperial between 1949 and 1962. The three-CD Disky collection collects
Domino's ABC and Sonet tracks into a neat package.

JACK DUPREE
New Orleans Barrelhouse, Columbia 5284.
Blues From the Gutter, Atlantic 8000002.
   The Columbia CD collects Dupree's earliest sides. The Atlantic CD was
recorded in New York in the 1950s, but has the fabulous sound and feel of New
Orleans.

SNOOKS EAGLIN
The Imperial Recordings, Capitol 33918.
Baby You Can Get Your Gun, Black Top 1112.
   The uneven Imperial recordings make up the Capitol CD. *Baby You Can Get
Your Gun* is Eaglin's best contemporary recording.

CLARENCE HENRY
The Best of Clarence "Frogman" Henry—Ain't Got No Home, MCA 9346.
   The MCA CD is a superlative representation of Henry's late 1950s and early
1960s Chess recordings.

IRONING BOARD SAM
The Human Touch, Orleans 1711.
   Unfortunately, a collection of Sam's early singles doesn't yet exist, but this
mid-1990s effort isn't all that bad.

AL JACKSON
Poor Man's Blues, Kolab 9101.
 Fine contemporary rhythm and blues with a vintage feel.

LITTLE FREDDIE KING
Swamp Boogie, Orleans 1611.
 A good collection of modern country blues..

MAC REBENNACK a.k.a. DR. JOHN
Mos Scocious, Rhino 71450.
 Like Domino, their is a daunting selection of Dr. John CDs. Most are enjoyable, but the Rhino CD is the definitive collection of his work as an R&B producer, arranger and artist. All of his other CDs are worth a listen.

AARON NEVILLE
Ultimate Collection, Hip-O 520 196.
 Sweeping nearly four decades, this CD collects some of his early Minit sides as well as his more recent AOR mega-hits. Also a few obscurities thrown in for the listener's enjoyment.

THE NEVILLE BROTHERS
Treacherous—A History of the Neville Brothers. Rhino 71491.
Uptown Rulin', A&M 069 490 403.
 The Rhino CD contains solo work by Art and Aaron and lots of early Neville Brother's sides. The A&M CD cherry picks the best tracks from seven A&M releases, including several from their break through, Yellow Moon.

ROBERT PARKER
Barefootin', Collectables 5163.
 Engaging soul and R&B from Parker's days at NOLA and Island.

TOMMY RIDGLEY
The New Orleans King of the Stroll, Rounder 2079.
Since The Blues Began, Black Top 1115.
 The Rounder CD contains Ridgley important early 1960s material on Ric. Recorded in the mid-1990s, the Black Top CD pairs Ridgley with a crack New Orleans band.

ROLAND STONE
Just A Moment—Something Special From..., Westside 577
Remember Me, Orleans 1111
    The Westside CD includes Roland Stone's early 1960s Ace material produced by Mac Rebennack. The Orleans CD is a reunion with Rebennack and features some great contemporary R&B.

THE SPIDERS
The Imperial Sessions, Bear Family 15673.
    Superb and complete chronicle of New Orleans' best vocal group led more often than not by Chuck Carbo.

WILD TCHOUPITOULAS
The Wild Tchoupitoulas, Island 7052.
    Landmark CD which features Big Chief Jolly, the Meters and all four of the Neville Brothers.

ANTHOLOGIES
Carnival Time: The Best of Ric Records, Rounder 2075.
    Superior sampling of this significant New Orleans label. Includes sides by Eddie Bo, Tommy Ridgley, Al Johnson, and Johnny Adams.

Creole Kings and Queens—Volume Two, Specialty 7038.
    Includes a superior choice of New Orleans R&B from the 1950s. Li'l Millet, Lloyd Price, Edgar Blanchard, Paul Gayten, Professor Longhair, Lloyd Lambert, and Guitar Slim among others are represented.

The Frisco Records Story, Ace 679.
    Including tracks by Danny White, Willie West, and the Rouzan Sisters, this is an introduction to the Frisco sound and good collection of R&B and early New Orleans soul.

Mardi Gras Essentials, Hip-O 314 545 684.
    Carnival classics from Al Johnson, Bill Sinigal. the Wild Tchoupitoulas, Al Johnson and the Neville Brothers among other New Orleans artists.

Mardi Gras In New Orleans —Vol. 1 & 2, Mardi Gras 1001 & 1005.
    Two essential collections of Mardi Gras music that belong in the collection of anyone with a taste for New Orleans R&B.

More Gumbo Stew, Ace 462.

The second of three fine collections of AFO material on Ace, it includes tracks by Prince La La, Mac Rebennack, Ronnie Barron, Wallace Johnson, Barbara George, the AFO Executives and Willie Tee.

Soul Stirring, Westside 541.

Great vintage Ace tracks from Benny Spellman, Chuck Carbo, Joe Tex and Lee Dorsey.

We Got A Party!:The Best of Ron Records, Rounder 2076.

Another sampling from an important New Orleans label. Includes classic material by Professor Longhair, Robert Parker and Irma Thomas.

Index